PRAISE FOR *POSITIVELY 4TH STREET:*
THE LIVES AND TIMES OF JOAN BAEZ, BOB DYLAN,
MIMI BAEZ FARIÑA, AND RICHARD FARIÑA

"This ambitious four-headed biographical narrative . . . vividly re-creates the folk era: the odd alliances the music forged between idealists and misfits, the convergence of rebels of varying talent and temperament."

—Terrence Rafferty, *GQ*

"One of the best books about music in America. [Captures] the self-delusion of the '60s counterculture, in which middle-class ambition and self-interest played at least as large a role as peace and love and flowers."

—Jonathan Yardley, *The Washington Post Book World*

"Think of *Positively 4th Street* as *A Little Night Music* scored for dulcimer and motorcycle. Or a pas de quatre, with wind chimes, love beads, and a guest-appearance entrechat by Thomas Pynchon. As David Hajdu . . . rotates among his principals until at last they settle down to play house in Carmel and Woodstock, he is such an ironist among blue notes, so knowledgeable about their performing selves on stage, in bed, and in our mezzotinted memories, that he seems almost to be whistling scherzos."

—John Leonard, *The New York Review of Books*

"A lovely madeleine of a book . . . [An] offbeat, compelling [story of] two sisters, their Machiavellian lovers and the assorted egos, ambitions, flirtations, rivalries and moments of musical genius that made those days so indelible."

—Janet Maslin, *The New York Times*

"Mr. Hajdu has the art of staging his moments without subjecting them to the embalming gaze of hindsight, and the result is a tonic freshness, the sense of a spirit recovered . . . He has clearly talked to everyone. No less importantly, he is able to channel the energies of that era convincingly. His weave of cultural history and dish creates a most poignant sense of coalescence and dissolution, both on the personal level, as relationships change and fray, and the larger cultural level, where—how to put it?—a whole larger feeling about things, the essence of 60's folk, emerges, flourishes and fades."

—Sven Birkerts, *The New York Observer*

"[In] a teetering stack of Dylan biographies and commentaries, [this is] the one new publication of distinction and clarity."

—David Remnick, *The New Yorker*

"David Hajdu makes a motley bunch of folkies—both naïve and ambitious, unquestionably talented and frequently unlikable—as memorable as any great fictional characters."

—Peter Terzian, *Newsday*
(selected as one of *Newsday*'s Favorite Books of 2001)

"From the sly Village title to the devastating New York characterizations, the probing, revelatory sentences, and the cruel plot, David Hajdu's *Positively 4th Street* recalls a lost Henry James novel transported to the 1960s."

—Robert Polito, *Bookforum*

"Hajdu adds an important chapter to the Dylan legend [and] deftly re-creates these era-defining characters and their world."

—Gregory Curtis, *Time*

"Absorbing . . . *Positively 4th Street* offers a window into the folk music scene of the early '60s, into which Dylan, cloaked in enigmas of his own devising, insinuated himself."

—A. O. Scott, *Slate* (selected as one of *Slate*'s Best Books of 2001)

"A sure classic of American popular history."   —Chris Fischbach, *Rain Taxi*

"An evocative picture of a time less innocent than we thought."

—David Kipen, *San Francisco Chronicle*

"A must for any folk fan willing to have some images tarnished."

—Michael Sangiacomo, *The Cleveland Plain Dealer*

DAVID HAJDU

POSITIVELY 4TH STREET

David Hajdu's first book, *Lush Life: A Biography of Billy Strayhorn*, won the ASCAP/Deems Taylor Award, was nominated for a National Book Critics Circle Award, and is being adapted for a feature film. Hajdu lives in Manhattan and writes for *The New York Times Magazine*, *Vanity Fair*, and *The New York Review of Books*.

4th Street

THE LIVES AND TIMES OF
JOAN BAEZ, BOB DYLAN,
MIMI BAEZ FARIÑA,
AND RICHARD FARIÑA

David Hajdu

NORTH POINT PRESS

A DIVISION OF FARRAR, STRAUS AND GIROUX

NEW YORK

North Point Press
A division of Farrar, Straus and Giroux
19 Union Square West, New York 10003

Grateful acknowledgment is made for permission to quote from the following:
"Another Country." Words and music by Richard Fariña. © 1964 M. Witmark and Sons. All rights reserved.
Used by permission.
"Celebration for a Grey Day." By Richard Fariña. First published in Atlantic Monthly. Used by permission of
Margarita M. Fariña, administrator of the estate of Richard Fariña.
"The Death of Emmett Till." Words and music by Bob Dylan. © 1963; © renewed 1991 Special Rider Music.
All rights reserved. Used by permission.
"Diamonds and Rust." Words and music by Joan C. Baez. © 1975 Chandos Music. All rights reserved. Used by
permission.
"11 Outlined Epitaphs." By Bob Dylan. © 1964 Special Rider Music. All rights reserved. Used by permission.
"The Field near the Cathedral at Chartres." By Richard Fariña. First published in Mademoiselle. Used by per-
mission of Margarita M. Fariña, administrator of the estate of Richard Fariña.
"Hard-Loving Loser." Words and music by Richard Fariña. © 1966 M. Witmark and Sons. All rights reserved.
Used by permission.
"Joan Baez in Concert, Part II" (liner notes). By Bob Dylan. © 1973 Special Rider Music. All rights reserved.
Used by permission.
"Little Nothing Poem." By Richard Fariña. First published in Long Time Coming and a Long Time Gone
(Random House, 1969). Used by permission of Margarita M. Fariña, administrator of the estate of Richard Fariña.
"Rainy Day Women #12 & 35." Words and music by Bob Dylan. © 1966 Dwarf Music; © renewed 1994
Dwarf Music. All rights reserved. Used by permission.
"Reno Nevada." Words and music by Richard Fariña. © 1964 M. Witmark and Sons. All rights reserved. Used
by permission.
"She Belongs to Me." Words and music by Bob Dylan. © 1965 Warner Bros.; © renewed 1993 Special Rider
Music. All rights reserved. Used by permission.
"Subterranean Homesick Blues." Words and music by Bob Dylan. © 1965 Warner Bros.; © renewed 1993 Spe-
cial Rider Music. All rights reserved. Used by permission.
"The Times They Are A-Changin'." Words and music by Bob Dylan. © 1963 Warner Bros.; © renewed 1991
Special Rider Music. All rights reserved. Used by permission.
"Troubled and I Don't Know Why." Words and music by Bob Dylan. © 1989 Special Rider Music. All rights
reserved. Used by permission.
"With God on Our Side." Words and music by Bob Dylan. © 1962 Warner Bros.; © renewed 1991 Special
Rider Music. All rights reserved. Used by permission.
"Positively 4th Street" is a copyrighted composition by Bob Dylan. The use of the title on this book is not in-
tended to imply endorsement by Bob Dylan.

Library of Congress Cataloging-in-Publication Data
Hajdu, David.
    Positively 4th street : the lives and times of Joan Baez, Bob Dylan, Mimi Baez Fariña,
and Richard Fariña.
        p. cm.
    Includes bibliographical references.
    ISBN 0-86547-642-X (pbk.)
    1. Baez, Joan. 2. Dylan, Bob, 1941–   . 3. Fariña, Mimi. 4. Fariña, Richard. 5. Folk
singers—United States—Biography. I. Title.
ML400.H335 2001
782.42162'13'00922—dc21
[B]   00-052085

Designed by Abby Kagan
www.fsgbooks.com
10 9 8 7 6 5 4 3 2 1

FOR KAREN

POSITIVELY 4TH STREET

I N THE WINTER OF 1949, when Joan and Mimi Baez were little girls, their aunt Tia moved in with them. She came through the chimney and brought music and ice cream in her carpetbag, or it seemed that way to them at the time.

Joan, who was eight, and Mimi, who was four, shared a bedroom on the second floor of the Baez family's clapboard house in Menlo Park, California, near Stanford University, where their father, Dr. Albert Baez, thirty-seven, worked in a cold war program to teach physics to military engineers in training. Their older sister, Pauline, ten, kept to herself in her own small room, a converted closet, and their mother, thirty-six, for whom Joan was named, tended to the house while listening to classical music on 78-rpm records a salesman picked out for her. The female contingent of the family submitted reluctantly to rooming-house life until the elder Joan's sister Tia, thirty-nine, joined them, freshly divorced for unimaginably adult reasons never to be discussed.

Sisterhood understitched the Baez household. The first of Joan and Albert's children had been named for Tia, whose proper name was Pauline Bridge Henderson (*Tia* meaning "aunt" in Spanish, Albert's native language), just as the third born had been named for their father's only sister, Margarita; Mimi was her middle name, which everybody in the family except Albert Baez preferred. Tia was fair and soft, with long, curly chestnut hair and the free-spirited poise of an artist's model; she somehow always seemed as if she would prefer to be nude and gazed upon. This may have come from experience: Tia had married a painter, traveled through Europe with him, studied dance with Martha Graham, written poetry . . . she had, that is, lived all her era's romantic feminine dreams. Sipping sherry in the kitchen of the boarding house, Tia would regale her sister and the girls—sometimes all three, more often only Joan and Mimi, since Pauline tended to play alone—with stories of her travels and readings from her notebooks. To Big Joan, the relief, the novelty, and the vicarious pleasures that Tia provided nearly outweighed the envy she incited. A strong, handsome woman, the former Joan Bridge had married young and with ambivalence; feeling sinful and confused for having loved another woman, she yielded to the overtures of a gentle Mexican academic who said he would accept her as she was. In the decade to follow, she fixed her resources on rearing children. "You could feel the house lighten up when Tia came in," Mimi would recall. "But Tia was not a worker, and so Mother was real resentful that Tia's role was to come around and be the clown, get everyone laughing and basically not hold her end up. Mother carried buckets of stuff, and Tia told stories—and we loved her, because she liked to have fun, and she would tell us stories that seemed really naughty, and she went out on dates with men."

For several years, Tia kept company with a fellow living in the boardinghouse, Rugger, a bit of a roustabout with a child's sense of abandon that delighted the Baez girls. "He'd take my sister and Joanie and Mimi out together, and they'd have a glorious time," said Big Joan. "He'd buy them all kinds of candy and ice cream, and he'd take them to double features. He'd ruin them! Their father was furious—'Why do they have to go to a double feature? Isn't one movie enough?' I couldn't explain it to him. The girls were still girls—they were supposed to have fun. He was beside himself. He was terribly jealous, and so was I." Evidently picking up glimmers of information from snatches of grown-up talk, Joan and Mimi seemed troubled by the family conflict over Rugger. "The girls were very upset that the adults were at odds," Tia remembered. "They thought they were doing something wrong because they were happy, or Rugger and I were doing something wrong because we were in love and enjoying it. I was afraid they were getting the impression that men and sisters don't mix, and I guess they did. But Mimi and Joanie were fine, as long as they got the same kind of ice cream and the scoops were the same size."

As they grew, Joan and Mimi drew closer, and their older sister turned inward. "When Mimi was very young, Pauline and I hated her," Joan remembered. "Mimi was the youngest and the prettiest, so Pauline and I conspired against her. That didn't last long. Pauline was a loner." When she was eleven, Pauline built a tree house and spent much of her time between school and sleep alone there; when Joan asked if she could play with her, Pauline replied, "Sure, you can be the daddy. Go to work. Bye!" At mealtime Pauline would construct a barricade of cereal boxes around her place setting. "After Pauline built that tree house, she never really came out," said their mother. "Mimi and Joanie discovered each other. They were very different, like my sister and me in a way, but very tight, like us." Because young Joan could draw (mainly clever, skillful sketches of her family, her classmates, and herself), she was considered the artistic one. Joan also had a quick, sassy wit and a knack for imitating voices—"Joanie was so funny," said Mimi, "she made you laugh so hard you almost didn't mind that it was at your own expense." A lovely girl with deep liquid brown eyes and an easy, disarming smile, Joan thought of herself as unattractive; surgery to remove a benign tumor had left a tiny scar on her torso that she saw as monstrous. She endured schoolyard taunts because of her Mexican surname and dark skin, and she coveted her little sister's fairer, delicate beauty. "Mimi was the pretty one," said Dr. Baez. "She looked like an angel. All three of my girls, they all were beautiful—Pauline, Joan, too—beautiful. But not like Mimi." She had physical confidence and poise; under Tia's patronage, Mimi had been studying dance since the age of five. She struggled with books, however, because she was an undiagnosed dyslexic, and her schoolwork suffered. Mimi envied her sister Joan's way with words and her ease in adult company. "Joan was very jealous of Mimi's looks. It was very hard for Joan. Joan always thought she was ugly," said their mother. "I think Mimi was just as jealous of Joan . . . [because] Joan was so talented. They were both talented, but—I don't know . . . I just know they loved each other so much, I thought sometimes they'd kill each other." The girls held hands constantly; once as they were walking, Mimi squeezed so tightly that her fingernails dug into her sister's palm, and blood smeared onto the sides of their dresses.

Encouraged by one of Albert's university friends, the Baez family started attending Quaker meetings, and they always brought the girls, all of whom endured the sessions dutifully and absorbed elements of the Quaker ideals that they understood and liked. "It was something we had to do, and it was a chore," Mimi would remember. "But all three of us seemed to get the basic idea that peace was a good thing. We basically made faces at each other [at the meetings]." Still, one speaker succeeded in capturing Joan's attention: a small, frail monkish fellow named Ira Sandperl. Moved by his lecture on pacifism, Joan asked him for advice in applying his principles to her life. "I asked him how I could learn to get along with my sister Mimi," Joan recalled. "She was very beautiful, and we fought all the time. It seemed so endless and unkind. Ira said to pretend that it was the last hour of her life, as, he pointed out, it might well be. So I tried out his plan. Mimi reacted strangely at first, the way anyone does when a blueprint is switched on him without his being consulted. I learned to look at her, and as a result, to see her for the first time. I began to love her."

All three girls showed interest in music. Pauline had taken some piano lessons and had practiced regularly but froze when it came to playing for her teacher. She and Joan (who had also studied piano briefly) both learned how to play the ukulele from a Stanford colleague of Albert Baez, Paul Kirkpatrick. "He taught Joanie and me the same thing on that ukulele the same day," remembered Pauline. "I became so concerned in doing my little three chords correctly, I didn't want anybody to hear me at all until I had it perfect. And Joanie picked up the thing and just started strumming away, and if the chords weren't quite right, it didn't matter—she played it for the people right off, you know. And then she just went on playing, because everybody clapped and cheered and said, 'Oh, isn't it great!' And me, I kept practicing my three little chords until they were perfect. I guess they didn't think I was very good, because they didn't

even hear me. But it was like that. Joan was 'Ta-da!'—center stage."
During one of these living-room performances, Joan decided to sing,
too. "Singing in the house while I played the ukulele—that was the first
time I remember people saying, 'Oh, you have a very nice voice,' " Joan
recalled. Mimi scored high on a third-grade music aptitude test and took
violin lessons for several years. "I did very well, but I was really more
interested in singing," said Mimi. "But that was more of Joanie's thing."

Late in the spring of 1954, when Joan and Mimi were thirteen and
nine, Tia and Rugger took them to a concert in the gym of Palo Alto
High School. It was an informal program of songs and talk to raise funds
for the California Democratic Party, featuring Pete Seeger. Tia considered herself politically aware and liberal, like Big Joan and Albert, and
she wanted Joan and Mimi to hear Seeger. "I liked him very much," Tia
said. "I thought if I still had some influence on those girls, they should
hear something they weren't going to hear on the radio." Indeed, Seeger
could not be found on any of the country's commercial stations, nor on
records from the major labels, in concert halls, or in nightclubs; he had
been blacklisted in 1952 for his association with Communism. Along
with Woody Guthrie and Huddie "Leadbelly" Ledbetter and folklorist
Alan Lomax, Seeger had been a central figure in the boomlet of folk-
style recordings and performances between the Depression years and the
beginning of the Second World War. By 1950 Seeger, as a member of the
Weavers (along with singer-guitarist Fred Hellerman and singers Lee
Hays and Ronnie Gilbert), had helped break folk into the pop mainstream with the quartet's hit records of "On Top of Old Smokey,"
"Wimoweh," and Leadbelly's composition "Goodnight, Irene," among
others. The accomplishment carried irony for a socialist such as
Seeger—a demonstration of his music's appeal to the masses through
commercial means that brought sizable profits to the record industry, as
well as to the Weavers. With the rise of the cold war and the intensifica-
tion of anti-Communist sentiment in the early 1950s, Seeger found himself liberated from the irony of mass popularity and economic success;
he was no longer welcome in most concert halls and nightclubs and returned to performing in community centers, schools, and private clubs

for modest sums, usually under the auspices of organizations associated with the left. At Palo Alto High School, the political component of his presentation was one of implication. "It seemed to me that I could make a point if I made it gently," Seeger explained. "I suppose you could say what I was doing was a cultural guerrilla tactic. I sang songs about people from all walks of life, and I talked about how anyone from any walk of life could sing this kind of song himself. What I was getting at was the idea of flip-flopping the power structure, so every individual had some power, rather than all the power being centered on a few organizations or just one. I said, 'Sing with me. Sing by yourself. Make your own music. Pick up a guitar, or just sing a cappella. We don't need professional singers. We don't need stars. You can sing. Join me now. . . .'"

The idea surely ran counter to the prevailing cultural tenets of glamour and professionalism: Down with the aristocracy of the Hit Parade, up with egalitarian amateurism. A message with appeal to the disenfranchised, the disconnected, and the tone deaf alike, Seeger's call for musical insurgency touched both Joan and Mimi Baez, as it would connect with many other young people who saw him perform during the 1950s. "Joan told me later that it was after that concert that she looked herself in the mirror and said, 'I can be a singer, too,' " Seeger recalled.

"I don't remember the actual concert anymore," Joan would say. "All I know is that was a major moment for me." (Mimi would not remember any of it.)

"I remember," said Tia. "Mimi and Joan both announced that they decided they wanted to sing. Mimi was not exactly a big out-there, out-in-front girl like Joan. But she really loved music. Pete's message was, you know, 'That's okay. You don't have to be a star to sing. Sing for yourself—that's what matters.'

"Joan came away with something a little bit different . . . 'Wow, maybe you don't have to look like a movie queen, and you can still be a star. I can sing. So I can go up there like Pete Seeger, and everybody will like me.'

"And I thought, 'Now, how different can two girls be and want to do the same thing?' "

SEEGER DESCRIBED HIMSELF as a sociopolitical Johnny Appleseed during the mid-1950s, "sowing the music of the people," and he would quickly have reason to claim more success than his metaphoric progenitor. At the end of the high school concert Joan and Mimi Baez attended, Seeger sold a copy of his home-published booklet *How to Play the 5-String Banjo* to Stanford sophomore Dave Guard; three years later, Guard and two friends, Nick Reynolds and Bob Shane, inspired by Seeger and the Weavers, formed a folk group and called it the Kingston Trio (to evoke the Jamaican township rendered voguish by Harry Belafonte and the calypso fad). A neatly groomed, collegiate, WASPy-looking group of athletic young men singing and playing traditional music in a robust, highly polished style, the Kingston Trio attracted national attention during an eight-month engagement at San Francisco's Purple Onion nightclub in 1957 and started recording for Capitol Records the following January. The group's first single, "Tom Dooley," an eerie late-nineteenth-century ballad about the hanging of Confederate Civil War veteran Tom Dula for the murder of his lover, became a number-one hit—after eighteen weeks on the pop charts, it joined "To Know Him Is to Love Him" and "The Chipmunk Song" as one of the top ten best-selling singles of 1958, selling more than two million copies. Johnny "Appleseed" Chapman had planted only fifty thousand trees.

Of course, the seeds scattered by Seeger (and at the same time by others, such as broadcaster Oscar Brand and record producer Harry Smith, creator of the six-record Folkways *Anthology of American Folk Music*, released in 1952) required the proper atmospheric conditions, nourishment, good timing, and the graces of the fates in order to take root. Fifties America provided them. "We were singing 'Tom Dooley' thirty years before the so-called folk revival," noted Agnes "Sis" Cunningham, vocalist and accordion player with Seeger and Woody Guthrie in the Almanac Singers. "I guess it *was* a revival—they were reviving our music. Then again, we stole everything, too, or changed the thing around to make it topical. After all those years, I think people were beginning to be enthusiastic about folk music because, you know, it wasn't the thirties or the forties anymore. It was the fifties. You know, the fifties were very fucked up."

There never was one single American folk music, of course, but rather a loose clump of threads extending from Appalachian mountain, hillbilly, cowboy, rural blues, urban blues, union, left-wing propaganda, military, hobo, and other kinds of music, intertwined and knotted. Still, there was a folk aesthetic as the music was understood in the mid- to late 1950s, and it was one styled as largely antithetical to the times—a core aspect of the music's appeal to young people seeking their own identity in the shadow of the World War II generation. As a music long associated with progressive politics, folk posed challenges to Eisenhower-age conservatism, explicit and implied. A rural vernacular music sung in untrained voices accompanied by acoustic instruments, folk put a premium on naturalness and authenticity during a boom in man-made materials, especially plastics. "It sounded real—it sounded like real people playing wooden things and without a lot of prettying up and fancy arrangements and gold-lamé outfits," said the singer and guitarist Tom Rush. "We'd go out and find these ancient records and play them, and the guitars sounded out of tune, and you couldn't understand the words. But it was more powerful than anything you'd hear anywhere else." A music that gloried in the unique and the weird, folk challenged conformity and celebrated regionalism during the rise of mass media, national brands, and interstate travel. "The part that attracted me and a lot more people than just me was the fact that this music hadn't been run through a grinder—it hadn't been made to stand up and salute," John Sebastian recalled. "It was unapologetically local in nature," said the singer and songwriter, who was raised in Manhattan. "Sleepy John Estes would be singing, 'Yeah, I like Miss So-and-so, she's always been good to me,' and it would be some kind of a thing about 'because she brings me cakes and feeds me when I'm workin' on the street.' It wasn't necessarily a love song. It was not trying to attract a mass audience. It was simply reacting to the needs, the musical needs, of a town, and there's something about that." A music historical by nature, it conjured distant times, often in archaic language, celebrating the past rather than the "new" and "improved," those ostensibly synonymous selling points of the postwar era. It was small in scale—a music of modest ambitions easy to perform alone, even a cappella, without a big band or orchestrations—when American society, with its new supermarkets, V-8 engines, and suburban sprawl, appeared to be physically ballooning. Folk music was down to earth when jet travel and space exploration were emerging; while Frank Sinatra was flying to the moon, Pete Seeger was waist deep in the Big Muddy.

Elvis Presley had helped introduce young people to aspects of the folk sensibility. The only singer since Rudy Vallee first crooned on the radio in 1927 to be a pop idol without Tin Pan Alley songs and a piano player, he had made rural music in general and the acoustic guitar in particular appealing to teenagers around the country. (Although "hillbilly" singers such as Tennessee Ernie Ford and Conway Twitty had broken onto the pop singles charts, their style was geared to adults.) "Elvis was a doorway into all these other types of music that up until then hadn't been available to young, northern white people—southern blues, country and western, and from there, bluegrass, old-time music, and traditional folk," said James Field, a Harvard student from a Boston Brahmin family who became a bluegrass musician. "I stopped listening to Elvis after high school, but my eyes had been opened. I was ready for the other stuff, even though I'm not sure I realized it yet."

Part of folk's appeal, particularly to young adults in the 1950s, was its antihero mythos—a sense of the music as the property of outcasts, drawn in part from the idiom's romantic portrayal of bad men and underdogs, murderers hanged, lovers scorned, and in part from the mystique surrounding folk characters such as Woody Guthrie, the hobo roustabout, and Leadbelly, an ex-convict. No wonder many people who emerged in folk circles during the late 1950s felt they had discovered the music alone and pursued it in defiance of their peers. Prep school students from the Northeast would stay up all night listening in the dark to WWVA out of Wheeling, West Virginia, a country-music station that broadcast north at 50,000 watts from sunset until dawn. (Forty years later, listeners from Boston could imitate the deejay, Lee Moore, "your coffee-drinkin' night hawk," and recite the commercials for a hundred baby chicks, just five dollars.) Suburban kids would take the bus to New York by themselves and shop at "the broken-record store" on Sixth Avenue and West 12th Street; there were Folkways albums in the bins, although they came without jackets; you could buy a plain-paper sleeve to protect the disk and send away to the record company for a sheet of information about the recordings, so you would know if that was Robert Gray or Horace Sprott playing the harmonica. "One of the things that made this music different and better than whatever everybody else was listening to was the fact that everybody else *wasn't* listening to it," said John Cooke, a New York blueblood who played bluegrass guitar at Harvard. (He was the son of writer Alistair Cooke and great-great-great-great-nephew of Ralph Waldo Emerson.) "It was not merely *not* commercial music," said Cooke. "It was *anti*commercial music. When you met anyone else who was into it, you were members of the same club, and I still thought of it as a very small club. There may have been a lot of us out there who thought that way, but we didn't know that. We thought we were special." Young northeasterners like Cooke and his friends apparently never realized that the music they revered as noncommercial (or anticommercial), the sound of rural artists that struck them as exotic and obscure, was really nothing of the sort in its time and place. Every track that Harry Smith collected for his Smithsonian Folkways albums was originally a commercial record, produced and distributed for profit; these were not field recordings by folklorists such as John and Alan Lomax. In West Virginia, WWVA was a commercial radio station, broadcasting songs its local audiences considered the hits of the day.

I N THE BEGINNING of 1958, a few months after *Sputnik*, the Massachusetts Institute of Technology hired Albert Baez to work on a federal committee charged with improving science education in American high schools, and that summer the Baezes moved from Palo Alto to Belmont, a wooded Massachusetts suburb populated mostly by Boston-area academics and their families. (The family had left the country briefly in 1951, when Dr. Baez took a UNESCO teaching post in Baghdad, then returned to Palo Alto.) The university found them a modern three-bedroom ranch house; it was plain and small by Belmont standards but a country manor in the Baez sisters' eyes, "the first nice, big house we ever had to ourselves," Joan said. With Pauline away at Drew University in New Jersey, Joan and Mimi, now seventeen and thirteen, got their own rooms, and both of them put their newfound privacy to use practicing the guitars they had gotten before moving east—Joan's a steel-string, folk-style Gibson, Mimi's a gut-string, classical-style Goya. "They wanted to switch from the ukulele and the violin and met in the middle, I guess, with guitars," their mother joked. "You'd walk by their rooms and hear them playing— sometimes the same song, like a duet, but with a wall between them." Albert Baez's role on the government committee was to help make educational films, produced at a converted old opera house in Watertown. Since her father was an employee of MIT (though not a professor there, as his daughters would often claim), Joan could attend any of several area colleges tuition-free; she was accepted at Boston University in April 1958 and enrolled for the fall. Mimi went to Belmont High School.

At freshman orientation that September, Joan was one of 2,500 incoming students corralled into Nickerson Field, BU's sports stadium. "Orientation—rah rah," recalled one of the initiates, Debbie Green. A pretty drama student with long, straight dark hair, Green was sitting on the ground with her friend Margie Gibbons, a classmate from the Putney School, and they had their red-and-white freshman beanies on their laps. "These very official-looking upperclassmen came over to us, and they started tapping us," recalled Green. "They were telling us we had to wear these beanies. We went, 'Oh, no.' But they said we had to put them on our heads—it was a school law, and if we didn't do it, we would be fined. We would have to pay a quarter every time they caught us without our beanies. And we said, 'No, we don't want to wear beanies.' And the only other people in the whole place who refused to put on the beanies were this girl and this guy with her who were huddled in the corner. It was Joan and a cute blond guy named Doug. They were the only people who fought back the same way we fought. We were outraged. We were shocked and mad. We all stormed out of the place together. We were the four radicals, fighting for our right not to wear beanies."

"We walked to Doug's car, and we got in the car, and Joan had her guitar on the backseat." Joan and her male friend sat in front, turned to face Debbie and Margie. "I went, 'Oh—do you play?' And she didn't really answer," said Green. "I went, 'I play,' and I picked up the guitar. She went, 'Oh, really?' And she was staring at my hands. That's how we met, and we became fast friends. For a while there, we were like sisters."

After several years of practice and some experience performing for classmates, Green could play guitar well—she finger-picked and knew how to use the whole neck of the instrument, instead of strumming elemental chords formed on the first few frets—and sang movingly in a misty voice. She had worked up a repertoire of songs from English, Appalachian, and other traditional sources well matched to her dramatic temperament: "Silver Dagger," a traditional English ballad about a mother's vow to protect her daughter from the evils of men; "John Riley," another English ballad, this of a maiden's loyalty to her long-missing betrothed; "Mary Hamilton," a Scottish tale of a woman condemned to death for carrying the king's child, one of the three hundred ballads collected by nineteenth-century Boston folklorist Francis J. Child in his five-volume series of books *The English and Scottish Popular Ballads*; "Henry Martin," another Child ballad; and others of like pedigree and morbidity. "My mother had a whole bunch of trouble in her life, and she was very emotional and did a lot of crying, so I had all this heavy weight on me," Green explained. "When I played the guitar and sang those songs of unrequited love, it was a release from all that sorrow." Sitting face to face on a bed in Green's dorm room, Joan and Debbie spent much of their first semester playing and singing songs, frequently skipping classes. Joan was in vocational training. "They were really a pair at the time—all they did was play guitar," recalls another BU freshman who befriended them both, Betsy Minot (now Betsy Siggins-Schmidt). "Debbie taught Joan absolutely everything she [Debbie] knew." But Joan knew more music than she disclosed to Debbie, Betsy, or any of her friends. Shortly before she moved east, Joan had learned about a dozen songs, including "La Bamba," Harry Belafonte's "Island in the Sun," and the rhythm-and-blues hits "Annie Had a Baby" and "Youngblood"—light folk tunes and danceable pop, music in a sexy and upbeat vein that she would quickly abandon in favor of a more serious approach all her own, or soon to be.

In the bohemian pockets of most major cities and college towns around the country in the 1950s, coffeehouses modeled upon European cafés emerged with foreign-film festivals and bookstores that sold imports of Henry Miller novels as outposts of intellectual and sensual dissent: the Blind Lemon in Berkeley, the House of Seven Sorrows in Dallas, the Green Spider in Denver, the Gas House in Los Angeles, the Laughing Buddha in St. Louis, the Drinking Gourd in San Francisco. "You could walk from New York to California by just stepping from one coffeehouse to another without touching ground," Oscar Brand joked. Their allure was conspicuously counter-American at a high point in the United States' world prominence—espresso and existential doubt, no cocktails, no glitz, an appealing combination to postwar college students seeking their own generational identity. The original sound of the milieu was jazz, a music recently abandoned by the mainstream American public. As folk surfaced, it spread into the coffeehouses; earthy, unpackaged, economical, and cool, it fit naturally with the Middle Eastern sweets and the cigarettes. In Cambridge, the center of artistic radicalism around Boston since James Russell Lowell wrote *The Biglow Papers* in the 1840s, the first European-style coffeehouse opened in 1955; run single-handedly by its owner Tulla Cook, the Coffee Grinder was a dim, unadorned place, no larger than a living room, on Mt. Auburn Street, a block from Harvard Square. There were no performers, just Tulla's AM radio. At the coffeehouses that opened after it—the Cafe Yana, the Salamander, the Golden Vanity, the Unicorn, and Club 47—music soon predominated. "One night I walked past the Cafe Yana and heard this jazz coming out and went inside—the room was full of conga drums," recalled guitarist Peter Rowan, who grew up in rural Massachusetts and visited Cambridge as a teenager. "Harvard Square was jazz music. It was mostly college people, and they were talking about William Burroughs and Allen Ginsberg, or trying to. It was turtlenecks and skinny girls. It was very Beat Generation. The next week I walked past and looked in the window, and some girl was playing the guitar, and there were fifty guys in tweed jackets smoking pipes sitting on the floor, and I said, 'Well, this is different.' " If the young scholars of Harvard Square were seeking something anti-intellectual as a respite from or a challenge to academic authority, they could no longer presume to find it in jazz, which had grown in esteem to be regarded as a highly advanced, serious music. In folk, however, Cambridge intellectuals could find all the anti-intellectualism they wanted.

Joan, Debbie, Betsy, and their friends spent nearly every night in the coffeehouses, soaking up the atmosphere and becoming familiar with the music and the Harvard boys. "If you were cool, that's what you did," Betsy recalled. "The best guys were there—that was the 'in' scene." For Baez, who still considered herself unattractive, the coffeehouses seemed an accessible route to social acceptance. "I knew I could do what [the folksingers] were doing and a lot better than them," Joan said. "In my mind, I was still the girl the kids used to taunt and call a dirty Mexican. But I could sing. I realized then that here was something I could do to show that I was valid, and I liked it a lot more than going to class."

A few weeks after the fall semester began, Debbie Green was singing at the Cafe Yana every Tuesday night. There was no cover charge, and Debbie was paid five dollars. One night before the end of October, she invited Joan Baez to sing a few songs with her. "She was just like a flower in the sunlight—when Joanie got in front of people, she bloomed,"

Betsy said. "Most people are nervous when they get in front of people. Joanie was a creature in her natural habitat."

Mimi played guitar every night at home. In school she struggled to parse the jumbled letters in her books and peeked at her neighbors to see when to turn the page. "I hated schoolwork so much," Mimi recalled. "I couldn't do it. I didn't understand it. It was very clear to me that I couldn't handle it, that I was dumb, and that I wasn't going to cut it, so it was just a daily uncomfortable situation. I always felt dumb, and Joan was so quick and funny—even if she didn't understand something, she could get away with it with a quick comment or something funny. She was so fast, she made me feel slower. I couldn't wait to get home from school and lock myself in with my guitar." Much like her sister, Mimi came to music naturally but sought to improve however she could without formal study. There was a popular folk-style guitar teacher in Cambridge, Rolf Cahn. A German-born, Chicago-bred singer-guitarist with horn-rimmed glasses and a big, sweet personality, he was considered one of the best and most successful folksingers in Cambridge, along with his frequent partner Eric von Schmidt. Cahn had an album of his own released on the Folkways label and a steadily growing roster of young guitar students, including a woman from Watertown a bit younger than Debbie and Joan, Wendy Robinson, who saved her parents money by passing what she learned at her guitar lessons on to her younger sister Susan, who, in turn, repeated it to her friend Mimi Baez. (Wendy and Susan Robinson inspired John Sebastian's "Did You Ever Have to Make Up Your Mind," a song often associated with Joan and Mimi.) "I was trying to learn guitar without leaving my room," says Mimi. Trained on the violin and practicing on a nylon-string guitar, she began to develop an intimate, chamber-style approach to the instrument, and it seemed to suit her voice as she sang alone on her bed.

Joan was learning fast from Debbie Green and beginning to see music as more than a social outlet. After a few more appearances together at the Cafe Yana, Joan and Debbie were asked to give a concert at a Harvard frat house after the Christmas break. Unfortunately, Debbie got mononucleosis. She went home to Staten Island for several weeks, returning in time for the show. Joan performed alone first. "I was sitting there in the audience, and I was listening, and the oddest thing happened," said Green. "She did my whole set. Every single song she sang was one of my songs, in my arrangements, and not only that, she sang every one the exact same way—not only the same songs, but the same interpretations, the same emotions. I'm talking *exactly*—the exact same inflection on the same word, the exact same pause at the exact same point. It was surreal. I was watching myself up there." At the end of her set, Joan introduced Debbie in the audience and invited her to take the stage. "What was I supposed to do? She had just done all my best songs. And no matter what I did, it would look like I was copying her. I didn't feel well when I got there. Now I was really sick."

They never disagreed on the reason they parted ways, only on its relevance. "It's true—when I first started, I used a lot from Debbie's act," said Joan. "But the alternative would have been codependent silliness. I mean, should I not have done it, to protect Debbie Green's feelings? She was modestly talented, but not ambitious. I was going someplace, she wasn't. I didn't hurt her. I only helped myself." Green, who lost her singing voice during a bout of asthma a few years later (but still stayed active in the folk scene as a club manager and occasional singer), assented: "I was never going to be a star—she's right. I never really wanted to. But she did hurt me—not professionally but personally."

Of course, folk music was by no means the creation of solitary artists communing with the muses; it evolved through the "folk process" of sharing and adapting songs and techniques over decades, even centuries. Joan had one foot grounded in this tradition as she began canvassing the Cambridge coffeehouses, picking up songs, finding her style, and she quickly surpassed Debbie Green. "Early on, she just devoured everybody's things," said Richard Zaffron, a Harvard philosophy major who sang and played guitar at Tulla's; a classically trained musician, he gave Joan some tips on the guitar in early 1959. "Our sources were records and the old songbooks. Those were the sources, and we all had a certain repertoire in common. But you didn't copy each other's signature pieces. Joan would take your stuff, and there would be your repertoire [in her shows]."

No more submissive to the ground rules of the folk tradition than she had been with the freshman guidelines at Boston University (or for that matter any rules she thought restricting), Joan built a repertoire of songs she liked, intuitively. "It's as if there were a mysterious string in me," she later explained. "If something I hear plucks that string, then I'll sing that song. The whole process must be instinctual. I have to admit that when people talk about the history of a song, I usually get somewhat bored. Sometimes I do wonder where a certain song came from and what it means beyond what the lyrics say. Yet this aspect of folk music has always been so secondary with me.

"I do feel kind of bad about being so bloody ignorant, because I'm that way about everything. I have a primitive way of going about everything. I can't force myself to do something in which I'm not really interested. Fundamentally, I'm lazy. I bought all the bound volumes of *Sing Out!*, the folk music quarterly, to learn more about folk material. But I never looked at them."

Whatever the degree to which Joan drew from the work of Debbie Green, Richard Zaffron, or anyone else in the Cambridge folk scene during her apprenticeship, her voice was her own—a ringing mezzo-soprano with an unusually forceful vibrato that Joan had trained herself to produce, in order to sound older. She was gifted with exceptional intonation, especially by the forgiving standards of vernacular music. Striking and clear yet tightly wrought, self-consciously projected, Joan's singing demanded attention without apology for its determination to get it. The forces at odds—natural ability and sheer will, nerve and insecurity—helped make her singing enigmatically compelling. There was also a detachment in her approach, an isolation from the emotionality of her material, that worked in congress with her taut stage manner to give Joan an air of regality or ethereality. In folk circles, where audiences had come to expect down-home characters groaning in and out of tune, Joan Baez seemed like the spirit of a child-queen, floating in off the moors.

"She was this little girl with a voice that would make angels cry— never heard such a voice on earth," said Clay Jackson, a Harvard student who took up bluegrass guitar. "Fantastic voice," said John Stein, a coffeehouse regular about Joan's age who would become a Baez family friend. "But her stage presence was sort of shy, you know. She gave off a kind of a vulnerability, which made her singing appear like kind of a brave act. You could see that there was an angst, some kind of anxiety," he said. "There was a certain kind of a hunted-animal feeling about her, like a beautiful bird that is terrified and doesn't quite know why." As Joan would recall, "I was always afraid. I was drawn to all that pathos and sorrow because that's how I felt. I didn't feel smart and attractive. I sang through my terror." The result, a bittersweet singing style informed by sadness and fear, suggests the Portuguese genre *fado*, a music of anguish, despair, and loneliness sung exclusively by women in black dresses, accompanying themselves on the guitar. (Joan said she never heard of *fado* till many years later.)

Dozens of Cambridge musicians first heard Joan's voice ringing through a coffeehouse when she was sitting in the audience and someone else was performing on stage. Their stories are virtually identical: Zaffron or Eric von Schmidt or Rolf Cahn would be singing when Joan would suddenly join in the song, drowning out the person onstage. (It was something she had done as early as her teens in northern California; while fox-trotting to a big band when she was sixteen, she starting bellowing a song from the dance floor, much to the horror of her date, a boy named Mark Spoelstra, who would become a folk-blues singer and guitarist a decade later.) "The first time I saw it happen, I thought it was a problem with the amplification," said Eric von Schmidt. A skilled realist painter and blues guitarist with a boyish enthusiasm for just about everything anyone mentioned, von Schmidt was, at age twenty-eight in 1959, an elder of the Cambridge folk scene and one of its most respected figures. He had been in the army and traveled through Europe painting on a Fulbright grant, a marvel to young people living away from home for the first time. Von Schmidt had a round, bearded face and a permanent grin; he looked like a big teddy bear, and the Cambridge crowd loved him like one. "All of a sudden, there's this other voice booming off the walls. I said, 'Hey, that must be feedback. Sounds pretty good, though.' Then I thought, 'Hey, that feedback is singing harmony. I got to get me an amp that does that!' "

Usually, the surprise duet would lead to an invitation for the gamine with the wonderful voice to join the singer at the microphone. "You got the feeling she really wanted to be on stage all the time," said von Schmidt, "and she didn't like anybody else being there. And when she got up there, she didn't really seem any happier."

As Joan advanced through the ranks of the coffeehouses, from Cafe Yana to Club 47, she refined a public image exquisitely in sync with the emerging campus folk audience in the late 1950s. "Joan Baez was more mysterious than anybody around—she really had that East Coast, dark, bohemian type of thing—and the beginning of the West Coast, sixties earth-mother thing," said Paul Arnoldi, the singer and guitarist. "She had what seemed like an incredible authenticity, partly because she was vaguely ethnic," said Joyce Kalina Chopra, who, with her friend Paula Kelley, founded Club 47. Because the Baezes were so thoroughly assimilated, however, Joan merely suggested the idea of being Mexican through hints in her appearance and her surname; this, of course, made her the ideal kind of Latino for white audiences: a wholly familiar, non-threatening abstraction. "And she never smiled once," said Chopra. "She was very serious, which was all part of the folk scene—very grave. And she was singing these songs most of us had never heard before. So when she sang about lost love, and she sang all these English ballads, it somehow seemed important. So that for young people at that time, who were searching for things to be serious about—that was very powerful."

In a review of a late February 1959 performance at Club 47 by Joan and Harvard undergraduate Bill Wood, a blues-oriented singer and guitarist known in Cambridge as the host of college radio station WHRB's weekly *Balladeers* program, a student critic for *The Harvard Crimson* strove to illuminate the melancholia at the heart of Joan's appeal:

Last Sunday evening the two young ladies of 47 Mt. Auburn St. removed the tables and hid the cups to make room for some 150 chairs and a platform for folksingers Bill Wood and Joan Baez. From the management's point of view, the evening was a success—standing room only and only one visit from Cambridge's

Finest. And from the audience's somewhat partisan point of view the evening was great. . . . Miss Baez with her long black hair and soft brown eyes has a following more prone to beards and souls and such. . . . Without trying to define just what it is that makes a folksinger better than the usual, finer than professional, suffice it to say that she can communicate a rare and beautiful sadness.

Breaking character, Joan occasionally startled her early audiences by bursting into parodies of teen radio hits; one of her favorites was "Goody Goody," Frankie Lymon and the Teenagers' bouncy trifle of *Schadenfreude* ("Well you lost someone and now you know how it feels / Goody goody!"). Her approach to this material was lacerating—dead-on mimicry of the pop acts' extravagant effervescence, performed with a merciless satirical edge. These digressions, which became rarer as she burnished her stage persona, were virtually the only times Joan allowed her Cambridge public to see the devastating humor for which she had long been known to her friends and family. Audiences seemed uncertain how to take the introduction of sarcasm amidst the melancholy; there were "darting eyes and nervous giggles," said Eric von Schmidt, "like, 'Where's this coming from?' "

Joan settled in as a weekly regular at Club 47, a sizable storefront on Mt. Auburn Street, a block east of Harvard Square, that had previously been Fournier's used-furniture shop. To darken the mood of the place, which had large commercial windows on two sides, its young proprietors hung long brown curtains and painted the walls glossy black. A photograph of the room taken in the spring of 1959 shows Joan standing along the rear wall, singing with her head bowed; more than a hundred young people sit listening, their eyes heavy, faces drawn. "Joan was a sensation," said Joyce Kalina Chopra. With no promotion beyond mimeographed flyers and little press coverage except items in a few of the college newspapers, the eighteen-year-old singer found herself performing to progressively larger and more responsive audiences, indicative of the Cambridge folk scene's growing popularity as well as Joan Baez's position as its chief beneficiary and stimulus.

Joan plucked lovers from her growing body of admirers, while seeing one Harvard undergraduate, Michael New, fairly regularly. A white
native of Trinidad one year older than Joan, New fancied himself a rebel
and poet. He read philosophy in Greek and the existentialists in French,
instead of attending class. (New would devote three years to his freshman studies at Harvard.) He was not handsome but beautiful; his long
dirty-blond hair curled around his ears, and he had a voluptuous lower
lip that made him look as if he were permanently on the verge of quot-
ing Sartre. Joan met him while she was playing her guitar on the banks of
the Charles River, and he approached her in a rowboat; Michael rowed
the boat ashore, and he and Joan kept close company until they succumbed to their mutual volatility. "We were passionately, insanely, irra-
tionally in love for the first few months. Then we started bickering and
quarreling violently," Joan recalled to a journalist. In her memoir, *And a
Voice to Sing With*, she wrote, "In my tender narcissism, I was reaching
out for . . . a 'tattered remnant of my own self'—an outlaw, a savage,
someone who understood what it was to be 'different' and could enter
my secret garden and leave the blemished and terrifying world of adults
and reality outside." The relationship did not last long, but neither
did the separation; Joan and Michael would split for months at a time,
often longer, then reunite briefly, only to perpetuate the cycle. Between
stretches with New, Joan saw no fewer than a dozen other men, by her
own estimate, and also experimented a bit with women.

She withdrew from Boston University before the end of her second
semester to pursue music full time, moving out of her BU dorm room
and back in with her family. A pack of Cambridge men on motorcycles
followed—Harvard undergraduate John Cooke and his friend Geno
Foreman on their Triumphs; Cooke's schoolmates Todd Stuart on a
Matchless 650-CSR and Jonathan "Gentleman John" Morse on a Velo-
cette; and others. The Baezes' house in Belmont became a satellite of the
Harvard Square scene; musicians traded songs in the living room as Joan
held court, her mother reveled in the excitement, and men discovered
Mimi, rekindling old rivalries between the sisters. "Their house was a
very welcoming sort of fun place to hang out, a place like the Club 47 . . .

not just a scene but also a place that was kind of a club in the best sense of the word," said Stuart. A freshman Romance language major who looked exactly like the young John Kennedy, Stuart dated Joan on and off for a few months, then started going out with Mimi. "Oh dear, there were just hundreds of boys," said Big Joan. "I loved it, because it was just wonderful. I used to make hamburgers by the thousands because I loved to have them stay. And they'd play—they'd start striking up the band. The whole thing was just fun, and Joanie ate it up. And someone would spot Mimi, and that would make some sparks." As John Cooke recalled his first visit to the house, "Geno and I came up to see Joan, but she was out. Nobody seemed to be home. Then, I remember, Mimi sort of wandered up to the door—this incredibly stunning teenage girl. We were just dazzled. I thought, 'Holy mackerel, you know, fifteen years old—whoa!' And she was a great guitar player, and nobody had any idea. We all went up there in love with Joan, and we left in love with her little sister." Naturally, Mimi relished the attention, as well as the momentary social triumphs over her revered sibling. "They would drop by the house to see Joanie, and I would manage to get into the living room and somehow get into the conversation and make myself available to talk and, ideally, play the guitar. And then often it would turn out that somebody would be impressed. There were a lot of Joanie rejects who came my way. That was fine—I didn't mind, because they were older and handsome, and Joanie didn't mind. The only ones she minded were the ones she wanted but [who] preferred me." The person in the house uniformly displeased was Albert Baez. (Pauline was still at Drew.) "Poor Al would come home, and there were his gorgeous girls just surrounded by men," said Big Joan. "He couldn't bear it, and he didn't care much for the music, either. He just wanted everybody to leave the house." After going out for dinner with Joan, Mimi, and their mother one evening, Todd Stuart drove the women up to the house and noticed, through the window, Albert Baez jitterbugging by himself.

At their male friends' urging, the Baez sisters often played and sang together during the living-room song sessions in Belmont and on several occasions performed as a duo in public. "The boys always wanted us to do something together," said Mimi, "so I chimed in with Joanie." Since Mimi's repertoire was smaller and somewhat less adaptable to duet settings than Joan's—Mimi liked quiet country blues and instrumental pieces—they worked up two-part arrangements of a dozen or so of Joan's songs; Mimi sang harmony and played a bit of counterpoint on the guitar. Their voices, close in timbre, blended naturally. "They meshed so bloody well," recalled Bob Siggins, banjo player for the Charles River Valley Boys, the Harvard bluegrass group. "Mimi was never as good a singer on her own as Joanie, but I thought the sum of the two parts was far greater than each." Wearing a pair of matching aqua-and-black dresses with a Googie print design, Joan and Mimi Baez played at a party in Harvard's Quincy House, did a set at one of the monthly hootenannies that Boston attorney Marcel Kisten organized in the basement of the Huntington Street YMCA, and performed once together at the Golden Vanity. Joan tended to dominate vocally, while Mimi made a notable impression on the guitar. "The Baez sisters—it was always Joan who could really sing and Mimi who could really play," said the guitarist Bruce Langhorne. "Mimi was really a good little player." The act, such as it was, remained mainly Joan's—the songs were Joan's, and Joan sang the melodies, soaring over her sister. "It was really Joanie's show," said Mimi. "She let me be a part of it, which was very nice of her. But I knew she didn't really want anybody else up there." Joan agreed to the joint appearances and enjoyed them, she said, "because it was fun, and it was good for my little sister, and it didn't really have anything to do with what I was doing by myself. It wasn't really something very serious for me."

Encouraged by the positive reaction to her first public appearances, Mimi told Joan she was beginning to consider the idea of taking up music once she finished high school. "She asked me whether I thought she should sing," recalled Joan, "and I said I didn't think so. I think maybe if I had been a supportive sister, a healthy, supportive sister, I would have said, 'Sure. Let me try to help you.' But I didn't want any competition. And I felt that my success would overshadow her. I was concerned that she wouldn't be able to have the same kind of success, and I wanted to protect her from the hurt of that." Not attuned to the benevolent portion of her sister's response, Mimi was crestfallen. "That was pretty hard to take," said Mimi. " 'Back to your room, little girl.' "

Joan worked with a few other musical partners in 1959. To help build an audience for the YMCA hoots he helped to promote, Boston entrepreneur Manny Greenhill put together an album showcasing several Cambridge artists, including Bill Wood and Ted Alevizos, a singer-guitarist on the Harvard library-science faculty. Greenhill had heard Wood perform duets with Joan on the *Balladeers* radio show and asked them to reprise those songs and do a few solo numbers on the recording. Taped in May 1959 for the local label Veritas Records, *Folksingers 'Round Harvard Square* featured Joan with Wood on three tunes ("So Soon in the Morning," "Kitty," and "Careless Love"), Joan, Wood, and Alevizos on one ("Don't Weep After Me"), and Joan alone on six ("On the Banks of the Ohio," "O What a Beautiful City," "Lowlands," "Black Is the Color," "What You Gonna Call Your Pretty Little Baby," and "Sail Away Ladies"), in addition to solos by Wood and Alevizos. Despite her relative inexperience—Wood, as a member of a Kingston Trio–style group called the Raunch Hands, had recorded two albums for Epic, and Alevizos, a generation older, had been performing professionally since World War II—Joan shines through the finished album. Her singing is dynamic and sure, and her voice has a youthful lightness. Her guitar work is simple but expressive, especially on "Black Is the Color." (Joan uses triplets effectively to give the accompaniment forward motion and keeps things interesting harmonically by intermittently adding a ninth to the tonic minor chord.)

"She learned quite a bit of guitar very quickly," recalled Wood; a smart and dedicated young man with Ricky Nelson looks, he was talked about as one of the few Cambridge locals with the potential for national success. "I think when we first met, I played better than she did, and she learned everything I knew in about three weeks. I would show her something, and she'd pick it up, and in twenty-four hours she'd be doing it better than I could. She was a great learner and really easy to sing with. You just had to assert yourself to hold your own with her." Alevizos, a

Juilliard-trained bel canto singer, projected so well that he nearly over-powered Joan. "We sang one song together at the end of the record ['Don't Weep After Me'], and I had kind of the lead on that thing," said Alevizos. "She got very upset about that, because she said I had the most gorgeous voice she ever heard. She used to tell me, 'How can you sing like that? I want to sing like that. How can you do that?' I said, 'I took singing lessons.' She said, 'Oh, no—no, no.'" However intrigued by Alevizos's vocal technique Joan may have been, her fear and insecurity outweighed her curiosity. "I don't know how to sing properly," she said. "It would be nice to be able to breathe when I'm singing. It'd be much easier if I knew how to breathe, and I'd probably sound better, too. I know I could improve my work, but the idea of training my voice doesn't appeal to me. As long as I can sing this well, I don't think I'll ever take lessons. I suppose I'm afraid that if I do start studying, I'll find out I'm really not that good to begin with."

Although it was small time and only marginally more legitimate than a vanity pressing, *Folksingers 'Round Harvard Square* lifted Joan a notch above the dozens of Cambridge coffeehouse singers who had not done any recording. Joyce Kalina Chopra masking-taped the record jacket onto one of the display windows in front of Club 47. On Tuesday nights, when Joan performed, Manny Greenhill stood outside by the door, selling records from a paper grocery bag. "It was kind of a big deal in our little world," said Betsy Siggins-Schmidt. "Joanie was a recording artist, even though she had to play with two other guys to get there."

Not many other folksingers were much more successful. The budding folk revival, while not quite Pete Seeger's proletarian dreamscape, had relatively few celebrities, and most of them were little known to the general public. The biggest names in the scene, beyond the Kingston Trio and veterans such as Seeger, Josh White, and Burl Ives, were Odetta, the folk-gospel guitarist and singer, who had emerged in the early 1950s; Bob Gibson, the banjo and twelve-string guitar player, singer, and songwriter, also a folksinger for nearly a decade; and Harry Belafonte, who was shifting from calypso to theatrical music and straight acting. (Mike Seeger, Peggy Seeger, Oscar Brand, Jean Ritchie, Dave

Van Ronk, Ramblin' Jack Elliott, and a few others hovered somewhere close.) Chicago nightclub owner and personal manager Albert Grossman, who represented Odetta and Gibson, saw untapped potential in Joan during a scouting mission to Cambridge and booked her for a two-week engagement at his club, the Gate of Horn, in June 1959. "Albert smelled a major opportunity in Joan Baez right away—he wanted her very, very badly, so he brought her out to his turf," said Charlie Rothschild, a personal manager who worked in association with Grossman for several years. During the engagement, Joan met both Odetta and Gibson; she had admired Odetta since high school and became smitten with Gibson. A roguishly handsome little man, Gibson was a robust, crowd-pleasing performer; he sang with a twinkle in his voice. "I had a terrible crush on him," said Joan, "and he was quite a charmer. I wasn't sure I'd get out of Chicago alive." Impressed by her performances at the Gate of Horn, Gibson invited her to do a couple of duets with him at the upcoming Newport Folk Festival.

George Wein, the jazz impresario from Boston already successful with the five-year-old Newport Jazz Festival, was about to try instituting a commercial version of the academically oriented folk festivals that had sprouted up in recent years at the University of California at Berkeley, Oberlin College, Swarthmore, and the Universities of North Carolina and Arkansas. Working out of a New York office in partnership with Louis Lorillard, the tobacco magnate, and Albert Grossman, who did most of the legwork for the festival, Wein put together a two-day program of folk concerts and workshops for musicians beginning on the morning of Saturday, July 11, 1959; performers included Pete Seeger, the Kingston Trio, bluegrass banjo master Earl Scruggs, the blues duo Sonny Terry and Brownie McGhee, and Bob Gibson. The setting, a Triple-A ball park on the Atlantic seacoast surrounded by the holiday mansions of Gilded Age barons, had helped make the Newport Jazz Festival a popular summer attraction for the suburban leisure class of the postwar boom economy; and the timing, between performing-arts seasons, served to magnify the perceived importance of the event. "All the reporters from the big newspapers and magazines, which were all based in New York, they all came to Newport—it was beautiful, and there was nothing else for them to write about," said Charles Bourgeois, director of publicity for Wein's organization. "The concert world was dead. Nothing was happening. Newport was *it*, man." In 1956 a fiery performance by Duke Ellington and His Orchestra at Newport had made the cover of *Time* magazine and sparked a renaissance in the bandleader's career. "We had the precedent with Ellington of being a place where things can happen," said George Wein. "When we started the folk festival the first year, some people had that expectation. Folk was becoming the big thing, and Newport was the place to be." An audience of some 13,000—mostly people of college age, a generation younger than the majority of the jazz festival crowd—attended the opening-day events, seemingly undaunted by intermittent rains.

"From the beginning of the festival, I remember, Joan stood right by the stage entrance," said George Wein, "and she was in bare feet, and she was there the whole time. She got to see and talk to every folk performer. She stayed there all day and night and danced during the music." It was not yet certain that she would get to do any other performing; although Bob Gibson had invited her to sing with him, he needed to square the plan with Oscar Brand, the festival's stage manager and master of ceremonies. "Bobby Gibson asked me if I could put her on," said Brand. "He took me aside, and he said, 'Listen, there is this girl. You know. She is very popular in Boston,' he said. He said, 'I would like to let her take part of my time.' And I didn't really think it was a great idea. First of all, it was a terrible rainy day, and we were running over. And when he came over with her, she was drenched. Her hair was wringing wet. She also had been dabbling in the mud, and she was not wearing shoes, and her feet were full of mud. Bobby said, 'Listen, I will work with her. I won't leave her alone.' And I said, 'Okay, what the hell,' if he was giving up his own time. It was a very loose program." Hedging her bet on Gibson, meanwhile, Joan asked several other performers if she could sing with them. Robert J. Lurtsema, a radio journalist for WBCN in Boston, watched backstage as she approached bluegrass banjo player Earl Scruggs. "He said no, and she moved on to the next guy who was going to be singing," recalled Lurtsema. "She wasn't leaving anything to chance."

Bob Gibson began his set early on Sunday evening and did about a dozen songs, singing and playing the twelve-string guitar. (Bassist Bill Lee, a virtuoso jazz musician best known in folk circles for having worked with Odetta, accompanied Gibson.) He wore a gray sports jacket and a tie, and he sang exuberantly. Gibson, who projected the friendly authority of a teacher whom students would invite to their parties, was usually a hit on college campuses; this evening, the audience (now more than 14,000, most of them young people) cheered him on with obvious delight. The rain had stopped, and a mist wafted through the stage light as he paused to tune up his guitar and announced, "Now, I want to sing 'Virgin Mary Had One Son.' There is a young lady from Boston whom I have asked to do it with me. Her name is Joan Baez." She strode out briskly in a long-sleeved red dress. She stood alongside Gibson, her hands dropped to her sides. They sang two verses together, and Gibson backed away from the microphone. Joan stepped forward, straight-backed, and sang full voice:

Some call him David
Think I'll call him 'Manuel
Oh, Lord, I'll call him 'Manuel
Oh, I'll call him 'Manuel
Glory be to the newborn king

Oscar Brand had brought his year-old son, Eric, to the festival and let him sleep on a couple of chairs offstage. "She sang with such a powerful voice that she woke him up," recalled Brand. "She woke everybody up all the way to Boston." As a follow-up, Gibson, seasoned in stagecraft, chose "Jordan River," a rousing, up-tempo gospel number; Joan let loose on the chorus, Odetta-style, and the audience roared in exhilaration. "The audience went crazy—mob psychology and great theater in perfect synchronicity," remembered Dave Van Ronk. "Newport absolutely exploded." In two performances of spirituals, Joan Baez made an evangelical debut.

"You have to understand this in its totality," explained Oscar Brand.

"It was the whole atmosphere of the occasion. It wasn't just that she was singing. The audience was surprised to see her—nobody said she was going to be there. It had been raining. Her hair was stringing down her face. And she stood there very, very simply, and the intensity with which she performed in front of that audience of thousands was just tremendous. It was like she had an aura around her."

Bob Gibson, though delighted for Joan, declined to take credit for the effect of her performance (that evening or in the years to follow). "If I hadn't 'introduced' Joan Baez, someone else would have," Gibson wrote in his memoir, *I Come for to Sing*. "It was like 'discovering' the Grand Canyon. I may have introduced her to her first large audience, but what does that mean? Do you think that girl was going to stay unknown in Cambridge?"

"There was no question that she had exactly what the young, new audience was looking for," said Jac Holzman, founder of Elektra Records. "When they came together, it was like a match and stick of TNT." Eager to sign her to his label, Holzman went backstage after he heard her sing, but he never saw Joan; she was lost in a mob of admirers.

Mimi had been at home all night, playing guitar in her room till bedtime. She had school the next morning.

As JOAN BAEZ SURFACED IN CAMBRIDGE, women like her played in coffeehouses and clubs all around the country. Jo Mapes in Chicago, Judy Henske in Los Angeles, Judy Collins in Denver—all capable, appealing, and young—carried on the tradition of strong female folksingers such as Ronnie Gilbert, Peggy Seeger, Odetta, and Susan Reed and added a youthful sensuality. In Greenwich Village, the largest and most celebrated community in the folk revival, a fair number of gifted women began to emerge by the end of the 1950s: Ellen Adler, Karen Dalton, Maria

D'Amato (later Maria Muldaur), Bonnie Dobson, Karen James, Molly Scott, Mary Travers, and the most prominent among them at that point, Carolyn Hester. Born about an hour's ride north of Austin, Texas, in 1937, Hester was nearly four years older than Joan and already known in folk circles when Joan made her Newport debut; since moving to Manhattan in 1956, Hester performed about a week each month in Village coffeehouses, as well as in cafés and nightclubs in Washington, D.C., Philadelphia, and Cambridge (Joan had seen Hester sing at the Golden Vanity); and she had recorded two solo albums of traditional songs, the first under Buddy Holly's producer Norman Petty. (Holly had watched Hester in the recording studio and had taken snapshots of some of her early sessions.) A womanly, voluptuous beauty with sculpted features and a mane of golden-brown hair, Hester had the commanding femininity of Merle Oberon or Rita Hayworth and was often asked if she was a movie star. She was so luminous a presence that people who met her briefly would mistakenly remember her as a blonde. Hester had taken a few acting classes at New York's American Theatre Wing but decided to concentrate on music, studying both voice and guitar with private teachers while she made the coffeehouse rounds. Performing a typical repertoire of traditional American and English ballads, she imparted the expected and the archaic with a fresh, contemporary feeling. Her singing was limber, seemingly casual, and friendly. Unlike many regional folk performers and urban revivalists of the time, she tended to sound as if she were enjoying herself—even on record, you can hear her smiling; Buddy Holly was indeed in the studio with her, in spirit.

"Carolyn was electrifying—set of pipes, very, very expressive," said Dave Van Ronk; at twenty-three in 1959, Van Ronk was known in the coffeehouses as one of the most charismatic and articulate figures in the New York scene. Nicknamed "the mayor of Greenwich Village," Van Ronk was so respected by the city's folk musicians that Robert Shelton, who covered folk for *The New York Times*, asked him to vet important pieces before the *Times* editors saw them. "Carolyn was a contender, no doubt about it," said Van Ronk, a hulking presence whose soft Brooklyn accent added just enough comic leavening to his bellowing gravel voice.

"Beauty, talent, charm—she had it all. If any of the folk girls was going to make the big time, so to speak, it was going to be Carolyn." Hester was less confident. "Pete Seeger was my idol and my role model," she said. "I've always loved traditional songs, and I loved singing them. I never expected to become famous singing folk music. Buddy was famous, I was the folksinger."

Hester shared a spacious nineteenth-century apartment on the Upper West Side with two friends from the Theatre Wing, but performed, studied music, and socialized almost exclusively in Greenwich Village. A fabled bohemia since Edgar Allan Poe and Walt Whitman squabbled in its basement drinking halls, the Village had long been infamously tolerant of cultural adventurism, including folk music. The Almanac Singers had used a loft on East 13th Street as their home base in the 1940s, and Alan Lomax and Harry Smith both worked out of the Village during the 1950s. A tradition of folk singing in Washington Square Park, the eight-block town square of Greenwich Village, began in 1945, when a professional printer named George Margolin started strumming a guitar and singing folk songs near the park fountain, according to Oscar Brand; Margolin evidently attracted a following and inspired imitators, whose numbers multiplied exponentially as folk grew in popularity. By 1960 hundreds of young people adorned with various stringed instruments congregated in Washington Square Park every weekend. Julius Zito, a Village baker, said the music carried over four blocks to his shop on Bleecker Street and slowed the rise of his bread on Sundays. An itinerant entrepreneur known as the Pick Man was understood to earn a living selling guitar and banjo picks in the park. "You couldn't turn around without bumping into a guitar," said Lionel Kilberg, a salesman for a Manhattan air freight company who, as washtub bass player for a bluegrass group, the Shanty Boys, featured prominently in *The New York News'* first feature on the Washington Square folk craze. "In the mid-'50s, more and more people from all over the New York area were coming to the park to play. Then more people started coming to hear them play. The next week, the same people who just came to listen would be back, only this time, they would have guitars, and they would be playing.

More people would be listening to them, and the following week they would have guitars."

Like good capitalists in a tourist economy, Greenwich Village shop owners acted quickly to accommodate the growing folk trade. The first coffeehouses in the district—two spare neighboring rooms called Edgar's Hobby and David's—had opened in the late 1940s for the area's Italian population. Their inheritors—more than a dozen places all around the Village with progressively whimsical names such as the Figaro, the Rienzi, the Caricature, the Cafe Wha?, the Dragon's Den, the Bizarre, the Why Not?, and the Hip Bagel—now offered folksinging (sometimes mixed with poetry readings, jazz, and comedy) to the mobs of weekend visitors, including uptown residents who would stroll around the Village, just minutes from their homes, as if it were a resort. The owner of a small garage on West 3rd Street, a block south of Washington Square, took a threadbare wool couch with one leg missing and miscellaneous battered furnishings from neighborhood trash piles, tacked a "Folk Music" sign on the front wall, and he was in the coffeehouse business.

For musicians (that is, anyone interested, this being folk music), there were also hootenannies from time to time at Cooper Union, the Henry Street Settlement farther downtown, and the American Youth Hostel on Amsterdam Avenue and 103rd Street near Columbia University, as well as frequent open parties by folk buffs such as Miki Isaacson, whose fourth-floor apartment at One Sheridan Square was essentially another youth hostel. "There was something going on all the time, if you liked the music," said Bob Yellin, a New York–bred son of a concert violist, who became the banjo player for the Greenbriar Boys bluegrass trio. "And there was traditional music of every kind. It wasn't just folk music like the Weavers. There was blues and old-time music and bluegrass and mountain music, and everything else. It was everything, nonstop." Even in private gatherings hosted by nonmusicians, folk music was a mark of egalitarian chic. "If there was a party in the Village," Brand recalled, "it was, 'You bring the folksinger, I'll bring the Negro.' "

One of the first important social centers of the Greenwich Village folk scene was Allan Block's Sandal Shop on West 4th Street between Sixth and Seventh Avenues, opened in 1950 by a self-taught leather worker who had learned country-style fiddle growing up in Oshkosh, Wisconsin. Passersby would hear Block playing "Sally Ann" or "Cumberland Gap" between sandal jobs and wander in. Just twenty feet wide and forty feet deep, the store had a few pine stools set in front of a shop table with a buffing wheel mounted on the side; on an exposed brick wall in the rear, Block hung some sketches of feet and sandal designs he had made. It was a work space, rustic and spartan. The smell of leather and glue, the sound of fiddle playing, and the sight of hand tools and pencil drawings worked in conjunction to attract a public veering from the regimented commercialism that midtown Manhattan seemed to represent. "In the beginning, most people saw sandals as something very European or feminine," said Block. "White men wouldn't buy them at all—only black men. Then, I think, people started relating the idea of exposed feet and natural leather and something handmade with folk music and crafts." By the mid-1950s, Block's shop became a meeting place for Villagers and tourists interested in folk culture; on Saturdays the store was overrun with musicians jamming, trading songs and stories. "God help you," said Dave Van Ronk, "if you wanted to buy a pair of sandals." In the free spirit the shop engendered, Van Ronk once picked up a banjo—not his instrument—and flailed away. "You know, you can't play the banjo," said a man in his mid-twenties whom Van Ronk had never met. "But you're the best banjo player I've ever heard." The fellow introduced himself as Richard Fariña, a writer who didn't play the banjo, either. Van Ronk roared as Fariña walked out of the shop.

Another store with a name that imparted institutional authority, the Folklore Center, became the nerve center of the Village folk community almost as soon as it opened in April 1957. "Within about three weeks after that opened, it crystallized the scene," said Ralph Lee Smith, a professional journalist who played the Appalachian dulcimer in jam sessions at Allan Block's Sandal Shop. "The scene was very scattered until then, and Izzy Young just walked right into the right place at the right time, and he became an instant crossroads, both in the Village and, quite quickly, nationally." An ebullient anarchist raised in a Jewish ghetto of the Bronx, Israel Young was a twenty-nine-year-old refugee from the Fourth Avenue bookstores when he opened the Folklore Center at 110 MacDougal Street, not far from Washington Square. The store was essentially an excuse for Young to indulge his own passions—books (he had carried so many around when he was a boy that neighborhood kids would try to push them out of his hands), folk music (and dance, especially English Morris dancing, of which he was an expert practitioner), and gossip (he was an obsessive diarist). A narrow shop with new and used instruments hanging on the walls and racks for records and all varieties of publications, the Folklore Center was invariably busy yet barely profitable. "The first place everybody with the slightest interest in folk immediately went was the Folklore Center," said Oscar Brand. "That was where you caught up on the latest news, speculation, and misinformation. If you stayed more than a minute, someone you knew came in. It was a social center, like an old eastern European town square, and just as profitable. Izzy was the worst businessman in the world. He sold everything at a discount, if he didn't give it away. If you wanted to sing in a coffeehouse, and you needed a guitar, Izzy would give you one and say you could pay him later. Of course, no one did." In the front of the store, Young held concerts—at least one a month, on average, many of which were the formal debuts of young singers new to the city. "I was a real schmuck," said Young. Tall and thickly featured, he had a disarming wit and moved speedily and gracefully with a dancer's physical confidence; it did not take him long to earn a reputation as one of the great lotharios of Washington Square. "I didn't know that I was doing everything wrong. But everybody else was schmuckier than me, because they came in and asked me for my opinion." Robert Shelton liked to bring in a sandwich and perch on the record bins, listening to Young chat with his so-called customers.

New York was not only home to the major record labels, the music publishing industry, and the national media, it was also the base of operations for Shelton, the only journalist and critic covering folk regularly for a major American newspaper. At age thirty-three in the winter of

1960, Shelton (born Shapiro), a Chicago-born graduate of Northwestern, had been contributing to the *Times* for nearly five years. His folk criticism, like much of the *Times*'s cultural journalism of the day, was restrained. He clearly saw his role as advocative; at his harshest, Shelton would describe an act he disliked as "promising." His enthusiasm for favorite artists led him to ethical lapses—he wrote some liner notes and press materials under pseudonyms for acts he reviewed—and his weakness for alcohol was well known among folk performers, including those eager to win his favor.

"Bob Shelton was infatuated with Carolyn Hester," said Charlie Rothschild, Hester's manager in early 1960. "He was always concocting phony business to be near her." In the first weeks of January, Shelton asked Hester to dinner, ostensibly to provide career counseling. "He was like 'Come and have dinner with me, and we'll talk about your music,' " recalled Hester. "What a come-on! I didn't like things on that level. He worried me, but I went. I was afraid it would come back to haunt me if I didn't." After a meal at a West Village spaghetti house, Shelton took Hester to the White Horse Tavern, a smoky pub on Hudson Street where young literary hopefuls congregated because they had heard that Dylan Thomas had dropped dead on his way out the front door in 1953. The White Horse could generally be counted upon to provide the presence of at least one writer who drank (usually Delmore Schwartz) and any number of drinkers who wrote, as well as a few Irish folk musicians (the Clancy Brothers, Tommy Makem) and New York University students. Shelton and Hester sat at a tiny oak-top table and watched a few men at the bar, one of whom was Paddy Clancy, singing Irish songs. Another of the group, a lean, dark fellow with longish black hair and a fiery glare, stepped forward and sang a vigorous rendition of "The Wild Colonial Boy." Shelton pointed him out to Hester as Fariña, one of the White Horse writers who drank, and introduced them. "I just was immediately drawn to him," Hester said. "Richard really stood out. His eyes were wonderful, and he was very bright, and he could make anyone laugh, and I loved to laugh. He couldn't sing, really, but he had real magnetism. He said he would come see me the next time I was singing in town, and I said, 'Great,' and I wished I was booked for the following night, so I would see him again. But I wasn't scheduled to play anywhere for a while, and he kind of disappeared."

RICHARD FARIÑA WAS BORN AT SEA. He spent his childhood traveling the world with his parents, his father a Cuban inventor, his mother an Irish mystic, and was educated by tutors throughout Europe and Africa. As a teenager in the early 1950s, he lived among the *barbudos* in the hills of Cuba and ran guns for Fidel Castro. Fariña returned to the United States to study at Cornell but was expelled for leading a campus riot. He fled to Ireland and joined the Irish Republican Army. Among other missions, he once swam the Irish Sea with timed plastic explosives strapped to his back and sank a British submarine. He had a child in Ireland with a woman whose name can never be revealed. Like his idol and mentor Ernest Hemingway, a friend from their days together in Cuba, Fariña loved to hunt; a rabid bear would surely have devoured him once, had he not inserted the barrel of his shotgun in the animal's rectum and pulled the trigger. He slept with a loaded .45 under his pillow, to protect himself from a jealous husband who vowed to kill him someday. Fariña had a metal plate in his head.

So he said, among innumerable other fantasies, partial truths, exaggerations, and appropriations from people he had met or had read about. "I think he rather self-consciously cultivated an aura of mystery," said C. Michael Curtis, one of his roommates in college—Fariña really did attend Cornell, and he was one of several students suspended for their involvement in a protest against university policies on parties held off-campus, although he later misrepresented both the event and his role in it. "He liked to be thought of as having lived the dangerous life. He could take the smallest detail and form it into a much more elaborate scheme. It is hard to know how much of this fantasy world he thought might actually have happened or how much of it was calculated. I've known liars, and I've known fantasists. He was more of a fantasist. There was something so boyish and irrepressible about his fantasies, and he wasn't aggressive about pushing them. He would sort of drop a lot of vague hints that would encourage you to think things, and he would say, 'I can't talk about it,' and he would give you a quizzical smile, and then he would go on to change the subject. There were times when I thought that he really considered himself as someone who had done all these things and whose life might actually have been in danger. And there were times when he seemed to want to let everybody in on the fact that everything he said was a grand joke.

"He had a strong sense of himself," said Curtis, "and it had a wonderful effect. I mean, he mesmerized you. He was so likable that most people were happy to accept whatever he said. He was just wonderfully charming and lovable."

In truth, Fariña was born and raised in a pleasant Irish Catholic pocket of Flatbush, Brooklyn. Like the Baez sisters, he was a first-generation American of Anglo-Latin descent: his mother, Tessie Farina, a high-spirited beauty christened Theresa Crozier, came from a family of fishing people in County Tyrone, Northern Ireland; and his father, Richard Farina, Sr., a rakish go-getter born Liborio Ricardo Fariñas, was reared in a brood of workers living on the Stewart Central sugar plantation in the Matanzas province of Cuba. (When Richard Sr. came alone to the United States at the age of eighteen in 1925, he adopted an Americanization of the family name, Farina; his son reclaimed the tilde, but not the *s*, after college.) An only child in an environment with a tradition of big families—his father was one of at least eighteen children—Richard came early to an attitude of entitlement. (Tessie Farina had a hysterectomy as a result of problems during Richard's birth.) His father's position as a tool maker (not a laborer, like many men in his sphere, but someone who constructed the machinery the workers used) gave the family some status in the neighborhood, and his mother, alone in the house with her only child, coddled the boy. "He could have anything he wanted—any toy, any game," said his father. "He knew he could have everything the other boys and girls couldn't have. And his mother took care of him day and night. He was all she had. For her, the world revolved around him. That's the way he grew up." Over the course of his childhood, Richard was diagnosed with asthma and allergies to numerous foods, including eggs, mustard, garlic, and brussels sprouts. Tessie Farina, following a doctor's recommendation to give the boy a change of climate, took him to spend a few weeks with his father's relatives in Cuba; as his cousin Severa Fariñas Lugones remembers the visit, Richard, who was eight years old and did not understand Spanish, was too shy to go to the outhouse without his mother (or, for that matter, to go drinking with Hemingway). At home in their five-room modern apartment on Linden Boulevard in Flatbush, his mother protectively restricted Richard from most outdoor play, and he developed an active internal life. "He had quite an imagination," recalled Richard Sr.'s nephew Humberto Fariñas, a frequent household guest. "One thing I remember about him, he would be very concerned about the funnies. He was that type of boy, you know, because he would spend so much time reading funnies and playing with toys by himself and stuff like that. His mind was always on something that was not real." Richard attended Holy Cross Catholic Elementary School and was an altar boy and sang in the church children's choir, the only sign of interest in music his father would later recall; the first thing his parents remember him saying he wanted to be when he grew up was a priest. Around the age of ten, Richard invented his own comic-strip characters and drew their adventures on sheets of construction paper he taped all over the walls of his room. His father went into Richard's room to fetch him for dinner and found his son lying on his back on the floor, gazing at his creations.

From his father, Richard inherited a force of will to match his sense of exceptionalism. "I think we had the same character—the same drive," said Richard Sr. "I taught him, when you want something, don't stop until you get what you're going after. Be very dedicated to whatever you do. And he wouldn't stop until he accomplished what he was after. He got that from me. Another thing I told him, if you want to do something great and improve yourself, you have to have the right friends. I used to watch him and his friends. I told him, 'Tell me who you go around with, and I'll tell you who you are.' "

Richard attended the academically exclusive Brooklyn High School of Technology, where he excelled, and he was accepted in the electrical engineering program at Cornell on a New York State Regents Scholarship, which covered most of his tuition. "I wanted him to be an engineer because of my technical background," said Richard Sr. During the military-industrial expansion of the early cold war years, moreover, the applied sciences were thriving fields of study. "If you were a smart young man at that time, the thing to do was be an engineer—that's where all the action was, and that's what Dick had in his head when he came to Cornell," said one of Richard's engineering classmates, Paul Cleaver. The school, historically one of the most diverse in the Ivy League, also had fine literature and writing programs, distinguished by professors such as the poet W. D. Snodgrass; short-story writer James McConkey, founder of the Morehead Writers' Workshop; and Vladimir Nabokov, who, having just published *Lolita* the year Fariña entered college, was revered in international literary circles and feared on campus but was not yet broadly known. Richard floundered in the Darwinian competition of the Cornell science curriculum but thrived in writing class. When he took the final exam for his first-term sophomore chemical engineering class in December 1957, he used the two and a half hours of test time to compose a free-verse poem about why he should not be studying chemical engineering and handed it in. Impulsive, daring, and wildly imaginative—or desperate, irresponsible, and dangerously susceptible to delusions of exemption?—Richard, with one dramatic gesture, earned a transfer to the creative writing program, with McConkey as his faculty adviser. His father, less impressed, made the five-hour drive to the Ithaca, New York, campus to meet with McConkey. "His dear father—very earnest," remembered McConkey. "He wanted my assurance that his son had genuine talent as a writer and prospects for success. I told him honestly that, yes, his son had a real gift and could be quite successful." Richard discovered the undergraduate literary scene in the local bohemia, four blocks of row houses, pubs, and shops geared for students called College Town, and joined in with confident élan. He wore a beret. He appeared engrossed in the world of words: over drinks at Johnny's Big Red Grill (Richard ordered Ballantine ale—whenever there was a choice of brands, he had a preference, and it was always important), he conducted conversations peppered with lines from Dylan Thomas and oblique references to the high modernists Joyce, Pound, and Eliot, whom he would casually mention like colleagues, and he carried a spiral notebook into which he would scrawl verse or bits of short stories between sips.

Richard became something of a Heathcliff figure at Cornell. "He walked and talked as if he had been born wearing a cape," said Kristin Osterholm White, a gifted Cornell writer who was one of Richard's closest college friends. "At Cornell, the women were outnumbered by the men, many of them richer, more dependable, and more attractive than Dick in a conventional way, but at parties he seemed always to slip away early with the most perfect, unapproachable woman in the room. I'd see them together a week later, and the girl would have a warmth about her I hadn't seen before." (While at Cornell, Fariña was briefly engaged to Diane Divers, a monied beauty and academic star, but her parents disapproved of Richard and had the engagement broken. Eventually Divers would marry an heir to Arkansas's Tyson Foods and become one of Bill and Hillary Clinton's closest friends.)

"Dick was grand company but had to have what he considered his fair share of the limelight," said White. "He knew when to back off and yield the floor—but while he listened appreciatively and intently to the yarn you spun, his mind would be whirling ahead. When you came to your punch line, he'd have a better line of his own all prepared. Everyone we knew was young and had talent, but Dick had an adult kind of ambition, too. Often he came across as a show-off and opportunist, but the ambition was genuine. He took himself seriously and, when he wanted to be, could muster immense discipline. Being clever, quick, and talented in a general way was not enough for Dick. He set out to measure his strengths and define his possibilities, and instead of taking them or himself for granted, he worked at his gifts. Competition brought out the best in him, Hemingway style."

Early in the spring of his junior year, Richard won Cornell's annual undergraduate short-story writing competition with a romantic memoirish story, "With a Copy of Dylan Under My Arm." The story, while indebted to Fariña's major influences, Dylan Thomas and Ernest Hemingway, has a confident voice that belies the author's youth; published in the March 1958 edition of *The Cornell Writer* (along with two poems by Fariña, "Out By McGuckins" and "The Priest that from the Altar Burst"), it quickly established Richard's campus literary reputation. In a review of the story in *The Cornell Daily Sun*, the student newspaper, Kirkpatrick Sale wrote, "If there is any one person in this issue of *The Writer* who really shows the ability to become a first-rate author, it is Farina. There is none of the simple surface glitter, the empty polish, the pseudo-stylization that is too often found in the false and phony prose of the collegiate literati." Eight more of Richard's stories and poems appeared in the next three issues of *The Writer*. Much of his verse, such as the poem "Away in the Highlands," traded on his Irish heritage:

Away where the men with their swollen fists
  Clutched tankards to warm their lives,
And the white waxed flame of the darkened church
  Offered bread to the mouths of the wives,
My Mary and I strolled by and by
And there with the sun and oat we'd lie.

"He was Irish," Kirkpatrick Sale recalled. "We never heard anything about his Cuban side." In much of Fariña's prose and some of his free verse, however, he probed a range of more contemporary styles, particularly in the lyrical memory story "Mary Anne and Me" and the adventurous prose poem "The Very Last Thoughts of One Now Dead." For the premier issue of the Cornell literary journal *The Trojan Horse* in December 1960, he contributed a parody that painted T. S. Eliot with the same tar as the Beats, "The Dream Song of J. Alfred Kerowack":

In the room, the cats eat mad spaghetti
Talking of Lawrence Ferlinghetti

He cultivated relationships with faculty members and fellow students who he thought could help realize his literary dreams. "He talked about Hemingway a lot," recalled Herbert Gold, the young novelist and essayist who joined the Cornell faculty when Nabokov left, at the Russian author's recommendation; an esteemed writer, virilely handsome, a spirited conversationalist, and a contributor to *Playboy*, Gold was, perhaps more than Hemingway, Richard Fariña's literary ideal. "But his conversation about writing was mainly 'How do you get an agent?' 'How do you get to an editor?' And 'How do you make it?' " At Beebe Lodge, a student hangout overlooking a lake on campus, Richard spun aspirational fantasies with David Leshan, a literature major from Manhattan. "We talked there, and we would go canoeing on the lake, and we talked about Hemingway, whom he admired," recalled Leshan. "What we talked about most was his future career. But he saw a role for me. He thought of me as—I don't think I had much of a track record for this, but he saw me as the great editor. I would be the editor, and I would edit his work, and he would be the novelist. It was a kind of fantasy, and most of my contact with him had to do with these sorts of fantasies."

In the summer of 1958, Richard Fariña and Mike Curtis rented one of the roomy old student apartments on Linden Avenue in College Town. Raised by a maternal aunt in rural Arkansas, Curtis had been educated at a high school with ten students in the graduating class. He read an article about Cornell in *Reader's Digest* while working as a short-order cook and arrived at the school alone with three dollars left after paying for one-way bus fare; he had not heard about the convention of applying to a college and had taken no entrance exams. Following the advice of a Cornell counselor, he put in a year at Ithaca High School while working full time as a bellboy at the Clinton House hotel, was then accepted at Cornell, and eventually became associate editor of the school literary magazine, associate editor of the humor magazine, coeditor-in-chief of the yearbook, and editorial writer for the *Sun*. "I had a lot of energy, and so did Dick," recalled Curtis, who, with his chiseled looks, fierce intelligence, and country-boy charm, was nearly as much of a social magnet as his roommate. They shared a first-floor place with two bedrooms and a parlor filled with furniture they had stolen from public spaces around campus. The next fall, a friend from one of their writing classes, Thomas Pynchon, joined them on and off. Like Curtis, Pynchon had the maturity of someone a bit older than many of his classmates. He liked to spend the time by himself, reading. While he was known to have a few Red Cap ales at Johnny's or pick up a guitar at a party and strum a standard such as Rodgers and Hart's "I Wish I Were in Love Again," Pynchon, in contrast to Fariña, was clearly most comfortable in the smallest groups. "He was a real observer of life in some kind of way that I thought is what a real author is," said David Leshan. "He seemed more aware than other people, and people listened to him."

Their mutual passions for literature and women brought Fariña and Pynchon together, as their friend David Shetzline observed. "I think Tom recognized that Richard had a magic with language, that he was genuinely gifted, and I think Tom recognized that Richard worked with his gifts, he worked consciously to hone them," said Shetzline (who would remain close to both Fariña and Pynchon and publish two novels himself after college). "Tom always hung back. You didn't find out much about his writing from him, but he was always complaining that he wasn't getting enough writing done, and that is the tip-off that somebody is absolutely haunted as a writer. Richard knew Tom was as serious about writing as he was. I think Pynchon was also fascinated with Richard's effect on women, which was powerful. Pynchon developed a capacity to appeal to women who would then sort of go after him."

To Pynchon, "What determined our relation as writers seemed to be the immediate polarities. Not to overstate things, Fariña in college was a total Hemingway maniac—I may have posed as Scott Fitz, but the opposite number Fariña really had me figured for was Henry James. He was the crazy one, I was the rationalist—he was *engagé*, I was reserved—he was relaxed, I was stuffy."

Their tastes in music appeared irreconcilable. Pynchon was a fan of jazz, bebop in particular. Fariña, while attracted to the tragic romance he saw in the jazz life, listened to pop radio in the apartment and frequently accompanied his younger schoolmate Peter Yarrow to the Sunday-evening "sings" at Cornell's Folk Song Society. "Fariña had no respect for my ear, and his own tended to bewilder me, and there it rested," said Pynchon.

Beyond palling around like typical college friends—popping up at James McConkey's home to help their teacher fix his garage roof, horsing around in an outdoor production of Dylan Thomas's *Under Milk Wood*—Pynchon and Fariña took each other seriously enough to provoke each other. "In college one or another of us would come on like [a critic] every once in a while," Pynchon recalled, "and there would always be Dick, pointing his finger, laughing, yelling, 'Critic!' 'Who,' you would say, 'me? Not me, man.' 'Eclectic,' he would yell back, 'academic, pedant. Ha!' He'd be right, of course. It helped keep you straight, if that was something you worried about. He was like a conscience."

After three years at Cornell (he did not graduate), Richard visited his mother's family in Ireland for a few weeks and returned to College Town (not enrolled in classes) with a souvenir bag of stories about his various activities with the IRA. He told no fewer than eleven versions of the submarine-sinking incident—it was a reconnaissance ship, it was a bridge, he used a hand grenade, he was the signal man—as well as a tale about a revolutionary leader bayoneting a traitor that he would later transpose to Cuba. There is no knowing what he did while he was not in his relatives' company, of course, and it is feasible that Richard's daring and sense of adventure led him to some involvement with the IRA. All his parents knew from the letters they received from Tessie's family was that Richard made his bed every morning and helped with the dishes after supper. Richard may or may not have gone to Cuba around this time as well. One of his Cornell classmates, Paul Cleaver, would later provide a credible account of a trip to Havana with David Leshan and Richard during spring break, 1958. Leshan, while corroborating other of Cleaver's particulars, insisted that Fariña was not on the trip. None of Richard's Cuban relatives who eventually moved to the United States would acknowledge having seen him in Cuba at any point after his childhood visit, and his father would not say he knew for sure if Richard returned a second time. Perhaps Richard was on a secret mission for Castro, and his family and David Leshan were protecting him (and themselves) with their silence. "That could be true," said Cleaver. "It's definitely what Richard would want us to think."

Richard started working at J. Walter Thompson after spring term, 1959, living for a while in a loft on lower Broadway with the painter Wolf Kahn —"no furniture, 3,000 mice, and occasional other guests," Fariña wrote in a letter to his writer friend Peter Tamony. In the evenings that summer, Richard tried to launch a literary magazine, which he wanted to call *Boo*; but he never pulled it together.

Richard, who was working on the Shell Oil account, kept in touch with Pynchon, who was working on a novel later published as *V.*, and tried enticing him to join him in the advertising business. As Pynchon recalled, "About once a week Dick would call up and say, look man, you really have to come down here, I have this job set up and all, and I would say, well I don't know. I really didn't. Advertising sounded like fun, but in back always there was that nagging doubt, and as it turned out it was there for Dick too, only like always he was trying it, grooving along, seeing what it would turn into, how long it would take before it got on top of him. It bothered him to see what it was doing to guys he worked with. I remember him trying to talk about it over some very noisy, too tightly arranged group playing intermission for Ornette Coleman, who at the time was coming on new, revolutionary, for some messianic. We would go down and listen a lot. He never had any what you could call illusions about the ad business, more a willingness to wait and see instead of condemning it out of hand, like me and others we knew—not accept the folklore about how it was all lies but to go in and see for himself. Impatience with hearsay or secondhand data, is what I'm trying to say, and that of course carried over into his writing. Most of us, me included, were not so skeptical, and unhappily that carried over into our writing too. . . . It never occurred to Dick to go at things any other way—he had it instinctively. But more and more the job at Thompson started bugging him, till he didn't take it seriously anymore.

"He hung out a lot at the White Horse. . . . He seemed to know everybody in the Village. One morning he laid out from Thompson and we all went down to see a guy and his wife off to England on the *United States*, which Dick had come back from Ireland once on and so felt attached to. We jammed into this little tiny cabin and drank gin earnestly till sailing time, lurched off, waved good-bye, sang along with the band, wandered over to the next pier and found the *Île de France* or one of them had just pulled in. It seemed a good idea to try and sneak on board, only the quarantine guys had other ideas, chased us around awhile. That was how that went, rollicking around the streets of New York. A funny time."

IN ITS FIRST YEARS, the Greenwich Village folk scene, much like the one in Cambridge, adhered to the labor theory of value. Pete Seeger had reason to be proud: most musicians sang and played for free in Washington Square and passed a basket for change in the coffeehouses (or "basket houses"). The principal measure of success for the majority of folksingers was peer approval. It was a system largely untainted by professionalism, until nightclubs such as the Village Gate and the Blue Angel began booking, paying for, promoting, and charging audiences to see folksingers as well as comedians and bebop combos. From his crow's nest at the Folklore Center, Izzy Young saw the spread of folk into the terrain of jazz and cocktails in Manhattan night life as proof of the music's commercial potential and an opportunity to expand his own enterprise. "All the folkniks were running around the schmucky coffeehouses," said Young, "and the nightclub owners were giving people folk music—and booze and a place to meet other people so they could get laid, instead of sitting there in the afternoon sipping espresso. But they weren't doing it right, because they didn't give a shit about the music. I said, 'Hey, I can do that better than them.' " Working in partnership with Tom Prendergast, a sharp-dressing advertising executive with an interest in folk, Young made a deal with Mike Porco, the owner of a bar and pasta house at 11 West 4th Street and Mercer Street, two blocks east of Washington Square, and set up the first folk-only nightclub in Greenwich Village. Porco, an irrepressible man with a Calabrese accent that he thickened and thinned like marinara to suit his needs, had been struggling for a few years, since the nearby factories that employed his regular customers began closing down. With handshakes, the three partners agreed that Young and Prendergast would book and pay for the acts, handle all advertising and promotion, and take home what they collected at the door ($1.50 per head, no charge on Mondays); Porco would keep all he made from the sale of drinks and food. "It was a good deal—for me," Porco recalled with a grin.

Izzy Young called the room the Fifth Peg, a banjo reference, although most everyone continued to use its old name, Gerde's. It was a cozy place, about thirty-five feet across and fifty feet deep. The walls were covered in a maroon flock-paper design, and the tables had red-checkered covers. The air was a soup of cigarette smoke, beer, and garlic. Gerde's exuded ascetic integrity. A three-foot-high oak-beam partition separated the bar area from the restaurant and performance space on the right; it was a cultural divide between Porco's old regulars, most of them Italian laborers, and the young Village folkies. The musical link between them—the performers on the right were singing about the working people on the left—seemed lost on both sides. "They tended to tolerate each other with benign amusement, complete ignorance, and fear," said Dave Van Ronk. In the back by the end of the bar, a narrow door led to a basement, a musty windowless area with two benches where waiters and waitresses changed clothes and musicians warmed up or gathered to play informally. "When you walked in from the street, the featured act was singing, and it was a scene," recalled John Herald, the Greenbriar Boys' guitarist and singer. "Then you'd go downstairs, and people would play for another two, three hours down there. It was unbelievably damp, unbelievable, and there was a mysterious gray area all the way in the back that was real dark and dank. You'd be playing the guitar, and you'd hear sounds from back there—some people were smoking dope or fucking—and you'd keep playing."

During its first few months of operation in early 1960, the Fifth Peg presented Ed McCurdy, Cynthia Gooding, Brownie McGhee, the Weavers (with Erik Darling in place of Seeger on banjo), Tommy Makem, Cisco Houston, and more than a dozen others. Business was brisk and improving but still disastrous for Izzy Young and his partner, who had underestimated both the expense of booking talent (twenty-five to fifty dollars a night, depending on the performer) and the aptitude of the folk audience for inventing reasons to enter for free. When Young tried to renegotiate his terms, Porco decided to pull out of the deal. "I had nothing against the man," recalled Porco. "But I didn't need him anymore." A category-three storm raged for a few weeks; "everybody was supposed to choose sides," said Dave Van Ronk. "If you bought a guitar pick in the Folklore Center, you couldn't be seen in Gerde's." In an advertisement in the May 12, 1960, issue of *The Village Voice*, Young announced, "I feel bad. Everything I do turns out to be successful—artistically only. Now the Fifth Peg is added to the list." Two weeks later Porco was ready to reopen without Young and Prendergast. The club had a new name, Gerde's Folk City, and a new booker, Charlie Rothschild, hired (for a flat fee of fifty dollars per week) at the recommendation of Tommy Makem, who knew the twenty-one-year-old entrepreneur from the White Horse. For its debut show on May 30, 1960, Folk City presented Rothschild's most popular management client, Carolyn Hester.

A good thirty or forty people came to Gerde's Folk City for opening night, by Porco's count—nearly as many as had come to the Fifth Peg for the Weavers, but different; they were younger, freer with their money, and, the owner thought, better looking: "pretty girls and boys." The evening was misty and cool. When Porco opened the front windows, the clamor from Gerde's rang off the walls of 4th Street's vacant factories. Always quick to recognize a scene in the making, Richard Fariña invited Pynchon and Kirkpatrick Sale to join him at the club, and

Sale came. Richard had been poking around folk circles, looking for a point of entry, since his encounter with Dave Van Ronk at Allan Block's shortly after he had moved to Manhattan. Oscar Brand recalled having met him at one of the Sunday hootenanny/cookouts the veteran singer hosted on his thirteen acres in Croton-on-Hudson upstate, knowing only that he was in advertising. The night Hester opened at Folk City, Richard spoke with Charlie Rothschild for some time and seemed to dodge the matter of what he did for a living. He talked vaguely about "pursuing the arts"—but which ones? Literature? Theater? Music? Only his immediate object of pursuit, Carolyn Hester, seemed clear. "You couldn't fail to be taken by her charm and beauty," said Kirkpatrick Sale, who was then working as an associate editor of *The New Leader*. "It was Dick's nature, of course, to find the most attractive thing and go after it. The minute he saw what Carolyn could do and the effect she had on others, he had to have her."

Eighteen days later, Carolyn Hester and Richard Fariña would be married. "There he was at Folk City, and there I was, and I came offstage and I saw him, and of course I realized who it was, because I thought he was so remarkable looking," Hester recalled. "His mouth was open. This was the strangest thing. He was looking at me, and his mouth was open. And so I said, 'Oh, hi,' and I patted him on the shoulder, and I walked past him. And he went back in the kitchen, where I went, and then more or less he didn't let go of me. And that was it. That was it. The next day, he told me he had been living with another woman but moved out that morning, because of me. I think it was true, because he didn't have anywhere to live after that—he stayed here and there, with friends. He asked me out, and we went to a wonderful Spanish restaurant [the Casa Madrid on West 14th Street], and he fed me some fabulous Spanish food and some great shrimp in green sauce. He knew all about everything and just bowled me over. I thought he was so gorgeous and charming and witty and talented and all that. We were having dinner, and he was staring at me, so romantically, and he said, 'You know, if you're going to keep a nice figure, maybe you shouldn't eat so much. You sure do eat a lot.'

"I liked having a strong man in my life—I'm from Texas—and being with Richard was magical, so much fun. He was controlling, but I didn't really pick up on it. I was always very careful about everything, and here was a wild, wonderful wildman, and I thought that was good for me. I felt like I could do anything when I was with him. Nothing was impossible with Richard. He asked me to marry him, and we had to do it right away, because we were so much in love. He had everything worked out. We went to Central Park and walked around Cleopatra's Needle, and he told me all about the life he had planned for us. He would quit his job at J. Walter Thompson, because now he knew what his path was. He would help me with my music career, and I would set the world on fire, and he would write. I would be a famous writer's wife, and we would have lots of kids. We walked around and around in a circle, and he talked, and the next thing I knew, we were getting married. He told everyone in the Village right away, and he made all the arrangements." Risking no recurrence of his last experience with marriage plans (when the parents of his college girlfriend broke off their engagement), Richard allowed no time to meet Carolyn's family in Texas and deftly avoided them when they came to New York the day before the wedding.

The ceremony, a small Anglican rite for the couple's immediate family and about a dozen friends, was held in the St. Ambrose Chapel at the Cathedral of St. John the Divine, the huge, unfinished Romanesque-Gothic landmark near Columbia University; Richard had arranged to have a simple, easy, economical wedding with an aura of monumental grandeur. C. Michael Curtis served as best man, and Beth Suckow, one of Carolyn's roommates, was maid of honor. The reception was a clambake (Richard's idea) at Robert Shelton's one-bedroom apartment on Waverly Place (Shelton's suggestion, "because he felt responsible for introducing us," said Hester). On the way Richard and Carolyn stopped to pick up their wedding cake from a bakery in an underground corridor of the Herald Square subway station; they balanced it on their laps in the back of a taxi, and the top layer slipped off during a turn. They patched it with a can of whipped cream at Shelton's before the arrival of the guests—about fifty friends of theirs and Shelton's, including Kirkpatrick Sale, Tommy Makem, Judy Collins, Logan English, Erik Darling, and

Cisco Houston. (Pynchon had recently left New York for the West Coast.) Beth Suckow and Carolyn shucked ears of corn in the kitchen while Richard filled tumblers with Irish whiskey in the living room. "We didn't have much space, but everybody was very jolly—it couldn't have been more fun," recalled Carolyn. "All I remember," said Kirkpatrick Sale, "is that it was a wonderful drunken singing party. I don't remember anything specific because it was so successful." After cutting the cake, Richard recited some pertinent Yeats from memory, dipped away for an instant, reappeared with his wife's guitar, and handed it to her dramatically. Tentatively at first, Carolyn sang a verse of "Once I Had a Sweetheart." On the second verse, Richard sang along.

The theme of things borrowed and blue carried through their honeymoon. Richard spent the morning after the wedding at the office of a "drive-away" service for transporting automobiles and got four days' free use of a new-model Pontiac that needed to be delivered in Miami. "He was resourceful," said Hester. "He didn't have anything, but he could make anything happen. It was always an adventure with Richard." Somewhere along Route 1 in Georgia, he pulled the car into a gas station where a circus convoy was parked, and there he saw some monkeys in a cage. "He had a horrible fear of monkeys, and he went crazy," recalled Hester. "He was very disturbed about it. He was really upset. He couldn't breathe. It was like he was having an asthma attack, and he said, 'We are going to have to find another station. We have to get away from here,' and we did. He was very shook up all night—very, very shook up. That's when I found out he would have nightmares about monkeys. He thought it was a terrible omen that we saw those monkeys. I tried to help him deal with that, and that was the first time I was beginning to see that he was kind of tortured inside."

In Miami, Richard and Carolyn delivered the car and picked up another, which had to go to New Orleans. "So we went all across the beautiful beaches of Florida, the Panhandle there and stuff, and we got to New Orleans, and we found a folk club," said Hester. "He said, 'Hey, why don't you do a gig?' And I said, 'I don't know, Richard—it's our honeymoon, you know.' And he said, 'Come on—let's see if they'll give us some money. We could use the money. Come on. . . .' I felt it was something I shouldn't be doing. I was a bride on my honeymoon. But he kind of wanted to show me off, and he kind of wanted to get some money for us, and he kind of wanted to see if I would do it. So I did it, and it went real well—it was fun, and we made some money." After the performance Carolyn and Richard talked with the room's booker over complimentary snacks. Hester was invited back to perform on a formal bill the next time she was in New Orleans. "Thank you," answered Richard. "But we have other plans." Although his wife had no idea what he was talking about, as she later recalled, she thought it sounded thrilling.

IN THE YEAR FOLLOWING HER DEBUT at the Newport Folk Festival, Joan Baez dominated Cambridge—lines of up to two hundred people and sometimes more, nearly twice as many as Club 47 could hold, purled along three blocks of Mt. Auburn Street for her weekly Tuesday-evening appearances. *Time* magazine, in a mildly reactionary one-page report titled "Folk Frenzy," published a photograph of Joan looking seraphic on the Newport stage and reported that her performance with Bob Gibson "tagged [her] as one of folk music's most promising talents." As the article noted, however, "So far, she is best known in the coffeehouses of Harvard Square." A regional phenomenon and the talk of folk cognoscenti elsewhere, Joan remained far less known than pop singers of the time such as Connie Francis and Brenda Lee, each of whom sold millions of records in 1960. The bridge between them was a commercial recording contract, and Albert Grossman, the Chicago club owner whose interest in Baez had led her to Newport, was convinced that Joan should and could get one, with his help. As Grossman's Newport partner George Wein recalled, "I wanted to book Joanie in a folk room I started in Boston, and Albert said, 'No, you leave her alone. I want to go after her.' I said, 'Okay.' He wanted her very badly. He really wanted her. He recognized her talent and her beauty and her youth, and he knew the record industry hadn't really caught on to folk yet. The whole thing was wide open, and he wanted in with Joan. I cannot tell you how much he wanted her."

Joan was working without a manager or an agent, although she liked dealing with Manny Greenhill, who booked her regularly, and she would call him for business advice when she felt she needed it, which was not often. Raised in Brooklyn during the Depression, Greenhill had worked in New York iron mills and shipyards until he discovered political theater and folk music through his participation in socialist activities. He sang in a New York production of Marc Blitzstein's leftist musical *The Cradle Will Rock* and took a few guitar lessons from Josh White. After moving to Boston in order to run a foreign-language newspaper-publishing business there, he shifted to promoting folk and blues concerts and representing artists; Greenhill became known (and respected or disdained, depending upon the observer's views) for taking on Negro blues acts, some with troubled histories, and doing right by them. He had the thick build and the jagged features of a middleweight a bit past the time to quit, but his mind was keen and probing. A good Marxist, he wore the same gray tweed jacket every day and kept a tie rolled up in the inside pocket. Greenhill stood along a side wall of the YMCA during the concerts he sponsored, smiling as he squinted to study the proceedings; he kept both hands in his pockets, and he rocked slowly, heel to toe, heel to toe.

Albert Grossman was a portly, mop-haired businessman with an intemperate urge to control. A high school graduate raised by a tailor and his wife in a middle-class Jewish section of Chicago's North Side, Grossman attended the Chicago Central YMCA College and DePaul and graduated from Roosevelt College with a bachelor's degree in commerce. He came to affect the manners of a high-born sophisticate. He held a cigarette with the tips of his thumb and his first three fingers. An expression of permanent bemusement took root in his brow. Grossman exuded menacing charm. "Albert was easy to deal with," said Dave Van

Ronk. "It wasn't till maybe two days after you would see Albert that you'd realize your underwear had been stolen. There you are—'Shit, man, my pants are on. What happened to my shorts?' Albert was easy." In negotiations one of Grossman's favorite techniques was silence. "He mastered the art of mystery," said Charlie Rothschild. "He would simply stare at you and say nothing. He wouldn't volunteer any information, and that would drive people crazy. They would keep talking to fill the void, and say anything. He had a remarkable gift for tipping the balance of power in his favor." In Greenwich Village, Grossman's nickname was "the floating Buddha."

Manny Greenhill and Albert Grossman plied the same trade in the same field at the same time and did virtually nothing the same way. "They were opposite ends of the spectrum," said Richard Waterman, a photographer and writer who served on Greenhill's staff in the early 1960s. "Manny negotiated in private, Albert negotiated in public. Albert knew exactly what he wanted to do and then did it with great flair, with great pizzazz. Manny looked at all the options and then quietly gave them all the proper consideration. With Albert, you had to accept the fact that he had divine knowledge. In other words, you had to surrender to the fact that he was in total control, that you were not going to have input. Manny listened. When you were talking to Albert, you never knew what he was thinking, and you always ended up doing what he wanted. But whatever it was, it was always the best deal for his artist."

Indeed, Grossman sometimes appeared treacherously devoted to his clients' satisfaction. "I walked in on a conversation between Grossman and Joan at Newport [in 1959] when he was trying to lure her in as a client," said Rick Stafford, the Boston-based photographer who shot the Folk Festival every year. "It's remarkable but revealing that he let a stranger hear a conversation like that. He said, 'Look—what do you like? Just tell me, what do you like? I can get it for you. I can get anything you want. *Who* do you want? Just tell me. I'll get you anybody you want.' "

Grossman had sold his interest in the Gate of Horn and moved to New York, and now he was focused on expanding his list of management clients with promising folk newcomers. Joan, though vocal about her discomfort with Grossman and his methods, indulged his offer to introduce her to his contacts at the big record companies. They met in midtown Manhattan shortly after Newport 1960, in order to capitalize on Joan's lauded appearance as a solo performer that year. (To ensure that she did not go unnoticed, Joan had gone to the festival in her friend John Stein's 1952 Cadillac hearse, with Mimi accompanying her as a nonperforming guest; Joan and her group, inspired by a promotional sign on the Staple Singers' tour bus, had used silver adhesive tape to inscribe MISS JOAN BAEZ on the sides of the hearse.) Grossman brought Joan to Columbia Records' headquarters in Rockefeller Center. "I could sense that folk was coming on," said David Kapralik, Columbia's vice president of artists and repertoire at the time. "I talked to John [Hammond] about looking into the people with the best potential and [asked him to] get back to me with a recommendation. He said we should talk to Joan Baez or Carolyn Hester—one or the other, not both, because they were too similar. Carolyn was very well liked in New York, but Joan had made a splash at Newport, and she came in first." John Hammond, a great-great-grandson of "Commodore" Cornelius Vanderbilt, the railroad baron, was the model of blueblood urbanity that Grossman emulated. Associated with Columbia since 1939 (with periods at other labels, including a stint with Vanguard in the 1950s), he was a mythic prince of the record industry for having discovered, taken credit for discovering, or helped to popularize a succession of jazz greats, including Count Basie, Lionel Hampton, Billie Holiday, Teddy Wilson, and Charlie Christian. When Grossman escorted Joan into Hammond's office, she had a phobic reaction to the atmosphere: Hammond and Grossman's talk of how the powerful record company could "make things happen" triggered images of corporate bullying, the air conditioning gave her a chill, and the gold records on the walls seemed to glare like royal plunder. "I began to feel ill," she said. "I told Albert I wanted to think about it, and they had a contract ready for me to sign. Everywhere I looked, there was gold. I had to get out of there." At Joan's insistence, Grossman took her to Vanguard Records. (By her account, Joan declined Columbia's offer, but

John Hammond would later say he rejected her. In his memoir, *John Hammond on Record*, written with Columbia executive Irving Townsend, he claimed, "I passed on Joan Baez, whom I had heard at the Newport Folk Festival, because she was asking a great deal of money while still a relatively unknown artist. . . . I decided to look further.")

Joan regained her health in the homey clutter of Vanguard's offices on West 14th Street off Eighth Avenue, the low-rent northwest corner of Greenwich Village. She said she felt more comfortable with the scale of the modestly prosperous classical music label, and she liked Maynard Solomon, the boyish intellectual who had founded the company with his brother Seymour in 1950. Maynard Solomon was soft-spoken, wry, and casually erudite. If he could not answer a question, a rare occurrence, he might say, "I am unable to respond to that, either theoretically or methodologically," and he would sound humble. Maynard Solomon wore sneakers and sweaters to the office when male rock and roll stars were still dressing in jackets and ties. New acquaintances were sometimes taken aback by the contrast between his collegiate attire and his hair, which had turned white as a result of an auto accident trauma in 1959. Joan knew that Albert Grossman and Maynard Solomon despised each other, and she found that heartening.

Vanguard had a reputation for maintaining high artistic and technical standards—its slogan was "Recordings for the Connoisseur"—and had some success in folk with the Weavers, whom the Solomons had signed in 1956. Joan Baez and her approach to traditional music appealed to Solomon as much as he and his company did to Joan. "Apart from her being a great singer, in terms of pure vocal production, and having an extraordinary sound and a range that was even from its lowest chest tones to its soprano register, she sang with a depth of feeling that reflected an inner depth and sensibility that was not readily available among other singers," Solomon explained. "There were other singers who sang the same repertory, and Joan used part of that repertory. But the distance between the pool of other female folksingers and Joan was one that could only be measured in light-years. Joan had a sense of refinement and passion that was available in no one else. It didn't matter that they were singing the same songs. I thought the most thrilling aspect of Joan's performances was the sense of a controlled passion, a reaching of a depth of feeling without giving way to overstatement, and projecting the depth of that feeling through the most subtle vocal techniques and with a purity of voice and a purity of personal presentation that was absolutely unique.

"There was also a feeling of sympathy between us, both as human beings and as carriers of aesthetic feeling. I think we met in an aesthetic dimension that really was like a mingling of extremely sympathetic individuals—extremely sympathetic."

From Joan's point of view, Vanguard provided more than Columbia by offering less. "John Hammond and Albert kept talking about everything they could do for me, and the impression I got from Maynard was that they could benefit more from our association—I could do something for them," Joan said. "There weren't any gold records up on their walls." She had Albert Grossman negotiate a contract with Vanguard but declined to employ his services further.

Joan recorded her first solo album in the ballroom of the Manhattan Towers hotel, a gray, smoke-steeped old waystation for transients and nocturnals from the pages of Lion Books, on Broadway and 76th Street. The space was affordable, available (except on bingo nights), and some kind of miracle of acoustics. Over three days of taping, Joan sang nineteen songs. She accompanied herself on guitar, "live on tape," without overdubbing; at Maynard Solomon's suggestion, the Weavers' Fred Hellerman played guitar fills on about half the tunes. Solomon selected thirteen performances for release, six of which included Hellerman. Apart from the second guitarist's presence as a polishing agent, the album, entitled *Joan Baez*, is a Tuesday evening at Club 47: the selections all came from Joan's set list of traditional ballads ("Silver Dagger," "All My Trials," "Mary Hamilton") and songs of similar ilk ("Donna Donna," the Spanish-language "El Preso Numero Nueve"). It is a dark, gravely serious record overall, despite a couple of relatively light moments in "Wildwood Flower" and "Rake and Rambling Boy." Of the remaining eleven songs, six are in minor keys, and the melancholy lyrics of the major-key songs are laced with disquieting imagery. Joan's singing—confident and precise—lost none of its urgency in the translation to vinyl; in fact, she sounds more expressive than she tended to seem when she sat stoically, motionless, onstage.

Shipped to record stores in November 1960 with no promotion beyond free review copies for a few dozen publications, *Joan Baez* found an audience first among responsive critics. Robert Shelton raved in *The New York Times*:

> This disk sends one scurrying to the thesaurus for superlatives. It represents one of those beautiful folk performances that one could give to the most conservatory-oriented listener, yet at the same time commands the respect of the most tradition-directed auditor. . . . At the age of only 20, Miss Baez has truly arrived. . . . Miss Baez has made a recording that is this corner's strongest current recommendation for people who hate folk music, and for those that love it as well.

While no folk performer of any legitimacy could convert anyone who hated folk music, there was some prescience in Shelton's hyperbole: as a recording artist, Joan Baez quickly attracted a national following beyond the core folk audience, increasing the prominence of folk in the process. Her album made the *Billboard* album chart and stayed there for 140 weeks; it hit number fourteen and earned well over a million dollars. Vanguard got a gold record to hang up. Like all hits, this one was a beneficiary of timing—Joan, an exquisite reflection of her generation's self-image at the cusp of the 1950s and 1960s, performed a brooding music that artfully refracted their spirit. How many children of the cold war sat on the floor next to their record players, listening to Joan Baez murmur of fate, helplessness, and death, thinking, *Yeah—they're all my trials, too?*

"She in one way represented the folk tradition and, in another way, represented something of a younger generation that knew nothing about that tradition and wasn't really interested in it, in and of itself," said Sam Charters, the folk historian and musician. "It was a combination of things Maynard Solomon saw in her and provided for her to be able to express—the absolute clarity, the purity, of her ballad singing and also a distinct earthiness. On record, whatever sex appeal she had in person dissipated. That record was utterly devoid of sex appeal. A few years earlier, no one would have imagined that formula succeeding."

Joan was impressed herself. "Based on everything I had been led to believe about the music business, I could only go so far, because my image was [one] of innocence and purity," she said. "I was not about to change it, because I took that image very seriously, to the point of being obnoxious. I remember thinking, when people compared me and my image to the Virgin Mary, 'That sounds good to me. Hey—that took her pretty far.' "

The first hit record by a woman of her generation in the folk idiom—and a best-seller with virtually no advertising, promotion, or "tour support" (beyond a concert or two each month, mostly at universities)—*Joan Baez* was the talk of the coffeehouses. "When the record came out and it was this major smash, I was completely surprised," said Fred Hellerman. "I thought we made a good record. It was a nice record for a new singer to do. Then all of a sudden, everybody and his brother were listening to this record and talking about Joan Baez. I said, 'Wait a minute—something's happening here. It's not *that* good!' What I mean is, she was tapping something in the air that wasn't just musical."

For young women, Joan's ascetic grace and brooding musical persona appeared to serve as an antidote to the era's sexualized, glamorized formula for feminine celebrity. She was the negative image of Marilyn Monroe: thin, dark, strong, smart, virtuous—still, young and attractive to men. "Girls around the same age category and even younger were just knocked out by her, because she had this waif-gypsy image," said Barbara Dane, who had been singing folk music professionally for several years before Baez began performing. "She seemed like somebody who was absolutely free and in charge of herself, even though she was young. With the bare feet and the straight hair, she looked like this creature who could do her own thing. And that sad music—all the girls who were miserable with their lot in life were dying to cry along with her. The main thing is that I think young women were absolutely starved for and ready for an example of somebody like themselves who could walk out on the stage and dominate the stage and be a different kind of woman up there and also have the guys interested."

To some men, at least, Joan's virginal quiescence gave her reverse-psychology sex appeal; like Doris Day for men a bit older, Joan Baez was a vicarious predatory challenge. "Her whole image and everything she sang in the early days—they drove the men crazy," said actor and singer Jack Landron, who, as Jackie Washington, performed extensively in Cambridge. "The songs were never straight-across 'I love you, we're going to get together and fuck our brains out.' It was always, 'I never will marry'—it was all that—and she looked sad, the hair hung down, and the fellows were thinking, 'I can make it right for you.' She loved us collectively. We loved her one by one. She knew it, and that's the way it worked." Indeed, Joan said she enjoyed the sexual gamesmanship. "I was the virgin princess," she explained. "They wanted to sleep with me, and I could sleep with them if I wanted to. So I didn't *have* to do it with any of them. It's called control."

Among musicians Baez's age, particularly women, Joan's swift emergence as a recording star inspired hope and raised expectations as it provoked inevitable envy. "Joanie's success was the first indication that this stuff that we were just doing because we couldn't help ourselves because we loved it so much was anything viable—that anything could come of it," said Terri Thal, a musician-turned-artists'-manager who was married to Dave Van Ronk. "When people saw what was happening with Joanie, they started thinking maybe they could have a hit record, too. Everybody was a little jealous. It was kind of, 'Oh, my God!' I mean, here was this chick from Cambridge, singing English ballads. But there was less of that, really, than there was genuinely, 'Hey—somebody's making it. Great!' "

Within the record industry, Joan Baez established a new standard. "I had to get my own Baez," said Jac Holzman, head of Elektra Records, a folk-oriented label that already had Theodore Bikel, Oscar Brand, and Jean Ritchie in its catalog. "I'm quite sure every label in town felt that way." At Columbia, Joan's chart success prompted an especially competitive reaction. "The first thing I wanted was [to know] why didn't we get her," said David Kapralik. "I don't think John ever gave me a straight answer. I told him, 'The message here is that the kids want this kind of music,' and I knew Joan Baez was a lovely woman with a great voice, a great talent, but she wasn't the only one in the world. I told John, 'Someone else has just as much to offer. Find her, and let's sign her.' "

Opportunity seemed to await a gifted young woman who sang, played guitar, and looked like Joan Baez. However, Mimi was still in Belmont with a year and a half of high school to finish, and she was hardly certain she liked opportunity's terms. She watched her older sister's rise to fame anxiously, wondering about its bearing on her life and her own musical aspirations. "Joanie's success affected Mimi most [among members of the Baez family], because they had always been so close, and Joanie was succeeding at the same thing Mimi wanted to do," said their mother. "Pauline was very quiet about it, and she wasn't with us very much. She wasn't really a part of it. My husband just went on with his work—it didn't really have any impact on him. Of course, I was terribly pleased and proud. I thought it was the normal thing for it to happen to her, because she was always way up there in my eyesight, and the world was just catching on. For Mimi, I think Joan's success was awfully confusing at first. I could tell she liked all the excitement, and she was happy for her sister, but she didn't like to talk about it. I think she had a hard time figuring out where she would fit in." As Mimi recalled, "It was an exciting time. Joanie became *this thing*—she wasn't just my sister anymore, she was Joan Baez. Everybody knew who she was. It was strange. When we were singing together, it was Joan and Mimi. Now it was Joan, and I started to notice that people thought of her differently, and they would think of me differently. I wasn't Mimi anymore. I was Joan's sister now. That was all right, but I didn't like it when I played guitar and I knew people thought I was trying to be Joan. I was just trying to be me, and I started to realize how hard that was going to be from now on." A few weeks after Joan's Vanguard album was released, Big Joan was listening to it in the living room, and Mimi walked in with her guitar. When "Fare Thee Well" came on, she finger-picked some accompaniment; during "House of the Rising Sun," she played and sang a harmony part; before the side was over, she turned it off and played "Freight Train."

ART D'LUGOFF, who ran the Village Gate, had a rambling, six-room apartment in the Belnord, an early-twentieth-century building that occupied a city block on West 86th Street. It was an ideal place for parties, and D'Lugoff had a big one to celebrate the winter 1960 Christmas season. Since she was visiting New York on business, Joan Baez came; Robert Shelton was there, along with Charlie Rothschild and most of the rest of the New York folk intelligentsia. "Joan was the center of attention," recalled Rothschild. "People wanted to see and be seen by the queen." Carolyn Hester and Richard Fariña arrived late in the evening. As his wife chatted with a small gathering of admirers, Richard drifted off to meet Joan, who was talking to Charlie Rothschild at the time. Richard bantered casually and said he was interested in writing something about Joan. He wanted to discuss it with her in private someday, he explained. He kept his left hand in his pants pocket, and for the first time Rothschild could remember, Richard declined to mention that he was married to Carolyn Hester.

GO BACK TO THAT NIGHT . . . when Pete [Seeger] first met Woody Guthrie," Alan Lomax told a journalist. "You can date the renascence of American folk song from that night." Indeed, for decades after they first appeared together on the Forrest Theater stage (at a New York benefit for migrant workers) on March 3, 1940, Seeger and Guthrie served as living symbols of the folk spirit—dual spirits, actually: a diptych of reverse images. Seeger, born to the folklorist Charles Seeger and the violinist Constance de Clyver Edson Seeger in 1919, was a bookish Yankee, educated at Harvard. Like Karl Marx himself, Seeger was a Marxist raised in bourgeois comfort. Shy, especially with women, he took up performing as an act of virtue; he said he believed a song could change the world. "It's not how good a song is that matters," Seeger explained, "it's how much good a song does." He had a genial tenor voice and played the banjo with exuberant vigor. When Seeger performed, he stood straight, stretched his neck, and peered skyward, as if to demonstrate that his purpose was uplifting. Guthrie, seven years older than Seeger, was raised in rural Okfuskee County, Oklahoma, by his parents Charles Guthrie, an entrepreneur who went bankrupt, and Nora Belle Tanner Guthrie, who was admitted to a mental asylum during Woody's childhood. (She suffered from Huntington's chorea, the hereditary disorder of the nervous system that eventually crippled Woody Guthrie.) A student of experience, Guthrie quit high school and spent his twenties roving the country by thumb and freight car with his guitar, occasionally laboring as a longshoreman or migrant worker, learning tunes and picking up ideas that he would put to use in more than a thousand original songs. Guthrie appreciated strength in women and drink, and he submitted to them heartily. Onstage he lurched over his guitar and sang in a sharp, dry voice that cut with the precision of truth. Pete Seeger embodied idealism; Woody Guthrie, realism. The majority of Seeger's best compositions are political homilies—"Where Have All the Flowers Gone," "Turn, Turn, Turn," "If I Had a Hammer" (written with the Weavers' Lee Hays); Guthrie's were poetic reportage—"This Land Is Your Land," "Pastures of Plenty," "Roll on, Columbia" (not to mention "V.D. Blues"). Although they became good friends, traveled thousands of miles singing together, and shared an ardent commitment to socialism, their approaches to both art and politics were distinct. "You know how Woody had a sign on his guitar that said, 'This machine kills fascists'?" said Oscar Brand. "If Pete had one, it would say, 'This machine encircles fascists and persuades them to lay down their arms.' " The young people drawn to folk music through the influence of Seeger and Guthrie were not so much Pete and Woody's Children as Pete's Children *or* Woody's Children. Joan Baez said, "We all owe our careers to Pete Seeger," and she is right about many of the singers of traditional songs who emerged in the late 1950s, including the Kingston Trio (and its offshoots, such as the Brothers Four and the Chad Mitchell Trio), Carolyn Hester, Bob Gibson, Jackie Washington, and Jean Redpath. (For women, Seeger's style of gentle persuasion may have been more palatable than Guthrie's more assertive approach.) But another realm of performers, most of them young and rising as the 1960s began, owed a greater debt to Guthrie: Ramblin' Jack Elliott (the elder of the group), John Sebastian, Phil Ochs, Tom Paxton, and the most devout of the Guthrie acolytes, Bob Dylan.

Born Robert Allen Zimmerman on May 24, 1941, Bob was just about four months younger than Joan and started taking folk music seriously nearly two years after she had. Raised in Hibbing, Minnesota—a Mesabi Valley mining town drained of the iron ore that had been its lifeblood—Bob grew up in comfort. His father, Abraham Zimmerman, ran a furniture and appliance business with his two brothers, Paul and Maurice; and his mother, Beatrice (Beatty) Stone Zimmerman, held a clerical job at Feldman's Department Store. They lived in a two-story, tan stucco house on a corner of a middle-class block; there was a terrace on the second floor and a rec room in the basement. Bob had one brother, David, five years younger, and innumerable relatives on his mother's side. The Zimmerman boys were part of a big, close Jewish family. (Defensive about his family's relative prosperity, Dylan would later insist, inaccurately, "Where I lived, there aren't any suburbs. There aren't any suburbs, and there's no poor section, and there's no rich section. There just is none. There is no one side of town and another side of town. There's no wrong side of the tracks and right side of the tracks. As far as I knew, where I lived, nobody had anything that anybody else didn't have, really, and that is the truth. All the people I knew had the same things.")

From early childhood through his four years at Central High School, Bob was considered a creative and solitary boy. He wrote poems, he drew (mainly pencil sketches of cowboys and horses), and he liked music; he listened to hillbilly radio and what rhythm and blues he could find in local record stores, and he taught himself how to play elementary chords on the family's Gulbransen spinet piano. In his teens, Bob was not rebellious so much as absorbed with the idea of rebellion, particularly as something central to the mystique of celebrity antiheroes in the teen culture of the 1950s. He went to the Lybba theater (built by Bob's maternal great-grandfather and named for his wife) to watch *Rebel Without a Cause* at least four times, according to one of his high school friends, Bill Marinac. He cut out magazine pictures of its tortured young star, James Dean, and framed them in his bedroom, and he bought a red vinyl motorcycle jacket like the one Dean wears in the movie. When he was sixteen, his parents bought him a used Harley Davidson model 45. Bob liked to ride his Harley up and down the Hibbing strip, Howard Street, glowering at the road. He was not a strong rider, his friends said; he looked uneasy on the bike and got thrown off once while he was trying a stunt near a passing train.

Bob had started singing, crooning along to the radio, at the age of ten or eleven; his childhood idol was Hank Williams. (He also liked Hank Snow, Hank Payne—"all sorts of Hanks," he said—as well as Lefty Frizzell and Jimmy Reed.) When rock and roll emerged, connected to motorcycles and red leather as a symbol of teen insurrection, Bob became obsessed with the music. He learned how to bang out three-chord songs on the piano well enough to front a string of garage bands: the Shadow Blasters (formed when he was fifteen; "We were just the loudest band around," Bob said), the Golden Chords, the Satin Tones. Bob wore a pink shirt and a bow tie. For the Rock Boppers, which Bob organized in the summer of 1958, he decided to start using a stage name, Elston Gunn. (Elston is an echo of Elvis, obviously; *Peter Gunn*, a television drama about a hipster detective, first aired that year and had a driving, jazzy theme song that became the source for two hit singles.) On a home recording made that year by his high school buddy John Bucklen, Bob can be heard playing, singing, and raving about rhythm and blues in adolescent rapture. Asked what kind of music is the best, he blurts, "Rhythm and blues! Rhythm and blues is something that you can't quite explain— see? when you hear a good rhythm and blues song, chills go up your spine. You wanna cry when you hear one of those songs." His piano work was a functional approximation of the Little Richard style of blocking major chords, without his speed or facility, and his voice was sweet and buoyant—he sounded something like Buddy Holly. (A big Holly fan, Bob went to see him perform at the Duluth Armory on January 31, 1959; with Holly's death at twenty-two in a small-plane crash three days later, Holly joined Hank Williams, who had died en route to an engagement when he was twenty-nine, and James Dean, who had died at twenty-four, also on the road, as the third of Bob's youthful heroes to be immortalized by a premature death while traveling. He had "a preoccupation with death, out of Hank Williams," his brother said; when Dean died, "Bobby's whole world crashed in," and after Holly's death, "Bobby just went into mourning.")

By September 1959, when Robert Zimmerman, age eighteen, entered the University of Minnesota and joined Sigma Alpha Mu, the Jewish fraternity, rock and roll had done nothing to keep up with its maturing fans. Indeed, during the four years since the first major rock hit, "Rock Around the Clock," the music had not merely stagnated, but regressed; neutered and prettified by record companies for the thirteen-and-a-half-year-old girls they identified as their most profitable market, late-1950s rock had little to do with rebellion, aside from having revolted against its original sensibility. Many of the genre's charismatically threatening founders were gone—Elvis Presley drafted, Jerry Lee Lewis and Chuck Berry banished because of sex scandals, Little Richard retired from music (temporarily) to beome a minister—and replaced by nice, pretty boys such as Ricky Nelson, Frankie Avalon, and Bobby Rydell. For college students in Minneapolis, just as in Cambridge or New York, rock and roll was a happy memory you left at home with your skates and high school notebooks. The music of preference at UM, especially in the artsy off-campus area called Dinkytown, was folk.

When Bob started performing publicly in Dinkytown early in his freshman year, he was strumming a flat-top Gibson acoustic guitar. "Elston" had gone the way of Elvis, Jerry Lee, and the other figures of Robert Zimmerman's teenage dreams. He replaced his motorcycle jacket with a dirty gray tweed sports coat from the Salvation Army and let his hair dangle, uncombed. Bob was a folksinger now. His small but fast-growing repertoire—rural blues and rhythmic, gospel-tinged material he picked up from Odetta records, as well as folk standards—hinted at his past musical identity, while he began to craft a new one.

By the beginning of 1960, Bob had moved out of his fraternity house to live with a shifting assortment of fellow artists and bohemians above Gray's Drugstore in Dinkytown, and he was appearing regularly at the local coffeehouse, the Ten O'Clock Scholar. Essentially Club 47 trucked a thousand miles west, the Scholar was a dark, narrow storefront with too many tiny round tables and benches along one side; the walls were painted flat black, and a plate-glass window faced the street. Sometimes the owner, David Lee, taped a sign with the name of a performer on the glass, and the sign occasionally read "Bob Dillon." Like Gunn, Bob's latest alias was the name of a television character: Matt Dillon, the stolid sheriff of Dodge City portrayed by James Arness on *Gunsmoke* (the most popular show that year); he had shifted the dramatic milieu from the modern city to the Old West, befitting the young musician's transition from "Buzz Buzz Buzz" to "Muleskinner Blues."

"He was just taking everything in—he listened to everybody, and he had an incredible ability to take things in and absorb them and turn around and put them right back out there like they had always been a part of him," said "Spider" John Koerner, the blues guitarist and singer who showed Bob dozens of songs in his Dinkytown apartment. (Teamed with two other local musicians, guitarist Dave Ray and harmonica player Tony Glover, Koerner would later tour extensively and record several well-regarded country-blues albums for Elektra.) Beginning in February 1960, he and Bob appeared often at the Ten O'Clock Scholar as a duo. "He liked all kinds of songs, and he sang in a real sweet, pretty voice. He had a very nice voice, but he didn't really know what he was trying to do except be a folksinger, because that was what you were supposed to be. I think he was writing some original material—simple, gospel-style stuff with an easy beat, like Odetta [performed]. I was never really sure if he really wrote any of it or not, but I didn't care about any of that." In their performances together, Koerner and Dillon sang, among other songs, "They Call the Wind Maria," the Frederick Loewe and Alan Jay Lerner song from the Broadway musical *Paint Your Wagon*.

It was early autumn 1960 when Bob, now spelling his name as Dylan ("because it looked better"), began to present a full-on musical persona, although that persona was not his own. At the recommendation of David Whitaker, a Minnesota graduate who had stuck around, Bob read Woody Guthrie's 1943 memoir, *Bound for Glory*—an epiphany. Bob appeared instantly and wholly consumed by idol worship; he had the book in hand for several weeks, poring over it, again and again. While he had not only known about Guthrie but had been performing a handful of his songs (including "Pastures of Plenty," "Car, Car," and "The Great Historical Bum," as well as "This Land Is Your Land"), Guthrie's music evidently never struck Bob as deeply as his picaresque tales of life on the road. In Guthrie, Bob found more than a genre of music, a body of work, or a performance style: he found *an image*—the hard-travelin' loner with a guitar and a way with words, the outsider the insiders envied, easy with women, and surely doomed. An amalgam of Bob's previous heroes, the Guthrie he found in *Bound for Glory* was Hank Williams, James Dean, and Buddy Holly—a literate folksinger with a rock and roll attitude.

"He's the greatest holiest godliest one in the world," Bob said of Guthrie—a "genius genius genius genius."

Examining his Guthrie fixation several years later, Dylan explained, "Woody turned me on romantically. As far as digging his talent and what he could do, in all honesty, I would just have to laugh at it [now]. The fundamental objection is that I can see why he wrote what he wrote. I can see him sitting down and writing what he wrote, in a very calm kind of a way. I'm not putting him down. I'm not copping out on my attraction to him and his influence on me. What drew me to [him] was that, hearing his voice, I could tell he was very lonesome, very alone, and very lost out in his time. That's why I dug him. Like a suicidal case or something. It was like an adolescent thing—when you need somebody to latch on to, you reach out and latch on to them."

Guthrie's footprints provided Dylan with a path, for a distance. He dropped out of school and decided to take to the road. "I really have no respect for college," Dylan later explained. "It's an extension of time. I hung around college. It's a cop-out, you know. It's a cop-out from life. It's a cop-out from experience." In mid-December 1960, Bob told friends he had telephoned his ailing hero at Greystone Park Psychiatric Hospital in northeast New Jersey, and had arranged to visit him there. He headed east by bus, stopping in Chicago, where he performed a set of Guthrie songs at a sorority party before changing his mind and hitchhiking toward home. On the way back to Minnesota, he stopped in Madison, Wisconsin, to check out the local folk scene and met a young political activist from the state university at Madison, Fred Underhill, who was about to drive home to New York; Bob went with him. They arrived in Manhattan on January 24, 1961. The weather was as cold as the North Country—fourteen degrees Fahrenheit, twelve degrees below normal for the day, with nine inches of snow in the streets; undeterred, Bob and Underhill trudged to the coffeehouses. At the Cafe Wha?, each of them was allowed to sing a few songs.

After that Dylan rarely left the Village. "It was like Dylan was in all the places all the time—all the coffeehouses," said John Herald. "The first time I ever saw Dylan, he was standing in front of the Folklore Center on MacDougal Street playing the fiddle. Not a great fiddle player. He was kind of unusual in the fact that he was 'out of town,' he wasn't 'New York.' But you couldn't escape him." He played somewhere—the back room of the Folklore Center, the Commons, the Gaslight, the Lion's Head, Mills Tavern—virtually every night for basket change or ten or twenty dollars from a generous manager, sleeping on couches and floors provided by hospitable folk buffs such as Miki Isaacson, as Guthrie had during his years on the road. (Eventually he found a one-bedroom railroad flat at 161 West 4th Street for eighty dollars per month.) Dylan's appearance and manner, both onstage and off, were vintage Guthrie. "He got up to sing one night at the Cafe Wha?, and he was singing Woody Guthrie songs, and his imitation of Woody was a hundred percent of what he thought Woody was, but it wasn't quite working for that crowd, and it wasn't even working for me," said Mark Spoelstra, who had recently arrived in New York from northern California. Less than a year older than Bob and already a virtuoso blues guitarist, Spoelstra would become one of Dylan's closest friends in Greenwich Village. "And a bunch of us just sitting around the table just went into stitches. I am sure he saw that, and I'm sure it hurt his feelings, and I felt bad about it at the time. But he never made that mistake again. Whatever it was that he was doing, he didn't do it that way again. Next time he was a much better Woody Guthrie." Dylan visited his idol fairly regularly, first at Greystone, then at the home of folk buffs Sidsel and Bob Gleason in New Jersey, where Guthrie often spent weekends, and later at the Guthries' bungalow on Coney Island and at the Brooklyn State Hospital. "Man, I could whip anybody—I was at the high point of my life from seein' Woody," he crowed; and the more time Dylan spent with Guthrie, the more the acolyte seemed to resemble the debilitated master. "It's interesting—he was visiting Woody Guthrie, and I was visiting Woody at that time also," said John Cohen, guitarist and singer with the New Lost City Ramblers. (Before Dylan's pilgrimage, a small group of young folksingers had been visiting Guthrie for several years.) With his bandmates, the banjo player Tom Paley and the multi-instrumentalist Mike Seeger (Pete's half-brother and son of the classical composer Ruth Crawford Seeger), Cohen had helped to revive the "old-time" string band music of the first decades of the twentieth century. "I had known Woody five or six, maybe eight years by then, and you could see all that jerky stuff starting to happen in his body. And then when Bob stood up to the microphone and started jerking around, tilting his head this way, and making these moves—I'd never seen anything like that except in Woody. When I first saw him, I said, 'Oh, my God, he's mimicking Woody's disease.' "

Dylan was nineteen years old now and becoming known around the

Village. But his first major work of imagination—his own persona—took shape slowly. "He seemed like a baby-faced kid, a little wet behind the ears, blowing things out of proportion," said John Herald. "You could not talk to him personally. You could not ask him personal questions. He'd always joke, or he'd tell you something like he used to be a miner—something like that. If you'd ask about his parents, he'd say he had none, or he'd make a joke, or he'd change the subject, or he'd put you on. If you asked him anything, you would get nowhere." ("I shucked everybody when I came to New York," he later admitted. "I played cute.") To those he thought had due grounds for inquiring about his life (such as Robert Shelton and Izzy Young) and others who pressed hard enough, Dylan mustered a parade of colorful fantasies: he was an orphan, born in Chicago or raised in a New Mexico orphanage or in various foster homes; his Semitic features were the mark of Sioux Indian blood in the family; one of his uncles was a gambler, another a thief; he had lived in Oklahoma, Iowa, South Dakota, North Dakota, Kansas, and on the Mississippi River; he joined a carnival at age thirteen and traveled with it around the Southwest; he had played the piano on Elvis Presley's early records. If an acquaintance said something that touched upon Bob's childhood or background—"Did you ever have to sing in church?" "Kid brothers are a pain, aren't they?"—he would snap back, "Dig yourself."

Performers had always changed their names and adopted professional images that diverged from their biographies. Indeed, transformation has always been part of the American idea: in the New World, anyone can become a new person. The irony of Robert Zimmerman's metamorphosis into Bob Dylan lies in the application of so much elusion and artifice in the name of truth and authenticity. Archie Leach and Norma Jean Baker became Cary Grant and Marilyn Monroe when they went into show business; but folk was supposed to be neither business nor show. Embraced as an alternative to mainstream commercial entertainment by a generation that considered itself smarter and more serious than its predecessors, the folk movement propagated an aesthetic of veracity. It ostensibly celebrated the rural and the natural, the untrained, the unspoiled—the pure. Popular and easy to learn, it happened to attract an ambitious, middle-class college kid from the suburbs, just as it had drawn a New York–bred physician's son, Elliot Adnopoz, who became Ramblin' Jack Elliott. (With their Jewish names, neither of them was likely to be accepted as part of old-time America.) Folk would accommodate them and their ambitions, no matter who they really were, as long as they could create the illusion of artlessness, and Bob did so giftedly. As the cowboy singer and sculptor Harry Jackson told folksinger Gil Turner when he saw the young Dylan perform, "He's so goddamned real, it's unbelievable."

He performed in work clothes—frayed blue denim pants, overworn tan boots, and stained khaki shirts, sometimes dressed up with a brown suede vest or a gray wool scarf—although his body appeared to have endured little hard labor. Pallid and soft, he seemed childlike, almost feminine. What conferred the impression of a life lived hard was his filth. "He looked like he could really use some help around the house," said Terri Thal. "He looked totally helpless." Inverting the physics of his raucous teen performances in "just the loudest band around," Bob gave the appearance of being just about the shyest, quietest folkie performing in the Village. He lowered his head and watched his right hand strum as he sang, and when he did look out at the audience, he had a lost look in his eyes. This was largely because he played without his glasses and could see for only a few feet without them, but virtually no one watching him knew that, and the effect was magnetic. "He in a sense was not a communicator," said Theodore Bikel, the Vienna-born actor and folksinger. "You had to come to him all the way. He didn't say, 'It's nice to be here.' He didn't reach out to touch you. You had to come to where he was." Nearly half his usual set comprised tunes either written by Guthrie or indebted to him, including some of the first songs Dylan wrote himself—a small handful of Guthrie-style "talking blues" numbers and the poignant ballad "Song to Woody." Bob murmured the words in a raw Dust Bowl twang. Between songs, he fidgeted with a funny corduroy seaman's cap he wore everywhere; a few times a night, he would pull it off, look at it or lay it on a knee for a moment, and tug it back on. He often started telling a story, somehow connected to a song, presumably, only to drift off in the midst of a thought or puff a bit on his harmonica. The audience, uncertain of what he was doing with that hat or what he was trying to say, watched ever more closely to find out.

Offstage he was even more agitated. Recalling Dylan socially—sipping red wine at Gerde's or playing chess at the Kettle of Fish, a bar with folksinging on MacDougal Street—his Greenwich Village friends recited a litany of nervous tics: he tapped his feet, one knee was bobbing, his head darted back and forth, he scratched, he wiggled in his seat. "Dylan was always hopped up, you know—I don't mean high, necessarily, hopped up," said John Herald.

"To put it frankly, he was a nervous wreck," said Oscar Brand. "He came on my radio show, and he said nothing but lies about his life. Naturally, he was nervous all the time. He was living with these enormous lies. Here he was, a kid from Minnesota, and he came here to a climate where a number of people were already quite seasoned. He was afraid he couldn't compete and afraid he wasn't good enough, so he lied, and that made him afraid he would be caught and we would judge him. I don't think many of us really believed he was that Dust Bowl character he pretended to be. Nobody really cared very much one way or another, because everybody was faking something and afraid in our own way. But he didn't know that."

In conversation, which he generally avoided, Dylan was scattered and cryptic but sometimes disarmingly witty. "When he got to know you, he could be very funny—really clever, fun, smart," said Jim Kweskin, who performed as a duo with Dylan at the Kettle of Fish. "Because he was so smart and perceptive of other people, he could say something funny about them that really cut to the core that was funny but at the same time embarrassing or hurt their feelings. He could be very, very cutting, but very funny."

Like many performers in the coffeehouses, male and female, Dylan had little difficulty attracting the opposite sex. His public image of unwashed timidity also proved a Freudian advantage. "He was like a hopeless little boy," said Barbara Dane. "All the women wanted to mother him. I think he knew that very well and really worked it." Uncommitted after a couple of flings in New York, he sat with Mark Spoelstra at the Café Figaro early one morning, about two or three a.m., and declared abruptly that romance was like hitchhiking. "I don't know why," said Spoelstra. "We were tired. We were pouring our hearts out about girlfriends and how hard it was to find the right one. I told him about the one I dated back in California that I still had a crush on. 'I went out with this girl Joan, and she was wild. Man, she was beautiful and real talented.' I told how we went to that dance, and we were slow dancing, and I was really into it and loving being with her and holding her, and she started to sing at the top of her lungs while I had my arms around her. 'Joan Baez.' He didn't seem to recognize the name, or he didn't show it if he did. I said, 'She could kill with that voice. Man. And she has this little sister. One time I picked them up, and I drove with her little sister on my lap. I wish she'd been a few years older. I guess she is, now."

Dylan knew who Baez was; he was just indifferent to her music. "Her voice goes through me. She's okay," he said, as Izzy Young logged Bob's comments in his diary a few weeks later. "Woody [told Dylan he] doesn't like Joan Baez or the Kingston Trio—Baez for her voice is too pretty and Trio because they can't be understood." At the same time, Bob followed Joan's career with interest. "He was more into the hardcore blues and gutsy stuff," said John Herald. "Most of her stuff did not appeal to him at all. Most of it, there's no roots in it—no blues, no gospel, no jazz, no roots. He was interested in her success—how she got to be so famous."

They met on April 10, 1961. It was a Monday, "hoot night" at Gerde's, and Joan and Mimi were in New York with their friend John Stein. He had driven them from Boston in his hearse the previous day, so they could be in Washington Square to protest a community measure meant to restrict folksinging in the park. They arrived too late for the Sunday rally but stayed in Manhattan as houseguests of their Cambridge friend Geno Foreman's father, the political activist Clark Foreman. Most of the Village folk community, energized by the past day's protesting and the socializing around it, gathered at Folk City in high spirits. Virtually every singer who was in town performed two or three songs: Doc Watson, Gil Turner, Dave Van Ronk, Mark Spoelstra (nervous in the same room as his old crush), Bob, and Joan. (Carolyn Hester and Richard Fariña were out of town.) Mimi, largely unknown in New York and not asked to perform, sat quietly with her sister and Stein and studied the competitive Village camaraderie. "There was a kind of an edge that was very different from Cambridge," she said. "I was happy not to sing there." When Dylan performed a couple of Guthrie songs, Joan was impressed. "He had that silly cap on, and he seemed like such a little boy," she said. "But he was a joy to experience. He was captivating. He made me smile." Joan rose to take the stage at the end of the night, the finale. As she sang, Dylan pulled a chair alongside John Stein. "He tugged my sleeve a lot while she was playing," said Stein. "Bobby was very bouncy and twitchy and cute—he was sort of an elf and cute, and he seemed younger than the rest of us, although we were all about the same age. He said to me, 'Hey, man, I wrote a song, and I want Joanie to hear it.' " By the time Joan finished a few numbers, it was nearly two a.m. Stein escorted the Baez sisters out the door, and Bob sprang up to follow them—so quickly that he had not taken his guitar. On the sidewalk, Bob asked if he could play a song for Joan. She said "of course" and took her Gibson from its case for him. Bob dropped his left knee onto the pavement and balanced Joan's guitar on his right leg. He seemed certain to tip over while he was singing, "Hey, hey, Woody Guthrie, I wrote you a song . . ." Joan, Mimi, and Stein looked down attentively. "It was like Bobby's little command performance," said Stein. "Joanie said she liked it very much, thank you, and Bobby said, 'Ya can sing it if you wanna.' " The hour being late and the night being unseasonably chilly and damp, Joan excused the group. Bob turned to Mimi, as she recalled, and said, "Hey, do you want to go to a party with me?" Joan answered for her, "No—she can't." She was too young, Joan snapped, and it was already past her bedtime. "It was a little weird that he was hitting on me," said Mimi. "Joanie was very upset." As they rode uptown with Stein, Joan fumed. "I don't want you to see him or talk to him ever again," she instructed her sister.

The next day Dylan started telling his friends that Joan Baez wanted to record "Song to Woody." But he wasn't going to give her the permission, he said, because Guthrie didn't like her, and Bob wanted to record the song himself.

THE PROBLEM with folk, Richard Fariña announced to a congregation of musicians at a table in the Gaslight, was that it needed a beat. Compared to the music of some other cultures—Cuba, for instance—American traditional music sounds like "nursery rhymes," he said. Richard darted a glance at one of the group, Fred Neil, a firebrand young singer and songwriter with an open affection for commercial pop music (and unfortunately for his art and his health, a surpassing passion for heroin). "Is this guy for real?" Neil asked himself. "The guy's a short-story writer or something, and he's telling all these musicians [that] what they're doing is kid stuff." Richard wrapped an arm around the waist of a passing waitress (Penny Simon, who later managed the club) and pulled a couple of dirty plates off her tray. He wiped them off with a soiled napkin and flipped them upside down on the table, as if he were beginning to perform the shell-game con. "American folk music is square on the beat," Fariña said. With the palm of his left hand, he patted out a simple four-quarter time pattern on the bottom of one of the plates: *one*, two, *three*, four . . . "In Cuba, they play two rhythms simultaneously." Richard dropped his head back and closed his eyes and, while patting in four-quarter time with his left palm, began a three-quarter pattern with his right. The table rumbled in polyrhythms as Richard swayed in time. At the White Horse Tavern a year earlier, among writers at the Dylan Thomas shrine, he had been a half-Irish poet; here, in the company of bohemian musicians, he was a half-Cuban percussionist. Caught up in the moment, possibly, or competitively motivated, Richard's table mates started joining in. "All the musicians around him couldn't keep up with him," said Neil. "None of them could do the two different beats at the same time. That was Fariña, man—you thought he was full of shit, then he delivered the goods and knocked everybody out." Richard opened his eyes to find a circle of musicians concentrating intensely and counting time under their breath, tapping on the table, rapping their thighs. While the racket of erratic attempted rhythms swelled, he waved the waitress back and ordered a round of drinks for his *compadres*.

Richard and Carolyn Hester had been married for nearly a year by spring 1961. With his left hand, he continued to pursue a career as a writer of serious fiction and poetry; he spent virtually every morning at the typewriter. He had a short story ("The Vision of Brother Francis," a lyrical account of a battle between soul and flesh) and two poems ("The Flax Long Ripe," one of his Irish period pieces, and "Celebration for a Grey Day," a muted account of a quiet afternoon with Carolyn) accepted for publication (in *Prairie Schooner*, *Transatlantic Review*, and *The Atlantic Monthly*, respectively). "Celebration" is most impressive for its gentleness and simplicity:

> *We know days pass away because we're told.*
> *We lie alone and sense the reeling earth.*
> *(You whisper in my ear it has some worth)*
> *And I lean near to keep you from the cold.*
> *There are so many things that must be told.*

(Richard used the fifty-dollar payment from the *Atlantic* to buy a very used gray 1950 Dodge; Carolyn would always call the car "the poem," as in "I'll park the poem," or more often, "The poem is broken.") Richard was also now more than a hundred pages into a novel, a picaresque about a libidinous radical at a university like Cornell.

With his right hand, simultaneously, he had taken up music; Richard was playing the dulcimer. A three-string, wooden instrument little changed from the rudimentary device of the Middle Ages that inspired it (called the *Scheithold* in Germany), the dulcimer was made known in

American folk circles by rural singers, especially women, in Appalachia. "Dulcimer? That was the holy province of the baptized southern mountain lady WASP," said bluegrass banjo player Jim Connor. While harmonically limited, intended for playing melodies and counterpoint phrases rather than chords, it produces a thin, droning sound that can be eerily beautiful. The dulcimer is the "easiest to play of any creative instrument," according to singer and musician Jean Ritchie, who was born to a family of dulcimer builders and musicians in Elkhorn, Kentucky. One lays it on one's lap, presses upon the strings with an outstretched finger or a thin rod, and strums; anyone should be able to pick up a dulcimer for the first time and play it, Ritchie said. Learning rudimentary guitar may have seemed like a painless route to musicianship—"Folk music is the shortcut to becoming an 'entertainer' these days," wrote *Village Voice* columnist Bob Reisner; "Express yourselves! Make girls! Get a record contract! You buy a guitar, learn three chords, and you are set." What could beat an instrument that you need not even learn? The dulcimer appealed to Fariña when he first saw Ritchie perform at a party in Manhattan; a few months later, Carolyn gave him an instrument handmade by one of her friends, George Emerson. Richard took to it, practicing for a while after finishing his day's writing. He largely ignored the dulcimer tradition and never listened to records of dulcimer players or learned music composed for the instrument. Using a chopstick as the "noter" and a guitar pick to strum, he played his own way, with a vigorous attack and propulsive rhythmic feeling. Hester listened in disbelief as he experimented, sometimes improvising instrumental dulcimer versions of "Hound Dog" or "Blue Suede Shoes," sometimes chanting the words of poems he had written over modal tones and a driving beat.

As his father had advised him in his youth, Richard capitalized on his personal associations for self-advancement. His college friend Thomas Pynchon, who had had a couple of short stories published in *New World Writing* and *The Kenyon Review* in 1960, was working on a novel of his own while making a living as an engineering aide for Boeing in Seattle. Richard sent him the completed sections of his novel in progress and asked for Pynchon's help in shopping it to publishers. (Pynchon referred him to his agent, Candida Donadio, and Fariña sent her about a hundred pages of the manuscript, which she declined to take on; although the book had commercial potential, she said, she found its treatment of sex and drugs sensationalistic.) His wife, Carolyn, provided his entrée to music. At most of her performances now, Richard was acting as emcee and sidekick. He adopted a new peasant look: he grew a mustache and wore a fisherman's turtleneck sweater and a black woolen cap onstage. Richard would introduce Carolyn with an elaborate anecdote and reappear between her songs to recite bits of verse, perhaps staying to join in a number or two, sometimes even doing his a cappella "The Wild Colonial Boy." (He did not play his dulcimer in public at first, although he liked to hold it onstage during his monologues, Jack Benny–style.) Hester's act was becoming a duo, through Richard's initiative and his wife's begrudging acquiescence. "He had his work, his writing, and I got to type the manuscripts," said Hester. "I had my music, and he had to have that, too. I couldn't resist, because he was so charming, and the audiences enjoyed him."

Offstage as well, Richard insinuated himself into his wife's business affairs, much to the distress of her manager, Charlie Rothschild. "Mister Far-*eeen*-ya," Rothschild said, "decided that he wanted to be in the music business. I was representing Carolyn Hester. He wanted to represent Carolyn Hester and Richard Fariña. If he took over her artist management, he could become a manager and an artist in one swell step. Unfortunately for him, Carolyn already had a manager, and that was Charlie Rothschild, not Richard Fariña, and I was doing quite well for Carolyn without him." Indeed, in midsummer Rothschild arranged for Hester to meet John Hammond, who was eager to sign an attractive and talented young female folksinger to Columbia in the wake of Joan Baez's success with Vanguard. For the negotiations with Hammond, Rothschild enlisted the help of his colleague Albert Grossman. "John Hammond knew he blew it when he lost Joan, and Albert reminded him of that," said Rothschild. ("We were looking for a replacement for Joan Baez," affirmed Hammond's boss, David Kapralik.) Accompanied by Rothschild and Grossman, Carolyn met Hammond in his office. (Her husband was not present.) She signed with Columbia, with Hammond to be her producer. To celebrate, Carolyn and Richard had a rare dinner out and steak, at that. "I guess we thought I could afford it," said Carolyn. "He was very happy for me. Richard thought this was the greatest thing. I never felt competitive with Joan, but it seemed very important to him that I do better than her. He was very excited about the record. He had a lot of ideas, naturally—we can do this, then we can do that. The one thing that upset him terribly was Albert's involvement. He didn't want Albert to have anything to do with me. He had a fit about it, actually. He didn't want Albert to have anything to do with our business. He said Albert was too controlling—he'd take over, he'd have his hands in everything. He thought Albert was domineering. I thought, 'Well, maybe Richard's right. This is something he seems to understand.' "

In early May, Carolyn Hester was scheduled to perform at a folk club in Springfield, Massachusetts, for a couple of nights, followed shortly after by a few nights at Club 47 in Cambridge, her first appearance in Joan Baez's domain since 1959. The last time, she had been the featured attraction and Joan the unknown who had knocked on her dressing-room door, eager to sing for her. Now John Hammond was telling Charlie Rothschild he thought Carolyn could become "another Joan." Carolyn and Richard drove "the poem" from Brooklyn, where they were staying for a while with Richard's mother (now divorced from Richard Sr.). They shared the ride with Terri Thal. A part-time artist's representative as well as first lady of Greenwich Village, she was trying to promote Bob Dylan, who had been eating meals at the apartment she shared with Dave Van Ronk and sleeping on their couch. Thal wanted to play a tape recording of a Dylan performance for Paula Kelley, in hopes that she would book him at Club 47. "Bobby hadn't played in any clubs beyond the Village since he came to New York, and I thought he was good enough," said Terri Thal. "Nobody ever heard of him, so he was a hard sell, and he didn't quite come across on tape. I knew I might be wasting my time going all the way up there, but the ride was fun." Richard did all of the driving and most of the talking, except for a stretch when Thal practiced her Bob Dylan sales pitch.

When she returned to New York, Terri Thal reported to her client that Paula Kelley, underwhelmed by his work as it sounded on Thal's portable tape recorder, wanted to see him perform before deciding whether to hire him; he was welcome to sit in between a featured artist's sets, if the other performer agreed. Since Carolyn and Richard had decided to stay in New England for a few weeks, Thal encouraged Dylan to go to Boston soon; if Hester had a booking, she would likely allow him to do a song or two, since Hester and Fariña had met Dylan casually and heard all about Bob on their drive with Terri. Dylan took a train in early June. However, Hester and Fariña were out of town, house-sitting for friends of Carolyn's on Martha's Vineyard. Dylan looked up the folksinger Robert L. Jones, whom he had recently gotten to know at the Indian Neck Folk Festival in Connecticut, and Jones introduced him to his brother-in-law Eric von Schmidt. (Jones's sister Helen was von Schmidt's wife.) Being in Massachusetts during the summer, they played a game of croquet at Jones's house—"Dylan was like a little spastic gnome," said von Schmidt; "he couldn't hit the ball" (perhaps because he wasn't wearing his glasses)—before taking out their guitars. Dylan seemed less interested in demonstrating his approach than in hearing what the Cambridge players, especially von Schmidt, were doing, Jones recalled. Von Schmidt obliged and taught Dylan a couple of his favorite songs: "He Was a Friend of Mine," a prison blues he had learned from a Library of Congress recording, and "Baby, Let Me Follow You Down," von Schmidt's adaptation of another blues, "Baby Let Me Lay It on You" (attributed variously to Blind Boy Fuller and the Rev. Gary Davis). "He didn't know a lot of country blues," said von Schmidt. "He seemed very impressed by the fact that I was playing black music. I don't think he knew much about the black strain in folk music, but he was obviously very drawn to it. I know he was surprised to find somebody doing it in Cambridge. The scene pretty much revolved around Joan Baez, and he was really having a hard time being heard." Dylan went to Club 47 with Jones and von Schmidt that evening, but he never got a chance to perform.

That August Carolyn Hester was booked back at 47; Bob Dylan

heard and took the train back to Boston. On the second or third night of her engagement, he showed up at the door with his guitar. The room was full, he was told, sorry. Dylan insisted that Carolyn was expecting him, although she was not—Terri Thal had not called to prepare Hester for his arrival; he was allowed to stand along a back wall. Carolyn, casually beautiful if unseasonable in a dark wool skirt and a long-sleeve gray sweater, sang no more than two songs before Richard, collegiately over-dressed in a white sweatshirt with a polo shirt underneath, joined her to recite some Yeats. They were together onstage so much that Eric von Schmidt assumed they were a duo act. To close the first set, Richard sang the Irish ballad "Johnny's Gone to Hi-Lo" to Carolyn's guitar accompaniment. It was "beautiful," von Schmidt said—"the real highlight, very intense. The energy went from professional to sky high." When von Schmidt noticed Dylan, still against the wall, he thought Bob "looked like a frightened puppy" and decided to keep him company for the rest of the evening. "Neither of us had ever seen Dick perform before," said von Schmidt. "Dick had this lusty presence. He didn't sound like any of the rest of us. Dick was coming more from a European idea and an Irish-English thing. This kind of impressed us. We couldn't keep our eyes off him. He had a kind of presence that you either have or you don't, something mysterious, and a real feeling of mystery and intellectual depth that wasn't the common thing in the folk world. Bob was fascinated. He studied him." Dylan never got to sit in; he had barely talked to Hester and Fariña. At night's end, however, von Schmidt invited all three visitors from Greenwich Village to join him, his wife Helen, and their eight-month-old daughter Caitlin for a picnic at the Atlantic seashore the next day.

Helen von Schmidt refused to go on sanitary grounds. Eric's plan was to take his guests to Revere Beach, about three miles of public resort area that lay ten minutes north of Cambridge and was popular among working-class families and folksingers. (Joan and Mimi Baez, Debbie Green, and their friends used to gather on towels and play guitars in swimsuits there; crowds of young men would appear around them and, presumably, listen.) Undermaintained and overcrowded, Revere Beach had an unsavory reputation that enhanced its appeal among Harvard Square's young bohemians. "It was fun for people our age," said Helen von Schmidt, "but I would never let my child set foot on that filthy place. You could get polio from that water." Eric von Schmidt made ham sandwiches and a jug of "punch" from a quart of orange juice and a fifth of rum, and he collected Hester, Fariña, and Dylan in his old Buick. Sitting semicircle in street clothes on a bedsheet von Schmidt laid on the sand, the four artists spent the afternoon soaking in the sun and the alcohol. (No one had brought a guitar, out of fear of damaging it from exposure to wet bodies and the damp salt air.) "I remember it was the first time that I had really seen Dylan in the daylight, because we'd meet in the Village at night," recalled Carolyn Hester. "In the daytime, he looked so pale, his skin was almost transparent."

Fariña and von Schmidt, both talkative, gregarious creatures, dominated the conversation. Dylan listened passively, acknowledging occasional comments with a few words—"Yeah, man," "Dig it," "Fuck that," "Fuck them"—or a giggle. Hester rested and flipped through a magazine she had brought. As the jug got lighter, Fariña and von Schmidt grew more animated, Dylan more withdrawn. "Bob was sort of sitting there staring at his toes," said von Schmidt. "He didn't look like he was having a good time there by the water. He sat there looking emaciated with his shirt off and just sort of kept to himself, just sort of obviously not feeling very comfortable, and he didn't really have anything to talk about."

To Fariña, Dylan posed a threat to both of his guiding principles:

1. Celebrate every day.
2. Never permit anyone the luxury of boring you.

Richard treated the outing, like most social situations, as a combination brainstorming session, business meeting, exercise in improvisational theater, and party in his honor. "He moved fast. Nothing shy about him," said von Schmidt. By six p.m., when the area closed and the bleary group drove back to Cambridge to prepare for another evening at Club 47, Fariña had made future plans with both of his new friends. He and von Schmidt would collaborate on a book—Fariña's novel in progress, reconceived that day as an adventurous union of prose and illustration. "He was writing a novel," said von Schmidt. "Sure, uh-huh—everybody you met was writing a novel. Next topic. But he was talking about Cornell and Nabokov, and okay, well, maybe. . . . Next thing I knew, the two of us were inventing a whole new genre. We decided to do a book that was extensively illustrated, and the illustrations would advance the text. They wouldn't be just decorative. They would stand alongside the text as equally creative and important. Hey—wow! We reinvented literature, and it only took one bottle of rum!" Fariña promised to mail von Schmidt the chapters he had written so far when he returned to New York. Von Schmidt could begin sketching ideas for scenes to insert.

After deciding on how to reinvent literature, Fariña turned to Dylan with an idea for reinventing music. He was experimenting with poetry, folk music, and rhythm, Richard told Dylan and von Schmidt. "He had really published real poems and short stories, which made him a real writer. That impressed the heck out of Dylan," said von Schmidt. "Dick said, 'We should start a whole new genre. Poetry set to music, but not chamber music or beatnik jazz, man—music with a beat. Poetry you can dance to. Boogie poetry! Yeah!' He was wild—a wild, improvising, egomaniac madman. Dylan was stunned. Like, how's he going to do that? On the dulcimer, the fucking dulcimer? But he had something. For all I know, Dylan had the same idea. A million people might have had the same idea—I don't know. But nobody else I knew was talking that way."

Dylan told Fariña he had a more immediate challenge. "He said, 'I'm having trouble finding gigs,' " Hester recalled. " 'Would there be any gigs you know of? Is there anything that you're doing, you could bring me on?' I said, 'Well, I just got a record contract, and I'm going to start recording when we get back to New York.' " She and Richard had been discussing ideas for bringing a fresh touch to her Columbia debut, and Fariña was keen on Dylan. "Richard and I were talking about what could be acceptable to the folk crowd and still be a little advanced commercially—to reach out, to be a little different from Joan Baez, say," said

Hester. "I put a lot of faith in Richard's judgment. He was able to zero in on who was doing *it* and who wasn't, and who was somebody we ought to be friends with. The fact that Richard was fascinated by Dylan was good enough for me." Carolyn invited Dylan to perform as her guest at Club 47 that evening and to play harmonica on a few tracks of her album when she started recording in a few weeks. "Yeah," Dylan said, grinning. "Dig it!"

Unlike virtually every notable folksinger in the Village, Dylan had not done any professional recording, not even as a sideman. Vanguard, in a series of showcase albums called "New Folks," had begun an effort to introduce others in Dylan's peer group, including Robert L. Jones, Hedy West, Lisa Kindred, and Phil Ochs. Dylan had been passed over. "We were recording people who had potential but were not yet there—people who we felt did not quite deserve an LP," said Maynard Solomon. "Bobby was desperate to be included, but I thought, in my arrogance, that he wasn't ready." Dylan had tried to see Moe Asch at Folkways, but literally couldn't get in the door. "I heard Folkways was good," he told Izzy Young. "Irwin Silber didn't even talk to me. Never got to see Moe Asch. They just about said, 'Go,' and I heard that *Sing Out!* was supposed to be helpful and friendly. Big heart. Charitable. I thought it was the wrong place and Sing Out! was on the door. Whoever told me that was wrong." (In 1958 Asch had hired Irwin Silber, editor of *Sing Out!*, to work in marketing for Folkways; as part of their arrangement, Asch entered into a publishing partnership with Silber.) One of Dylan's most enthusiastic early boosters, Izzy Young arranged for Dylan to see Asch—and soon after to meet Jac Holzman of Elektra. (Holzman would never recall any such meeting.) Neither signed him. "Nobody wanted to touch Dylan," said Young. "All the geniuses—none of them thought he was good enough."

At the end of Carolyn's first set at Club 47 that night, Richard took the microphone and launched into a monologue about the afternoon at Revere Beach, dropping casual references to the book he and Eric von Schmidt were going to do and Hester's record date. "We asked Bobby to be part of it," he said, "and we'd like to show you why." As he beckoned Dylan up to the stage, Richard led Carolyn off.

Dylan sang four or five songs that night, including one original, "Talkin' Bear Mountain Picnic Massacre Blues," a wry talking blues in the Guthrie style. Paula Kelley finally got to see him perform in person, and she declined to invite him back.

IN 1936 George Gershwin moved to Beverly Hills. Prospering from his innumerable Broadway hits, the thirty-seven-year-old composer bought an expansive Spanish-style estate on North Roxbury Drive, off Sunset Boulevard; there were palm trees lining its private road, formal gardens on the grounds, a swimming pool, and a tennis court—everything a fan-magazine photographer could want. Gershwin's old musical colleague Jerome Kern lived nearby, and so did their mutual friend Irving Berlin, and so did Harold Arlen. For all of them, New York–bred composers who rose out of Tin Pan Alley to redefine popular music in the first half of the twentieth century, moving to California represented professional success and social ascension. Amidst the glamour, the opulence, and the luxury of Hollywood—the world of all those songs they wrote for Fred Astaire and Ginger Rogers—the voices of the Jazz Age found affirmation on the terms they put to music.

During the summer of 1961, Joan Baez left Cambridge and moved to California. She had a hit album, and her performances at concert halls and university theaters around the country invariably sold out. "She was a star," said her manager, Manny Greenhill, who set her standard fee as high as he dared: $1,200 per concert. With her father about to take on another new job (this one in Europe to help UNESCO improve elementary-level science education in developing countries), Joan found the timing good for making a change. "My parents were going to be taking Mimi out of the country, following my father's work. I figured, 'Now's the time.' " She rented a house in the Carmel Highlands, a pic-

*Joan and Mimi Baez posing with their guitars and,
below, playing together in Cambridge in 1959*

*Bob Dylan's first
recording session,
backing Carolyn Hester,
with Bruce Langhorne
and Bill Lee. Left,
Richard Fariña recites
poetry in a London folk
club*

*Ethan Signer (back turned), Martin Carthy, Fariña, Dylan,
and Eric von Schmidt commandeer the Troubadour in London.
Below, Mimi and Richard in Tom Costner's Paris flat*

Joan and Bob at the 1963 Newport Folk Festival.
Below, the "We Shall Overcome" finale: Peter Yarrow, Mary Travers, Noel "Paul" Stookey,
Baez, Dylan, the Freedom Singers, Pete Seeger, and Theodore Bikel

Mimi and Richard celebrating their second wedding, top, and relaxing at home in the Carmel Highlands

Bob and Mimi by the pool at Newport, 1964

Richard and Mimi Fariña, folk duo

Joan and Bob sitting in at Club 47 in Harvard Square

turesque rock pile of about seven square miles overlooking a cove
sculpted artfully by the Pacific. It was a pine saltbox, painted light blue.
You drove to it up an unpaved road that became the lawn, a small clearing of gravel and earth with hopeful green patches. Someone had once
positioned a nearly four-foot-high whitish oblong rock a few feet to the
left of the house, and it remained there, immovable and puzzling, like a
ruin. When you looked at the front of house, you were facing west, and
you could hear the ocean about half a mile behind a thicket of tall cypress and redwood trees; you saw a narrow plank door and, to its right,
one horizontal window. The roof was eight feet from the ground on the
left side and ten feet high on the right. The house had one room, and it
measured twelve by twelve feet, about the size of the Baez parlor in Belmont. For heat and cooking, there was a wood-burning stove. Joan
found the house through Michael New, who had a friend at Harvard
from the Highlands, Richard "Red" Williams. She rented it from Red's
parents, Cynthia and Russell, heirs of the Carmel pioneers Michael and
Peggy Williams, for thirty-five dollars per month.

Clearly, moving to California meant something different to Joan
Baez than it had meant to George Gershwin and his peers half a century
earlier. "I think a big reason for the move for me was my general terror
of the whole business of being a star," said Joan. "I may have wanted it,
but I wasn't prepared for it. So I chose to move away and live in some
obscure place where there were no photographers." (Despite her fame,
Joan remained pathologically insecure about her appearance. "It wasn't
the invasion of privacy, although that was there, too," she said. "I
couldn't stand the way I looked in pictures, so I projected it back at the
camera." At the sight of a camera about to click, she would routinely
turn to the lens and make a funny face, scrunching her nose or sticking
out her tongue.)

"Everything was happening too fast," she said. "I just told Manny,
'See you—I'm moving out west.' He said, 'What about your concerts?' I
said, 'Oh, yeah—call me. I'll have a telephone.' I was like, 'I don't want
to think about the music business. I'm going to escape it all. Michael is
right—it's all wickedly commercial, and I'm going out west to live the

pure life.' I associated California with some kind of purity. The West Coast for me was like that, something pure. I didn't really have any intention of stopping my music. I was touring the country, but I was not at home as much as I wanted, and I needed to retrench and stop and think about what I was doing and why I was doing it. I had to go somewhere that was home for me, an escape from the wicked world, and for me, that meant the West Coast." Michael New accompanied Joan to Carmel, but as usual for them, they did not stay together long.

The Highlands had long been the least Beverly of hills. Historic as California's "bohemia of the seacoast," the Carmel area had been a haven for artists and the aesthetically inclined since the early part of the century, when it was settled by the poet George Sterling, the novelist Mary Austin, the photographer Arnold Genthe, and their partners and friends. Henry Miller found literary and sexual inspiration in Carmel, and Harry Partch set hobo speech to music on instruments he hand-built there. Exquisitely rustic and hospitable to creative adventurers, Carmel appealed to Joan Baez far more than had Cambridge or, for that matter, any other place on the East Coast; it was a part of California—an aspect of the state's character, as much as a location—in keeping with Joan Baez's sensibility and image. She had been performing in bare feet; here no one else seemed to wear shoes, either. She had been singing about rural life; now she could begin to live it. At the same time, while Carmel was decidedly not Hollywood, it was no more the Ozarks; as an artists' colony, Carmel upheld its own tradition of intellectual elitism. Joan Baez, the supremely gifted and intensely driven and competitive celebrity earth child, felt at home, and she was welcomed as one of Carmel's own.

"No one in Carmel Highlands knew much about Joan, aside from the facts that she was friendly with my son and she was a musician," said Cynthia Williams, a strong, small woman fiercely protective of her family's heritage. Cynthia invariably spoke with deliberate authority; when answering a letter, she wrote her reply on the unused space on the first correspondence with circles marking the writer's errors and critical comments in the margins. "We were aware that she had been mentioned in

Time magazine. But many residents of the Carmel Highlands were covered often in the press. This meant little to us. Joan was not very different from any of us, although I don't think she did a great deal of reading. I know she enjoyed playing with the dogs." The locals' many pets freely roamed the neighborhood. "She came here to get away from it all. This was a fine place to do it." Joan made sure not to wear her hair shirt too tightly, however. Since her house was up a mountain road, she needed a car and bought, with cash, a new-model Jaguar XKE roadster (list price: $5,685). George Gershwin's Jaguar was a Swallow Seven 90.

ALBERT GROSSMAN came to Gerde's for lunch once that summer, a rare afternoon intrusion upon the neighborhood laborers by one of the night people. He ordered the most expensive dish on the menu, breaded veal cutlet, six dollars, and extended his hand to Mike Porco when the owner walked by. Grossman invited Porco to sit down and join him. Although the place was busy and a liquor delivery had just arrived, Porco took a seat in honor of his patron's atypical largesse. Grossman said he had been watching Gerde's success. "He told me Folk City was the best around," Porco recalled, beaming when he told the story a decade later. "He wanted his entertainers here, because this was number one." While continuing to manage the veteran acts he had signed in Chicago, Grossman was fixed on expanding his influence in Greenwich Village. He had already retained Peter Yarrow, Noel Stookey, and Mary Travers and refashioned them as Peter, Paul and Mary; now he was looking to groom a few other young newcomers. "Albert wasn't interested in established or recognized artists," Travers explained. "He was much more clever. [His approach at the time was to] find a nobody that he could nurture and make famous. Then they'd be forever indebted to him, so he thought." While his veal was being baked, Grossman mentioned the progress the new trio was making in rehearsals and brought up Dylan, speaking as if he represented him. "Nobody had to tell me about Bobby," said Porco. "It was me—I gave him his start." Grossman added that he had privileged information: Robert Shelton was interested in giving Dylan "a big write-up" in *The New York Times*, Porco recalled, "and this would be a big thing for me. I told him, 'Good, because I was planning to bring in Bobby for a couple of weeks.' " Porco left the table and attended to the delivery. In conducting the transaction, he was told that a hundred dollars of the cost of the liquor had been paid for by the heavyset fellow at the table over there.

A few weeks later, just back from Cambridge, Dylan announced to Terri Thal, who was still acting as his representative, that "Grossman wants to be my manager," and he said he had decided to use him. (Dylan would sign a ten-year contract with Grossman for management and representation.) "I was pissed," said Thal. "I thought [Dylan] should have talked to me about it earlier, when he was talking to Albert, instead of doing it in secret and just laying it on me like that. But that [anger] didn't last long, and I said, 'Oh, that's good, because he can do more for you than I can, the snake.' "

FRESH FROM HARVARD, Pete Seeger first earned credibility as a folksinging banjo player when, at age twenty-one, he spent a year or so roaming with Woody Guthrie from the redwood forests to the gulf-stream waters. The image of the rootless troubadour, never settling—never resting, never compromising—had long been integral to the folk ideal. Around Greenwich Village in the early 1960s, it was a token of status to have no residence or to pretend you had none. Bob Dylan was by no means the only young vagabond to eat and sleep at Dave Van Ronk's, the Isaacsons', and the Gleasons'; Mark Spoelstra, Fred Neil, Phil Ochs, and John Herald all took turns on the same couches. To Carolyn Hester, Richard Fariña's habitual transience seemed typical, for a while. Richard always carried a little black book labeled "People with Pads," through whose hospitality he had lived since coming to Manhattan. More than a year after Carolyn and Richard married, however, they were still living out of the book, and she was feeling debilitated from and embarrassed by the incessant moving. They returned from Cambridge to Richard's mother's house in Brooklyn; next, Richard arranged for them to house-sit for Ned O'Gorman, one of Fariña's drinking-writer friends, who would be traveling in Africa for two weeks. "We were living like gypsies," said Hester. "That wasn't the way I was raised. I couldn't stand it anymore, and I started to rebel. I was feeling better about myself since John Hammond signed me. I was feeling more independent, so Dick got more controlling.

"He started insisting that I lose weight. He wouldn't let me eat. I had to sneak food—anything I could find anywhere. If we went to a party and all they had was cookies, I'd eat ten cookies behind his back. I lost twenty pounds in no time. I was absolutely starved. In a way, Richard had a point. He was trying to protect his interests. You need to not be enormous, if you're going to be in the public. But I was pretty thin before I lost a pound. I was beginning to feel ill, just as we were starting to prepare for the sessions."

As self-appointed creative consultant, Richard accompanied Carolyn to a rough run-through of some material for her new album with Bob Dylan at the apartment at One Sheridan Square where the sisters Carla and Susan Rotolo lived with their mother Mary, a journalist for an Italian-language newspaper, recently widowed. Dylan had just begun spending time with Susan, a demure seventeen-year-old with long auburn hair and a cheering, sunny face. Like Joan Baez, Susan was one of a pair of competitive artistic sisters in a matriarchal and politically progressive Old World household. Raised with Puccini on the record player, Romantic poetry on the bookshelves, and impassioned left-leaning conversation at the dinner table, both Susan and her sister Carla, twenty, gravitated naturally to the Village folk scene. "It was all music and poetry and politics all rolled in to love," said Susan, who went by the nickname Suze (pronounced like "Suzie"). She saw something of her late father, an amateur painter and social idealist, in Dylan's quiet determination; and he seemed to draw strength from her joyful encouragement. "We had differences that made us good for each other," she said. "In other ways, we were very similar. I didn't have a place of my own, and he didn't have a place to live. We were both not very verbal. The way we understood each other—there was something." Although Suze thought her mother distrusted Dylan, Mary kept a warm Italian home, and everyone was welcome. Dylan invited Carolyn and Richard over during the afternoon, while the Rotolo women would all be working (Carla as an assistant to folklorist Alan Lomax, Suze doing clerical work for the Book-of-the-Month Club).

Describing the work session to Robert Shelton, Fariña said, "I felt [Carolyn] should be doing something with the blues, but she didn't know any blues songs. Carolyn said to Bob, 'I want to learn some blues,' and he sang around fifteen or twenty at her." Carolyn liked "Come Back, Baby," a sultry plea recorded by Muddy Waters and Walter Davis, among others, and Dylan taught it to her. They devised an arrangement around Dylan's twining harmonica lines and made a date to meet the following week to work up more songs with a couple of other musicians who would be recording with Carolyn.

At the request of Carolyn and Richard, Hammond had agreed to include a second guitarist on the album: Bruce Langhorne, the versatile improviser (on both guitar and country fiddle) who worked regularly at Folk City as a one-man house band. One of the few black musicians in the Village coffeehouses, he felt a kinship to Fariña because of Richard's Cuban ancestry. "It was a very white scene, and the two of us didn't quite fit in," said Langhorne, "and we were both pretty wild." (Early one morning after Gerde's closed, Langhorne and Fariña rode the guitarist's Volkswagen Beetle up the New York State Thruway; taking turns, one drove while the other popped through the sunroof with Langhorne's hunting rifle and shot at road signs as they sped past.) Hammond brought in Bill Lee. Since Hester and Fariña were staying at Ned O'Gorman's apartment and it was big, a floor of a townhouse on West 10th

Street off Fifth Avenue, they invited the musicians there to rehearse on Thursday, September 14. Hammond invited himself, to hear how the group's sound was taking form. "He was a little worried, because he didn't know anything about Bobby," said Carolyn, "and he wanted to hear what we were up to before we all sat down in the studio and tape started rolling." (Actually, Hammond's nineteen-year-old son, John, a skillful blues singer and guitarist, had mentioned Dylan favorably to his father.) Dylan, who certainly knew Hammond's importance, took a seat next to him on an antique bench in O'Gorman's living room and softly finger-picked his guitar.

"I went to one of [Hester's] rehearsals and heard a kind of folk music I knew nothing about," Hammond recounted in his memoirs. "One member of her group was Dick Fariña, a writer, poet, and lyricist. . . . There were two other guitar players. One, a young fellow wearing a cap and a harmonica holder, was a friend of Fariña's. I watched him for a while and found him fascinating, although he was not particularly good on either guitar or harmonica." After about an hour, Hammond got up to leave, satisfied. "Okay," he announced, as Hester recalled. "I like the way it's going. This sounds good. I can see this. This has a sound of its own. Okay." Hammond said he would book a studio to begin recording in a couple of weeks, and he left the musicians to finish their work.

I T SEEMS POSSIBLE, though not certain, that Albert Grossman invested at least two hundred dollars to launch Bob Dylan's career at Gerde's Folk City. Mike Porco said he understood that Robert Shelton received the same amount as his liquor distributor to help defray the cost of coming to see Dylan. Many insiders had heard that Shelton accepted payments from record companies for public relations services and that he worked under pseudonyms to dodge the *New York Times*'s editorial ethics guidelines. Some knew, too, that his main job at the newspaper was proofreading and that his reviewing was a sideline. By the end of September, the coffeehouses were humming with rumors that Grossman had joined the record companies as one of Shelton's freelance employers. Then again, all that talk might have been envy.

On the evening of Tuesday, September 26, a clear, brisk autumn night, Bob Dylan began a two-week engagement at Folk City as opening act to the Greenbriar Boys. Everyone on the bill had heard that Robert Shelton had promised to review the show. Dylan was frenzied. "Oh, it was a big deal to him," said John Herald, the Greenbriar Boys' singer and guitarist. "He was a guy at the Gaslight until that. This was a real big deal, and he knew it. He was excited. He dressed a certain way. He asked everybody what he should wear that night, what he should sing— 'Remember when I sang that song a couple weeks ago? Should I do that?' He was hopped up, excited, about the whole thing." He decided on a blue dress shirt, properly unpressed and frayed; a tie, an old foulard that had a brown pattern or coffee stains; a charcoal sweater vest; khakis; and as always his little sailor's cap. For his first set, he chose songs darker and more weathered than his outfit: among them, a couple of bleak Woody Guthrie tunes (including "Hard Travelin' "); several traditional blues numbers; and four songs he had written himself since coming east: "Song to Woody," "Talkin' Bear Mountain Picnic Massacre Blues," and two similar, cynically humorous talking blues, "Talkin' New York" (a litany of his hardships in Manhattan) and "Talkin' Hava Negeilah Blues" (a swipe at singers of "ethnic" folk songs such as Harry Belafonte and Theodore Bikel). The dominant themes were woe and despair: the world can be cruel to its children, particularly to Bob Dylan. While tuning his guitar to an open chord to play the blues lament "This Life Is Killing," he announced, "Here's a song suitable to the occasion."

Dylan's performing style, as it had come together over the past months, was of a piece with his appearance and his material: refined asperity. His guitar playing was erratic; the beat slowed and sped, frets buzzed, dead strings thumped. When a simple minor chord, perfectly executed, rang for a moment, it would seem a kind of miracle. He used the harmonica to produce battlefield sound effects—explosions, rebel yells, and death moans tangentially related to the notes of the musical scale. (While conventional players traditionally blow into the instrument, blues musicians also inhale through it; Dylan did both with equal urgency, breathing in and out through the harmonica as if it were a life-support device. Jarring to his early audiences, Dylan would soon be the best-known and most-imitated harmonica player around.) His voice was rawer still, a pinched mountain holler; melodies came out as nasal moans or growls—at a dramatic point, a yelp. If he wanted, though, he could murmur in a fragile voice of startling beauty, and he would relieve the melancholy with bits of Chaplin-style physical business.

Like Joan Baez only more so, Dylan seemed to embody the rising generation's rejection of prettifying artifice. (*Sing Out!* would report, "His night club appearances at Gerde's Folk City have attracted predominantly youthful and enthusiastic audiences while the elders in the crowd seem puzzled at his style of singing. . . . The largest portion of his growing following is made up of persons near his own age.") Indeed, Dylan appeared even more authentic and important—purer, in his acridity—than the beatific, dulcet-toned virgin of Newport. Next to Bob Dylan, Joan Baez was as lightweight as one of the 1950s pop stars she liked to parody.

Although the Greenbriar Boys were the headliners, Shelton decided to do an interview with Dylan, whom he knew only casually, and they conducted it in the club's kitchen between sets. Dylan grabbed facts from the air as if they were Gerde's mascot flies: he had been a farmhand; he had run a steam shovel; he had cleaned ponies; he had played piano for Gene Vincent in Nashville; he had learned his songs straight from their creators, Mance Lipscomb, Blind Lemon Jefferson, and somebody named Wigglefoot, in his ramblin' days. Still talking when the Greenbriar Boys came onstage, Dylan and Shelton moved to a table and continued the interview while the trio played.

Robert Shelton's review was published in the *Times* on Friday, September 29, under a three-column headline: "Bob Dylan: A Distinctive Stylist." Beneath it there was a photo of the singer in his hat and tie. "A bright new face in folk music is appearing at Gerde's Folk City," Shelton began, adding among the 400 words devoted to Dylan before getting to the 250 about the Greenbriar Boys:

> Although only 20 years old, Bob Dylan is one of the most distinctive stylists to play in a Manhattan cabaret in months. . . . There is no doubt that he is bursting at the seams with talent. . . . If not for every taste, his music-making has the mark of originality and inspiration, all the more noteworthy for his youth. Mr. Dylan is vague about his antecedents and birthplace, but it matters less where he has been than where he is going, and that would seem to be straight up.

Friday, September 29, was also the day Dylan was supposed to record with Carolyn Hester at Columbia Records' Studio A on Seventh Avenue and 52nd Street. The sessions were not going well when Dylan walked in—"bounced in," Hester recalled—with a copy of the *Times* rolled up in his back pocket. He had been carrying it around all morning, waving it at storekeepers through their windows and stopping friends on the sidewalk so they could read it while he watched the expressions on their faces change. Carolyn and Richard had seen it already, of course. (Among all the Village folksingers, they were the "most enthusiastic" about the review, Shelton later wrote.) At the moment, however, Carolyn's career had priority to Hammond, and it seemed at risk. Light-headed from stress and hunger, she was having trouble concentrating. Richard bore down on her and prodded Hammond to record second and third takes. "I didn't like the way Hammond was running the session," Fariña said. "I got agitated with Hammond saying, 'That's a take,' when I knew that the song was nowhere near finished. Finally he asked me if I wanted to go into the control booth. At that point, I also talked to him about Bob and said, 'He's not just a harmonica player.' Between takes, I chatted to Hammond about Dylan and said, 'When this is all over, you ought to listen to Dylan.' What happened in the studio after we left I would not know. All I know was that I said to Hammond that he ought to listen to him."

It is hard to believe that John Hammond had not yet seen Shelton's review. Rarely engaged by the recording process, Hammond was notorious for reading the *Times* during studio sessions; he was more likely to know what was in the paper than what his artist was singing. According to Dylan, he pointed out Shelton's praise himself. "Showed the article to John Hammond," Dylan told Izzy Young. " 'Come in and see me,' [Hammond said]." By the end of the day's sessions, Dylan had played harmonica breaks on three songs, "Swing and Turn Jubilee," a square-dance number associated with Jean Ritchie; "I'll Fly Away," a gospel tune recorded previously by the Blind Boys of Alabama; and "Come Back, Baby," on which Dylan's solo is a fearless single note for six bars; and he stayed in the studio to confer with Hammond when the session was finished. "He asked me what I do," Dylan recalled. There is some confusion over related details. Dylan subsequently claimed that Hammond offered him a record contract on the basis of the *Times* piece, without having heard him sing—improbable, even by Hammond's laissez-faire standards. Hammond later claimed he asked Dylan to audition—more likely, although there is no record of an audition in Columbia's logs. In any case, Dylan was soon telling friends that he was going to be recording for John Hammond. "The following day," Fariña said, "we were sitting at the Gaslight, and Bob said that he had just been offered a Columbia contract, and he came over and hugged me."

That autumn Dylan and Fariña crossed paths at Gerde's and the Gaslight now and again, usually in the company of mutual friends such as Bruce Langhorne and Jim Kweskin. Once or twice they huddled briefly and discussed creative ideas and career plans—Richard's, naturally. Bob was loath to talk much about his work with anyone, even Suze, and his recent breaks drove a wedge between him and the Village folk community, Richard included. "They weren't together very much at that time, but I remember Bobby liking [Richard] a lot," said Suze Rotolo. (As Dylan told Robert Shelton, "He's very groovy. He's a kind of writer like Dylan Thomas.") "They hung around, and I think they went onstage with a bunch of people and sang a few times. That's what was going on. But we didn't think of [Richard] as a musician, even though he did play. I remember them showing each other their writing—to polish, one writer to another. Bobby liked him. They were kindred spirits. He had a lot of respect for him as a writer. Richard came over to the apartment on 4th Street once with a story he had written, and Bob loved it. He said, 'This is great—it's *poetry*.' Fariña was writing his novel, and Bobby was starting to write songs seriously. They helped each other." (Suze Rotolo would not recall what writing they exchanged, and Dylan would never discuss it.) As Bruce Langhorne said, "Richard had that aura of being a writer, and Bob was very plugged into that. I think Bob wanted to see what he could learn from this guy."

Fred Neil, who went drinking at the Gaslight with Dylan, Fariña, and a few others around this time, recalled Richard suggesting a career idea to Bob that he surely would not have wanted Suze Rotolo to hear. (Mary Beal, who married Fariña's college friend David Shetzline, would remember Richard's recounting the same tale.) "Fariña gave Bob this lecture," said Neil. " 'If you want to be a songwriter, man, you'd better find yourself a singer.' You see, Bob and me, we were both writing, but I knew how to sing. Fariña told him straight, 'Man, what you need to do, man, is hook up with Joan Baez. She is so square, she isn't in this century. She needs you to bring her into the twentieth century, and you need somebody like her to do your songs. She's your ticket, man. All you need to do, man, is start screwing Joan Baez.' "

According to Neil, Dylan joked, "That's a good idea—I think I'll do that. But I don't want her singing none of my songs."

MIMI BAEZ'S FRENCH SOJOURN began like one in a pulp romance. Traveling under the auspices of UNESCO, she and her parents sailed first-class on *La Flamberger*, an opulent small ship designed in the 1930s to the specifications of French diplomats. She had a shipboard *amourette* with a sensitive young Frenchman named Pierre. They held hands and gazed at the sea. "What are you thinking?" Mimi asked. "I am thinking," replied Pierre, as she recalled dreamily years later, "about all the ships of the past that sank and are lying at the bottom of the ocean." They kissed a great deal, and when they parted, he gave her a postcard of a castle that he said was his home. *This,* Mimi thought, *is so . . . French.*

Once Pierre returned to his castle (or wherever he lived) and Mimi and her family settled in, she began to feel isolated and helpless. The Baezes were staying in a meticulously appointed, three-story fieldstone house in Le Vesinet, an upper-class residential district outside Paris; they rented the bottom two floors from the owners, a fastidious elderly Alsatian couple, who lived on the top floor and, in Mimi's mind, seemed to hover over their tenants in judgment, like angry gods. Away from her sisters and her American friends, unfamiliar with French culture and unable to speak the language, at sixteen too young to drive, Mimi spent most of her days walking alone, smoking Kent cigarettes she sneaked from her mother's pocketbook. She still had a year of high school to complete but was not allowed to attend the local French schools, so her mother enrolled her in a correspondence course run by the University of Nebraska. Neither Mimi nor her parents yet realized she was dyslexic. "I only knew I was miserable, and I couldn't learn anything," said Mimi. "That was the worst possible way for me to try to learn."

Around ten o'clock one morning, Mrs. Baez came to Mimi's room while she was studying. Big Joan had telephoned Joan in California to ask her advice. "I told Joanie, 'I know Mimi's unhappy,' " she recalled. "Joanie said, 'I can't sit and talk to her. Why don't you? Go have a cigarette with her.' I said, 'But I'm not supposed to know she smokes. Joanie said, 'Mother—have a cigarette with her. She needs somebody, and I can't be there. You're going to have be her sister for me.' " Mimi went with her mother to the kitchen, and they had a smoke and traded open secrets: they were both lonely and depressed. They had to find a new place to live, closer to Paris. The next morning they took another cigarette break together. Things were picking up. Soon Mimi started calling realtors to try to find an apartment for the Baezes in town. "That was when I miraculously learned how to speak French," said Mimi. Newly conversant, or now motivated to try to be, she found a dance studio and enrolled in a class. A young woman who knew of Joan from Club 47 was visiting Paris and, hearing that the Baez family had relocated, tracked them down at their house in hopes of finding Joan there. She found Big Joan instead, and they had an affair. Mimi found further hope in a letter from Todd Stuart: he was coming to visit her soon. "Things were definitely picking up," said Mimi. For the first time since she arrived in Paris, she unpacked her guitar.

BOB DYLAN AND JOAN BAEZ gave their first major New York concerts in November 1961, seven days and a world apart.

In the weeks after the publication of Robert Shelton's review of Bob Dylan at Folk City, when every conversation at the Folklore Center seemed to end up about Dylan, Albert Grossman persuaded Izzy Young to present his unofficial client in a venue suiting Dylan's current status. (Grossman's encouragement was purely verbal, according to Young.) As Young wrote in his diary:

> After listening to Jack Elliott for two nights last week I now think he will not "make" it. Grossman thinks that Bob Dylan has a much better chance of making it. He thinks "Peter, Paul and Mary" will be one of the top commercial groups. . . . I just made an arrangement with Bob Dylan to do a concert early in November. Grossman spurred me to do it.

Young reserved Carnegie Chapter Hall, an elegant little chamber music room adjacent to the historic main hall on West 57th Street in Manhattan, and he made up posters announcing, "The Folklore Center Presents Bob

Dylan in His First New York Concert. 8:40 p.m. All seats $2.00." Already convinced of Dylan's gifts as a performer and optimistic about his commercial prospects, Young, much like Shelton after his session with Dylan in Gerde's kitchen, seemed mesmerized when he interviewed him for the concert's program notes. (This time Dylan had formerly been a motorcycle racer in the Dakotas, and Carl Perkins had sung songs he had written in Nashville.) Ten days after he had logged his notes about Albert Grossman initiating the concert, Young wrote:

> I am very excited by Bob Dylan. I am producing the concert so I can hear him entire. Purely from the way he talks he seems to have greatness in him—an ability to stand on his own.

Five days before the concert, however, Young reconsidered:

> Tickets aren't selling well for Bob Dylan's concert.

"I guess nobody reads *The New York Times*," Izzy Young later joked. "If they did [read Shelton's review of Dylan], they didn't take it seriously. Meanwhile all the Village folkies were jealous of Dylan because he's the one who got the big write-up, and he got the record contract with Columbia. They boycotted the concert. That's a good theory. But there's a better theory: The schmucks in the Village won't go uptown, because they think it's the North Pole." Fifty-three people came to the concert on Saturday, November 4, 1961; just as well for Dylan's reputation. Perhaps shaken by the poor attendance or simply unnerved to be attempting his ragged music in such a stately setting, Dylan gave a tense, bloodless performance. His voice quavered and broke, even on such standards of his repertoire as "Gospel Plow" and "This Land Is Your Land." He sounded distracted, as if his mind, like the crowd from Gerde's, was elsewhere that night.

The following Saturday, Joan Baez appeared at Town Hall on West 43rd Street, a ten-minute walk away. The 1,700-seat theater sold out quickly, and more than two hundred people (more than enough to fill

Carnegie Chapter Hall) in the queue outside were turned away. "I read in the trade papers that the show was SRO, and I couldn't figure out what it meant," said Joan. "Finally I decided it meant 'Sold Right Out.' But I couldn't reconcile the fact that so many people were coming to see me. All those people coming to the concert seemed like something happening to somebody else, and I was singing, yes, but I couldn't put the two things together. I really didn't think of myself as worthy of all that." Timed to help promote her second Vanguard album, *Joan Baez, Volume 2*, which had just been released, the event featured most of the songs on the recording ("Wagoner's Lad," "Once I Knew a Pretty Girl," "Old Blue," more Child ballads) and the same musicians; in addition to Joan, singing and accompanying herself on guitar as usual, the Greenbriar Boys added a feeling of back-porch fun to a couple of songs ("Banks of the Ohio" and "Pal of Mine"). As Robert Shelton wrote in his review of the concert for the *Times*,

> That superb soprano voice, as lustrous and rich as old gold, flowed purely all evening with a wondrous ease. Her singing [unwound] like a spool of satin.

The reverent audience, a mix of ages, clung to Baez through four encores. If the Folk City cognoscenti had declared the elegiac beauty of her singing outmoded by the sound of Bob Dylan, the news had not made it past 14th Street.

Joan Baez, Volume 2 became a hit just as Dylan began recording his first album. (Baez's second gold record, it would peak at number thirteen and remain on the *Billboard* pop charts for more than two years.) Irrespective of their differences, Dylan was contracted as a performer in the same essential tradition as Baez, and he and John Hammond approached their recording sessions much as Joan and Maynard Solomon did. Dylan was known as a guitar-playing singer who played other people's music, not his own; although he had written songs in the style of his idol, two of which ("Talkin' New York" and "Song to Woody," both based on simple, bass-note-driven chord progressions) made it onto his album, the music he recorded, drawn from his coffeehouse repertoire, was virtually all traditional ("House of the Risin' Sun," "Man of Constant Sorrow," "Freight Train Blues"). Like Baez in the Manhattan Towers ballroom (where she continued to record), Dylan performed all the material for his album quickly—eighteen songs in two three-hour sessions at Columbia's Studio A on November 20 and 22—singing and accompanying himself on guitar as if he were doing sets at Gerde's. Columbia Records' production costs were reported to be $402. The album is, true to Shelton's words, the work of a distinctive stylist: Dylan sounds like no other interpreter of the folk canon, with the exception of Woody Guthrie (and by extension Jack Elliott). Yet as a collection of spirited, if frequently overwrought, renditions of more traditional songs about death, *Bob Dylan* offers little evidence that the round-faced twenty-year-old singer on the cover was "bursting at the seams with talent."

Columbia Records, its management fearful that John Hammond's mythic golden ears had corroded, delayed the album's release until March 19, 1962, four months after it had been recorded—about a month longer than usual. "We almost didn't release it at all," said David Kapralik. "John fought for it tooth and nail. But he was really fighting for his reputation. He was deep in the doghouse for losing Joan Baez. All anybody talked about was folk music and Joan Baez. John couldn't tolerate any more damage to his reputation." Issued with virtually no advertising or promotion, *Bob Dylan* sold poorly (fewer than five thousand copies in its first year); it was stamped as a discount-record "cut-out" and shipped to appliance stores like Zimmerman Electric and Furniture. The reviews were scant and mostly noncommittal, with some praise for the two songs Dylan had written himself.

Dylan, though taken aback, found consolation in the undiminished esteem of his Village peers and friends, especially regarding the songs he was writing. "He was obviously disappointed, although he didn't talk about it," said John Herald, who noticed that Dylan, sitting in the Gaslight, would mutter something unintelligible and take a sip of jug wine when the subject of his record arose. "But I think he really dug the attention the songs of his own on the record got. He was still something special on the scene." Indeed, few of the other folksingers at Gerde's were doing their own songs; the idea seemed anathema. How could a song written just last week by a twenty-year-old in a New York apartment qualify as a song of the folk? Dylan began writing in the spirit of idol worship: he was, he said, "writing like I thought Woody would write." (It was a fitting tribute to Guthrie, who once admitted, "I steal from everybody. Why, I'm the biggest song stealer there ever was.") In the course of his emulation, however, Dylan was developing a growing reputation as an original. "I thought he was a terrible singer and a complete fake, and I thought that he didn't play harmonica that well," said Bruce Langhorne. "I didn't really start to appreciate Bobby as something unique until he started writing. Bobby was one of the first people to say, 'Hey, I'm a folk. I can write this shit.' "

It helped Dylan considerably to have a strong personal manager with designs on the music publishing business. Using his orchestration of Dylan's Folk City breakthrough for leverage, Albert Grossman persuaded Dylan to enter into a comprehensive contract for management, representation, and accounting services. In his first formal deal, he arranged, through an acquaintance, one Artie Mogull, an executive at Witmark Music, for Dylan to join Cole Porter and Leonard Bernstein on the prestigious publishing firm's roster of composers. "As I recall, the first person who ever called Bob Dylan a poet was Albert," said Charlie Rothschild. "I don't know if Bob Dylan had written enough for anyone to come to that conclusion. Albert wanted to get into music publishing, which is where all the money is in the music business in the long term, and he started looking to sign folksingers who could write, and he started calling them poets. Bob Dylan was the first." Encouraged by his new manager, Dylan began carrying a spiral notebook around, as Richard Fariña had been doing since college. Dave Van Ronk noticed the book lying next to Dylan's glass of burgundy late one night at the Gaslight, and he asked him what was in it. Dylan said, "My novel."

In the four months between the recording sessions for his Columbia debut and the album's release, Bob Dylan introduced eight to ten new songs in his performances, including "Hard Times in New York Town" (derived from the traditional "Down on Penny's Farm"), "I Was Young When I Left Home," "Poor Boy Blues," "Standing on the Highway," and "Ramblin' Gamblin' Willie." All are musically and lyrically modest laments about the hard life and romantic outcasts—folk clichés—with one exception, "The Death of Emmett Till." At the initiative of Suze Rotolo, Dylan had accepted an invitation to perform at a benefit for CORE (the Congress of Racial Equality), the civil rights organization that the Rotolo sisters aided as volunteers, stuffing envelopes, passing out flyers on the street. Dylan wrote the piece, a declarative account of the 1955 murder of an innocent Negro man that Rotolo had described to him, performed it for the first time at the fund-raiser (held at City College on 137th Street in Harlem on February 23, 1962), and incorporated it into his usual set. The lovely minor-key melody and chord progression are a straight lift from a song that Len Chandler, a musically sophisticated folksinger and composer, had written and taught Dylan in the poker room upstairs at the Gaslight; and the lyrics are simplistic and heavy-handed at points:

> If all of us folks that thinks alike,
>   if we gave all we could give
> We could make this great land of ours a greater place to live

Still, Dylan seemed to take special pride in "The Death of Emmett Till." He told Izzy Young, "I think it's the best thing I've ever written." The song was certainly a departure for Dylan—a strong, explicit statement of social protest—and it marked an evident rise in Suze Rotolo's influence on his music. "How many nights I stayed up and wrote songs and showed them to her and asked, 'Is this right?' " Dylan said. "Because I knew her . . . mother [was] associated with unions, and she was into this equality-freedom thing long before I was. I checked the songs out with her. She would like all the songs."

By the spring of 1962, Suze and Bob had known each for about six months and had grown close, despite Dylan's reluctance to reveal much about himself. He tested his songs on her, played Elvis records for her to hear, and brought her to Gerde's; she loaned him books of poetry and took him to CORE meetings. "A lot of what I gave him was a look at how the other half lived—left-wing things that he didn't know," said Rotolo. "He knew about Woody and Pete Seeger, but I was working for CORE and went on youth marches for civil rights, and all that was new to him. It was in the air, but it was new to him. And poetry, we read a lot of poetry together"—Lord Byron and Rimbaud, as well as playwrights, especially Brecht, "a lot of Brecht." As Dylan prepared to begin recording again, the failure of his first album still fresh, he focused on writing his own songs. Perhaps Albert Grossman was right: he was a poet. And Suze might have a point: social protest was in the air.

W HEN RICHARD FARIÑA WAS A BOY, he put on shows for his parents, portraying characters he had heard on the radio. He stood in front of the living-room curtains and imitated the Lone Ranger, rustlin' the ottoman and shootin' at the lamps. At the conclusion of the scene, he would bow grandly, then quickly disappear into the coat closet. The door would open, and he would be another character, Superman or Jack Armstrong, All-American Boy.

Having made some progress with the dulcimer, Richard started experimenting seriously with setting his poetry to music, in the months after Carolyn finished recording all the tracks for her Columbia album. He told her in the first week of 1962 that he wanted to leave the country immediately. "He was ready to be a musician," Carolyn said. "I guess he thought he could go away and come back as somebody new." Setting out to become a singer and songwriter in the folk clubs of London, Richard sailed out of New York on the *United States* with money from his father. Carolyn, who had to stay behind to honor a few weeks of bookings, saw him off—Richard threw a bon voyage party for himself on the Manhattan pier where he had caroused with Pynchon—and stayed in Brooklyn with Richard's mother while making plans to fly to London to meet her husband as soon as possible. In traveling by ship rather than air, Richard said, he stood a better chance of averting British authorities on the lookout for him because of his IRA adventures, and he could more easily sneak his pistol into England, for protection from English assassins; moreover, air travel posed a risk that, because of the metal plate in his skull, his head would explode. When Carolyn arrived in London about a month after Richard, she found her husband better known in the half-dozen London folk clubs than he was around Washington Square and not as a writer, nor as Carolyn Hester's husband. (Paul Simon would succeed in a related metamorphosis shortly after Fariña; he would arrive in London as a struggling Brill Building pop tunesmith, author of "Lone Teen-Ranger" and "Get Up and Do the Wobble," and he would return to America as a folksinger with a portfolio of delicate, cerebral songs indebted to English traditional music.) Richard had shaved his mustache, which had given him a European appearance in New York, so he looked more American in London.

"Richard Fariña—delightful character," said Anthea Joseph, manager of the Troubadour, one of the best-known London clubs. "I didn't realize he had a wife, until he asked me to hire them both. I thought he was trying to give her a break, let her in on his job." A dark, woody, late-Victorian place in Earls Court, an after-work stop for tea or even coffee, the Troubadour had a room in the basement—a low, windowless space with warm acoustics—that was the proving ground for English folk-singers such as Martin Carthy, Bert Jansch, and Davy Graham, much as Folk City was for Village musicians. Shortly after Carolyn arrived, Richard arranged for the two of them to appear at the Troubadour, billed as a duo, Carolyn Hester and Dick Fariña, justifying the move as a means of doubling their income. "He told me, 'They'll pay us twice as much for two people, and you only have to do half the work you used to,'" Carolyn recalled. "We needed all the money we could get, so I went along with it. But I had just about had it with his hogging in on my thing." By March, Richard had pushed his wife's tolerance to its limits:

he set up a concert at Cecil Sharp House, a hub for folk music and scholarship in London (named for the Cambridge-educated turn-of-the-twentieth-century folk song and dance collector who is considered the father of English folk scholarship), with four performers—Carolyn Hester, Dick Fariña, Clay Jackson, and Peter Stanley—billed individually. Each of the artists performed a solo set, followed by some work together. Now Richard was not just hogging Carolyn Hester's thing but laying claim to a thing of his own, equal to hers. "I had the impression they were both folk stars in the States," said Stanley, an English banjo player and singer. Clay Jackson, a guitarist and mandolin player for the Charles River Valley Boys who was passing through London smuggling hashish, knew better and resented Fariña for his presence onstage, but he was too stoned to speak up or to perform long before dropping the twelve-string guitar he had borrowed for the show.

At the end of the concert—a success, judging by the raucous applause from the near-capacity crowd of more than two hundred English folk enthusiasts—Carolyn and Richard had a blow-out backstage. He complained that her voice sounded strained, because she was singing in the wrong keys. "You could tune a guitar to Carolyn's voice," said Peter Stanley. "Her singing was perfect, and they had this big row. Carolyn was screaming, 'What do you know about singing? You don't know what a key *is*!' And she stormed out. Richard shook his head coolly and said, 'Screaming like that is not going to help her voice.'"

In a gesture of reconciliation, Richard suggested to Carolyn that they take a romantic trip to Paris. They could stroll along the Seine, make love on the banks of the Seine, sing at a few cafés overlooking the Seine, and since they had no other engagements in London, they could leave as soon as they packed; Carolyn just had to strap his pistol into the small of her back, in case would-be assassins followed them across the English Channel. "I don't know how he talked me into these things," she said. "We were taking a vacation to Paris, and I was smuggling arms across international borders." By French law, transporting a concealed weapon into the country could be deemed an act of terrorism (especially then, only a few weeks after France signed the Algerian War cease-fire) punishable by up to twenty years in prison. They reached a cheap but atmospheric hotel in the Sixth Arrondissement without incident and scouted the Parisian folk scene, which amounted to ad hoc performances in and outside of cafés by whatever musicians from America or the United Kingdom were passing through. At the moment, John Cooke of the Charles River Valley Boys was spending a summer in Paris before his senior year at Harvard, and so was his friend Todd Stuart, whose primary interest in Paris was in seeing Mimi Baez. Enough folk expatriates were close by that, Richard said, a party was clearly in order. Carolyn and Richard had never met Mimi and Todd, and Mimi and Todd had not met Alex Campbell, a Scottish folksinger whom Carolyn, Richard, and John knew. Richard suggested having a picnic, because he loved the Georges Seurat painting *A Sunday Afternoon on the Island of La Grand Jatte*; and John Cooke recommended driving to Chartres Cathedral, because he had just purchased a new Volvo with an inheritance payment, and he wanted to break in the engine.

On a warm, hazy morning in April 1962, a couple of weeks before Mimi's seventeenth birthday, John Cooke pulled up to the Baez house in the Volvo with Alex Campbell in the front seat and Carolyn Hester and Richard Fariña in the back. They had come to rendezvous with Mimi and Todd, who would be riding on Todd's motorcycle. But since Chartres was an hour's drive away on winding country roads, Mimi's parents forbade her to ride with Todd. As the smallest person in the group, just over ninety pounds, she was relegated to the hump in the rear seat of John's Volvo, between Carolyn and Richard. "I had been told by Todd that it would be nice for Carolyn and me to meet, since she was a folksinger and all," Mimi recalled. "But she wasn't too happy to meet me, probably because of her rivalry with Joanie." It was a tight squeeze in the backseat; Mimi could tell Carolyn's crinoline slip was crinkling under her skirt when the car veered to the left, and she could feel Richard's leg, taut in his starched black jeans, pressing against her when the car angled to the right and staying there just a moment longer than necessary. John drove leisurely, reporting periodically on the odometer reading and the behavior of the engine. Richard, seeing the French countryside for the first time, seemed to have an improbable historical anecdote about every sight they passed. Once at Chartres, Mimi waited awhile for Todd, who had slipped far behind the Volvo, then decided to go into the cathedral without him. She walked slowly up the right aisle of the old tower of the High Gothic monument. Ten-meter-tall stained-glass windows, glowing softly under the day's cloudy skies, cast a wash of multicolored light through the thick, incensed air. "It was a little scary," said Mimi. "Soon I heard Dick coming up from behind me, and he started explaining what everything was. He was a Catholic, so he knew all about the saints and all the strange stories of their lives, and the candles and what everything means. And he's being very attentive, asking me a lot of questions about what I thought, and we strolled through the whole cathedral." As they walked together, side by side, Mimi could hear Carolyn's high heels, about three steps behind them in the darkness.

Once Todd Stuart caught up with the rest of the group at the cathedral, they all took off again to find a spot for their picnic. John Cooke saw a clearing in an apple orchard and pulled over. Carolyn laid out the blankets, John and Alex unpacked the sandwiches, Richard uncorked the first of several bottles of table Bordeaux. Mimi smoked one of her mother's Kents, and shortly afterward another, then drank some wine; "Things started looking very pleasant and very humorous," recalled Mimi. "Everything started to get light and silly. I was sixteen and having a fabulous time. Todd was politely lighting my cigarettes for me, and I was getting light-headed and drunk. And Dick started getting very entertaining. He was telling stories and embellishing and carrying on and getting us all laughing. At one point, I laughed so hard that I threw up my sandwich in his face. I was just kind of losing it, and he just wiped it off his face, laughed really hard, and then went on with his story." As the afternoon wound down, Richard drifted off alone for a walk through the trees. "The poet communing with nature," said John Cooke. A few minutes later, Mimi went for a walk. In her haze, the orchard looked like a ballet troupe, and she decided to join it. As she danced with the tree trunks, Mimi noticed Richard, who stood watching her a short distance away.

Dusk approached, and the picnickers assembled, packed up the car, and headed toward Paris. About halfway back, somewhere in the province of Yvelines, they found traffic slowed to a stop; a parade was passing through a cross-street ahead of them. A throng of revelers celebrating a town fair surrounded the idling vehicles. "Damn!" burst John Cooke. "We could be stuck here for hours. How long is this going to last?" He rolled down his window to make an inquiry to a group of townspeople standing near, and they threw handfuls of confetti into the car. Mimi, squeezed between Carolyn and Richard in the back again, ducked her head. As her brow pressed against the side of Richard's face, she could feel him breaking into a broad, cheeky grin. "Oh, no," John groaned. "Now I have to pick all this confetti out of the car."

The next day Carolyn and Richard said nothing about Mimi. They had a quiet dinner at a noisy Mediterranean restaurant in the Latin Quarter that Americans in Paris liked and called "the Greeks." Avoiding each other's eyes, they glanced around as they nibbled at stuffed grape leaves. Carolyn recognized William Burroughs sitting with a couple of teenage boys a few tables away. Richard noticed a young woman in a sleek black dress. "Look at that girl over there," Richard told Carolyn. "She looks so stylish and sexy. That's the way you should look. I want you to start dressing like that."

"What?" snapped Carolyn as she dropped her fork.

Richard took another bite of his food. "All I'm saying," he responded calmly, "is that I'd like you to look more like that girl."

Carolyn rose and stormed back to the hotel and started packing. When Richard opened the door to their room a short while later, he found Carolyn sitting on the bed, facing him, with his pistol pointing at his face.

"I would have shot him," recalled Carolyn. "But he talked me down and convinced me that it was okay if I killed him—he understood that—but if I missed his head, the bullet could go through the door and hurt an innocent person." As she calmed, Carolyn reverted to her initial impulse to leave Richard, alive; moreover, she later recalled, it struck her that "he would have loved to have gone out that way, murdered in a jealous rage, and I was not about to give him the satisfaction." Carolyn had planned to return to the States soon anyway; the mayor of the city of Austin, Lester E. Palmer, was about to proclaim May 8, 1962, Carolyn Hester Day, and she was scheduled to participate in the festivities, including two concerts. (Carolyn had to go back to the U.K. by September, however, to honor a commitment that Richard had made for the two of them to perform together at the Edinburgh Folk Festival.) Richard decided to stay abroad and returned to London, where he knew a few people with flats.

"Obviously, Richard was working real hard at getting into folk music through Carolyn," said Clay Jackson. "The one problem with that was Carolyn. She wasn't just any girl—she was a Texas girl. Carolyn was a lot stronger than Richard gave her credit for, and she wasn't going to turn over her career to him. I think when he realized that, he knew he had to make another plan. He had to get into the folk music world another way." While Carolyn Hester received fond recognition from the people of Austin, Richard Fariña appeared determined to have his day as soon as possible.

Richard reintroduced himself to Mimi with a poem, which he wrote as soon as his wife left Paris and which Mimi received within a few days of her seventeenth birthday.

> *And now as breezes shudder in the orchard,*
> *thick with rhyme and loosed of somber reason—*
> *thought and motion raise their head as one.*
> *Your sudden dance is free of all design.*
> *Young girl, you chose the amber coil of wish,*
> *unlocked it with the cocking of a heel*
> *and stepped away. While in the lunge of flight*
> *I know the tale in your dark body's book.*

(Titled "The Field Near the Cathedral at Chartres," it would be published in *Mademoiselle*, with a dedication to Mimi Baez. "You might like to know," Richard wrote in a note to Madeline Tracy Brigden, an editor at the magazine, "the poem comes directly out of my growing relationship with the Baez family; out of Mimi's dancing, Joan's singing, the parents' belief.") To Mimi, receiving a poem in the mail was nearly as romantic as having a fling on an ocean liner. "I never had a poet writing poetry to me," she recalled. "I knew he was married, and I was nervous. I didn't know what was happening, really. But he was so incredibly appealing—I couldn't help thinking about him and fantasizing about being with him and maybe even spending my life with [him]. He was exactly the kind of guy a girl dreamed of marrying." It was, of course, early for her to be planning her adult life. She would not be twenty-one until 1966.

A FEW WEEKS AFTER Carolyn Hester flew home from Europe, leaving Richard Fariña in Paris, Suze Rotolo sailed on the USS *Rotterdam* to visit relatives in Perugia, Italy, leaving Bob Dylan in the Village. This was no breakup—Suze and her mother had been planning for her to spend time with her Italian cousins. Yet Dylan's rapid ascension in the Village was beginning to strain the couple's relationship, and Suze welcomed the separation. "It was a hard time, because he was becoming famous, and it was hard to deal with it—for him and for me and for everyone around us. He became *something*. That was hard. Suddenly everybody was making all this noise about him. It became odd that there was all this focus on him—very odd. You know he's just a guy, and you hope that he's just going to go back [to being his old self], but it's hard. It made me crazy. I couldn't stand the idea of being called 'his chick.' It was good to get away." Dylan, meantime, lamented the absence of his lover during his first brush with success. "Things were starting to happen for him, and he wanted Suze at his side," said Terri Thal. "He was a little down for a while and just spent all his time writing songs."

Yet most of the songs Dylan wrote over the next few months were not expressions of longing or unrequited love. (The gently mournful

"Tomorrow Is a Long Time" was a notable exception; related pieces such as "Don't Think Twice, It's All Right" and "Boots of Spanish Leather" would come a bit later.) He was writing furiously and concentrating almost exclusively on the protest songs Suze had prompted him to write, advancing the approach he had tried with "The Death of Emmett Till" in a series of increasingly persuasive statements of social commentary and dissent. Was he honoring his muse by carrying on Suze's kind of work? Or much as he had changed instruments, jackets, and names before, was he adopting something new for the potential glory in it?

By April 1962 the nascent discontent on college campuses (initially associated with civil rights and the cold war) was beginning to take form as a movement of sorts, one of a distinctly postwar American character—a mobilization in the name of political and moral principle that was also a fashion trend and a business opportunity. Student-written editorials denouncing nuclear arms and instructional articles on avoiding selective service appeared in college newspapers such as the Brown *Herald* and the Rutgers *Targum*, sparking administration reprimands and debates over student liberties. Thousands of young people from the North, many of them white, spent spring break that year joining freedom marches in Atlanta and Birmingham and voter-registration rallies in several southern states. Under pressure from college students who were adopting the appearance of rural working people, Northwestern, Princeton, and Georgetown Universities amended or revoked their dress codes. Annual sales of dungarees had increased nearly 50 percent in 1961, and sales of dress shoes reached a historic low for the industry in the same year. Recognizing the challenge, the advertising agency for the Thom McAn chain hired the Village singer and songwriter Bob Cohen and his group to record a new jingle with flat-top guitars and a banjo. A million Americans were now purchasing guitars every year, and they all seemed to be sitting on college grounds in blue jeans and no shoes, strumming "Where Have All the Flowers Gone" and "This Land Is Your Land."

There was a breach between the singers and the songs, though. All those idealistic students were young, in their late teens or early twenties.

(Indeed, the political bloc they became, the New Left, was somewhat uncommon historically as a force promoting radical change to be distinguished mainly by age rather than by race or class.) Most of the songs of idealism they were singing, however timely, were written by members of their parents' generation: "Where Have All the Flowers Gone," by Pete Seeger, whose hair was going gray; "This Land Is Your Land" by Woody Guthrie, who was dying. More to the point, something about the songs was old-fashioned—not simply old, as all folk music is supposed to sound, but out of fashion—for a generation that grew up on rock and roll. Perhaps it was the singsong quality of the melodies, with their suggestions of children's music and summer camp; or maybe it was the wry puns of the lyrics, which wink in the direction of revolutionary ideas but seem afraid to speak them, let alone scream them out. These were songs that had survived the blacklist and could escape another one, on their tip-toes, whispering. They were songs that had never seen Elvis on TV.

Late in June, Bob Dylan went to Witmark Music's offices on West 28th Street and made a demonstration record of one of his new songs of dissent, "Blowin' in the Wind." Musically it is modest: a pretty and memorable, if repetitive, adaptation of the traditional antislavery ballad "No More Auction Block" that Dylan would later say he composed in ten minutes. Owing mainly to its simple poetic lyrics—oblique provocations in keeping with "Where Have All the Flowers Gone"—"Blowin' in the Wind" was an all-purpose protest anthem. Dylan explained its theme plainly: "Your silence betrays you," an echo of the Talmudic precept that one who can protest an injustice and does not is an accomplice to it. For all its obtuseness (Where are the answers? "Blowin' in the wind . . ."), the song makes a sweeping indictment: When evils exist, and they always do, everyone but the protester is to blame. Who could dare not to join in that chorus? (" 'Blowin' in the Wind' was a lucky classic song—no more, no less than 'Your Cheatin' Heart,' " Dylan would later claim. "What it conveys is no more, no less than that. It is one-dimensional, that's what it is.")

He hammered out topical songs like journalism—five songs before breakfast, he joked on a radio program to benefit *Broadside*, a new magazine devoted to topical songs, edited and self-published by Sis Cunningham of the Almanac Singers and her husband, the writer Gordon Friesen. (Dylan would nurture friendships with Cunningham and Friesen, who would print virtually all his early protest songs, as well as prose-poetry he wrote for *Broadside*; in addition, he performed regularly on the "Broadside Ballads" LP series, recording under the pseudonym Blind Boy Grunt to dodge restrictions of his contract with Columbia.) Discussing his new songwriting focus in an interview for *Sing Out!* with Gil Turner, the singer and songwriter, Dylan said, "I don't have to B.S. anybody like those guys up on Broadway that're always writin' about 'I'm hot for you and you're hot for me—ooka dooka dicka dee.' There's other things in the world besides love and sex that're important too. People shouldn't turn their backs on 'em just because they ain't pretty to look at. How is the world ever gonna get any better if we're afraid to look at these things?" In describing his inspiration for one song, "The Ballad of Donald White," a reportorial account of another unjust murder of an innocent Negro (sung to a melody taken from singer Bonnie Dobson's arrangement of the traditional "Ballad of Peter Amberly"), Dylan acknowledged his debt to Suze Rotolo. "I'd seen Donald White's name in a Seattle paper in about 1959," Dylan told Turner (bolstering his talk of wandering the country by placing the newspaper in Washington State). "It said he was a killer. The next time I saw him was on a television set. My gal Sue said I'd be interested in him so we went and watched. . . . He murdered someone 'cause he couldn't find no room in life. Now they killed him 'cause he couldn't find no room in life. They killed him and when they did I lost some of my room in my life. When are some people gonna wake up and see that sometimes people aren't really their enemies but their victims?"

One by one Dylan's songs of protest and social commentary veered further from tuneful intimations of Seeger and Guthrie toward a bolder style with the bite of rock and roll: "Long Ago, Far Away," an enumeration of ancient horrors that had parallels in the early 1960s (war, poverty, racial conflict); "Ballad of Hollis Brown," another newspaper-clipping story, this of a South Dakota farmer driven by hardship to unthinkable

violence, told in blues-style AAB refrains; "Let Me Die in My Foot-
steps," a stand against fallout shelters that mixes zealous protest language
("I'd throw all the guns and the tanks in the sea / for they are mistakes of
a past history") with passages of striking lyricism ("Let me drink from
the waters where the mountain streams flood / let the smell of wildflow-
ers flow free through my blood"); and a better song about nuclear fallout
that, along with "Blowin' in the Wind," began to cement Dylan's status
as a young folk composer of substance, "A Hard Rain's a-Gonna Fall."
Although the music and lyric structure are derived from "Lord Randal,"
one of the Child ballads, "A Hard Rain's a-Gonna Fall" proved Dylan to
be unique among his peers in protest music, a writer interested in craft-
ing words to provoke feeling and thought as well as action: "I saw a
room full of men with their hammers a-bleedin' / I saw a white ladder
all covered with water / I saw ten thousand talkers whose tongues were
all broken / I saw guns and sharp swords in the hands of young children." Clearly he was reading Suze's volumes of Blake; but in the year
and a half since he had arrived in New York imitating Guthrie, Dylan
had been learning how to assimilate and recombine his influences rather
than simply reproduce them. He used "Lord Randal" and Blake, among
other sources, and he mixed them with elements that were becoming his
signatures: a dark tone, rhythmic verve, and a mercurial point of view, as
well as occasional carelessness and a penchant for verbosity.

"I didn't think much of him until I heard 'A Hard Rain's a-Gonna
Fall,'" said Liam Clancy. "I heard him sing it, and I told him, 'Bobby,
you have a great gift. Those wonderful words just flow out of you. But
do there have to be so many of them?' All those verses!"

Albert Grossman initiated an organized program to establish Dylan
as a composer. He had demo records of "Blowin' in the Wind" and several of Dylan's other new songs pressed and mailed in bulk to singers
and their agents. The cover letter declared, in essence, "Bob Dylan is no
longer available for public appearances. But here are his songs," recalled
the singer Mitch Greenhill, whose father, Manny Greenhill, received the
demo disks for the artists he represented. "By doing that mailing, Albert
started really building an aura around Bob," said Mitch Greenhill. "He

became the mysterious, reclusive composer." Although Dylan continued to perform to packed houses at Gerde's and the Gaslight every few weeks (hardly unavailable for public appearances), Grossman inspired him to write, praised him to his contacts as a "great poet," and closely supervised his client's catalog at Witmark. In another genre of music thirty years earlier, Irving Mills, an artists' manager with extensive music publishing interests, had encouraged one of his artists, Duke Ellington, to compose; Ellington's contemporary, Louis Armstrong, had a different manager, Joe Glaser, with ties to theater chains. Ellington composed (and secondarily performed), and Armstrong performed (and secondarily composed). "Bob Dylan became the composer, and practically everyone else was just a performer," said Mitch Greenhill. "Suddenly, being a performer looked like it was a little less than it used to be."

Manny Greenhill saw Joan Baez during her next visit to Boston, and he asked her to listen to Dylan's demo of "Blowin' in the Wind." She had already heard the song, repeatedly, performed by local folksingers in cities all around the country who had picked up on it by word of mouth. It seemed to have spread with the speed and the impact of that rain Dylan wrote about. "The boy's coming along," Joan said. "I didn't know he had it in him."

At the end of August, the first profile of Bob Dylan for a major magazine was published in *Seventeen*. If revolt can be style, as the poet Thom Gunn once wrote, the twenty-one-year-old folk rebel was now stylish enough for teenage girls. The photograph accompanying the article— suitable for framing, as Robert Zimmerman did with his magazine pictures of James Dean—shows Dylan wearing his cap and a dark bulky knit turtleneck; he looks chiseled in three-quarter view, and his lips are pursed; from the opening paragraph, the text focuses on the cerebral authority of his songwriting: "[Dylan's] intense homespun ballads sear the mind like a hot iron." The messages of the presentation conjoin in combinations unseen in earlier issues of *Seventeen*: creative intelligence is sexy, radicalism is cool. In addition to the usual nonsense about his background as a carnival roustabout and the like, Dylan mentions his first record dismissively and sounds perplexed by the songwriting process. "I seem to draw into myself whatever comes my way, and it comes out of me," Dylan said. "Maybe I'm nothing but all these things I soak up. I don't know."

IN THE MONTHS following her afternoon at Chartres Cathedral, Mimi Baez found new reason to overcome her reading trouble. Richard Fariña was writing her letters from London every day, twice a day, sometimes every few hours, and she tried to answer each one. An epistolary courtship with a poet, across the English Channel—what could be dreamier to a seventeen-year-old girl? Richard was certainly expert at conjuring an air of romantic fancy. He wrote poems to Mimi on the back of his envelopes and doodled around the addresses on the front; on one envelope, he drew pen-and-ink sketches of two men from Rembrandt's *Staalmeesters* (the Dutch Masters cigar-box painting) and put word balloons in their mouths to show them giggling, "he he he." Every few days, a letter would include a Cracker Jack surprise, such as a small wildflower that Richard said reminded him of Mimi when she danced. "Reality plays a large part [in life], yes, but so does the magic," he wrote to her. "And if things are right, it's the wild, seemingly irrational kind of magic that often gives such depth of meaning to the Reality." For a twenty-five-year-old married man seducing a teenage daughter of Quakers by mail, magic would come in handy.

Mimi had no trouble falling in love, she wrote to her diligent suitor; to the contrary, she said, she was unable to think of anyone she had ever had occasion to dislike seriously, other than her sister Joan. That was, Mimi explained, because she and Joan had an exceptional closeness, one that "went beyond love." Richard responded with a statement of intent: "Above all, you nut, keep from turning me into a brother. I'd never do it. If you've never been able to dislike anyone but Joanie, and you do insist on loving so many people, then please, dislike me." Joan hovered just beyond most of the correspondence between Mimi and Richard, conspicuous for her absence in Richard's letters. He mentioned her so rarely and with such apparent unconcern that Mimi asked for an explanation. Richard wrote:

> I think of her to begin with as your sister Joan, see? Like your mother—who is someone I'd like very much to know—I can only imagine, & in turn see her through you. Which is of course the only way I want it. In both their cases. (Since you love them as you do, & the expression of theirs is such a truly important part of your own well-being, happiness, and like that.) Still, what I'm saying is if I come to know them, no matter how well, they will first of all be your sister and your mum, since that's the way I'm put together. O.K.?

If Mimi needed reassurance that this fellow was different from all the boys in Cambridge who never could decide which Baez sister they really wanted (including Todd Stuart), Richard made sure she had it; he was wholly interested in Mimi and always would be, he made clear, even if he came to know Joan, and no matter how well.

They got to see each other again in the first week of September. Richard invited Mimi to come to see him perform at the Edinburgh Folk Festival—with his wife, who flew back to the U.K. in order to appear at this high-profile engagement and to test the prospects for a reconciliation. "I came back [to England], and we had a lot of arguments, and I knew it was never going to last and whatever," said Carolyn. "When we got to Edinburgh, well, Mimi was there." To escape her parents, Mimi had convinced them to send her to a Quaker summer program in Newcastle—close enough to Edinburgh. Todd Stuart, still motorcycling around Europe for the summer, picked her up at her dormitory and accompanied her to the festival. All four principal players of Chartres convened again. This time, though, there was no surreptitious coquetry between Mimi and Richard. In groups they gazed at each other, and they kept disappearing into corners to talk. Sharing a car ride from the festival to a party with Richard, a couple of his friends, and Todd, Mimi sat on Richard's lap. Todd saw no point in intervening for the sake of a relationship that he was unlikely to continue himself; besides, he felt a strange empathy with Mimi in her attraction to Richard. "He was a pretty appealing figure," said Todd Stuart. "He seemed smart and talented and incredibly spontaneous—very emotional, very giving, and a little mysterious. You know, here was a guy who seemed to come from nowhere, who had an interesting background that you didn't know much about, except these little pieces you heard all sounded pretty intriguing and romantic. There was a lot of unpredictability about him. I sort of responded to that in a positive way. Dick to me was just bubbling over with this creative, spontaneous attitude . . . you know, anything's possible, in the best sense—'Let's get on the back of a motorcycle and just kind of go off, and who knows what will happen?' That's pretty hard to resist." As for Carolyn, Richard's caddish behavior only made her more determined to get back to Texas and find one of those Mexican attorneys who specialized in quickie divorces.

THE EDITORS OF *TIME* MAGAZINE had an informal policy of scheduling stories on popular-culture subjects near holidays, when young people were home from school, and they deemed the folk boom worthy of a feature story in the issue published during the 1962 Thanksgiving weekend. On the cover, there was a painting of Joan Baez—an eerie Goya-style oil (by commercial illustrator Russell Hoban) that could have been a thought projection of Joan's distorted self-image. She is repellent, a skeletal ghoul clinging to a guitar. Joan had been recovering from an intestinal virus when she posed for the portrait; still, the published image seemed less intent on capturing its subject than on caricaturing her—and by extension the folk movement she was said to represent—as something grotesque and infectious. The article inside, written by John McPhee (who, as *Time*'s "show business" correspondent, had contributed recent cover stories on Sophia Loren, Jackie Gleason, and Lerner and Loewe), depicts Joan and the folk "cult" more accurately and thoroughly, with only intermittent patronization (mostly inserted by editors). Despite the unsettling cover picture, the article was the formal coronation of Joan Baez as queen of the movement.

"I appreciated it as something positive—'That's nice, thank you'— but I didn't really comprehend the value of something like that," said Joan. "All I thought about was how dreadful I looked on the cover." In Paris her parents (who had been interviewed by *Time* reporters) and Mimi (who had not) did not see the magazine right away. "We were out of the country for so long, we didn't realize how famous Joan had become," said her mother. "I didn't see the magazine till I came back to America for a visit, and I was astonished. Couldn't they make her look prettier?" Mimi, distracted by her blooming romance with Fariña, seemed non-plussed. "I was so happy at the moment and busy writing letters," she said. "I just thought, 'Well, if that makes Joanie happy, great.'"

At Gerde's the *Time* cover story was dismissed as old news; such was envy. "Nobody in the know was talking about Joan Baez anymore," said Dave Van Ronk. "On the street, most of the real talk revolved around Bobby." One of the innumerable staff researchers assigned to contribute to the *Time* piece had submitted a brief about Dylan that focused on his songwriting:

Bob Dylan, 21, is the hottest new property around. A singularly unattractive man . . . he writes umpteen songs a week. . . . He writes, so they say, "stunning poetry" and has a great sense of in-volvement (anti-Establishment involvement). . . . [I] expect we re-ally should have gone to see him at least to talk to.

The published article, however, mentions Dylan as "a promising hobo" who sings "in a studied nasal that has just the right clothespin-on-the-nose honesty to appeal to those who most deeply care." In fact, there is no mention of contemporary folk songwriting in the five-page, five-thousand-word article, aside from a paragraph devoted to comedian Allan Sherman's parody record, *My Son the Folksinger*. "I presume my reaction was fairly typical," said Van Ronk. "I read it and I thought, 'Well, Joanie made the cover of *Time* magazine. Now, she's finished.' "

A PART FROM HIS FAMILY and his old acquaintances in Hibbing, few people knew how good an actor Bob Dylan was. His rustic vagabond persona, a character he invented and cloaked in the folk movement's ethos of naturalness and honesty, was so convincing that Albert Grossman could arrange for the BBC to cast him as a "type" in a TV drama by the Jamaican playwright Evan Jones, *Madhouse on Castle Street*. The role of "an anarchic young student who wrote songs" was essentially the same character *Seventeen* magazine had recently profiled. Dylan took the job with glee—he crowed in the Gaslight that he was going to be paid a lot of money (five hundred pounds) to be on TV—and flew to London in mid-December 1962 to play himself playing himself and, while he was at it, to see some of Europe for a few weeks. The moment may have seemed inevitable: virtually every major American singer before him had taken up acting, from Al Jolson through Bing Crosby, Frank Sinatra, Nat Cole, and Doris Day to Elvis Presley. (Even the country singer Eddy Arnold and the jazz vocalists Billie Holiday and Ella Fitzgerald took "straight" roles in films, with limited success.)

Rehearsals went badly. Apparently unable or unwilling to remember his dialogue, Dylan mumbled cryptic improvisations and soon found his part reduced to one line: "Well, I don't know—I'll have to go home and think about it." Was he overtaxed, or was his erratic unprofessionalism part of his portrayal of an anarchic young man who wrote songs? "He gave the impression of being hopelessly lost," recalled David Warner, a young actor in the production whose role grew as Dylan's shrank. "No one had the slightest idea why he had been sent there. When he started singing, it began to become clear." Indeed, producer Philip Saville, who put Dylan up at his own home (in part to ensure that the unpredictable young American arrived on the sound stage), was impressed when he heard him sing "Blowin' in the Wind" in private, and he had the broadcast open and close with scenes of Dylan performing the song.

At night Dylan roved the London folk clubs. Virtually every evening for a couple of weeks, he went to at least one of the half-dozen places offering traditional music: the Troubadour, Bunjies Coffee House, the Establishment, Les Cousins, the Roundhouse, and the Singers Club (owned by the Scottish songwriter Ewan MacColl and his wife, Peggy Seeger, Pete's half-sister). He listened closely to folksingers he had never heard, absorbing new material—the centuries-old ballads of the British Isles, with which he had been familiar mainly through their Appalachian adaptations and mutations—and he took the ones he liked and further adapted them himself. From Martin Carthy, Dylan first heard "Lord Franklin" and "Scarborough Fair," and he used them to write "Bob Dylan's Dream" and "Girl from the North Country." (Dylan would soon tell a radio interviewer that he felt as if his music had always existed and he just wrote it down, and he was literally correct, to some extent: much of his early work had existed as other writers' melodies, chord structures, or thematic ideas.) From Carthy's friend Bob Davenport, Dylan learned "Nottamun Town" and "Poor Miner's Lament," and he turned them into "Masters of War" and "Only a Hobo." (Jean Ritchie would later charge that Dylan derived "Masters of War" from her arrangement of "Nottamun Town," a possibility, although Dylan composed his antiwar song shortly after hearing Davenport.) From Nigel Denver, he picked up "The Leaving of Liverpool" and changed it exiguously for his "Farewell," as well as "The Patriot Game," which became "With God on Our Side." (According to the Clancy Brothers, Dylan first heard "The Patriot Game" from them; as Dylan's esteem as a songwriter grew, it became a source of pride to be a victim of his thefts.) "I believe Bob Dylan wanted to gather as many songs as he could," said Troubadour manager Anthea Joseph. "I read *Sing Out!*, so I knew who he was. When he came in [to the Troubadour], I told him he didn't have to pay if he sang something. Dylan didn't seem as interested in performing as he was in listening. I felt quite like a native in the presence of an anthropologist."

He performed a few songs at virtually every club, to inappreciable effect. As in Cambridge and Greenwich Village, the folk scene in London was protective of its own and resistant to intrusion; Dylan was no more welcome at the Troubadour than he had been at Club 47. What was more, the clubs in and around the West End were less a single folk community than an archipelago of distinct and independent-minded groups centering around a neighborhood or a pub; Jo Ann Kelly, a regular at Bunjies, was no more welcome at the Troubadour than Dylan was. His coarse and highly American style, difficult for many even in New York, alienated Dylan from the London club audiences nearly beyond hope. "The first time I heard Dylan perform in the Singers Club, I thought he was awful," remembered Karl Dallas, the English folk music historian. "Everyone appeared to agree. He went to many of the clubs, and he learned a great many songs, and he played some of his own, and he was greeted with derision wherever he went. I was at the Singers Club, which was a very staunchly traditional club, and he sang, 'Hey, hey, Woody Guthrie, I wrote you a song,' and everybody said, 'Big deal.' You know, who cares?" Dylan fared best at the relatively untraditional King and Queen pub, where Martin Carthy, the local favorite, endorsed him. Carthy and Dylan spent New Year's Eve at the King and Queen, ringing in 1963 with songs and mugs of ale that Dylan always seemed to leave somewhere after a few sips. At midnight they joined the crowd in song, although Dylan stopped singing after the opening bars. " 'Should auld acquaintance be forgot,' " he sang, " 'and never brought to mind . . .' " Carthy saw Dylan shrink for a moment; his eyes receded, as if something had just been brought to mind, and he turned away. Carthy wondered if his new acquaintance might be thinking of old ones he had forgotten, but Carthy would never ask him.

While Dylan and Martin Carthy were bellowing "Auld Lang Syne," Eric von Schmidt was celebrating with a miniature bottle of bourbon on a BOAC flight to London. Richard Fariña had invited him to pick up their plan for revolutionizing literature. In the sixteen months since their day at Revere Beach, Fariña had finished about 220 pages of his novel, and he had sent it to von Schmidt. "I learned my first lesson about Richard—he followed through," said von Schmidt, who worked up a dummy edition with sketches of illustrations, suitable for presentation to a publisher. Fariña, working through someone or other he knew somewhat somehow, had set up a meeting with an editor, a Miss Allison, at Weidenfeld & Nicolson, which published Peter Wildeblood and Saul Bellow in the United Kingdom. As further motivation for von Schmidt to spend a month's earnings on transatlantic air travel, Richard wrote that he had landed a record deal with a label in London, and he would bring von Schmidt in on it. However, Eric, who had learned to recognize a bluff playing poker in the army, never believed that part. "It was 'You gotta come over here, man! We'll get our book published, and we'll make a record! We'll make music and get drunk. There's women—man, we'll tear the joint up! You'd better hurry!' " recalled von Schmidt. "He wrote all these letters, and he had all these inducements to come on over. I was interested in film at the time, and I was working on an animated short based on the song 'The Young Man Who Wouldn't Hoe Corn.' Dick said, 'We can record the soundtrack here, man.' It was like everything I could want, Dick had waiting for me in London. I would never have done anything like that—I didn't have the kind of money it took to fly in those days. But my wife and I were splitting up, and I was a wreck over it, and I wasn't thinking right. So it all made perfect sense, and I hopped on the plane." Delayed in the air because of a blizzard over London, von Schmidt's flight landed in midafternoon on New Year's Day. Fariña docked at Folkestone on the Channel ferry from Paris two hours later.

They convened, per Richard's instructions, at an exquisite townhouse on upper-class Tregunter Road—the London residence of the McEwen family, wealthy Scots. Two young McEwens, the brothers Alex and Rory, were folksingers whom Fariña had met in the London clubs. (Upper-crust folksingers in a highly class-conscious culture? To make their affluence more palatable to the folk audience, Alex and Rory claimed to be related to the makers of McEwan's ale, a product much beloved in the after-work pubs where they played. No one seemed to notice that the last names were spelled differently, and few people knew that the real beermaker's only heir had died in 1942.) Richard and Carolyn Hester had performed with Alex and Rory at the Edinburgh Festival and briefly experimented with them as a quartet, recording four songs together in a London studio. Rory, a painter as well as musician (his specialty was scientifically detailed watercolors of botanical subjects), lived in the townhouse for most of the year. But since he was visiting his family in Scotland, Fariña explained, Rory invited Richard to stay on Tregunter Road. Eric was dazzled by the McEwen residence's imperial opulence. The walls were covered in red silk, and the doorknobs were ivory. Every element of the house seemed to be a souvenir of a different outpost of the British Empire; there was an enveloping air of conquest. "It was Dick's kind of place," said von Schmidt. "He loved being the lord of the manor, and I didn't mind being there myself." Both of them drank up the luxury, played music together through the day, and gallivanted in the folk clubs every night.

Although he was not only a Yank but far less experienced a musician than von Schmidt, Fariña played up his Irish side and managed to win over the London club audiences. He held his own through force of will and personality. At the Troubadour, Jim Connor, who knew Fariña as a writer, watched especially closely when Fariña did a few solos and von Schmidt sat out. Connor's skepticism regarding Fariña's musicianship approached contempt, but it quickly dissolved into respect and, ultimately, admiration. "I assumed he couldn't play anything—otherwise he would be playing a guitar, or a banjo, instead of the dulcimer," Connor said. "But when he got up there, he really enjoyed what he was doing, and it was good. He was irresistible. It was just his natural raw talent, his ability to make people love him at that moment, or go with him with whatever he was doing. It was a devil-may-care venturesomeness that he had. In the movies, Errol Flynn had it. The guy would show up drunk on the set, Jack Warner or whoever was producing the movie is pulling his hair out. The guy smells, he hasn't shaved, you know he hadn't studied the script. And then he combs his hair and he goes out there and gives a performance that gets an Academy Award. That was Fariña at the Troubadour. When he came out, you thought he could fall down dead any minute. Then he gave this incredible performance." Defying the prevailing rules as well as expectations, Fariña ended his brief set with an energetic rendition of a rock and roll song, Buddy Holly's "Oh Boy." He flipped his dulcimer on the side and played it like a guitar, and he growled the lyrics: "All my love, all my kissin', you don't know what you've been missin' . . ." The audience seemed uncertain how to take this transgression; there were chuckles and a moan or two. What was Fariña doing? Was it a parody of that adolescent music, rock and roll—an ironic affirmation of folk's superiority? Or a taunt—an imputation that the folk audience didn't know what it was missin'?

Chatting during one of von Schmidt's numbers, Anthea Joseph mentioned to Fariña that Bob Dylan was visiting from America, too. She said she had no address or phone number for him, but she agreed to pass along a message from Fariña the next time Dylan came into the club: *Von Schmidt and I are here to make a record. Come to the McEwens' pad. Free beer.*

"We were really living it up," said von Schmidt. "We were lounging in the grand parlor of this house every day, and finally Dick said to me, 'There's something I have to tell you. Have you ever noticed that we never do the dishes, and they're always clean, and the end of the toilet paper is always folded neatly, and the towels in the bathroom are always warm?' I said, 'Well, now that you mention it, come to think of it, yes.' He said, 'Well, there's another person living with us. There's an invisible butler. He's here to serve our every need. But he's invisible.' "

To von Schmidt's amazement, Fariña really had a record deal. One of the people Richard knew with a pad in France was Tom Costner, an American lawyer working in the Paris office of Hays and Busby, a corporate law firm that also had offices in New York and Washington, D.C.

Costner, a doggish adventurer four years older than Richard, found jurisprudence loathsomely tedious but valued its ability to support his great passions: travel, music, and French clothes. He was gay and had a sweet Parisian lover, Yves Chaix, who was an aspiring painter and also masseur for the Claridge hotel; Chaix's massage clients included celebrities such as Yul Brynner and Sugar Ray Robinson, and Costner liked knowing that. As part of an effort to branch into the field of show business representation, Costner had written a pitch letter to Carolyn Hester before she and Richard had come to Europe; Fariña had answered on his wife's behalf. "I was trying to target the next big thing, the genius that I was," Costner said drolly. Tom Costner said everything drolly. "I knew it was going to be Carolyn or Joanie. Which one, I wasn't sure. I suspected it would be Joanie, so I pursued Carolyn. I have a weakness for underdogs, and I recognize that they tend to have the greater need for me. I don't remember what I said to Carolyn—something like 'Come on over, and let me con you.' " Richard responded that his wife had no need for representation or management, since he was handling her business; still, when Carolyn and Richard came to Paris, they met Costner for lunch at a café on the Boulevard Saint-Germain. "He was a dynamo," said Costner, "very strong and surely very dangerous, I thought."

The first business to transpire from their association was a writing job for Fariña. Costner had just produced a record for his only clients as an artists' representative, Jim Connor and Richard Lockmiller, and he needed liner notes for the album, which was about to be issued by Folklore Records in England. "He was kind of a hot young writer and a friend of Bob Dylan and all that," said Costner. "I was impressed, and he graciously offered to write these liner notes. I didn't suspect that lurking in the background was going to be 'P.S.—I'm next.' " (On the initial release, the brief text on Lockmiller and Connor's album jacket was attributed to Richard Fariña and Carolyn Hester; on subsequent printings, Hester's name was removed.) Fariña leveraged his friendship with von Schmidt to Costner, just as he had leveraged the record contract to von Schmidt, winning them both over without drawing attention to his own inexperience as a musician. "He hit me up—you know, 'You did it for them. Von Schmidt's much bigger than them!" Costner recalled. "Front a few lousy bucks, and we'll all get rich and famous.' " With a total investment of 250 pounds for recording and manufacturing, Costner contracted Richard Fariña and Eric von Schmidt to record an album for Folklore. Von Schmidt would design the jacket, Fariña would write the liner notes, and neither would be paid an advance. "It seemed to make sense at the time," Costner said. "The only thing I hadn't quite figured out was what Richard Fariña was going to do in the recording studio."

One afternoon in the first week of January 1963, Bob Dylan arrived at the McEwens' townhouse. He had his guitar case in one hand and a note with the message Richard had given Anthea Joseph in the other. Since the butler was still invisible, Eric von Schmidt greeted Dylan and hurried him through the foyer into the parlor to see Fariña, who was lounging in a grand chair with leather upholstery. Richard blurted, "Hey, man!" and began to rise to hug his guest as Bob took a seat in a chair about six feet to Richard's left, facing the same direction as Fariña. Dylan ignored him and looked straight ahead as Richard stared at the side of his face. Eric poured glasses of gin for all three, passed them around, and sat in a third chair across the room, facing Richard and Bob. "And Dick says, 'Hey, how you doing man? What's going down?' " von Schmidt recalled. "And Dylan said, 'Hey Eric, I didn't know you were in London.' He didn't pay any attention to Dick. It was like he wasn't in the room. Dick was pretty taken aback, you know. And so Dick started talking to me, and I answered Dick, and then Dylan said some more, and it ended up like I'm translating from Dick to Dylan and back and forth, like I was the only one who spoke the common language. And this went on for like fifteen minutes. And then Dylan said to me, 'Hey, you want to hear a song that I just wrote?' I said, 'Yeah—great, man. Get out your guitar.' And so he gets out the guitar and plays 'Don't Think Twice, It's All Right' and beautifully, and the instrumental part, everything is perfect. And I say, 'Oh, man—that's fabulous.' And Dylan says, 'You like that?' Now Fariña is talking to me—'Wow, what a song!' And then, finally, it was like Dylan all of a sudden realized Dick was there, now that Dick had said how much he liked the song. And they started talking like old friends." (A year later Dylan would build a song around the idea of pretending to have never met someone; in "I Don't Believe You [She Acts Like We Never Have Met]" he characterizes the role playing as a punitive act: " 'It's easily done / You just pick anyone / An' pretend that you never have met!' ")

"I think that was a trick Bob learned from Grossman," said von Schmidt. "That was Grossman's famous trick, ignoring you. I think it blew Bob's mind to see how Dick and I were living. He wasn't exactly setting the house on fire in England, and I think it bugged him to see Dick living like a king. I don't think he wanted to hear all about Dick's novel—and [how Fariña] was involved with the most beautiful young woman in the world. It was pretty obvious that there were two huge egos butting heads there, and Bob had to spray his territory."

In a letter to Mimi describing the encounter, Richard multiplied the duration of Bob's pose by a factor of sixteen and probably exaggerated Dylan's subsequent behavior at least as much. If Dylan indeed said much of what Fariña attributed to him, he was surely pulling another prank:

Dylan was real cool for maybe four hours, then ran over to me . . . and TALKED, asking questions, telling me things, & holy Christ, do you know what? He said all over the east coast there's talk about my book, & people already know [the main character] Gnossos' name, & that he's never heard so much gobbling about a guy who wasn't AROUND as he'd been hearing about Frina [sic]. And *why?*

"You *know* something," he said.

"Maybe," I said back.

"There's this guy [John] Stein, you know him?"

"Only his name."

"Well, Stein, he came up to me and said What do [I] know 'bout a guy named Frina, and I told him, and Stein said Guess Who he's with. You'll never guess in a million years but guess anyway, because it's so crazy and improbable you won't believe it. So I said who, and he said Mimi Baez, that's who, and I said, Wow, things don't happen that good. You know Dick?"

"No, but I keep hearing things," said Stein.

[Later] . . . I overheard Ric say something to Dylan that filled me with good feeling from nose to kneecap. He said, "Bobby, Dick is doing a beautiful thing in this book."

And Bob said, "You know how they talk about him in the States? They say he's stepped out."

Evidently, Dylan and Fariña were both absorbed with this notion of "stepping out." Bob discussed it further with Richard in London, as Fariña later quoted him (in an essay he wrote about Dylan for a prospective book about folk music, never published). "Man, there's things going on in this world you got to look at, right?" Dylan said, according to Fariña. "You can't pretend they ain't happening. Man, I was in New York when that Cuba business came over on the radio, and you think that don't put something in your head? Man, you can keep on singing about Railroad Bill and Lemon Trees, or you can step out, right?" In a pointed variation on the same idea, Dylan made an example of Joan Baez, as Fariña (in a different piece of writing) quoted Bob as having said in London: "Take Joanie, man. She's still singin' about Mary Hamilton. I mean, where's that at? She's got all kinds of feeling, so why ain't she steppin' out?"

Acquaintances of Richard's from the London clubs rang Tregunter Road through the evening of Dylan's visit, and Fariña invited them all to come over with their instruments and friends. Soon there was a party. (Those five words are the caption to the mental picture most people had of Richard Fariña.) Strangers commandeered the kitchen to cook a pot of bean stew. Von Schmidt had everyone stomping and hooting to the blues, and Fariña and Dylan got stoned. "There was grass all over the place, singing, jumping, yelling," Richard wrote Mimi. Dylan stayed the night. The following day all three musicians (a fair term for Richard now, he proved) jammed till nighttime. There were more parties, first a musical bash at the home of folksinger Susan May; she played piano, Dylan and von Schmidt traded off on the harmonica, Fariña strummed his dulcimer, and various participants took turns on guitar. Breaking for a late-evening dinner, Richard, Eric, and Bob downed some cheeseburgers at the Wimpy bar. Then more music, alcohol, and pot at singer Jon Shear's flat. "Still more grass," Fariña wrote, "and Dylan & me getting into a Thing of story-telling and everyone laughing hard, almost cackling, falling on the floor and suddenly it was nine o'clock [in the] morning."

Their fondness for marijuana united Richard and Bob. (Von Schmidt rarely smoked marijuana; "I had trouble inhaling it," he said. "I was a peyote head.") Still widely seen as an exotic, potentially insidious indulgence of jazz musicians and other degenerates, marijuana was just beginning to emerge in casual social gatherings of folk enthusiasts, as it was starting to pop up amidst the alcohol and cigarettes at college parties. In the 1963 edition of *Roget's Thesaurus*, "marihuana" was cited once, under the heading "Poison," as a synonym for bacteria, hemlock, mustard gas, and radioactive fallout. Fewer than four million Americans were estimated to have tried the drug (half the number estimated five years later). Fewer still knew how to purchase it or dared to carry it with them (especially on foreign soil), as Fariña did; to be the one who had the stuff was a mark of high cool. As for Dylan, he seemed far more interested in the literal effects of the drug than in its social cachet. "I don't know how much pot Bob had ever smoked before," von Schmidt said. "I don't think very much. He was like somebody just discovering something they couldn't get enough of."

When Dylan heard about the album Fariña and von Schmidt were about to record, he asked them if he could be a part of it. Richard and Eric, though surprised, welcomed Bob happily; at the same time, von Schmidt was doubtful that Albert Grossman would approve of his important client's participation in such a low-wattage endeavor. "Bob was the one who invited himself to the session," said von Schmidt. "He just said, 'You're going to do a record? Hey—can I be on it? I'll be on that record. What do you say?' I was a little startled that he was so enthusiastic about it. He had his own contract with a big record label. And we just said, 'Yeah, sure, come on in—do the record with us. Great!' I think he was expecting it to be a kind of band thing, like we were going to be a group, the three of us. But that wasn't what Dick and I had in mind. Dick asked me to do a record with him, and this was going to be our record, and we had already talked to one other person [Ethan Signer of the Charles River Valley Boys, who was visiting London with his wife Barbara] about playing with us, and we weren't even sure Dylan would really show up for the sessions."

Tom Costner came from Paris on the Air France shuttle to finalize details of the recording sessions and was tickled to learn of his good fortune as an entrepreneur—the much-discussed Bob Dylan was going to be involved in *his* production. Then he met Dylan, pubbing with Fariña. Costner found him "detestable," smug and discourteous. "He was so fucking rude," recalled Costner. "They were still the days when there was a facade of politeness and 'Hello, how are you?' and such. Dylan wouldn't even look at me." Fariña, though cursorily hospitable to Costner, cocooned with Dylan. "They were very buddy-buddy, annoyingly—speaking their own secret code and laughing at all of us who didn't know what they were talking about," said Costner. Could they have been drunk or stoned? "Oh, hell, yes—that's how they prepared for the record," according to Costner. "They were in their own world, and they should have stayed there and never gone to the recording studio."

In the middle of the second week of January, a few days before Fariña and von Schmidt were scheduled to begin recording, the butler at Tregunter Road achieved visibility. He and Rory McEwen had been in regular contact by telephone, the butler said, and Mr. McEwen would like Messrs. Fariña and von Schmidt to know that they are not welcome to live in his house, nor were they ever. Mr. McEwen requested that they leave immediately. Would the gentlemen be needing any assistance?

"I hated their strained hospitality & fled," Richard wrote Mimi, "even though Ric dug the luxury." After a few nights in the homes of others Fariña knew, more or less, he and von Schmidt took a small suite in the Hotel de France, a cheap French-owned kindling pile of rooms near the South Kensington tube station—"a maniac place," as Richard romanticized it to Mimi, "run by a fat little woman from Calais who loves me, where we took the best suite of rooms in the building and got so many phone calls, telegrams, & urgent messages in the first 48 hours that we felt obliged to inform them of how famous we were, from which time they began serving us breakfast in bed." Sitting face to face on Richard's bed, they rehearsed about a dozen songs: "Jumping Judy" (aka "Drive It On"), a prison work song von Schmidt had picked up from a Library of Congress recording; "Overseas Stomp," a 1927 Memphis Jug Band tune on Harry Smith's *Anthology of American Folk Music*; an adaptation of the Rev. Gary Davis's version of "Cocaine," which von Schmidt had learned from Davis at the 1960 Indian Neck festival; the Negro hymn "Glory, Glory"; and a twelve-bar blues Fariña had written and titled "Xmas Island"; among others. To see how they sounded with Dylan and Ethan Signer, Richard and Eric met them at the Troubadour and did a few numbers on the evening of Saturday, January 12, two days before their first scheduled recording session.

After the performance, two men in their early twenties who were going to school outside London invited them to a party at their flat. "There weren't any chicks at the club," said von Schmidt, "so we thought, 'A college party—great!'" Signer took a cab to meet his wife at their hotel, and Richard, Eric, and Bob rode with the students for about an hour. The party turned out to be just the five of them and two other young men. "It was nothing, just these four English guys staring at us like specimens in a bell jar. We were pissed. No chicks, just these four guys treating us like some kind of freaks." Fariña, undoubtedly offended by the promise of a party unfulfilled, turned to von Schmidt and Dylan, and said, "Well . . . why don't we sing a song? I know something suitable for the occasion. Let's do 'The London Waltz.'" He laid his dulcimer on his lap and started strumming a three-quarter time pattern. Von Schmidt recognized an improvisation in the making and took out his harmonica. Richard started with a chorus—"We're doin' the London Waltz, doin' the London Waltz, doin' the London Waltz . . . Can't think of nothin' else"—then he and Dylan took turns ad-libbing words that mocked their hosts with deepening sarcasm. "They just ripped into those jerks," said von Schmidt. "Really funny and lacerating stuff." When the objects of Fariña and Dylan's ridicule declined to drive their guests back to London, Richard telephoned for a taxi. The three Americans slid in with their instrument cases, and von Schmidt pulled out a flask of gin. After a few swigs all around, Eric felt inspired to do an a cappella rendition of Frederick McQueen's song "In Them Long, Hot Summer Days." That was the cue the others needed. For the rest of the ride, the three of them sang, drank, and laughed into each other's faces. Fariña and Dylan broke into "The London Waltz," improvising about a dozen more verses. Someone pulled the cab windows down, the biting night air rushed in, and the drunken trio's voices bellowed out into the suburbs as the cab sputtered toward the city.

On the evening of January 14, Richard and Eric took the tube to meet Ethan, Bob, and Tom Costner and make their record. They had to wait until six o'clock to begin, because the sessions were to be conducted in the basement of the Dobell record shop after it closed. Folklore (not to be confused with Moe Asch's American company, Folkways, a giant by comparison) was a record label by only the most generous definition. It was owned and run almost single-handedly by Douglas Dobell, a forty-five-year-old music enthusiast and amateur boogie-woogie piano player who had inherited a respected bookstore on Charing Cross Road and made it a hub for collectors of jazz and folk records. Dobell had placed chairs here and there around the store, and he kept a bottle of scotch in the drawer of his desk to share with his regular customers, who included the tenor saxophonist Ben Webster. "He ran the store like a pub," said Brian Peerless, one of his record salesman. "He loved musicians and was a bit of a pushover when it came to them." In the late 1950s, Dobell started making records in the shop's basement—a handful of New Orleans–style jazz releases by little-known English artists and two or three folk things. The "studio" was a space of about three feet by six feet between bins of used records, and the sound equipment was a monaural Ferrograph tape recorder with one input and a microphone on a stand.

Fariña ran the sessions. (The production master tapes were labeled

"Dick Farina.") He and von Schmidt faced each other on straight-back chairs, as they had on their hotel beds, and ran through most of their repertoire, which would take up one side of a long-playing record. In a few hours, they taped several versions of ten songs, including a drastically abridged version of "The London Waltz." Fariña sang with a lilting fervor that made every selection sound a bit like "Will Ye Go, Lassie, Go," and his dulcimer playing was sprightly and inventive (particularly on his showcase, "Old Joe's Dulcimer," a medley of traditional themes associated with the instrument, including parts of "Old Joe Clark" and "Darlin' Corey"). His strength as both vocalist and instrumentalist was rhythm; there was a dance-beat pulse in his phrasing, even on ballads. Fariña struggled to sing on key, however, and tended to fail. Von Schmidt was in good form, crooning some of his favorite traditional songs in his slightly sour buttermilk voice. His guitar playing was masterly offhanded, "loosey-goosey," he would say—ideal for this record. Ethan Signer filled out the songs on mandolin, fiddle, and guitar. ("I played a lot of instruments adequately," said Signer. "That's why they asked me along—they got a whole band for nothing.") Both Dylan and Costner arrived late, as the session was winding down. Bob was carrying a crate of beer, which was empty within ten or fifteen minutes.

They went to the Troubadour, without Costner, to celebrate. Judy Silver, a petite Israeli singer and guitarist, was performing one of her Yiddish-language specialties when the Americans strode in. She sat on a stool in a brilliant red wraparound dress. "Now there's something you don't see every day—a Jewish folksinger," Dylan told his friends, who chuckled blithely, unaware of the comment's irony. As they stood watching Silver from a back wall, Peter Stanley came up to Richard. Stanley, the English banjo player who had performed with Carolyn Hester, Fariña, and Clay Jackson at Cecil Sharp House, had a bag of marijuana and wanted to impress Fariña with it. There was a furtive exchange of information, and Fariña and Dylan followed Stanley into a small side room painted bright green. Perhaps twenty minutes later, the foursome returned. Silver was leading the audience in a sing-along to "Tonts! Tonts!" or some such children's song.

"Fuck this," Dylan said. "Let's go up and play."

Richard, Eric, and Ethan followed Bob onto the stage, although Silver was still sitting at the microphone. While Fariña charmed her into stepping down, his friends powwowed, trying to agree on a song they all knew. They settled on "Cocaine." Their choice of a drug song may have been intended referentially: Fariña and Dylan had gotten very high. You could tell from a snapshot someone in the audience took that night. Richard and Bob are standing together in the center of the group, but just barely standing. Fariña, who is dressed in a plaid shirt, a bulky sweater, and a wool cap, like an Irish peasant with a college scholarship, seems about to topple over. Dylan, next to him in a khaki work shirt and a high, narrow-brimmed leprechaun hat, seems to be having trouble keeping his tongue in his mouth. Their eyes are pencil-line slits, and they're smiling like tickled babies. Both of them are cupping harmonicas in their hands; in a nearly identical picture, they're wailing on their harps in unison.

Fariña, von Schmidt, and Signer played a few of the songs they had recorded earlier in the evening, with Dylan blowing harmonica. Then they left Bob to do a couple of songs alone. He took out his guitar, plopped upon the stool without looking behind him or feeling about to make sure the stool was where it needed to be, and began finger-picking the introduction to his recent, unrecorded song, "Don't Think Twice, It's All Right": G, D, E minor . . . Peter Stanley, observing in fascination from a few feet away, laughed as he watched Dylan stare at his fingers, evidently amazed by their activity. "My fingers are moving sooo sloooww," Dylan announced. Gazing up in due time, Bob shifted his glare onto one of the walls. "Where are we—are we underwater?" he continued, still finger-picking the same three chords. Dylan was either having his first public drug experience or giving a performance of one.

"We're all underwater," Dylan announced. "We're all in a submarine."

"This is no submarine," someone yelled from the crowd—a young Scot in a kilt, Peter Stanley recalled. "This is Mayfair!"

"Who's talking to me?" Dylan said, glaring blankly, still finger-picking. "Are you a fish?"

"I'm no fish, for fuck's sake! Who do you think you are?"

. . . two, three, four . . .

" 'It ain't no use to sit and wonder why, babe, if you don't know by now . . . ,' " Dylan began singing, using the heckling as his introduction; there was even tenuous thematic continuity. "It was the most amazing piece of stagecraft," said Peter Stanley. "The others got stoned and played while they were fucked up, and they gave fucked-up performances. Dylan got stoned, and he instinctively *used* it. It gave him material." After "Don't Think Twice," Dylan played a languid version of "Blowin' in the Wind." While the audience was still applauding Dylan, his friends shuffled around him to play another tune together. Fariña cued the group to do "The London Waltz."

The musicians regrouped the next day to finish recording. This time Dylan was involved from the beginning, playing background harmonica and singing in the background of four songs: "Cocaine," "Overseas Stomp," "Glory, Glory," and Fariña's "Xmas Island." His role was colorative; as von Schmidt put it, "Bob's job was to jump in and go 'Hey hoo ha! Whoop de doo!' " He did so with infectious conviviality, revealing a playful side unheard in most of his own work since he had given up Little Richard songs. The record complete, Fariña, von Schmidt, and Dylan headed off to the folk clubs again. They chose Bunjies Coffee House as the site of this evening's havoc, the last mess they would be able to make together in London. Both Eric and Bob had flights departing for the States the next morning.

There were loose ends. Von Schmidt still had to design the album cover; Fariña had to write the liner notes; Douglas Dobell had to choose which tracks to issue; and Costner had to clear all the necessary rights, including permission from Albert Grossman's office to use Bob Dylan's name on the album. Costner needed to find an American distributor for the record, too. Beyond the album, as well, the matter of Richard and Eric's book remained unresolved; Weidenfeld & Nicolson rejected the project on grounds that illustrations would be too expensive to print. ("Those are your hang-ups, not mine, nor any writers," Fariña told the Weidenfeld & Nicolson editor, or so he claimed in a letter to Mimi.

"Meanwhile," he assured her, "the reputation of the thing grows underground, the People Who Know are extra confident, & my price, ho he, goes up."

Fariña and Dylan had already started talking about their next project together, though. Now that Bob was an actor, Richard decided to write a treatment for a film geared to the singer's persona. It would be a Western about a peace-loving cowboy who never carried a gun but had to take up arms to save his father, as Fariña described it to Tom Costner. (This was a variation on a story-poem of Richard's, "The Ballad of the Last Caution Gunbattle," which *Mademoiselle* had rejected the previous year.) Dylan loved the idea, Richard said. The movie would be called *The Kid*, and the Dylan character would die a heroic death—shot in the back, he would fall off his horse in the last scene of the film. That part was Bob's idea, Richard told Costner. Fariña just needed a quiet place to write. He was wondering, could he stay in Tom's apartment in Paris for a while, only long enough to finish the script?

AMONG THE IDEAS Pete Seeger planted in thirteen-year-old Joan Baez's mind, the notion that folk music was easy to perform took root quickly. However, the precept Seeger considered paramount—that the music could be a force for social change—spent some time germinating. Joan's first two albums, like her concert programs, were wholly comprised of traditional material devoid of overt relevance to the issues of the day. The ethereal Baez conjured the otherworldly and the past, but rarely the here and now. She was the image of passivity, not advocacy—until that seed of social advocacy sprouted within her, just as it did within so many others coming of age at the time of the civil rights movement and the cold war.

Since moving to her cabin in the Carmel Highlands, Joan had used ude to reconsider the course of her musical career. She and

Michael New split again—this time, surely, for good; he went to Europe, met a Venezuelan woman, and moved to her native Mérida with her. Joan rented a nicer house about a mile up the road from her one-room saltbox, an airy modern place owned by the photographer Brett Weston. "I needed to start over," Joan recalled. "I had gotten everything I had set out for, and what did it get me? Money? I've always loved to shop, but that wasn't enough. I felt empty. I thought of giving up music completely. It wasn't doing it for me to keep doing the same old songs."

Joan's growing disenchantment with the music she had been singing for several years began to taint her performances. Being the poster girl for the folk craze assured her success at the box office: the Joan Baez concert at Carnegie Hall in the fall of 1962 sold out two months in advance, and two hundred chairs had to be set up on the stage. Still, some critics, including a few of her earlier champions, detected something mechanical in Joan's singing. She started getting lukewarm reviews. As Robert Shelton wrote of the Carnegie Hall concert in *The New York Times*:

> She appears, because gifted with such a great voice, to lean too heavily on vocalism alone. There are many more things—in folklore, personality, projection and stage presence—to make a totally rounded folksinger. Further, she tends toward a monochrome mood of melancholy that should be relieved with some other hues.

She was growing weary of singing the same old songs, and critics seemed to be getting tired of hearing the same old Baez. How long would audiences keep listening before they were all spent?

"Her moment was essentially over—that's what those of us in the field were beginning to think and say, among ourselves," recalled author and musician Sam Charters. "Once the novelty was over of this great presence, this beautiful young girl with this absolutely unforgettable voice, singing these traditional songs, what the hell do you do next?"

Inspired by her Quaker parents as well as by Seeger—and no doubt by others in her sphere who were socially and politically conscious, including Manny Greenhill and Clark Foreman—Joan began using her celebrity to promote an inchoate social agenda. She had never been much of a reader and was not about to undertake a scholarly study of nuclear proliferation and race relations; intuitive, decisive, confident, and iron-willed, Joan dove into her new pursuit, like so many crusaders before her and around her, on faith. "The basic issues were clear, and they were indisputable," she said. "Peace. Equality. There was no question about the issues. I felt them in my bones. I knew what I had to sing about."

For the third Joan Baez album, Maynard Solomon had several of Joan's live performances taped; the result, *Joan Baez in Concert*, was released for the winter 1962 holiday season. The record included Baez's first performance of a topical song: "What Have They Done to the Rain," a melodic, poignant evocation of nuclear disaster by Malvina Reynolds, a contemporary of Pete Seeger and Sis Cunningham who had written "Sally, Don't You Grieve" with Woody Guthrie. The rest of the album comprises Joan's usual mix of folk standards such as "Kumbaya," "Black Is the Color," and "Copper Kettle"; Child ballads; and a Portuguese-language traditional, "Até Amanhã." Although it became a top-ten hit and was nominated for a Grammy Award as best folk recording, *Joan Baez in Concert* got a mixed response from an increasingly wary press. As Henrietta Yurchenco wrote in *Musical America*, "[Joan's] mild manner does not do justice to the more energetic numbers on this otherwise excellent disk."

With Reynolds and many of her Almanac-era contemporaries still writing political material and a young breed following suit, Joan had a wealth of topical protest songs to choose from if she so wished. *Broadside* magazine was publishing the words and music to half a dozen new songs every month. Unfortunately, few of them appealed to her. "Most of the first protest songs [of the 1960s] weren't great songs," Joan said. "I couldn't sing them. They didn't have to be sung—you just chanted them. There was no beauty in them and no complexity, musically or lyrically." The first contemporary song with a social statement that Baez heard and immediately wanted to sing was "With God on Our Side," one of the songs Bob Dylan crafted from a tune he had heard in London. It was a song that, as the Quakers say, spoke to Joan's condition.

The source of the song, Irish folksinger Dominic Behan's "The Patriot Game," echoes a theme Behan drew from Samuel Johnson: Patriotism is the last refuge of a scoundrel. Dylan reworked that idea, lambasting the use of religion to rationalize war as the refuge of the patriot. ("With God on Our Side" adheres closely to Behan's melody, which, in any event, resembles that of at least one earlier composition, "Magyar Himnusz," the Hungarian national anthem.) The song is a sarcastic cousin to the musing "Blowin' in the Wind." Its point is clear and expressed with cogent vigor:

> *The cavalries charged*
> *The Indians died*
> *Oh the country was young*
> *With God on its side*

In the fifth of nine verses, however, the song takes an unexpected turn. Challenging the liberal orthodoxy of the day, it ridicules America's postwar rapprochement with Germany:

> *When the Second World War*
> *Came to an end*
> *We forgave the Germans*
> *And we were friends*
> *Though they murdered six million*
> *In the ovens they fried*
> *The Germans now too*
> *Have God on their side*

Beyond evoking the historic Holocaust while most protest-song writers were fixed on the ostensibly imminent nuclear one, Dylan dared to part from the obligatory pacifism of the *Broadside* crowd. Not all actions can be forgiven, Dylan said, and not all people can be friends.

Joan heard the song for the first time when she was visiting Cambridge the day after she gave a concert in Boston and Bob was in town to play at Cafe Yana. Baez and Dylan both went to Club 47's weekly hootenanny on Sunday, April 21. When Joan wafted in, wearing a light body-formed jumper and high heels, Dylan was doing a song (something old and rousing) with von Schmidt and Ramblin' Jack Elliott. Eric had trouble looking in Joan's direction and strumming simultaneously, such was her allure. With word out that Joan Baez might be coming tonight, the club was packed with folksingers: Jim Kweskin, Bob Siggins, Maria and Geoff Muldaur, Jim Rooney, John Cooke, Joe Boyd, Bob Neuwirth . . . If you came without a guitar, you had to stand outside and wait for a turn to peer through the window in the club's front door, and what you saw was like a yearbook photo of the Cambridge folk scene. Before the midnight closing time, Joan joined the dozen or so singers onstage and wailed along. (No one would remember if Dylan was part of that group, nor what everybody was singing, although it was something old and rousing, too.)

After the hoot, Sally Schoenfeld, a Cambridge singer, threw a party in the apartment she shared with Joy Kimball, also a musician, and Susie Campbell, who worked at Club 47. They had a floor above a dry-goods store on Harvard Square, and that was where Baez and Dylan got their first chance to talk at any length. (By Joan's recollection, she had spoken to Bob at Gerde's on two occasions prior to this: when they first met in April 1961, and a few months later; the second time, Dylan began their conversation by asking if Mimi was on her way. "I was quietly jealous of his interest in her," Joan said, "but managed to laugh and tease him.") Dylan was jamming with Kweskin, trading verses of a Gary Davis song in one of the bedrooms, surrounded by fellow blues enthusiasts, including Mark Spoelstra, who was in Cambridge to play at the Cafe Yana. "Bob was squaring off with Jim," Spoelstra recalled. "They were singing there with their noses three inches apart, proving to each other how many lyrics they knew to all these songs or something. It was just ridiculous. It wasn't fun. It was tense, and Joanie walked in on that." Baez listened quietly and intently. "I remember really looking forward to seeing her," continued Spoelstra. "We hadn't really talked in all those years, since we dated when we were kids. But she was more interested in that battle between Bob and Jim. She really seemed to enjoy watching that." It is unclear who won; in Kweskin's mind, Dylan was no competition. "It was more like I was teaching him songs," Kweskin said matter-of-factly. In Spoelstra's recollection, Dylan plopped his guitar down on the floor, as if he were spiking it in triumph.

Catching Joan's eye as he leaned back in his chair, Bob said to her, "Hey, how ya doin'? Is your sister here?"

Joan said, "No," flatly and finished the sentence with a glare that expressed, in essence, *and fuck you for asking.*

"Wanna hear a song I wrote?" Bob responded.

Dylan nestled his guitar on his lap and began strumming a C chord in three-quarter time. He repeated it until the small room hushed, then he slid into the opening of "With God on Our Side." By the end of the song's nine verses, Joan Baez was no longer indifferent to Bob Dylan or irked by his crush on her sister Mimi. She was startled by the music she heard and fascinated with the fact that that enigma in the filthy jeans had created it. "When I heard him sing 'With God on Our Side,' I took him seriously," said Joan. "I was bowled over. I never thought anything so powerful could come out of that little toad. It was devastating. 'With God on Our Side' is a very mature song. It's a beautiful song. When I heard that, it changed the way I thought of Bob. I realized he was more mature than I had thought. He even looked a little better." Social consciousness as an aphrodisiac? *Seventeen* magazine must have been on to something.

Dylan played a few more of his topical songs, including "The Death of Emmett Till," "A Hard Rain's a-Gonna Fall," and "Masters of War." They astounded Spoelstra, who had not kept up with his old Village cohort's development as a songwriter, and they seemed to overwhelm Baez. (In one interview, Baez recalled "The Death of Emmett Till," not "With God on Our Side," as the Dylan song that changed her view of him and prompted her to take up protest music; "I was basically a traditional folksinger," she said. "I was not 'political' at that time. When I heard 'Emmett Till' I was knocked out. It was my first political song. That song turned me into a political folksinger." Although the songs varied in separate recollections, the same point remained: one of Dylan's early protest songs inspired Baez to rethink her career.) "Joan was not somebody who was easily impressed," said Spoelstra, "and she was not somebody who was ever at a loss for words. She just sat there with her mouth open."

"You like 'em?" Dylan asked.

Baez just nodded, smiling, while Spoelstra and a few other musicians who had gathered in Schoenfeld's study watched in fascination. "It's fair to say [that] I fell under that spell of his," said Joan. "Nobody was writing like that. He was writing exactly what I wanted to hear. It was [as if] he was giving voice to the ideas I wanted to express but didn't know how." Joan had to leave soon; it was after two a.m., and she had an early-morning flight back to California. But she wanted to hear more of the songs Bob was writing; perhaps he could teach some of them to her at another time. They should get together again, she told him. He was going to be in New York for a while, recording songs for his next album; then he was going to California. He was supposed to play at the Monterey Folk Festival in a few weeks, he said. She should come and hear him. She could sing something with him, if she wanted to. Joan thanked him and said she liked that idea. She lived near Monterey. In fact, she said, he was welcome to come to her house and visit, while he was in the area. Bob said sure, that sounded cool, and almost smiled.

IN COMPLIANCE with the terms of Bob Dylan's contract with Columbia, Tom Costner learned, Dylan's name could not appear on the album he had recorded with Richard Fariña and Eric von Schmidt. Dylan told Costner to use his usual pseudonym, Blind Boy Grunt. It seemed to fit in with the spirit of the cover text Fariña wrote to explain the album's bacchanalian content:

. . . singing, shouting, & playing American ballads, worksongs, & blues, with Ethan Signer, & occasionally Blind Boy Grunt. Instruments include mountain dulcimer, three mouth harps, two Spanish guitars, fiddle, mandolin, kazoo, & Gordon's Gin.

Von Schmidt's original album design (revised before printing) included a second hidden message. For the cover art, Eric made a black-ink drawing of a horse, and he put the words of the album title—*Dick Farina & Eric von Schmidt*—directly above the animal, tracing its shape, with the last part of the second name curving down along the tail. Each of the letters of the title alternated in color: black, ocher, black, ocher, a design that made every other letter difficult to read. The title read as *D-c-F-r-n-a & r-c o* . . . , then, <u>dangling vertically next to the horse's backside</u>, . . . <u>*S-h-i-t.*</u>

WHEN MIMI BAEZ was doing her dance exercises and her thoughts drifted into fantasies of a life with Richard Fariña, he sometimes turned into Rugger, the boyfriend her aunt Tia had brought into the boardinghouse in Menlo Park. Mimi would find herself in Tia's role, and her sister Joan would be her mother (Tia's own sister Joan). Richard/Rugger would take Mimi/Tia for ice cream and hold her hand, catering to her, loving her. Joan/Big Joan would fume. For a moment, Mimi might be in the daydream as both Tia and her childhood self watching the adult sisters in confused distress.

The arrival of a man rarely improves a relationship between sisters, and males had been igniting sparks between Joan and Mimi since the teenage Mark Spoelstra took his date's little sister for a car ride on his lap. Separated by five thousand miles and leading increasingly different lives, Joan and Mimi had been growing apart for a while. Richard seemed unlikely to draw them closer. Anticipating trouble, Mimi opted to reveal little about this romance in her occasional letters to Joan, although she did ask her a few questions about sex, phrased in hypotheticals. "I didn't really want to share much with her," explained Mimi. "I felt that she would put a damper on it, and I wanted the excitement. She was so influential in our family that I knew if I shared too much more, there would be more words against him, and I was already getting enough from my father."

Most of what Joan first learned about Mimi and Richard, then, came in correspondence from her parents, both of whom had met Fariña during his visits to Paris and found little to their liking. In Albert Baez's eyes, he was simply unworthy of his daughter, although perhaps no less so than any other man. "I probably would have objected to anybody," said Albert Baez. "I thought that he was spinning tales about himself—in other words, I sensed a form of self-promotion. I can't say that I really liked him. I didn't dislike him. I guess I just somehow wished Mimi had chosen somebody else." To Big Joan, danger seemed to lurk in Richard's magnetism. "He wasn't terribly handsome," she said. "But neither was Hitler. Hitler had charisma. Richard was terrifically charismatic, but I didn't think he was a very honorable person. He'd go off and send letters or something that made me suspicious of him. He had this strange thing. There was something about his eyes that looked strange, but he made himself attractive. I think I'd be scared of him if I lived with him."

Although Joan and Richard traveled in overlapping circles and had chatted once in Art D'Lugoff's apartment, she remembered nothing about him, and virtually everything she heard recently was damning. Richard, in his letters to Mimi, exaggerated the amount of gossip they inspired—"Did you know the whole fucking WORLD seems to be talking about us?" Still, acquaintances of the Baezes in Cambridge and New York, a sizable group, appeared to be absorbed with the news filtering in from Europe about that writer Carolyn Hester had married and Joan Baez's sister Mimi. "It was the hot topic [in Cambridge] for a while there," said Betsy Siggins-Schmidt, who was managing Club 47. "Joan asked me what I'd heard [and] what I thought. I told her. Mimi was just a little kid, and the next thing you know, she was engaged to Dick Fariña.

She was *so* young, and he was pushy and aggressive—and amusing. Amusing, pushy, and aggressive. He was an opportunist—most people seemed to think so, and the perception was that he just dumped Carolyn because there was a larger opportunity [in Mimi]. Most people thought he was using Mimi to get to Joan."

Fearing as much, Joan interceded with a rare telephone call from California to Paris, a dramatic act at the time. She was livid and immovable. Scolding her sister like a mother, Joan ridiculed Fariña as a glory-hungry bluebeard who had to be stopped before he hurt the whole Baez family. "I didn't trust him, and I was very hostile," Joan recalled. "I didn't want anybody walking off with my little sister, and I was feeling protective. I also sensed his wanting to be part of the family and getting in too fast. I didn't want him near me." Mimi recoiled, barely responding to her sister's diatribe. "Maybe she was right—I didn't know for sure," Mimi said. "But there was a voice inside me saying, 'She's more worried about protecting herself than me. Why is she making this about herself?' Of course, that was a voice that stayed inside." Joan spoke her piece, and Mimi listened passively, then handed the phone to her mother, who said, "Yes . . . yes," nodding for a minute or so, and hung up. Albert Baez, who had been standing nearby without getting involved, said he wondered how much that telephone call would cost.

"The girls were really split about Dick," Big Joan said. "When they had problems in their life in the past, they could turn to each other. With this thing, they each really thought the other one had deserted them—I heard it from them both. It was very hard for me to be caught in the middle. They each thought the other girl was trying to ruin her life. I tended to agree with Joanie."

Among the adults in Mimi's family, Tia seemed most open-minded about Fariña. She came to Paris to visit for a few weeks and met Richard twice or more. "He was very theatrical. He was a creative character, and my sister and her husband didn't know what to make of him—he scared them," Tia recalled. "I got a charge out of him, and Mimi fell in love with him. I told [Big] Joan, 'Let her go. Let her find her happiness.' But [Big Joan] wasn't ready."

While Joan, Mimi, their mother, and Tia parried over Richard, the question remained: How long could any number of Baez women maintain a defense against Fariña? He was determined to marry Mimi while she was still writing him that she was not even sure if she loved him. "And what do you mean you *think* you love me, girl, you know goddamned well you do. As much as I do you," he lectured in a letter, early in 1963. He played to her youth, adopting a child's spelling in a note in which he appeared to empathize with his seventeen-year-old girlfriend's trepidation about entering the adult world so soon. "I just do not want you to feel you OUGHT to BEHAVE more SENSIBULL because yore going to be MAREED," he wrote; and he used Joan as a role model: "Yore not running away just to freedom and sex. Yore sister, for Jesus' sake, ran away, n' she got her freedom and sex *and* her art hasn't suffered any! I mean am I right?" In spite of his talk about magic and his reputation for spontaneity (as he wrote Mimi, "The right chords in the wrong order, together with a wish for Somethin Good, gets you just about anything"), Fariña approached an important objective methodically, as a tactician.

By spring Richard was living in Paris full time. Tom Costner let him use the flat on the Quai des Orfèvres while he returned to the United States for a two-week business trip; Richard made a nest in a tiny alcove. Neither of them mentioned the situation when Tom returned; Fariña's intent was apparent, Costner's discretion considerable. A tourist postcard sold at the time (and for three decades to come) shows the exterior of the building as a pristine example of seventeenth-century Henry IV elegance. Marc Chagall lived nearby, and so did Yves Montand and Simone Signoret. The four rooms Costner rented were on the fourth floor of a six-story townhouse facing the Seine; though small, the flat appeared spacious through the use of few and delicate furnishings: a single bed, a Louis XVI commode across from it, and a small Louis XIV writing table in front of tall windows that opened over the river. Richard set up an Olivetti portable typewriter on the table and worked virtually every day while Costner was at his law office—he continued adding to his novel, he fleshed out the story for his Western movie idea for Bob Dylan, and he started work on another book he wanted von Schmidt to illustrate: a collection of ruminative essays about folk musicians. (Von Schmidt, once bitten, never did any of the illustrations, although Fariña drafted a couple of sample chapters, including one about Dylan in which he wrote, "Years ago, people like Dylan were supposed to have lit their candles at both ends. Today they light them smack in the middle, with a blowtorch. The risk may be mortal, but more people see the flame.") Richard even made some money by writing scripts of fairy tales such as "Rumpelstiltskin" and "Hansel and Gretel" for children's records (ten contracted at eighty dollars apiece). Through careful timing, Costner and Fariña essentially lived like one person; Richard would go out for the evening when Tom came home. Nighttime could be awkward, however, because Yves Chaix usually stayed with Costner on a small bed a few feet away from Richard. Fariña proved capable of considerable discretion himself.

Whether or not Richard was plotting to insinuate himself into the Baez fold, close to Joan as she suspected, Mimi's intentions toward Fariña were no more pure. "On a very pragmatic level, I had to get out from under my parents, and here was a possible solution," Mimi said. "I think that's a good part of what was going on for me, in all honesty." Still, as they came to spend time together—strolling all over Paris, joking about the people they passed, taking baths together in Costner's tub, making love on Richard's cot—Mimi and Richard grew closer and closer. "On the deepest level," Mimi said, "there was this giant friendship between us. We really got along and loved being together, and we were good for each other. Here was somebody who was old enough to take care of a lot of stuff I didn't understand, like how to cook food, how to go shopping, how to live in the world, who felt like taking care of me—and who was professing to a kind of commitment that I was shocked by at first but that I absolutely needed. I needed to be loved, and we really did start to love each other very much. I would sense that he thought I was beautiful, and he liked my creative side, he appreciated it. And the letters convinced him that I had character or that I was interesting. I know that it was a temptation for everyone to feel that it was because of Joanie that he was interested in me, and I'm sure that there was some element of that. But we were good for each other—we gave each other exactly what we needed. I got a sense from him of wanting to hold my hand and lead me into a life." Mimi told her parents her bedroom was too warm, and she started sleeping on the couch in the living room, where the telephone was. She hid it under the cushions to muffle the ring when Richard called, so she could talk to him for hours at night.

Fariña could hardly avoid this family as he had the parents of Diane Divers and Carolyn Hester. Mimi was still a minor, spending her days at home doing high school work. While he courted her, he had to woo her parents. "Dick couldn't have been more attentive and charming," Big Joan said. "I felt quite flattered." He cooked dinners with her and, clowning in the kitchen once, showed her a few steps of the tango. Upon convincing the producer of the fairy-tale albums he was writing to hire him to record the voices, too, he invited Big Joan to take part, and she played the Queen of Hearts to Richard's White Rabbit on the record of *Alice in Wonderland*. With Albert Baez, who liked neither the tango nor reciting puns in a funny voice, Richard resorted to restraint; at dinner one evening, he asked, most respectfully, if Dr. Baez would grant him the honor of having his daughter's hand in marriage. "I appreciated the way he did that," Albert Baez said. "I still didn't like him. But I valued that he showed me that respect, and Mimi seemed very fond of him." (In his letters to friends, Fariña referred to Dr. Baez as "the Aztec hatchet-man.") After a bit of debate among the three vocal parties—Mimi observed quietly, gripping Richard's hand firmly on the top of the table—it was decided: Big Joan and Albert would consent to the wedding, if only because Mimi seemed likely to proceed with it after her eighteenth birthday anyway. But Mimi and Richard were to wait until the summer; by then, Mimi would have earned her high school diploma and Albert would have begun a leave of absence from UNESCO, so the whole family could gather in California for a wedding near Joan's house. Fariña agreed enthusiastically: they could even set up housekeeping in Carmel, he said, so Mimi would be near her sister. After dinner, Richard gave Mimi a ruby engagement ring: an heirloom from a wealthy uncle in

Cuba, he explained. (It was red glass, as Mimi discovered when she had it appraised many years later.)

They were both radiant for days. "I danced everywhere," Mimi said. Fariña kept Costner awake into the morning while he sat up in his alcove typing notes to friends, including a letter to Thomas Pynchon, who had just published his first novel, *V.*, asking him to be the best man. Herbert Gold, the novelist, who had clashed with Fariña at Cornell, was visiting Paris at the time, and he was waiting in the mail line at the American Express office when Richard strode in. "Herb!" Fariña barked across the room. "Guess what? I'm going to marry Joan Baez's sister!"

When Joan learned of the California plan in letters from Mimi and their mother, she made another transatlantic call, this time to Richard at Costner's flat. Wasn't marrying her sister enough for him? Why did he want to move to Carmel? Where did he expect to live—in Joan's house? How was he going to make money? Or was he planning on living off Joan? When was he going to stop? If she had any say in the matter, there wasn't going to be any wedding, no, not in her backyard.

Late that night, April 2, 1963, Richard turned his conversation with Joan over in his mind and wrote Mimi a rambling letter:

I'm sitting up in bed, baby, & . . . I can't shake this DOWN feeling. . . . The call from Joanie . . . Everybody has been hung up; and me, I've been in left field alone—hoping with every ounce of life in me that people would start to understand I wasn't only TALKING love, I was in it. . . . I wanted to take YOU girl, from Paris to California. Because California was where yore sister was. . . . No parent things, no hangups, just us, out there, with horses an' dogs an' sun. . . . Thing is, Mishka mine, I'm weary of hopping around the cities of this tired world & not knowing what was happening 'fore I got there. For me alone I guess it's all right but I'm not me alone anymore. I'm with you; with all my soul I'm with you; and I want our start to be a little like we've said it would be. I've put my whole mind & body into making it happen, taking humiliation from your father, rushing a divorce, working at a wheelbarrow full of job-things. But some of it, like you 'n' Joanie, is yore affair more than it can ever be mine, and I can't control it. Nor do I want to. Take my hand a little, baby, and squeeze it some. An' . . . let's do together what we can.

Unsure what to do, Mimi asked her aunt Tia for advice. They went for a walk, smoked a few cigarettes, and talked. "This has gone beyond anything you can change," Tia told her. "Do what you have to do."

Early on an afternoon a few weeks later, Mimi Baez put on a pretty white dress that her friend Wendy Robinson had handed down to her in Belmont, and she took two rings out of her jewelry box: a silver band that had lain in the box for a few years and a gold (or gold-plated) one, another hand-me-down from Wendy, that had always been too big for her. She was going out for a walk, she told her mother. Be back soon.

Mimi took the metro to Costner's apartment, where Richard Fariña was waiting with Tom Costner and Yves Chaix. The men were wearing suits and ties, Fariña's borrowed from Costner for the day. The four of them joked nervously and grinned as they walked a few blocks to the *mairie*, the city hall of the First Arrondissement, located between the Samaritaine and the Louvre, for an appointment they had made with a municipal official. He was a stout little fellow who wore pince-nez eyeglasses. Yves did the talking. Yes, the papers required for marriage seemed to be in order. Richard had the proper documentation from the attorney who had represented him in the Mexican divorce Carolyn Hester had arranged, Amado Jasso Linares of Ciudad Juárez, Chihuahua. Costner had handled the rest of the legal work, and he and Yves would be the witnesses.

The official held an enormous book with both hands and read from it grimly in French. "Say '*oui*,' " Yves told Mimi and Richard. "*Oui.*" "*Oui.*" And they were married.

The four conspirators were about to exit the building when Yves mentioned that the bride and groom had not yet kissed, whereupon Mimi and Richard devoured each other. She neatened her dress in preparation to go home, alone, in time for dinner, when Yves interceded again, insisting that there be some kind of celebration. That role would ordinarily be Richard's, but he seemed atypically quiet all afternoon. "He was rather visibly scared out of his wits, although he was also obviously thrilled," recalled Costner. "I presume the thrill was connected to the fear." At Richard's suggestion, the group hustled to one of Mimi's favorite spots, Le Rigodon (French for bull's-eye), a tearoom in the Place Dauphine. Yves ordered a bottle of champagne, which a waitress had to run out to buy. Since there was no time to chill it, everyone sipped it warm. But Mimi really had to go now, she insisted. She kissed her husband again, and he held her hand as he walked her to the metro station. Richard went back to Costner's to eat with Tom and Yves. Mimi got a scolding for coming home forty-five minutes past dinnertime, had chicken and potatoes with her parents, and did her history homework during the remainder of her wedding night.

I N THE ROCK ERA, popular music always tended to lighten with its listeners' study load. The "summer single," a record geared for teenagers on vacation from high school, became a genre of its own—bright, frothy pop for and usually about cruising, dancing on the beach, and necking under the boardwalk. It was a striking sign of shifts in the teen-culture paradigm that Warner Bros. issued a 45-rpm record of Peter, Paul and Mary singing "Blowin' in the Wind" for the summer of 1963. (Said to be Warner's fastest-moving single to that time, it would sell more than a million copies and reach number two on the pop charts.) Kids seemed to want to do something unusual while school was closed that year: think. (This would be in addition to cruising, dancing, and necking, of course; the Surfaris' "Wipe Out" and Lesley Gore's "Judy's Turn to Cry" accompanied "Blowin' in the Wind" in the top five.) For Albert Grossman, the record signified complementary personal triumphs: another number-two hit (following "Puff the Magic Dragon") for the group he had created and a demonstration of Bob Dylan's potential as a composer that was far more impressive than those acetates he had been mailing to recording artists.

Grossman arranged for Dylan to appear on the same stage as Peter, Paul and Mary just as the group's rendition of "Blowin' in the Wind" began airing on the radio (a month in advance of the record's official release date, June 18). On May 17, 1963, the trio headlined the opening day of the Monterey Folk Festival, a new three-day event spun off from a successful jazz festival, as Newport had been; the following evening Bob Dylan would appear on a bill with the Weavers, the New Lost City Ramblers, and veteran blues singer Mance Lipscomb, among others. This would be the Greenwich Village phenomenon's first appearance in California, as the *Monterey Peninsula Herald* pointed out:

> Bob Dylan, 20, makes his West Coast debut at the festival as a singer, guitarist and harmonica player. Termed the Jimmy Dean of the folk world, Dylan has been called one of the most compelling blues singer[s] recorded. . . . He is noted for his highly colorful style of dress, sporting a "Huck Finn" type of corduroy cap.

Dylan traveled from Los Angeles to Monterey with Victor Maymudes, the founder of L.A.'s pioneering coffeehouse, the Unicorn; twenty-nine and impressively conversant in liberal politics, Eastern thought, beat literature, and everything else modish, he kept Dylan company and attended to professional details under Grossman's auspices. Like many of the men with whom Bob made friends—Van Ronk, von Schmidt, Fariña, Bob Neuwirth—Maymudes was a talker. Dylan seemed to want constant stimulation with minimal expenditure of effort himself. "Bob [was] a very internal being," Maymudes recalled. "When we drove, I don't think he said much of anything to anybody. He was always *processing*." Dylan and Maymudes shared the ride with Jac Holzman of Elektra, and Holzman's colleague Jim Dickson, a personal manager planning to scout the upcoming festival for new clients; Maymudes, Holzman, and Dickson took turns driving Jim's overridden Ford

Falcon, which was molting parts on highway 101, while Bob quietly finger-picked his guitar in the backseat. "He was very private and with-drawn," Holzman said. "I think he was writing songs while we were talking. I remember wondering if I was going to hear my own conversation in the next song of his." On a roadside in Buellton, the crew had lunch at Andersen's Pea Soup, which provided all you could eat for fifty cents. "Dylan was determined to get his money's worth," Holzman said. "He forced the stuff down." Back on the road, Bob would occasionally hum a melody idea softly, and Jac mistook the sound for vomiting.

Joan Baez was waiting for Dylan in Monterey. Taking him up on his offer to sing something together at the festival, she had learned "With God on Our Side" from one of the demonstration records Grossman had sent Manny Greenhill. The two of them reunited backstage, both acting cool among the dozens of assembled musicians, friends, and members of the festival staff, and they ran through the song together quickly. When it came time for Bob's fifteen minutes onstage, Barbara Dane, the festival's host, introduced Dylan as the man who had written Peter, Paul and Mary's new single. Scattered mumbles. He shuffled out and did three of his hardest-hitting protest songs: "Talkin' John Birch Paranoid Blues," "A Hard Rain's a-Gonna Fall," and "Masters of War." Yet the Monterey audience, which was largely unfamiliar with Dylan's style, re-sponded poorly, talking loudly over his singing. "He went over very badly," Dane recalled. "He didn't play very long, and it felt like he was on for an hour. I think people were laughing." To Jac Holzman, "They just seemed in shock. The West Coast people weren't prepared for how he sounded."

Joan walked out, with no introduction, to murmurs of surprise and eager applause. As Bob began strumming the opening chords of "With God on Our Side," the crowd quieted. Baez, standing alongside him, inched near his microphone to make an announcement. She wanted everybody to know, she said, that this young man had something to say. He was singing about important issues, and he was speaking for her and for everyone who wanted a better world. They should listen, she said— she ordered them, nearly: Listen! Dylan began singing, "Oh, my name it is nothin' / my age it means less . . . ," and Baez joined in, singing harmony. "I had barely finished memorizing [the song], and the [weather] was very hot," Joan recalled. "There was perspiration running down the small of my back and behind my knees. I was nervous, excited, and exhilarated." Their voices were odd together, a mismatch—salt pork and meringue; but the tension between their styles made their presence together all the more compelling.

"They were a mysterious thing together," Barbara Dane said. "Her fans couldn't figure out what he was doing there. People who saw Bobby as the hip new thing didn't understand what he was doing with Joan Baez. Everybody was interested. 'What's this? I don't know, but it's great.' " They left the stage with 20,000 people cheering.

The following day, Joan and Bob watched the festival's last performers—old-time music veterans Doc Watson and Clarence Ashley, gospel singer Bessie Jones, and some others—and talked. They strolled part of the grounds (twenty-three rolling acres of oaks, twisting Monterey cypress trees, and lawns), gorging on hot dogs and laughing at the amateurs in the "song swap" under the concession tent. Bess Hawes, who sang in the "Gospel Get-Together" that evening, saw Joan and Bob huddling together and assumed they were longtime lovers. Although this was essentially their first date, Baez and Dylan appeared intimately attached, and Joan's prominence (especially there on the West Coast) ensured that everyone noticed. One of the Monterey newspapers published a schedule of events, printed next to a news item about a visit to New York by Princess Grace and Prince Rainier of Monaco; the former movie star and her royal husband were attending a Broadway show during the last night of the Monterey festival, but they could not have sparked more fervent curiosity than Baez and Dylan did at the hot-dog stand.

Bob accepted Joan's invitation to visit her house in the Carmel Highlands. She drove him in her XKE, and she cooked a pot of stew. He played and sang his songs. They sat on the wide-plank pine floor in the living room, surrounded by windows that restrained encroaching eucalyptus trees on all sides. Dylan taught her the chords to half a dozen or so of his songs and wrote down the lyrics for her. They tried singing most of them together, experimenting with arrangements and harmonies. "It was very exciting but challenging," Joan recalled, "because he never wanted to do the same thing the same way twice."

After a couple of days together, playing music almost constantly, Joan found herself captivated equally by the power of Dylan's music (especially his protest songs) and the enigmatic fragility of its composer. "I was falling in love," she said. "When I heard those songs, I melted. They were manna from heaven to me, and he was so shy and fragile. I wanted to mother him, and he seemed to want it and need it. He seemed so helpless."

Dylan's feelings toward Joan were unclear. Back in New York, Bob had begun seeing Suze Rotolo again after her return from Italy, although their relationship was no longer what it had been. Joan could only assume or hope that Bob had affection for her and that perhaps it was growing quietly. "We didn't need to make love," she said. "The music seemed like enough at the time." Like Scheherazade, Dylan may have called upon the muse to postpone something for which he was not quite ready.

Reinvigorated by their musical collaborations, Joan told Bob she had a concert tour of the Northeast coming up and she wanted him to join her on it. She was now singing to audiences of 10,000 and more, she explained. She could introduce him to all those people. Bob said hey, yeah, cool—and they had a deal. Joan drove him back to Monterey, so he could connect with Dickson, Holzman, and Maymudes and ride back to Los Angeles.

Joan seemed obsessed with Bob Dylan after he left. She walked to the Williamses' house, the town square of the Highlands, and announced to the neighborhood that she had discovered a genius. Perfectly accustomed to having great minds wandering the vicinity, Cynthia Williams told her that "he sounds quite worth listening to, if he's remotely as brilliant as you say he is." As for Bob, he sat in the back of Dickson's Ford playing his guitar quietly again, and he never mentioned Joan Baez during the seven-hour ride to Los Angeles. "Did he seem any different on the way back?" said Jac Holzman. "Was he affected in any way by his visitation with the queen? To tell you the truth, we didn't even know he stayed with her. He didn't utter her name. He was exactly the same—quietly working on his music. Whatever he was thinking, he was putting into his songs."

WITH THE HELP of her secret husband, who wrote her book reports, Mimi graduated from her high school correspondence course in early June 1963. She put her new free time to use, practicing the guitar in earnest again. Joan occasionally mailed some albums that record companies had sent to her, and Mimi looked forward to receiving the latest batch to hear what American folk musicians were doing, learn songs, and pick up riffs. One of the records her sister sent her that month was *The Freewheelin' Bob Dylan*, which had been released on May 27. Joan had clipped a note on the sleeve: "My new boyfriend." The announcement seemed to Mimi like a competitive taunt; when she had met Bob at Gerde's Folk City, he had flirted with her, not Joan. It was puzzling, too; if Joan was Bob's girlfriend, who was the cute brunette on the album jacket, walking arm in arm with Dylan through the snow?

If the cover photograph of Dylan and Suze Rotolo on Jones Street the previous winter was out of date, the album captured Bob well in his most recent incarnation, a socially conscientious composer. The follow-up to Bob's unsuccessful Columbia debut had been a long time coming. Recorded over a period of twelve months, it began under John Hammond's supervision as a collection of traditional songs and Guthrie-influenced apprenticeship pieces ("Sally Gal," "Ramblin' Gamblin' Willie," "Talkin' Bear Mountain Picnic Massacre Blues") on April 24, 1962, and it ended under producer Tom Wilson (sent in by a frustrated David Kapralik) as a portfolio of mature original songs ("Blowin' in the Wind," "Don't Think Twice, It's All Right" "A Hard Rain's a-Gonna

Fall," "Masters of War," "Girl from the North Country," and seven more, plus one adaptation of a romantic blues by Henry Thomas, "Honey, Just Allow Me One More Chance") on April 24, 1963. It is a thoroughly persuasive declaration of Dylan's seriousness of purpose—ambitious, musically varied and nuanced, and literate, a demonstration of Dylan's ability not only to change but to grow. Could the singer and musician executing the delicate melody and graceful, intricate guitar patterns of "Don't Think Twice" really be the same one who scratched out "You're No Good" a year earlier? Could the author of the dense, impressionistic lyrics of "Hard Rain" really be the kid who used to keep singing, "Hey, hey, Woody Guthrie, I wrote you a song"?

Disciplined and pointed, the album is "freewheelin' " mainly in its approach to genre. At least two of the tracks make nods to rock and roll (past and future): "Corrina, Corrina," in its use of rock instrumentation, a full band with piano and drums; and "Masters of War," in its driving beat and ranting lyrics, spewed out. Lyrically, the songs are personal ("Girl from the North Country," "Don't Think Twice") as well as social and political, although reviews of the album tended to concentrate almost exclusively on the protest material. ("He stands outside his problems and writes a credo for people to live by," wrote Linda Solomon in *The Village Voice*. "The emotional understatement in his voice emphasizes the power of his lyrics and his genuine concern with the state of the world.") Moreover, virtually all of the songs blur distinctions between popular music and literature, at least in intent, if not always in execution. Dylan was clearly seeing himself as a writer, not solely as a songwriter, with literary aspirations and a flexible, playful conception of category. As Nat Hentoff quotes him in the record's liner notes, "Anything I can sing, I call a song. Anything I can't sing, I call a poem. Anything I can't sing or anything that's too long to be a poem, I call a novel. But my novels don't have the usual story lines. They're about my feelings at a certain place at a certain time."

Richard Fariña, who was working on songs, poems, and a novel of his own, took the album as a challenge. When Mimi played it for him, he seemed to her impressed by Dylan's achievement and inspired to try besting him. Richard said something about this being a good time to be a poet, and he asked her if she thought her guitar playing was up to the kinds of songs Bob was doing.

A ROUND MIDNIGHT on June 12, 1963, just hours after President Kennedy finished his first nationally televised address on civil rights, a white segregationist murdered Medgar Evers, a field representative for the NAACP in Jackson, Mississippi. The depravity of the killing, Evers shot in the back on the front lawn of his home, provoked immediate and widespread outrage. Bob Dylan watched the news about Evers on television while he was visiting Peter Yarrow in Woodstock, and he wrote a ballad about it, "Only a Pawn in Their Game." As in his earlier story-songs about slain men, "The Death of Emmett Till," "The Ballad of Donald White," and "Who Killed Davey Moore?" Dylan portrayed Evers reverentially; but he went further this time, using Evers as a touchstone to explore the web of culpability in a world fraught with racial conflict and poverty. The opening words of the song describe the killer (Byron De La Beckwith) taking aim at Evers from behind a bush, only to conclude, "But he can't be blamed / He's only a pawn in their game." Dylan continued to exonerate a southern politician preaching racial superiority; in fact, he devoted three out of his five verses to a sympathetic treatment of poor whites in a song titularly about the death of a Negro martyr. There are no easy answers in "Only a Pawn in Their Game," not even on the matter of "their" identity. Instead of formula sentiment and finger-pointing, "Only a Pawn in Their Game," raises thorny questions: Where does social responsibility begin and end? Can exploitation be excused? When does the one in power become a pawn?

These are themes that would infuse Dylan's own life as his relationship with Joan Baez progressed.

On Friday, July 26, nine weeks after Joan joined Bob on stage in Monterey, they reconnected at the 1963 Newport Folk Festival. It was the first event after a two-year hiatus during which George Wein had overseen the transfer of authority over the festival to the Newport Folk Foundation, a not-for-profit group run by a board of directors comprising folk musicians (Pete Seeger, Theodore Bikel, Bill Clifton, Clarence Cooper, Erik Darling, Jean Ritchie, and Peter Yarrow). Wein, who retained an active role as "technical producer" (and the option to reclaim the Newport Folk Festival in the future, should the foundation opt to relinquish it), marveled at the failure of the event to function on a not-for-profit basis. "Of all times to give the thing up," he said, "I had to do it at the peak of the folk boom." An estimated 47,000 paid attendees and another 5,000 latecomers allowed in for free overflowed the three-day festival—more than five times the capacity of the festival's main venue, Freebody Park, and 17,000 more than had come to Wein's for-profit Newport Jazz Festival three weeks earlier. Seventy acts were scheduled to perform over three days and nights, so many that at least ten performers appeared in each evening's main concert. (Under Seeger's decree that all the performers be paid equally—fifty dollars apiece, plus food, lodging, and some expenses—the foundation would end up with a $70,000 surplus to spend on scholarships, library endowments, and preparation for the next year's festival.)

Baez returned to the site of her breakthrough in the role Bob Gibson had played in 1959: "What I wanted to do was help Bobby," she said. Dylan was hardly an unknown; Peter, Paul and Mary, whose record of "Blowin' the Wind" was high on the charts, had been raving about him in concerts around the country. He was all the talk at Newport, and the festival program (edited by Robert Shelton under one of his pseudonyms, because he was assigned to cover the event for *The New York Times*) devoted a page and a half to a rambling prose-poem by Dylan, "—for Dave Glover." (Written in loping Okie speech patterns, the piece is a somewhat defensive rumination on traditional folk music and Dylan's shift into topical songwriting—"An all I'm sayin is 'at I gotta make my own statement about this day.") Joan, however, was now such an institution that her influence permeated the festival. When Boston radio journalist Robert J. Lurtsema approached her near one of the Newport stages to request an interview, he was told, "I'm sorry, I'm not Joan Baez." He looked closely and realized he was not talking to Joan at all, but to another woman who had modeled every aspect of her appearance on Baez. Lurtsema glanced around and saw Joan Baezes everywhere.

Bob and Joan opened and closed the festival together, singing the same song on both occasions. On the first day, Baez participated in an afternoon panel discussion and song demonstration on the topic "Whither Folk Music?" conducted at the Newport Casino Tennis Club. She surprised the audience of about five hundred by introducing Bob Dylan to join her in a song she said best represented the current state of folk music, "With God on Our Side." While honoring Dylan, the gesture made a statement about Baez as well: she was more than a famous face and the star of Newport four years earlier; if folk was heading witherward to Bob Dylan, it was going toward, not away from, Joan Baez. She was connected to him.

That evening Dylan performed a brief set of his own, sardined in a ludicrously overpacked bill (Bill Monroe and His Bluegrass Boys, Doc Watson, Brownie McGhee and Sonny Terry, Peter, Paul and Mary, and five other acts). Peter Yarrow, who was serving double duty as a master of ceremonies and performer, ended the concert by asking the audience to sing "Blowin' in the Wind" with his trio, and he called a select group of compatriots onstage to join them: Seeger, Bikel, the Freedom Singers (Rutha Harris, Bernice Johnson, Charles Neblett, and Cordell Hull Reagon), Baez, and Dylan. As an encore, they all locked hands and sang "We Shall Overcome," swaying in time. The image of this assemblage at Newport would become one of the primary symbols of the 1960s folk revival: the old guard joined with the new, the commercial and the Communist, black and white, leading a sea of young people in a sing-along for freedom. "I think of that highlight of the 1963 Newport Folk Festival, that stunning, stirring ringing out of "We Shall Overcome'—as the apogee of the folk movement," said Theodore Bikel. "There was no point more suffused with hope for the future." Yet the moment had

another dimension. Despite the defiant words the group was sing
civil rights anthem adapted from Charles Tindley's 1903 spiritua
Overcome Some Day") and the physical posture it adopted (a line of
solidarity traditionally employed to resist police), this was as much a
crow of triumph as it was a rallying cry. The performers holding hands
onstage could well have been singing, "We *Have* Overcome." From the
Newport stage on July 28, 1963, Seeger was essentially proclaiming the
triumph of the political folk diaspora. It had overcome the blacklist, television, the Hit Parade, Tin Pan Alley, and rock and roll; it had never
been so prominent—indeed, no other music in America was as popular
as folk.

On Sunday Joan Baez closed the final concert of the festival. She
wore a simple knee-length white dress that clung to her body, and she
sounded as stunningly unadorned as she looked. At the conclusion of a
set peppered with the Bob Dylan songs she had been learning, including
a pointed "Don't Think Twice, It's All Right," she thanked the audience
effusively. "Tonight is one of the most beautiful nights I've seen," Joan
said with a broad smile. "I'm all up here with it. I feel sort of like exploding." She bounded offstage and came right back with Bob Dylan in
tow. He was wearing the same short-sleeve khaki work shirt and grimy
blue jeans he had had on two days earlier, when Joan introduced him at
the "Whither Folk Music?" workshop, and they sang "With God on Our
Side" again. It was the last song of the festival, the final impression made
upon the 13,000 listeners at Freebody Park, the sixty-eight other musicians, and the press. As Robert Shelton and several others wrote in virtually identical words, "Baez, the reigning queen of folk music, had named
Dylan the crown prince."

Backstage during the festival, Bob spent much of his free time playing with a twenty-foot black leather bullwhip. Geno Foreman, Joan's
devilishly eccentric old friend from Cambridge, had brought it to Newport; it was his idea of provocative fun. Dylan coveted it, so Foreman
gave it to him, and for three days Bob carried it with him, even to the
pool at the Hotel Viking, and practiced making cracks and whipping
nearby targets such as folding chairs and guitar cases, when they were

empty, as a rule. The sight of Dylan going through motions usually associated with lion tamers and practitioners of sadomasochism surely ran counter to his popular image as a sensitive folk poet. What was he doing? "The whip? Well . . . ," Baez said. "What is a whip usually used for?" Asserting authority, training circus animals, spurring beasts of burden, punishment, threatening, inciting fear. "That just about covers it. All of the above." Boyishly shy and subordinate to Joan on the Newport stage, he apparently needed to show the folk community that there were other sides to Bob Dylan.

Joan stayed on the East Coast for the next few weeks, to be with Bob. On the way from New England to Manhattan, they rested for a day and a night at Albert Grossman's house in Bearsville, New York, near Woodstock. But they spent most of their time together in social settings. On July 30 Dylan videotaped performances of two of his songs, "Only a Pawn in Their Game" and "Blowin' in the Wind," for a local New York City television program on topical music, *Songs of Freedom*; Joan accompanied Bob to the studio and whispered with him between takes. On two evenings around then, Joan brought Bob to the homes of the activists Bernard Brightman and Corliss Lamont for fund-raising events to benefit the Emergency Civil Liberties Committee. On at least one other evening, they visited Clark Foreman at his grand apartment on Riverside Drive and talked politics all night. As they began keeping regular company, Baez and Dylan offered an image of courtship that was notably different from the dream dates at beaches and amusement parks in the teen movies that summer—*Operation Bikini* with Frankie Avalon and Tab Hunter, and *Fun in Acapulco*, starring Elvis. Joan and Bob showed that social and political ideas could stimulate and bring people of their generation together as well as (or at least in addition to) swimsuits and thrill rides.

Their peers were aggressively curious about the nature of this relationship. One night in early August, Joan and Bob showed up at Gerde's together, and so many of their Village friends seemed fixated on them that Joan excused herself and went to the rest room. She returned with a tablecloth rolled up under her blouse, looking pregnant. "They were driving us crazy," she said. "Everybody wanted to know what was going on between us. So now they knew—we were going to have a baby!" With all eyes on Joan and Bob, it was pointless for anyone else to try performing in their presence; they took the stage and sang a few songs, including a new tune of Dylan's that Joan had never heard before she found herself singing it, "Troubled and I Don't Know Why." A comic send-up of teen angst, it was lighter than anything they had sung together publicly—or for that matter, than anything either of them had ever recorded individually—the first public sign that, while saving the world, they were having some fun together:

What did the television squall?
What did the television squall?
Well, it roared and it boomed
And it bounced around the room
And it never said nothin' at all

As she had offered to do when they were in the Carmel Highlands, Baez brought Dylan along on her summer tour of the Northeast. Their understanding was that he would appear as a surprise guest, unbilled. After all, the four concerts she was scheduled to give in outdoor arenas and halls with 10,000 to 15,000 seats were all sold out in advance; Bob Dylan's name would contribute negligibly and perhaps even put off Baez's fans. "It would have just added confusion to put his name up there," Joan said. "My audience wanted to hear me."

The first of the concerts took place at the Convention Hall in Asbury Park, New Jersey, a majestic showplace at the center of a mile-long boardwalk, on August 10, high season for the Atlantic Coast resorts; Joan followed Frankie Valli and the Four Seasons by a couple of weeks and preceded Peter, Paul and Mary on the center's schedule. An hour's bus ride from New York City, just right for a weekend day trip, Asbury Park had more than forty concert and music halls, nightclub stages, and dinner theaters in the summer of 1963, and Joan Baez drew one of the largest crowds of the summer concert season. Ushers were still setting up seats to accommodate the audience of more than 5,000 when Joan began her first song. She asked them kindly to finish before she would continue singing; then she performed, alone with her guitar on the great Beaux Arts stage, for about an hour and gave a short speech about the man who wrote a number of the songs she had been doing, Bob Dylan. It was a refined variation of her lectures to the audiences at Monterey and Newport: You might not know his name, she said, but you should. Here's a young man with something important to say. . . . Bob dawdled out with his guitar to respectful, tentative applause. Joan gave him a kiss on the cheek and walked offstage, laying Dylan and her audience in each other's hands.

He looked terrified. "I remember him coming out with his humble attitude," Joan recalled. "He was really scared, and he couldn't hide it. He would never admit that, but he was scared. So he did his whole shy little poet thing." While Bob performed three or four songs (the one review of the concert did not cite the titles he sang, and there is no known recording), Joan beamed near the backstage steps. A reporter for the *Asbury Park Evening Press* was startled to notice the woman he had just seen perform so gravely now dancing by herself as Dylan sang.

"She was getting a kick outta having me coming up—baggy elephant me, come up and sing my songs, which nobody had ever heard before," Bob remembered. "And her audience, which are just like pieces of wheat, anyway, man—when they heard my songs, they were just flabbergasted."

Indeed, Baez's fans were not very receptive to Dylan, at first. Some talked while he was singing—an act of treachery in a setting where the ushers were prohibited from making a sound during the performance. A few even booed. "It was exciting for me to bring him out, but it was also a big challenge, because my audience didn't like it," Joan said. "They didn't want this scruffy little guy out there, singing off key. Some people would heckle him, and I would come out from the wings like a schoolteacher-type and scold them—'You're very lucky to be hearing him,' that kind of thing. 'You'll be hearing more of him. You'll be sorry!' "

Baez and Dylan were better received when they sang duets. In Asbury Park, Joan joined Bob on "Blowin' in the Wind," which seemed to click with the audience (surely in large part because everyone knew the song). For the subsequent shows—at the Yale Bowl on August 13; in Boston three days later; and in Forest Hills, Queens, on August 17—Joan expanded the portion of the concert she performed with Dylan from one to three or four songs. (At the Forest Hills tennis stadium, the only one of these concerts known to have been recorded, Dylan sang two solos, "Only a Pawn in Their Game" and "A Hard Rain's a-Gonna Fall"; Joan and Bob followed with three duets, "Blowin' in the Wind," "Troubled and I Don't Know Why," and "Farewell.") Their voices and styles seemed elementally incompatible, Joan with her ethereal tone and tight vibrato, Dylan talk-singing in earthy yelps; together they sounded like Glinda, the Good Witch of the North, and the Mayor of the Munchkin City. But they functioned more like another movie couple, Fred Astaire and Ginger Rogers. Joan seemed to soften Bob, and he emboldened her; as the Hollywood fan magazines used to say about Astaire and Rogers, Baez gave Dylan class, and Bob gave Joan sex appeal. Doing harmony with Baez, Dylan sang more melodically, applying himself to hitting the notes (or coming closer than usual), and he used warm, sweet parts of his voice that he had been keeping secret from audiences since he used to sing Buddy Holly songs in high school. At the same time, Joan's singing intensified; to be in sync with Bob, she adopted a charged, emphatic style of phrasing, and she abandoned her fixation on purity of tone; Joan's voice had not sounded this natural and unaffected, this appealingly imperfect, since she had taken up singing professionally. They both sounded like teenagers again.

Audiences responded to something about the combination of Baez and Dylan beyond the music, too. As Dylan said, "Now, me and Joan had this *thing*." But what was it exactly—sexual magnetism? There was that, certainly, although the romantically linked (and soon to be married) duo of Ian Tyson and Sylvia Fricker exuded far more heat than Joan and Bob. The chemistry between Baez and Dylan was more unconventional. As soloists, each of them had always had a public image that was elementally desexualized and androgynous—Joan the virgin enchantress, Bob the boy poet. The idea of either of them sexually engaged was not so much titillating as it was startling and puzzling: How will *this* work? Moreover, with Joan the more successful of the two, helping Bob by toting him along on her tour, the traditional gender roles were reversed, further warping this sexual picture.

Their union clearly benefited Dylan, as Bob acknowledged. "She brought me up, man," he said. "She recorded my songs, and she was . . . important on that level." John Cooke, who saw Baez and Dylan perform together on several occasions, elaborated, "Lo and behold, they joined forces, and the effect was far greater than the sum of the parts. But it was very clear that Bob was the primary beneficiary of this deal. What happens when you're this kid from Minnesota, and you've been walking around the streets of New York with Suze Rotolo, and you've had your first couple albums come out, and you're having trouble making it as a folksinger because your voice is so weird, and all of a sudden the opportunity for a quantum leap comes along? This gorgeous woman who is the icon of another aspect of this music latches on to you and says, 'I'll be your everything, including being your lover.' She adopted him. She found this guy who gave voice to all that powerful stuff, and she nurtured him in that role . . . because, by her lending her backing to Dylan's music, all of a sudden it attracted a much wider audience. It was like she gave it a stamp of approval and said this is important. He made out on every level." Still, their appearances together elevated both Baez and Dylan in public esteem. Reviewing their performance before 14,700 at the Forest Hills tennis stadium in Queens on Saturday, August 17, Robert Shelton wrote,

> Her enthusiasm [for Dylan] was contagious, [and] she has never seemed quite so relaxed and warm in a performance. . . . Miss Baez's ability to hold and move an audience by herself is widely known. To have her so closely align herself with Mr. Dylan's charismatic poetry resulted in an unforgettable evening.

Offstage Joan and Bob were playful and tender with each other—again, like teenagers. To warm up for a performance, they liked to sing pop-radio hits by two-part harmony teams, especially the Everly Brothers' "Bye Bye Love" (a rock and roll song about unrequited love—fun, but with an underlying layer of unease). Baez doted on Dylan, patting down his mutinous hair and tuning his guitar for him between sets; at least once she pulled off the khaki shirt he always wore and hand-washed it in his dressing-room sink. When they were with their friends or associates, they always seemed to be whispering conspiratorially and bursting into laughter for reasons no one around them understood. With Bob, Joan seemed to have found a way to enjoy the glass cage, pointing and laughing at the world around them. They are almost unrecognizable in the photographs that capture them amusing each other: exploding in open, toothy grins, their faces looked unnaturally contorted. When they were alone, though, they tended to be quiet and showed their gentle sides. A colleague of Bob's saw them from a distance in a hallway, waiting to go onstage together; they were sitting side by side in wooden rehearsal chairs. Bob had his head nestled on Joan's shoulder, and she was gazing at him as she caressed his hair. One of Joan's friends once began to open the door to Baez's dressing room and saw Joan and Bob slow dancing to a pop ballad on the radio.

"At that time, and it wasn't a long time, when he was on my tour with me and we were getting close, it was very sweet between us," said Joan. "I was very nurturing, and he was incredibly vulnerable and endearing. We didn't clash much at all, which is amazing, considering that we both had egos—and when we did, it didn't last long. A lovely thing was happening, and I didn't want it to end." After the concert in Boston, an outdoor affair at the Boston Common, Bob and Joan had a squabble over something small. They went to Club 47 together that night, barely talking to each other, and took a table. The evening's performer was Ray Pong, a Dartmouth-educated microbiologist and part-time folksinger; noticing Joan in the audience, he asked her if she would like to come up and do a song, but she declined. He asked Bob, in turn, and Dylan accepted. Bob struggled to work Pong's guitar strap over his shoulder; it was too tight for him and pulled the guitar up to his chest. Making do, Dylan crouched a bit and sang a couple of songs. Then he lit a cigarette and started a third song, singing through the corner of his mouth as he smoked: "It ain't no use to sit and wonder why, babe . . ."—"Don't Think Twice, It's All Right." As he continued the lament to a doomed romance (his own "Bye Bye Love"), Joan walked to the stage and sat in a chair next to Bob, on his right as he stood singing. "It was difficult to watch," said Richard Waterman, who tried taking some pictures of Joan and Bob that night. "It was kind of uncomfortable to see that she had come up so sadly. He was kind of angry, and she was upset and reaching out. It was the kind of thing you thought you should turn away from—you shouldn't see—and you couldn't take your eyes away from." Joan picked a tambourine off the floor and played it softly, tapping it against the side of the chair with her right hand. With her left hand, she began slowly rubbing the small of Dylan's back. Bob continued the song without acknowledging her, and Joan closed her eyes as he sang.

FOR THE YEAR AND A HALF he lived in Europe, Richard Fariña felt marooned by failure. " 'I can't go back to America yet,' " Carolyn Hester recalled him saying. " 'You can go back because you have your record and all that. But I can't go back, because I don't have a victory.' He had this thing about having a victory." Although his novel remained unfinished and not accepted for publication, and his album with Eric von Schmidt was yet to be released, Richard bought two tickets to return to New York on the *France* (a different ship from the *Île de France*, which had been decommissioned in 1959); he and Mimi Baez were going to have a wedding in California, no small triumph for either of them.

On the morning of the day they set sail, June 21, 1963, Mimi and

Richard mailed thirty or forty museum postcards of *Les fiancés à la Tour Eiffel*, Chagall's montage of a young bride and groom surrounded by peasant musicians. Each had a handwritten message in keeping with the folksy cheer of the artwork: "Hey guys," Richard scrawled on the card to Costner and Yves Chaix, "come to a wedding. Ahem. ñ & friend." Mimi and Richard packed virtually everything they owned—thirteen bags of clothing, records, books, and musical instruments—and Big Joan, who was still unaware that her daughter and Richard were already married, drove them to the train station for the hundred-mile ride to the piers at Le Havre. Albert Baez had, as always, gone to work that morning without saying good-bye to his wife and daughter. His avoidance, however, stung Mimi no less than her mother's dismay over her plan to marry Richard. As they hugged good-bye, Big Joan gave Mimi an envelope, which she opened on the train. It contained a little money and a note: "It's so hard to let go of you. I'm so sorry you're doing this. I know you think this is what you need. It will leave a deep hole in my heart." Mimi read it and cried for most of the next two days.

The Fariñas lived as husband and wife for the first time during their five-day transatlantic cruise. (If Richard had not really been born at sea, at least his marriage to Mimi was.) Reverting to their betrothal charade when they landed in New York, they dove into a swirl of introductory encounters with various friends and relations. Mimi's sister Pauline and her husband, the abstract painter Brice Marden, had recently moved to Manhattan and were waiting for them at Pier 88 on West 48th Street—a long wait, while customs inspected the contents of every bag Mimi and Richard shipped; Fariña's talk of involvement with the IRA may well have filtered to the American authorities. Primed by Joan and her parents to reject Richard, Pauline greeted him with dutiful contempt. "Oh, I was ready to hate that man," she recalled. "That terrible older man who was making off with my younger sister. Oh, I hated him so bad the first time I met him. I was ready to feed him mustard! And he knew it, and he was an absolutely magical wizard. Oh, he was amazing, 'cause he was just as warm and wonderful as could be. He was so interested in me. We drove them where they were going [to visit Richard's family in Brooklyn], and when we waved good-bye, I said to myself, 'What a nice guy.' " Mimi faced similar resistance from Richard's father, who was struggling to disentangle his loyalties; "I took Carolyn in as my daughter," he said, "and I didn't know anything about this [new] girl, except she was the famous singer's sister. I didn't know what Richie was doing. But he was my son." Only Richard's new stepmother, Lillian, a second wife herself, encouraged Mimi and Richard wholeheartedly. "They lived in this very plastic environment, but Lillian was just so loving and caring," Mimi said, "and I needed a mom pretty badly." While Richard was out of the house, collecting some housewares and odds and ends that he and Carolyn Hester had put in a storage center before moving to London, Mimi and Lillian sat on the steps of the Farinas' small back porch, smoking cigarettes, drinking 7&7s, and trading loving complaints about their men.

Using a "drive-away" service, as he had on his honeymoon with Carolyn Hester, Richard took Mimi across the country in a 1956 Falcon ("pisspoorly named," Richard wrote to von Schmidt) that threw a rod in Ohio and burst a pump in Winnemuca, Nevada; Mimi, who had not learned how to drive, wrestled with the road maps. After nearly a week, they reached the Carmel Highlands and began settling in, Mimi staying with her sister, Richard in a one-room cabin about thirty feet behind Joan's house on Brett Weston's property. Joan wasn't home; she was with Dylan on the East Coast. When she finally arrived shortly after the August 17 concert in Forest Hills, Joan made an appointment with Mimi and Richard to discuss these plans of theirs to get married. They agreed to meet at the Village Corner restaurant in Carmel, at three o'clock, immediately following Joan's weekly psychotherapy appointment; an outdoor café in the downtown shopping district, the Corner was easily the most public location in Carmel. Joan was waiting near the low, open fireplace on the restaurant's patio when she spotted her sister and Richard approaching her. "[I remember] being very huffy at this man who was going to marry my sister," Joan recalled. "He had to stretch it to win me over. Whoever it was wasn't going to be good enough for my sister. And I think his assumption was that he was part of the family, bang, even probably before they were married. But there he was, and the picture I have of him crossing the street was just cocksure—I'm the guy you've been waiting for, you know,' and I thought, 'Well, fuck you. You've got to jump over a few hurdles to get in this family.' And that's what it was, that he didn't have any idea of being cautious." Joan gave her sister a long, tight hug and Richard her hand.

The three of them sat talking for about an hour. Mimi and Richard had their arms locked the whole time; Joan was glacial and spoke with measured force. Are you really going to do this? And why? Fariña responded breezily. *Most definitely. We're in love.* How do you intend to live? *Very happily.* What do you want? *Right now, a sandwich. Let's get some menus. Are you hungry? I'm starved. . . .*

"He was used to coming up against adversity much more than either of us," Mimi said. "It didn't scare him away. I think Joan respected that." Indeed, although Joan kept up a resistant front, Richard was beginning to wear her down. "He was just so cheery and winning," said Joan. "That was the beginning of changing me around toward him." Before the wedding, planned for Saturday, August 24, at a small house in Portola Valley that Big Joan and Albert Baez had rented for the summer, Joan agreed to be Mimi's maid of honor.

Richard's best man, Thomas Pynchon, had been living in seclusion in Mexico City since leaving Boeing and Seattle in 1962 to write full time. With the publication of *V.* that spring, Pynchon seemed to burst upon the literary world as suddenly, magnificently, and disruptively as Joan Baez had upon the world of popular music; he had the success of Richard's fantasies. (The *Atlantic Review* predicted, "This work may well stand as one of the very best works of the century"; *V.* would win the William Faulkner Foundation First Novel Award.) At the same time, Pynchon's increasingly notorious secrecy (refusing to reveal his whereabouts, make public appearances, do interviews, be photographed, and so on) was giving him a reputation as exactly the sort of genius mystery man that Fariña had been trying to become through years of self-dramatization.

Richard, who thrived on attention, seemed to Pynchon dumbfounded by his old roommate's fear of its harmful effects. As Pynchon recalled (later, in a letter to Mimi), "I know it's dumb to have an anti-photograph Thing, but it's how I am. Dick used to kid me about it—what's the matter, you afraid people are going to stick pins, pour aqua regia? So how could I tell him yeah, yeah, right, you got it."

Pynchon entrusted Fariña with his precious secret addresses and phone numbers, and they kept in touch fairly regularly; Mimi would recall Richard calling him from Paris, using phone booths so Costner would not see Pynchon's home number in Mexico City on the telephone bill. They discussed the writing life, exchanging thoughts and criticism as they had in College Town, although Pynchon always remained the upperclassman. Fariña sent Pynchon a draft of his novel as early as April 1963, just as Pynchon's own first novel was being published; by his references to *V.* in letters, Fariña seems to have read a manuscript or proofs of Pynchon's book as well. "I heard them on the phone, and I remember thinking how grown up and what a comrade and how thoughtful that these two guys would get on the phone and ask each other's opinion," said Mimi. "They were tight, they were established friends, they obviously thought they both knew what they were talking about. They were reading each other's stuff and asking questions over the phone. They both had literary opinions about one another. I felt happy that he had someone he trusted in the literary world."

On his part, Pynchon recalled (again, in a letter written later to Mimi), "I wish I could tell you all the things I owe him, things I took from him . . . things both personal and writerly, so I could be worth his friendship, so we could continue some kind of dialogue as writers." Elaborating (years after that), he added, "If I [said] I took things from him, and that he would begin to appear in my writing, I must have meant that if I could somehow manage to be less remote in my work, more open to myself, to experience and so on, why I would owe this to Fariña more than to anybody else."

Having no driver's license, Pynchon traveled from Mexico (with a stop of unknown duration in Los Angeles or thereabouts) by bus. He arrived at the Western Greyhound Station in Pacific Grove, a few miles outside of Carmel, in the third week of August. Mimi and Richard had arranged for him to stay in a guest cottage that one of their friends, Colleen Creedon, had behind her house in the Carmel Highlands. Pynchon and Fariña spent a couple of afternoons catching up, drinking, trading thoughts on books they had read (both liked Oakley Hall's literary Western *Warlock*), and discussing Fariña's novel. While he was initially put off by the book's creative appropriation of some events and figures from Cornell, Pynchon was impressed by Fariña's achievement. He took it seriously enough to probe the work critically with Richard—so critically that Fariña mistook his response as disapproval. As Pynchon later clarified in a letter to Richard, "Did my reaction in Carmel seem less [than] enthusiastic? I was being analytical then. Because you had asked me to. And there is that bit of the nasty/analytical to us all, right? Not to mention, having been peripherally There Then, the temptation is to read it as a roman à clef, which of course it never was." Reporting on the book to Michael Curtis, Pynchon joked, "Reading it you feel like a Spaniard watching Charlton Heston play el Cid, or a Jew watching him play Moses, if you dig me. The protagonist, oddly enough, is a swarthy, heavy-set Greek named Gnossos, a transformation most shrinks I am sure would be beguiled by, not to mention us ordinary onlookers. This all sounds more wiseassed than is intended. It is, all sarcasm aside, a damn good novel, at least in the version I read in Carmel the drunken week before Fariña's boda."

On the evening of Wednesday, August 21, three days prior to the wedding, Fariña and Pynchon went to the opening of the Monterey County Fair, a five-day event in the earthy tradition of John Steinbeck's Monterey, with Joan, her friend and secretary (and sometime lover) Kim Chappell, a male date of Kim's named Marty something, the Baez sisters' old Cambridge friend Betsy Siggins, and Colleen Creedon's fifteen-year-old son Bart; Mimi, ill with stomach pains eventually diagnosed as appendicitis, stayed at Joan's house under the care of Richard's mother. (Big Joan was now with Albert Baez in Portola Valley, preparing for the wedding.)

Joan and Richard joked a lot, usually at the expense of the locals, improvising conversations they imagined the passing merrymakers to be having; to Bart Creedon, they "always seemed to be doing funny voices and making faces" and laughing at something he missed. Coming upon a booth promoting the John Birch Society, they could not resist initiating a confrontation: Joan glanced over their handouts and asked what they had on the subject of peace. Debate ensued, of course; soon one of the Birchers invited Fariña to continue their discussion alone in a nearby grove of sycamores. Richard would write an account of the event (to be published in the March 1964 issue of *Mademoiselle*), a polemic disguised as a recollection, in which the Bircher proceeded to try provoking a fistfight that Fariña resisted, Gandhi-like—and in which, elsewhere in the story, a racist fortune-teller ranted against the upcoming March on Washington. But none of Richard's companions saw either of these incidents, and he never mentioned anything about either one to his friends that night.

The night before the wedding, Pynchon played host to a bachelor party for Fariña, which Richard organized himself with help from Mimi, who had asked an old Palo Alto friend of the Baezes, Sandy Maw, if they could use his house; there was a rec room with a bar. Mimi, Joan, and Betsy crashed it and got filthy drunk with the men. Nauseated from the alcohol (its ill effects compounded by her oncoming appendicitis) and anxious about the day ahead, Mimi plopped onto Joan's bed around one in the morning. Her sister sat next to her. "Well," Joan said, "how are you doing?"

"I'm feeling funny," Mimi answered.

"I know," Joan replied, trying to comfort her. "Don't worry—you can still call it off."

The wedding turned out to be a happy affair on a heavenly California afternoon. Big Joan handled virtually everything. "Once I realized there was no turning back," she said, "I thought it should be as nice as we could make it. If she got divorced, she got divorced. In the meantime, I would give her a beautiful wedding." Albert Baez's sole contribution was financial: a hundred dollars, the entire cost of the wedding. Big Joan made small arrangements of Mimi's favorite flowers, daisies, and placed them around the lawn of the A-frame cottage; she played records she knew Mimi liked (there was no band); and the wedding cake was cheesecake, which Mimi loved. The bride wore a Spanish lace gown she had seen in a family friend's closet when she was four years old; Mimi had always said she wanted to wear that when she got married, and Big Joan saw to it. The groom's father bought him a sleek black suit, and Richard wore it with a white silk tie. Conducted in front of a cluster of cypress trees near the back door of the house, the ceremony was short; Fariña had written somewhat cryptic, haikulike vows, and a nonsectarian minister whom Big Joan had found did the officiating with friendly proficiency. There were forty or so guests—Joan's neighbors from the Carmel area, Tia and several old acquaintances of the Baez family from their early years in California, and a handful of the espouseds' friends who happened to be nearby, such as Jim Connor and Richard Lockmiller. In the pictures Lillian Farina took that day, everyone looks giddy. Mimi's face is all gleaming teeth, and Richard's eyes seem about to fly out of their sockets. Pynchon, dressed in a business suit with a plain dark tie, grins under a mustache so big, it looks like a costume-shop disguise (and well may have been). Standing near the newlyweds, Big Joan is laughing out loud, and Joan and Pauline both glow. Only Albert Baez is absent from view, having gone for a walk after the ceremony. For the reception, Big Joan brought out hors d'oeuvres, and the wedding party went indoors to change, returning in jeans and T-shirts and work clothes; how long could young revolutionaries be expected to stay in such bourgeois finery? The evening ended, naturally, with a jam session. Jim Connor and Richard Lockmiller played a few country songs, Steve Young did something he had written, Joan sang along with the others and did at least one tune herself, and Mimi and Richard harmonized on "Old Blue," their first performance together. Much like Fariña's wedding to Carolyn Hester, the occasion marked not only the formal union of a couple but the debut of an act.

FROM THE AUTUMN of 1962 to the end of the following summer, several of the nascent social-consciousness movement's core issues rose to the forefront of public discourse: civil rights, with the Kennedy administration finally drafting a comprehensive package of antidiscrimination legislation; the nuclear debate, made urgent by the Cuban missile crisis; and three issues illuminated in influential new books—women's rights (Betty Friedan's *The Feminine Mystique*); the environment (Rachel Carson's *Silent Spring*); and poverty (Michael Harrington's *The Other America*). When some 250,000 people rallied for a freedom march from the Washington Monument to the Lincoln Memorial on August 28, 1963, Baez and Dylan were together in the heat of it.

Joan, who convinced Bob to participate and kept him at her side offstage, performed a few songs solo at Lincoln's feet shortly after the marchers assembled on the mall in front of the memorial. Ferociously earnest as well as young and unassumingly beautiful in a plaid A-line dress, she dominated the next day's coverage of the entertainment program that preceded speeches by the movement's leaders, including the Rev. Martin Luther King, Jr. Dylan, looking homespun in a checkered shirt and a brown Western-style jacket, sang "Blowin' in the Wind" and "Only a Pawn in Their Game" and joined Len Chandler for the Negro spiritual "Hold On." But he was scarcely mentioned in the press. *The New York Times* got to Dylan twenty-three paragraphs below a quote from Bobby Darin, who attended the march but did not sing, and that reference to Dylan was intended to illustrate the program's diminishing energy:

> Bob Dylan, a young folksinger, rendered a lugubrious mountain song about "The day Medgar Evers was buried from a bullet that he caught." Mr. [Burt] Lancaster, Mr. [Harry] Belafonte and Mr. [Charlton] Heston found time dragging, stood up to stretch and chat.

Still, Dylan was seen doing something good and important, largely through Baez's initiative. Moreover, when he joined Joan to sing "We

Shall Overcome," a quarter of a million people watched them as partners, gifted young artists on fire. "I had to use Brando's cattle prod to get him up there, practically," Baez said, referring to the implement Marlon Brando brandished at the march to illustrate the severe control techniques southern police had been employing against Negroes. "But he did it. It wasn't really his thing, but he did it, and he was brilliant when we sang together. We had to look straight at each other when we were singing. It was just too moving to look out at that sea of faces. We never sang that way, staring straight into each other's eyes. We gave each other strength, and it was very intimate and the most public thing we ever did."

As young whites from the North, Baez and Dylan encountered a bit of cynicism about their motivations for championing the Negro struggle; Dick Gregory covered his ears during Bob's songs and turned away from him in private. "I preferred to see Odetta up there," he said. "She is a virtuoso musician, and she lived what we were there for. What was a white boy like Bob Dylan there for? Or—who else? Joan Baez? To support the cause? Wonderful—support the cause. March. Stand behind us—but not in front of us. If Bob Dylan and Joan Baez and whoever the hell stood out there with the crowd and cheered for Odetta and Josh White, that would be a greater statement than arriving in their limousines and taking bows." Harry Belafonte, in contrast, saw the white performers, Joan and Bob in particular, as key assets to the movement. "We were not there solely to send a message to ourselves," Belafonte said. "We were there to communicate something terribly urgent to the power center of the culture at the time, and that power center was white. Joan and Bob demonstrated with their participation that freedom and justice are universal concerns of import to responsible people of all colors. Naturally, the intrigue about their relationship added greatly to their appeal—every crusade needs a great romance. Were they taking advantage of the movement? Or was the movement taking advantage of them?" As Dylan had asked in song, who were the pawns in the game?

In mid-September Bob returned to the Carmel Highlands. He went by himself, with no concerts or other business on the West Coast, solely to be with Joan. This was more than a visit. Dylan virtually moved in, bringing not just the one pair of blue jeans, the work shirt, and the Martin guitar he usually traveled with, but a suitcase full of clothes and his portable Olivetti typewriter—practically everything he owned. "I lived with her, and I loved the place," Dylan recalled. "And, like, I lived with her. Hey, I lived with Joan Baez."

Their daily life was constructed around Bob, so he could write. (Though a model for independent women, Joan seemed to feel obligated to assume a subordinate role, supporting her man, at home.) Joan would get up first, around nine o'clock, to make coffee. When Bob awoke an hour or two later, they would have a light breakfast and spend some morning time together, and then he would start the day's writing. They had set up his typewriter on an adobe lamp-stand in the main room of the house, next to a row of windows overlooking the hills. Dylan stood while he worked, facing the machine like an adversary, glowering at the keys. He typed, using one or two fingers of each hand, in gushes and waves. The bottom half of his body seemed independently engaged in trying to rub away a bad rash. He sipped black coffee constantly until the afternoon, when he replaced his cup with a glass of red wine. Joan, meantime, busied herself around the house, attended to business on the phone, and made them snacks. "The only way I could get him to eat was to go over and eat right next to him, just peer over his shoulder and chew," said Joan, "and right away he'd start picking at whatever I had in my hand. So I made picking food. Otherwise, I'd say, 'You want something to eat?' and he'd say, 'No, no.' "

Working all day for weeks, Dylan concentrated almost exclusively on writing poetry and prose-poems. He was trying in seclusion to complete the transformation he had recently begun in public, like Fariña in London, but in reverse—Dylan, a folksinger becoming a writer. Most of the twenty or so short pieces he wrote during this period at the Carmel Highlands are free-form verse, loose impressionist takes on events and people in his life. Among them were the first of what would become "11 Outlined Epitaphs," sketches dealing with his youth in Hibbing, Woody Guthrie, and New York. At Joan's request, he also wrote the

Eric von Schmidt's poster for the 1964 Baez-Dylan tour

Richard and Bob take turns posing for a family portrait with
the Baez women: Mimi, Big Joan, and Joan

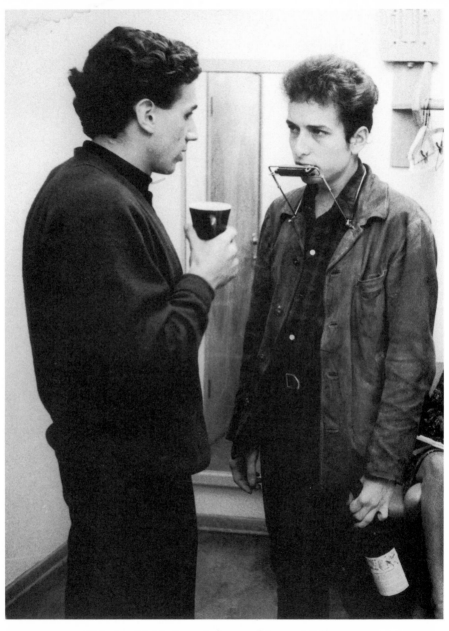

Richard and Bob backstage before one of Joan and Bob's concerts

Top, Joan and Bob prepare for a show, with Richard and Mimi (in the mirror).
Above, Joan and Richard telling a reporter about their "rock and roll" album

1965: Richard, Joan, and Mimi in the rain at the Newport Folk Festival, the afternoon before . . .

Bob, plugged in and wearing black leather, plays rock and roll

Mimi and Richard at Fariña's book-signing party, April 30, 1966.
Below, Bob and his Triumph in Woodstock, with Victor Maymudes and Bob Neuwirth

liner notes for her upcoming album, another collection of songs recorded in concert, including "With God on Our Side" and "Don't Think Twice, It's All Right." (Titled *Joan Baez in Concert, Part II*, the album was scheduled for release that November.) What Dylan wrote was an autobiographical prose-poem dealing with them and their romance:

> *So between our tongues there was a bar*
> *An tho we talked a the world's fears*
> *An at the same jokes loudly laughed*
> *An held our eyes at the same aim*
> *When I saw she was set t sing*
> *A fence a deafness with a bullet's speed*
> *Sprang up like a protection glass*
> *Outside the linin a my ears*
> *An I talked loud inside my head*
> *As a double shield against the sounds*
> *"Ain't no voice but an ugly voice*
> *A the rest I don' give a damn . . ."*

In Joan, Bob found unqualified support for his literary experimentation. Unlike Suze Rotolo, who had been early to recognize Dylan's potential as a writer and played a mentor role by introducing him to the work of several masters, Joan thought of Bob as a fully formed great poet. She read little; "We used to joke, if somebody bought Joanie a book for a present, they didn't know her," said her friend Nancy Carlen, a musician and entrepreneur in the Big Sur area. Moreover, Joan's own experience in music had convinced her that creative expression is a natural gift—one doesn't need training or experience to be brilliant and successful; one just needs to open one's mouth or, say, start typing. With Joan, Bob never had to suffer comparisons with Brecht or Lord Byron; all he had to do was write, and she told him he was "the modern Shakespeare." When Dylan was out of the house, Baez would rifle through the trash and pull out his abandoned ideas, first drafts, sketches, and false starts. She would flatten them and hoard them without Bob's knowledge, and she would take them out to show her friends, handling the flattened pages like a girlhood leaf collection. Read this, she implored Kim Chappell or Carlen—isn't this amazing? Would you believe he was going to throw this out? "Good or bad," said Carlen, "Joan saw no difference. It was all brilliant, because Bobby did it."

When Bob wanted a break, Joan would sometimes take him for a drive along the Big Sur coast, stopping whenever they spotted a promisingly ramshackle antique shop. Dylan was interested mainly in old Hawaiian and Mexican-made Spanish-style guitars, which rarely showed up in New York. He would pick every one up gingerly and test it with a few mariachi chords or a flamenco trill, surprising Joan; it seemed almost as if guitars were something magical with Bob, as if they had the power to change his personality. On a few occasions, Joan and Bob explored the coffeehouse scene in Cannery Row, taunting the locals with their presence but declining requests to perform; Bob had no choice, he told Joan: he had promised Albert Grossman he would never play in a coffeehouse again.

In the evenings, they socialized around the Carmel Highlands, most often visiting the Williamses. Once Joan brought Bob to meet a fellow writer, Alan Marcus, who lived with his wife, Lotte, and their three children a few hundred yards from Joan. A New Englander who had attended Brown, Marcus made his literary debut in 1948 with the acclaimed *Straw to Make Brick*, a novel inspired by the author's military experience in the Second World War. Since moving to the Highlands in 1958, Marcus continued to write serious fiction and essays while quietly milking Hollywood for relatively easy money. He was a thoroughly rounded intellectual of a kind seemingly extinct, versed in science, philosophy, politics, and the arts; yet he had a feeling for popular culture. Marcus tended to intimidate Joan Baez, because she did not intimidate him. Joan and Bob had apparently decided to treat this visit to the Marcuses as a joke; Dylan was wearing blue jeans, a work shirt, a bow tie, and a top hat. He looked like a scarecrow of Eustace Tilly. Were he and Joan simply in a playful mood, or were they parodying Alan Marcus as an intellectual elitist? They never said a word about Dylan's getup, and neither did the Marcuses. "I wasn't sure what effect they had in mind," said Marcus. "But it didn't interest me. She seemed to want to show him off, and perhaps show us off as the interesting family that lived up the road. So we sat back and waited for conversation to flourish. It didn't flourish. I think he was used to people being very obsequious with him, and I didn't say, 'Gee, can I touch you?' or anything like that. He obviously felt that he wasn't being celebrated enough, which he wasn't. So he just sat there staring at us." To break the mood, Joan walked up a set of stairs to a loft area overlooking the others and started to sing. When she was finished, she walked down, Bob got up, and they left.

Joan and Bob spent virtually all the rest of their time with Mimi and Richard. The newlywed Fariñas had just begun nesting in the small building next to Joan's house that Brett Weston had used as his photography studio. It was a one-room plywood cube with a low, flat roof. The only door emptied onto a narrow gravel driveway; if you pulled in with a big car and got out on the passenger side, you had to be careful not to scrape the front of Mimi and Richard's home with your door.

There was a thicket of eucalyptus trees between the two buildings and a dirt path, which Joan and Mimi bustled up and down once or twice a day, grabbing each other to share a thought or talk over a problem while Bob and Richard did their writing. ("In Carmel, I used to write about the length of time that he did," recalled Richard, who was working diligently every day to finish his novel and experimenting with music at night.) Being neighbors brought the sisters closer, on the whole. "I had gone through quite a bit, and she had been growing up away from me," said Joan. "We didn't really know each other like we used to, and that had created some tension . . . [and] misunderstanding. We needed to work those things out, and living right next to each other helped." The presence of two men—friendly rivals, at that—complicated this process, however. Although Richard was now a member of the family and Joan was warming up to him, the hard feelings between Mimi and Joan over Fariña were just starting to mend, and the issue of Richard's intentions toward Joan remained open. When Dylan arrived, meanwhile, he seemed to have the same old crush on Mimi. "He was obviously very interested in me and being kind of flirtatious in his mumbling Bob way," Mimi recalled. "So it was kind of weird between the three of us [Joan, Mimi, and Bob] at the beginning."

Mimi found herself alone with Bob once, because her husband was busy with Joan. Richard, in a visit to Joan's house shortly after he and Mimi had moved to the Highlands, had been surprised to discover Joan making pencil sketches for pleasure. He suggested they collaborate on a book: his poems, her drawings. Joan was flattered, the intended response, and agreed to give the thing a try. Richard pulled out a trunk idea—short, ephemeral "Little Nothing Poems," all somehow touching upon the theme of nothingness.

Nothing
could put
Humpty Dumpty
together again.
But there was a war on
so they had to try
all those other things

While Joan and Richard were reviewing poems for illustration ideas one afternoon, Bob wandered out of Joan's house and walked up to Weston's old studio to see Mimi. He moped around for a moment while Mimi finished some tidying, and Joan came in behind him. "That was the end of that!" Mimi said. "She just gave him one of those looks that would kill, and he just sort of shrank, and they left, and I burst out laughing. Then she kind of acted like it was all my fault, and there was a distance between us for about a day, and then that was over." Richard, despite all his own insecurities and Cuban-macho jealousy with women in the past (and with Mimi, at other times), took Dylan's attraction to his wife in stride; indeed, he appeared to find satisfaction in it. "Oh, it was fine with him," said Mimi. "People accused Dick of going after Joanie. Well, Dylan had Joanie, and he wanted me. Dick was very, very protective. He would never let anything happen. But I think he liked the idea that he had something Dylan wanted and would never get."

Although Joan tended to stay close to Bob when he finished his day's work, Dylan and Fariña found some time to try out the California experience together. Shortly after Bob arrived, Richard showed him Joan's Vespa motor scooter, and they went through the male ritual of inspecting the bike, pacing around the machine, and handling random parts decorously. Fariña, who had ridden other people's bikes a few times in Europe, was a novice rider but critical of Dylan's ability. "He would play around with that motorcycle," Fariña said, "but he really could not drive." Mimi and Joan watched from Joan's window as the men took turns spinning down Corona Road, wondering which one would crash first. "Neither of them knew what he was doing, really," said Mimi, "and they got on those things and thought they were Marlon Brando." Apparently looking for another hot-dogging opportunity for which they were equally ill prepared, they borrowed a Carmel neighbor's surfboard one night in early October and went moonlight surfing alone. "I remember that he had written 'Lay Down Your Weary Tune' at Carmel," Fariña later said. "One evening, we were out surfing with a surfboard, and he rode the motorcycle back and wrote the tune. I remember that because [Joan] was on her way to do a concert at the Hollywood Bowl, and he was very keen that she should sing it with him. But she was unsure of the song and the words and didn't want to do it yet."

A lament to the hazards of singing the same tired music derived from the gospel song "I Came to Jesus," "Lay Down Your Weary Tune" may have touched Joan all too deeply. Is that how Bob repaid her for her support, with a critique? Or was that his way of trying to prompt her to grow, as she had been motivating him? (Dylan seems to have written only one other song during this period with Joan, "The Lonesome Death of Hattie Carroll," another of his journalistic narratives about an unjust murder. He played relatively little music alone with Joan, either, and none with Mimi and Richard. Neither Bob nor Richard appeared eager to reprise their experience in Dobell's record shop.)

Since both men were concentrating on writing for the page, they occasionally compared notes and exchanged some work for comment. Richard was impressed by Bob's seriousness, as Mimi recalled; he complimented Dylan in general terms and volunteered bits of constructive criticism. Still, Fariña confided to his wife, he held back an opinion that Dylan's prose-poems were less inventive and moving than his songs. "He just felt that Bob's music was better than the kind of writing Bob was getting into," said Mimi, "but he didn't want to discourage him, so he just said something nice." Whatever Dylan thought of Fariña's novel, he never told Joan. To Richard, though, he mustered something positive. "Dylan saw [the book]," Fariña crowed in a letter to von Schmidt, "& I'm pleased to say it reached him where it was meant to."

On the evening of Saturday, October 12, Joan gave a concert at the Hollywood Bowl. She was the first singer to sell out the 17,000-seat outdoor theater since Frank Sinatra in 1944. Joan drove Bob, Mimi, and Richard to the show, the Fariñas scrunched in the XKE's miniature backseat during the 350-mile drive down the Pacific Coast. As her fans by now expected, Baez brought Dylan onstage as a "surprise," and they performed their usual duets, as well as Bob's new "Lay Down Your Weary Tune," which Joan stumbled through, as she had feared. After the show, Joan took up novelist Henry Miller on an invitation to meet at his big house in Pacific Palisades, bringing Bob, Mimi, and Richard. The visit was at once awkward, sexually charged, and mundane, much as one might expect with Henry Miller. Richard, the only one of the four conversant with Miller's fiction, cornered the seventy-one-year-old author and somehow managed to steer the conversation to an offer to help Miller get his unread work published in *Mademoiselle*. (That Miller might in turn help Richard someday was surely understood.) Dylan and Miller spoke little to each other but played a game of Ping-Pong. "Miller is a very good player," Fariña said. "As I recall it, there was no contact whatever [between Dylan and Miller]. The main reason for that meeting was that Henry Miller should meet Joan. Miller didn't know anything about Dylan or who he was or anything. If anything, he was only interested in Joanie and Mimi—in fact, he went after them both."

Bob left the Carmel Highlands to play a solo concert in Ann Arbor on October 19 and continued east to New York for work on his third album. But he told Joan he would come back soon, and she remained on his mind, even though he picked up his relationship with Suze Rotolo in the Village. As Dylan told Robert Shelton, "Like, I thought about her, and I called her, and shit like that." (He would be more eloquent, as usual, in the music he would write about Joan.)

Dylan and Fariña also had plans to reconvene, perhaps on the East Coast before the year's end. Photographer Barry Feinstein was going to be traveling with Bob on a college tour, and Fariña wrangled an invitation to join them; the idea was to pitch a magazine on publishing Feinstein's pictures with a road memoir by Fariña. *Life* said it might want to use the photographs if one of its own reporters wrote the text, but Dylan demurred, insisting that Fariña be the writer. "He's a very closed-in kind of cat," Richard wrote in a proposal to Madeline Tracy Brigden, his editor at *Mademoiselle*, "and he wants no one but me to do the story." Indeed, Feinstein recalled, "Bob really only liked to have friends like us around him. He had an image to maintain, and he protected it."

Returning to Columbia's Studio A for the first time since early August, Dylan recorded a dozen tracks in two all-day sessions conducted on October 23 and 24 under his new producer, Tom Wilson. With a few exceptions, including the graceful Latinate ballad "Boots of Spanish Leather" (left over from the *Freewheelin'* sessions), the majority of the compositions to be included on the new record were hard-hitting songs of social protest: "With God on Our Side," "Only a Pawn in Their Game," "When the Ship Comes In," "Ballad of Hollis Brown," "The Lonesome Death of Hattie Carroll," and the song for which the album would be titled, "The Times They Are a-Changin'." A mordant rallying cry in three-quarter time, this was by far the most fervent anthem Dylan had written:

> *Come senators, congressmen*
> *Please heed the call*
> *Don't stand in the doorway*
> *Don't block up the hall*
> *For he that gets hurt*
> *Will be he who has stalled*

When his old friend Tony Glover heard the tapes, he asked Bob about the title song. It seemed so zealously emphatic, almost strident, to Glover—more like Pete Seeger than Woody Guthrie, and not much like the Dylan with whom Glover used to spend hours playing country blues. Why would Bob write such a straight-ahead call to action? Dylan told him, coolly, "It seems to be what people like to hear."

I N 1963:

- More than two hundred albums of folk music were released in the United States, including *Jazz Meets the Folk Song*, *Soul Meeting Saturday Night Hootenanny Style* (with Jimmy Reed and John Lee Hooker), *Kiddie Hootenanny*, *Tommy Scott's Hollywood Hillbillies Hootenanny*, Kate Smith's *Hootenanny Folk Songs*, and *Hot Rod Hootenanny* (with the Weirdos and the Voice of Mr. Gasser, Ed Roth). *Show Business*, a trade newspaper, reported "Folk Music Craze Baffles Experts."

- The only new music program on national television was ABC's folk series *Hootenanny*, which broadcast college concerts to some eleven million viewers weekly. (Because Pete Seeger was black-listed from the show, neither Joan Baez nor Bob Dylan would per-form on it.)

- At least two dozen magazines about folk music were published in the United States, including *ABC TV Hootenanny Magazine* and *Hootenanny* (edited by Robert Shelton, with a monthly column of prose-poetry by Bob Dylan).

- The American Dairy Association promoted milk products with a full-page newspaper advertisement that depicted a young housewife in her kitchen, strumming a guitar. The headline asked, "Wish you could write a protest song about your family's eating habits?"

- Sam Katzman, producer of teen exploitation films such as *Don't Knock the Rock* and *Twist Around the Clock*, produced the movie *Hootenanny Hoot*. It starred Judy Henske and featured Johnny Cash in a story about the travails of undergraduate folksingers who like to play guitars in swimsuits on the beach.
- Cincinnati radio station WCPO went "100% Hootenanny" with "a new formula of all-folk music around the clock, seven days a week."
- Parkway Ford, an auto dealership in New Jersey, merchandised the year's new models with a Hootenanny Sale at which local folk performers sang while sitting on the hoods of cars.
- There were folksinger paper dolls, a Bally Hootenanny pinball machine, and a Hootenanny candy bar.

WHEN AN ARTICLE in the November 4, 1963, issue of *Newsweek* exposed him as a Jewish kid from the suburbs and not a part-Indian backwoods hobo, Bob Dylan went into hiding, staying with trusted old friends such as Dave Van Ronk and Barry Kornfeld for several weeks. He swore off any sort of press coverage, including the tour article he had agreed to do with Fariña, and he made relatively little music in public or private. After honoring a couple of major concert commitments in the days immediately following publication of the article, Dylan did about half a dozen shows in nearly four months' time, and he appears to have written no more than two or three songs (half his old prebreakfast output) in the same period. He was writing the whole time but continuing to concentrate on poetry, prose-poems, at least one play, and a novel.

Except for a few pieces, including a couple of poems about President Kennedy written on or shortly after his assassination on November 22, 1963, nearly all this work was personal. In a few "Outlined Epitaphs," he reminisced about Suze Rotolo, Eric von Schmidt, Geno Foreman, and other old intimates, and he ranted at journalists, striking back at *Newsweek*:

> *your questions're ridiculous*
> *an most of your magazines're also ridiculous*
> *caterin t people*
> *who want t see*
> *the boy nex door*
> *no I shall not co-operate with reporters' whims*

In style the pieces are casual, declarative, often verbose, and wildly uneven, closer to prose than conventional poetry, but most like the transcribed ramblings of an interesting person with a tape recorder and far too much tape and ego. The "novel," which Dylan was now talking up to reporters, was a hodgepodge of ideas, and at least one of the plays grew out of notions that he said began in the "novel." (Dylan talked about writing several plays during these months, although there is known typescript for only fifteen pages of one untitled, unfinished play, a political quarrel set in a "combination barroom-church.") As Dylan wrote in a six-page prose-poem published in the January 1964 issue of *Broadside* ("for sis and gordon and all broads of good sizes"):

> *anyway I'm writin a play out of this so called*
> *novel (navel would be better I guess)*
> *an I'm up to my belly button in it.*
> *quite involved yes*
> *I've discovered the power of playwriting means*
> *as opposed t song writing means*
> *altho both are equal, I'm wrapped in playwriting*
> *for the minute, my songs tell only about me an how*

I feel but in the play all the characters tell how
they feel. I realize that this might be more confusin
for some but in the reality of things it might
be much better for some too. I think at best you could
say that the characters will tell in an hour
what would take me, alone, two weeks to sing about

As a writer, Dylan was experimenting and trying to stretch, but he was also floundering. None of his recent work outside of music quite matched his songs in beauty, vigor, or distinctiveness. Unfortunately, in the wake of the *Newsweek* exposé, he seemed to have lost his musical footing. His folk vagabond pose was scarcely credible anymore, and the protest genre had always been too narrow for his tastes. "He really didn't know what to do," recalled Barry Kornfeld, one of the few friends he confided in during his seclusion. "I remember him saying all people wanted from him now were finger-pointing songs, and he only had ten fingers. He didn't want to do that anymore, but he didn't quite know where to go next, so he spent a lot of time at the typewriter. Everybody was saying he was a great writer. What does a great writer do? A great writer writes."

Fariña, at the same time, set aside his fiction and poetry to focus on setting words to music. In late November 1963 he told Robert Shelton that he had recently composed a "carload" of songs; Richard said he was caught in "a notion-storm and setting everything down as quickly as possible." Accompanied by Mimi on guitar, Richard played and sang the tunes to Joan as soon as he finished them, and she was "pleasantly shocked," Joan said, to find that "he was better than I ever expected . . . and better than a lot of people who had been at it for years." Joan so liked Fariña's music that she made demonstration recordings of five songs for Maynard Solomon, who operated Ryerson Music Publishers in connection with the Vanguard Recording Society. Solomon signed Fariña as a publishing client and promptly started submitting the work to singers on and off his label. Composed on the dulcimer, the songs are all highly singable, with memorable, lilting melodies equally indebted to Irish folk music and American pop. Musically, they are surprisingly adept, considering Fariña's lack of training and experience—tuneful, harmonically suggestive of something Middle Eastern, and in several cases intensely rhythmic. Fariña was finally writing the "boogie poetry" he had talked about with Dylan at Revere Beach two years earlier.

Joan immediately added Richard's one topical song, "Birmingham Sunday," to her concert repertoire. Inspired by the deaths of four Negro schoolgirls when a white racist firebombed a church during services in September 1963, the song is neither a straightforward reportorial account nor a protest anthem but a gently poetic evocation of a tragedy, set to a poignant melody in three-quarter time derived from the traditional Irish love song "I Once Loved a Lass." (Langston Hughes would describe it as "musically so beautifully understated . . . a quiet protest song.")

This first portfolio of Fariña's also included a song that Richard built around a comment he had heard from Mimi and Joan's sister Pauline: "Pack Up Your Sorrows." Buoyant and tuneful (with a well-balanced melody set to harmony that changes every two measures), it is a song of exceptionally infectious charm. When Joan gave it a try in concert, she was startled to find the audience singing along by the second chorus. Richard seemed to have a knack for this songwriting thing.

Dylan, seeking escape and rejuvenation after the *Newsweek* exposé, decided to do something dramatic and gathered four friends—Victor Maymudes, the writer Peter Karman, and the singers Bob Neuwirth and Paul Clayton—to take a cross-country road trip, a literal journey toward a psychic destination. They left from Manhattan on Monday, February 3, in the sky-blue Ford station wagon Grossman had bought for Dylan's touring, aiming to arrive in Berkeley to give a concert three weeks later. Heading south, they stopped in Virginia on February 4 to support striking miners by donating clothing Maymudes had collected in New York. In Hendersonville, North Carolina, two days later, Dylan knocked on Carl Sandburg's door, announcing that he was a poet, too; unimpressed, the eighty-six-year-old poet and folksinger turned Dylan away. The group timed a stop in New Orleans to coincide with Mardi Gras, the musical revelry of which inspired Bob to write a masterly, upbeat new song,

"Mr. Tambourine Man." In Colorado at some point in mid-February, they tracked down the site of the 1914 murder of striking miners and their families that Woody Guthrie had dramatized in his song "Ludlow Massacre"; and from Denver they headed west, then north up the California coast toward San Francisco. They were winding along the Pacific when a song came on the car radio that caught Dylan's ear: "I Want to Hold Your Hand." It was the first time Bob had heard the Beatles.

"He practically jumped out of the car. 'Did you hear that?' " Maymudes remembered Bob saying. " 'Fuck! Man, that was fuckin' great! Oh, man—fuck!' "

Maymudes, who was driving, reached over for the radio tuning knob. "Let me see if I can find it again," he said. "All the top-forty stations play the same songs over and over."

"Don't worry about it, man," Dylan said, staring out the window, as if he were replaying the song in his head. "We kept driving along," Maymudes said, "but we lost Bob somewhere back on Route 1."

After a brief stop in San Francisco to try to find another fellow poet Dylan wanted to see, Lawrence Ferlinghetti (who was not at home), they reached Berkeley on the day Bob was due to perform at the Community Theatre, where Joan, Mimi, and Richard were waiting. So were more than 3,500 fans, just nine months after Dylan had appeared in Monterey a virtual unknown. As much as the *Newsweek* article had upset Bob and fueled his critics, it hardly fazed the undergraduates who were beginning to see Dylan as their spokesman and who professed to distrust the mainstream press anyway. Baez joined Dylan for their usual duets, including "With God on Our Side" and "Blowin' in the Wind"; but she no longer had to hush the audience or lecture them about her protégé.

Bob and his traveling companions (except Peter Karman) spent the next day and a half with Joan, Mimi, and Richard in the Carmel Highlands. Big Joan, who was visiting, cooked up a stew, and the whole gang ate, joked, gossiped, talked about movies, and made music in Joan's living room all day and night. They all sang their new songs, including Richard, much to the others' surprise. "Suddenly, Richard was writing," Victor Maymudes remembered. "This was the first time we had ever seen him do his own thing. He played the dulcimer, and we heard his new songs for the first time—his own songs—and it was a great thing to see. Bob was really happy about it. He said it was great that Richard was doing his own thing.

"He kept playing new tunes, and they were amazing," Maymudes said. "He was a guy on fire, and we were discovering it at the same time he was. Bob knew he was on fire when he was eleven. With Richard, it was coming to him in his late twenties, I guess. That was a big deal, you know. We all got high, but not everybody went home and did something. A lot of people went home and did nothing or did more drugs. Only a few people went home and accomplished something."

After Dylan and his companions left on the morning of February 24, Fariña wrote a piece for *Mademoiselle* about Joan and Bob. In it, he gushed about the Monterey concert (especially the duet part) and described his sister-in-law and her friend as aesthetic counterparts to Dylan Thomas and Edna St. Vincent Millay, "purveyors of an enjoined social consciousness and responsibility" to their generation. The article is not really a portrait but worship liturgy, obviously designed to earn points with Dylan and Baez. Fariña portrayed Baez wholly in her self-image, the stoic altruist; when she read it, Joan told Mimi, "Dick is one of the only people who knows what I'm about." He glamorized Dylan, much the same, as the enigmatic rebel of Bob's adolescent male dreams—and Richard's ongoing fantasies about himself. "There was no sensation of his having performed somewhere the previous night or of a schedule that would take him away once the inevitable post-concert party was over," Fariña wrote. "There was, instead, the familiar comparison with James Dean, at times explicit, at times unspoken, an impulsive awareness of his physical perishability. Catch him now, was the idea. Next week he might be mangled on a motorcycle."

I N THE MONTHS following the Kennedy assa: President Johnson deepened the United Stat ment in the Vietnam War and the national mood grew darker and more anxious, Joan Baez found much to protest and more creative ways to do so. She had always had a flair for dramatic gesture—her Newport debut, the March on Washington. On April 15, 1964, she included a handwritten letter to the Internal Revenue Service with her tax return; it said, in part:

> Our modern weapons can reduce a man to a piece of dust in a split second, can make a woman's hair fall out or cause her baby to be born a monster. They can kill the part of a turtle's brain that tells him where he is going, so instead of trudging to the ocean he trudges confusedly towards the desert, slowly, blinking his poor eyes, until he finally scorches to death and turns into a shell and some bones.
>
> I am not going to volunteer the 60% of my year's income tax that goes to armaments.

The turtle imagery came from *Mondo Cane*, the Italian-made documentary film hodgepodge released the previous year, although the letter's passionately overripe language was Joan's own; and the idea to withhold tax payments proportionate to military allocations in the federal budget—a proposition almost childish in its simplicity—came to Joan through Ira Sandperl, the charismatic pacifist who had taught Joan how to look at her sister Mimi without hating her for her beauty when they were girls in Palo Alto. (Radicals had been withholding taxes in this way since the 1950s.) Joan and Ira had corresponded from time to time over the years and became reacquainted when Baez moved back to northern California. "Joanie was always susceptible to simplistic thinking," her father said. "Simple, overarching solutions appealed to her, and I suspect that's why she fell prey to that man [Sandperl]." To Big Joan, her daughter's association with Sandperl seemed to fit into a pattern of mothering eedy men. "I don't know why she was—for such a strong girl and a smart girl, she was always throwing herself at men who had to be pampered," she said. Ira Sandperl worked on and off as a bookstore clerk, subsidized by cash gifts from Joan when he said he could use them.

Joan's letter to the IRS, which was publicized in a press release from Sandperl complete with his home phone number for follow-up interviews, sparked intense controversy. Scheduled to perform on *The Tonight Show*, she was restricted from talking about politics or taxes on the air, "as a favor" to Johnny Carson. Baez, with one grand act of economic civil disobedience, was no longer just the most famous of the folksinging young idealists but, seemingly now, some kind of radical and perhaps a bit of a flake. To skeptics and her antagonists, the very notion of protesting war by keeping a significant amount of income raised doubts about her motivations: *Why did she keep the money for herself and not donate it to a charity?* She did give money to numerous charities and organizations whose causes she supported, including the NAACP and CORE; to Joan, though, the point was not where the money went— she still loved to shop, and she kept driving her Jaguar XKE—but where she prevented it from going, not positive action but negation. As women had long been relegated to relying on their sexuality as a source of power, she recognized the act of withholding as a force of influence.

Despite her stand against the new administration's military policies, Joan participated in a fund-raising "Salute to President Lyndon B. Johnson" at the National Guard Armory in Washington on May 26, 1964. (Whether the event sponsors invited Joan prior to her challenge to the IRS or despite it is unclear.) She agreed to perform in the program (which also featured Mahalia Jackson, Gregory Peck, Gina Lollobrigida, Mitzi Gaynor, and a sing-along of "Once in Love with Lyndon") with the intent of bolstering Johnson's support for civil rights legislation, while challenging the president on Vietnam. At the climax of her low-key set ("musically effective if a bit maudlin," *Time* reported), she urged the president to suspend American involvement in the Vietnam War, and she sang two Dylan songs, "The Times They Are a-Changin' " and "Blowin' in the Wind," staring straight at the president. Johnson met her eye to eye but carried on a conversation with an aide while she sang. Joan suspected that the president was saying something like "Keep a watch on that girl, she's a Commie," and she was proud to have made that kind of an impression.

Baez and Dylan by now seemed inseparable, even when they were apart; Joan praised Bob at every concert she gave without him, and Bob started dedicating his encores to Joan. Most new articles about one mentioned the other prominently, usually hinting at a romantic connection. The comedian Mort Sahl called them "the Liz [Taylor] and Dick [Burton] of the self-righteous set." *Hootenanny* magazine gave their relationship cover treatment, with text so fawning that *The Little Sandy Review*, Jon Pankake and Paul Nelson's independent-minded folk music journal, lashed back in ridicule:

> Baez and Dylan, Dylan and Baez. Robert Shelton tied the sappy symbolic knot in the March issue of *Hootenanny*. . . . The cover screamed, in the best Abbott and Costello or Frankenstein Meets Dracula fashion, "Joan Baez Meets Bob Dylan." Once inside, we got *True Confessions* and *Modern Romance*: "The voice meets the poet." "He speaks for me, she sings for me," *ad nauseam*. Nothing like it since the Monitor met the Merrimac, folks!

Professionally, at least, Joan and Bob were actually beginning to veer in different directions. While Baez was devoting more and more of her time to social and political issues, especially disarmament, Dylan declined to appear at any protests or rallies after the March on Washington in the summer of 1963. He felt especially uncomfortable as a white man in the civil rights movement; he could never understand the black experience, he said, and his own sympathies extended beyond race. "It's not that I'm pessimistic about Negroes' rights, but the word Negro sounds foolish coming from my mouth," he explained in an unpublished interview. "What's a Negro? I don't know what a Negro is. What's a Negro—a black person? How black? What's a Negro? A person living in a two-room shack with 12 kids? A lot of white people live in a two-room shack with 12 kids. Does this make them Negro? What's a Negro—

someone with African blood? A lot of white people have African blood. What's a Negro? An Ethiopian kind of thing? That's not Negro—that's ancient religious pajama-riding freaks. I've got nothing against Negro rights. I never did. [But] anybody who is taught to get his kicks off a superiority feeling—man, that's a drag." Could he have overheard Dick Gregory talking about him on the Washington mall?

For months, Dylan's poetry, prose-poems, and other literary experiments had been drawing him into personal creative territory (with the nominal exception of his unfinished poems about the Kennedy assassination). When he started writing songs in earnest again, he picked up where his work for the page had taken him, eschewing topical and political themes to write songs in a new style—introspective, ruminative work about his own life, with dense, symbolic lyrics and music drawing equally upon folk, blues, rhythm, and pop influences. Whether or not he thought he had found what he had been seeking on that cross-country road trip, the music Dylan wrote afterward was like a dream memory of his stops, a mixture of Carl Sandburg, New Orleans, Woody Guthrie, and the Beatles, filtered through his increasingly distinctive voice.

Bob wrote nearly all the songs for his next record in about a week at the end of May, while vacationing in Greece between engagements in a one-month tour of Europe. He returned to the United States in early June and, after attending his brother David's high school graduation in Hibbing, made the record in a single all-night session at Columbia's Manhattan Studio A on June 9. This was music that burst out of him like something pent up for years: "I Don't Believe You (She Acts Like We Never Have Met)," a passive-aggressive taunt set to an incongruously bouncy tune; "My Back Pages," a statement of personal emancipation phrased in often cryptic imagery ("Crimson flames tied through my ears / Rollin' high and mighty traps . . ."); "It Ain't Me, Babe," another, stronger vow of defiance sung to a clinging lover, perhaps representing the folk music audience; "All I Really Want to Do," a comic, Cole Porter–style "list" song celebrating fraternal love; "Ballad in Plain D," pure folk blues, but with Dylan's most declarative and personal lyrics to date—about his romance and breakup with Suze Rotolo, with a few piercing jabs at Carla ("For her parasite sister, I had no respect / Bound by her boredom, her pride to protect"); and "Chimes of Freedom," the only protest song, which he had written during his road trip to California. As recordings, many of the tracks—especially "I Don't Believe You," "It Ain't Me, Babe," and "My Back Pages"—seem incomplete; the arrangements are too spare for the pop-style melodies and song structures. On guitar Dylan mostly blocks rhythm chords like an ensemble musician. The music sounds as if it had been written for a band, and Dylan seems to be playing as if he were hearing one in his head.

Another Side of Bob Dylan was Dylan's first authentic album, one created not to reinforce a fabricated image or to raise universal questions but to communicate what it was like to be a confused and somewhat volatile twenty-three-year-old who was having trouble with his friends and his women. The "another side" it showed was his inside. "There aren't any finger-pointing songs in here," Dylan told Nat Hentoff, who interviewed him in the recording studio for *The New Yorker*. "Me, I don't want to write *for* people any more—you know, be a spokesman. From now on, I want to write from inside me, and to do that I'm going to have to get back to writing like I used to when I was ten—having everything come out naturally. The way I like to write is for it to come out the way I walk or talk. When I'm uptight and it's rainin' outside and nobody's around and somebody I want is a long way from me—and with someone else besides—I can't sing 'Ain't Got No Use for Your Red Apple Juice.' I don't care how great an old song it is or what its tradition is. I have to make a new song out of what I know and out of what I'm feeling.' "

"The songs [on *Another Side*] are insanely honest," Dylan explained to one of his friends, "not meanin' to twist any head, and written only for the reason that I myself, me alone, wanted and needed to write them. I've conceded the fact that there is no understanding of anything—at best, just winks of the eye—and that is all I'm looking for now, I guess." If, as he had told Tony Glover, he made his previous album, *The Times They Are a-Changin'*, because "it seems to be what people like to hear," this one seemed to be what he wanted to say, and it could not have been further from what Joan Baez was saying.

MIMI LIKED BEING A FARIÑA. For the first time since Joan had become famous, Mimi felt as if she were stepping out from her sister's shadow. Now nineteen herself, older than Joan in Mimi's mental image of the Club 47 days, Mimi was married to an adoring, dynamic man, while Joan lapped after that mumbling, roving-eyed character Bob Dylan. Admittedly, her husband Richard could be taxing, nearly smothering at times. Since they had bought a 1958 Plymouth on Cannery Row (for a dollar), they could finally attend to everyday tasks such as grocery shopping without borrowing Joan's jeep; however, Richard refused to help Mimi learn to drive. "He wanted to take care of me, and I appreciated it—he was so sweet," said Mimi. "And I guess he didn't like the idea that I would go out by myself. You know, Cuban jealousy." Their days were structured around Richard, as her sister's had been with Dylan; after morning coffee and cereal together, Richard would sit in his writing corner with his typewriter on his lap and spend about an hour trying to find an eraser or pursuing some other quotidian mission to release nervous energy, and Mimi would watch, pretending to read. She was not permitted to make noise while he was working. "He kind of thought whatever he was doing was more important than my stuff," she said, "and it was at first, till I found things to do. We both kind of focused on him." In his letters to friends, Richard sometimes referred to his wife as "MeMe." "I was mainly his wife after we got married," said Mimi. "But I wasn't just Joanie's little sister anymore."

By the summer of 1964, Mimi had begun to find stuff of her own. She was giving dance lessons several times a week at the Williamses' house, and with the money she made, added to what Richard picked up from publishing the occasional magazine article or poem, the Fariñas, now married a year, were able to rent a place about a mile away from Joan in the Carmel Highlands. (Joan was having a house built for herself in the nearby Carmel Valley and was planning to move off the Weston property soon, in any event.) The Fariñas' new home was Colleen Creedon's guest cabin, where Pynchon had stayed. Mimi and Richard could afford neither a phone nor a TV, but they went to the animal shelter and picked out a white German shepherd puppy to keep them company and complete their model of rustic domesticity. Richard named the dog Lush, because he would drink anything—milk, beer, dishwater, salt water—much like the equally furry and playful Eric von Schmidt, Fariña said. Mimi spent most of her free time alone in a small garden behind the cabin, quietly practicing guitar and teaching herself how to play the autoharp. A skilled guitarist when she had performed with Joan around Cambridge five years earlier, she was becoming superb on the instrument. Most nights she and Richard played together, workshopping Richard's new songs, experimenting with traditional material they knew, or taking off on French or Algerian tunes they remembered having heard on the Left Bank. Mimi devised an original arrangement of "Old Blue" that Richard enjoyed jamming over, and she loved to throw him a chord progression to hear the mock beat-poetry lyrics he would improvise about events of the day. Mimi's voice was pretty as ever, a bit warmer and softer than Joan's, if less commanding, and now that Richard was singing in earnest nearly every night with a partner who had good pitch, his voice was growing more musical and assured. As Richard wrote to Robert Shelton, "Mimi and I are getting more and more together on the dulcimer and guitar. Joanie told us straight out that it ought to be recorded, and we figured it was what we'd been waiting to hear."

While Joan was clearly impressed with the music Mimi and her husband were making, especially Richard's songs, she tempered the encouragement she gave Mimi, much as she had dissuaded her sister from performing in Cambridge. "[My] worry was that she would not have a career at the volume of mine or [with] the stature of mine," said Joan. "Mimi, I knew, would be hurt. I don't know why she did it."

Mimi was not entirely certain, either. "I really loved making the music, and I loved doing it with Dick," she said. "But I didn't really think about doing it to get famous, like Joanie. I don't think I wanted to *be* famous. That was more Dick's thing. He was always talking about making it. That was one of his favorite topics of conversation with Joanie. I didn't necessarily want that, but it felt nice to help him, and I really loved to sing and play. I basically just went along with Dick [into music], without thinking it [through] very far." If she just so happened to be acknowledged as being good at the same thing everyone worshiped her sister for, well, she thought "that would be nice," too.

The musical duo of Mimi and Richard Fariña turned out to be inventive, proficient, fresh, and appealing enough to succeed almost immediately with little help from Joan. Once when the couple was playing a few songs at the Williamses' perpetual house party, one of the guests was the singer Nancy Carlen, who had been working at the Big Sur Hot Springs and was organizing a folk festival on the grounds of the resort. She invited Mimi and Richard to perform—their first engagement anywhere— in a program with Joan, Mark Spoelstra, Malvina Reynolds, Berkeley folksinger Janet Smith, and Carlen herself. A strong, resourceful, openly gay woman with no experience at concert promotion but no particular concern for how anyone else might have done it in the past, Carlen saw a kindred spirit in Richard and asked him to brainstorm with her to plan the festival. "He was an extraordinarily creative guy who had an idea a minute," recalled Carlen, who credits Fariña with organizing a panel discussion with the singers on the bill, moderated by Ralph Gleason. "Dick and Mimi were a really unusual act," said Carlen (who went on to produce the Big Sur Festival for the next seven years). "Most people were doing a traditional thing or a blues thing or a protest thing. They were combining folk music with Eastern music and poetry and rock and roll. They were completely original and creative."

After a few weeks of running through songs at night, Mimi and Richard Fariña made their professional debut at the June 1964 festival. They performed a twenty-minute set of rhythmic, exotic-sounding instrumentals and songs by Richard such as "Pack Up Your Sorrows" and a graceful ballad titled "The Falcon." For their finale, Joan joined them and sang Fariña's "Birmingham Sunday" to Mimi and Richard's accompaniment. The audience of about a thousand warmed up to this new act's odd, unfamiliar music slowly, but they ended up calling for an encore that Mimi and Richard could not deliver, having already done everything they both knew.

The day after their performance, they were offered a contract to record for Elektra. Jac Holzman, who was in the festival audience, thought their adventurous music would fit well in his eclectic catalog. "I wanted them very badly," he said. "They were dynamic, and Mimi was hypnotic and immensely musical, and Richard—he was very charismatic. He was elfin, witty, and a fine writer, a very fine writer. Things glowed around Richard. Everybody felt better around him, because he kept the game moving. He kept everything lively." Tempted to sign immediately, they waited; because Richard was contracted to the publishing arm of Vanguard, he thought he should consult Maynard Solomon before signing with a different label, and Mimi wanted to talk the matter over with Joan.

There was a celebration dinner at the conclusion of the festival, and Mimi and Richard were invited to join Nancy Carlen, Mark Spoelstra, Joan, Kim Chappell, and one or two others. Joan was in a merry mood, teasing everyone mercilessly; she imitated the doe-eyed waitress behind her back and found something ridiculous about each item on the menu; among friends, Joan sometimes appeared to suspend her pacifism. Mark Spoelstra, still harboring glints of his teenage crush on Baez, was developing a migraine. By the end of the dinner, he was in too much pain to ride his motorcycle to Carlen's house, where he was going to spend the night. Kim offered to give him a lift in her sports car. Good idea, Richard said: he would accompany them on Spoelstra's bike. He was an old hand at motorcycling from his days in Ireland, he assured Spoelstra, and the way he emphasized Ireland, with a quick, affirming nod of the head and a stare, seemed to Spoelstra like a message: he had to be good, because he must have been doing something unutterably cool for the IRA.

Spoelstra's motorcycle was a 305cc Honda Dream, a light, small bike, and the road to Nancy Carlen's residence was Route 1, which whipped around the hills along the Pacific. Fariña rode slowly in front of Kim and Mark, practically stopping when he had to shift gears or navigate a turn. It was windy and growing dark. "He didn't look too good," said Spoelstra. "Gusts would come along when you went up some of those hills, and you go along the edge of the cliff on those turns, and he was really wobbly. A pretty scary sight. He was really having trouble keeping his balance, and we weren't going very fast. When we finally got to Nancy's driveway, he stopped the bike, and we pulled up next to him, and he said, 'Is this the driveway?' And I said, 'Yeah, this is it.' He said, 'Okay,' and he was staring at the turn into the driveway. I said, 'Why don't you just go ahead and pull in, and we'll come in behind you.' And he said, 'All right.' All he had to do was turn left and go into this dirt road. So he turned a little, but he kept going and ran right off the road onto the grass and fell down. He couldn't make the turn. He just went right over on his side, and the bike fell on him. There was no reason for him to lose his balance and fall like that. He just had no idea how to turn and keep his balance. I went, 'Oh, my God!' But he was all right. He had my helmet on, and thank God, he was only going about a mile an hour." Richard got up laughing and said something like "For my next trick . . ." (Mimi, who had gone with Joan on a different route, missed the fall and was never told about it.) "I remember thinking, 'Good thing he didn't get hurt,'" said Spoelstra. "At the same time, I almost wished he had gotten a few nicks. He didn't get anything out of it." Subjected to risk by his own delusions, Richard learned only that he was right: he was exempt, and no matter how reckless his behavior, there were no consequences.

In the weeks after the Big Sur Festival, Mimi and Richard kept Jac Holzman on hold while they made a demo tape and submitted it to Vanguard. Maynard Solomon wrote them promptly that he liked the Fariñas' "good fresh sounds, unpretentious and musical and very appealing," and he offered them a contract, which they accepted, encouraged by Joan's artistically satisfying and lucrative experience with Vanguard. Joan told Mimi she was pleased that her younger sister would be on her record label, where Joan could ensure that Mimi was treated right, and she recommended that Mimi and Richard use her manager, Manny Greenhill, too. Richard said he would prefer to be represented by Albert Grossman, who had done so much for Bob Dylan and Peter, Paul and Mary. But Mimi ruled Grossman out because she had heard so much bad about him from Joan. "I told him, 'I'm not going to sign with that fat pig,' " said Mimi, and Richard promised not to force the issue. They were now professional partners as well as husband and wife, even though Mimi was still under twenty-one.

Having had a victory, Richard started planning a trip back east with Mimi; it would be his first lengthy visit home since he and Carolyn Hester had moved to Europe two and a half years earlier and Mimi's first as an adult with a husband and a career. He tried unsuccessfully to persuade the *Atlantic* or *Mademoiselle* to cover their air fare, then settled on going by car again, this time sharing the driving with a friend he had met in Carmel, Alfredo Dopico. Richard and Alfredo were largely redundant: of Cuban ancestry, about the same age and size, strong-featured, impetuous, and volatile, they were both treacherously fond of beautiful women, marijuana, and Richard Fariña. They differed solely on matters of creativity and ambition, Alfredo having little of either, Richard more than they both needed. "Dick was always after something," Dopico said. "I was never quite sure what it was, but he was always going after something. I don't know if Dick ever knew. But I loved him. We were brothers—he treated me like blood. Being with Dick was a feeling. It wasn't something outside of you that you looked at or saw. It was something that went through you." Since Alfredo lived simply and worked as a waiter when he chose, he was free for open-ended travel or, for that matter, almost anything else, and he had a black 1955 Volvo coupe ("Alfredo's Italian chariot," Fariña called it) that was more reliable than Mimi and Richard's Plymouth. When Joan heard of Richard's plan, she offered her sister an alternative: if Mimi wanted to keep her company at the upcoming Newport Folk Festival, Joan would pay for the two of them to travel together by train; the women would have some rare time together while the guys (and Mimi and Richard's dog Lush) took their road trip.

Still titularly a forum for traditional music organized by a not-for-profit foundation, Newport was now also a presentation of mainstream popular entertainment, a big show featuring young singers whom folk music had made fairly prosperous and famous over the past year. In 1964 more than 70,000 people bought tickets to see Baez, Dylan, Peter, Paul and Mary, Johnny Cash, Judy Collins, Mississippi John Hurt, and some fifty others. If Joan was still the most famous, Bob now had the most respect. This year Baez performed on the festival's first evening, as Bob had a year earlier, and Dylan was granted the climactic closing-night slot.

Onstage Baez stepped up her political advocacy, calling upon the audience to protest the Johnson administration's military escalation in Vietnam. She did "Blowin' in the Wind," as usual mentioning Bob Dylan glowingly; but she chose a new song to close her set, "Birmingham Sunday," which, she explained, was written by another important young songwriter, Richard Fariña. For the encore, Dylan joined her to scant surprise; but the song they performed was nothing like anything they had ever done together in earnest: "It Ain't Me, Babe," a protest song of a most personal nature.

In his set the next night, Dylan continued to promote *his* agenda, introducing several more songs from *Another Side*, which was due to be released in a couple of weeks. He sang "All I Really Want to Do," "To Ramona," "Mr. Tambourine Man," and the record's one protest song, "Chimes of Freedom." Inevitably, Joan came out with him for the encore, "With God on Our Side." To the audience, they still appeared to be folk music's first couple.

Bob's Newport audience responded enthusiastically (as tapes of the performance bear out, despite claims in years hence that Dylan was poorly received). It was the political old guard of the folk world and their progeny, Seeger's children, who lambasted Dylan for betraying his—or their—ideals. "To the old left, Dylan was the second coming," said Oscar Brand. "He was a kind of a link to their own lost youth that validated them and gave them hope for their own resurgence." Bess Hawes of the original Almanacs said, "He brought something back for a lot of people who didn't want to lose it." With one twenty-minute set, Dylan seemed to have splintered the folk community into factions for and against him. "The political folkies were very black and white," said

Izzy Young. "Which side are you on? Which side are you on? They almost killed me for not choosing sides. That's what happened with Dylan. They had all decided he was on their side—oh boy! He's one of us! Then he sings a couple of songs that aren't about some dying coal miner, and now—oh, no! He's not one of us! He's a traitor, and he's a hypocrite, and he's good for nothing." In *Sing Out!* editor Irwin Silber derided Dylan's Newport performance in a long, patronizing "open letter":

> You seem to be in a different kind of bag now, Bob—and I'm worried about it. I saw at Newport how you had somehow lost contact with people. . . . Your new songs seem to be inner-directed now, innerprobing, self-conscious—maybe even a little maudlin or a little cruel on occasion. . . . Now, that's all okay—if that's the way you want it, Bob. But then you're a different Bob Dylan from the one we knew. The old one never wasted our precious time.

Ignoring the protest music he had made for a year, Dylan acted as if he and the social activists in the folk community never had met. "All I can say is politics is not my thing at all," Dylan explained after the festival. "I can't see myself on a platform talking about how to help people. Because I would get myself killed if I really tried to help anybody. I mean, if somebody really had something to say to help somebody out, just bluntly say the truth, well obviously they're gonna be done away with. They're gonna be killed.

"I'm not really part of any society, like *their* society. You see, nobody in power has to worry about anybody from the outside, any cat that's very evidently on the outside, criticizing their society, because he is on the outside, he's not in it anyway, and he's not gonna make a dent. You can't go around criticizing something you're not a part of and hope to make it better. It ain't gonna work. I'm just not gonna be a part of it. I'm not gonna make a dent or anything, so why be a part of it by even trying to criticize it? That's a waste of time. The kids know that. The kids today, by the time they're twenty-one, they realize it's all bullshit. I know it's all bullshit."

Twenty-five hundred miles away from Newport, cruising through Nevada, Richard Fariña scrawled a note to Mimi while Alfredo drove and Lush slept in the backseat. Richard described having a premonition about Bob, "a strange, uneasy, even ominous feeling about Dylan or something around him." It was hardly wild speculation; Bob often seemed on the brink of mischance. Still, clairvoyance was not one of Fariña's usual affectations. Had Fariña heard trouble in the catchy new songs Dylan played in California, or was the desert sun overheating the metal plate in his head?

Backstage at the festival, Joan and Bob remained intimate—indeed, closer than ever. "We were never more together than we were that summer," said Joan. They lounged side by side at the pool of the Hotel Viking, reading each other passages from the articles about themselves in newspapers and magazines (including the *Hootenanny* cover story on Bob and Joan, Fariña's piece about them in *Mademoiselle*, and an article in the *Playboy* imitation *Cavalier*, which Joan hoarded; self-conscious about her breasts, which she considered too small, Joan wore a light floral jumper over her bikini at the pool). Bob, looking comically seafaring in a white captain's cap, spent most of one afternoon on Joan's lap. He sipped Beaujolais, clowned, carried on conversations with his friends and Albert Grossman, and played the guitar for hours, nestled on Joan the whole time. Mimi sat next to them soaking in the rivalrous camaraderie and the attention of the men. In the evenings, Joan and Bob clung together backstage or watched the shows, encircled by Dylan's growing entourage and its adopted new member, Mimi. The Viking hotel management knew to leave messages for Miss Baez in Mr. Dylan's room.

Being close that summer may have helped Joan and Bob break away from what each represented publicly. Behind their supreme confidence, both of them had always been insecure, traits they recognized in each other. Dylan said, "She's very fragile," and Joan called him "infinitely fragile" and "as fragile as a winter leaf." As Bob ventured into a new creative area, probing himself in depth for the first time, Joan offered not only romantic love (which Suze had provided) but also support in the opposing camp and a powerful line of defense against his critics in the social activism ranks. How far could the king have fallen if the queen was still beside him? "Bobby was taking a deep dive here," said Dave Van Ronk, "and Joanie was a lifeline." At the same time, as Baez risked losing much of her audience by taking political actions considered radical, Dylan provided her with not only companionship (which Joan had with Kim Chappell) but a boost to her public image. How cold and fearsome could she be, if she was so involved in a romance with that kid folksinger? "I never knew what she saw in him," said Joan's mother. "But I know she was afraid when she took on the Internal Revenue Service. People turned on her. She needed someone, and Dylan was there. It's funny that they just started doing different kinds of things [in their careers]."

After the festival, Joan and Mimi spent a few days in Manhattan and rendezvoused with Richard while Bob made a grueling trip to and from Hawaii for a one-nighter at the Waikiki band shell. Dylan could have stayed on the islands for a while, having no more bookings scheduled until the end of September; but he rushed back to Bearsville, to familiar surroundings and the company of friends. Bob had Grossman's estate to himself for a month while Albert and his new bride Sally vacationed in Europe, so he invited Joan, Mimi, and Richard to house-sit with him. Alfredo drove the three of them and Lush from the city, then left. For most of the next several weeks, Joan and Bob and Mimi and Richard lived together, sharing the housekeeping and the cooking, eating at the kitchen table, idling away the time.

The house Albert Grossman used as a weekend retreat was a weather-seasoned, two-story farmhouse built in the early twentieth century. Surrounded by acres of pine woods, it was a rustic cocoon much like the house Joan rented in California. In fact, if Woodstock and Carmel were east-west parallels as rural artists' colonies (reputations a bit overblown in both cases), Bearsville was to Woodstock what the Highlands were to downtown Carmel. Joan and Mimi both loved Grossman's house and made themselves at home immediately; the first day they cleaned enough debris and algae out of the pool to risk swimming, and they washed all the bedsheets. (There were rumors of a gonorrhea epidemic at the house, and the sisters took no chances.) Because Dylan had stayed at the house so often—and perhaps because it belonged to someone who worked for him—Bob seemed to treat it with nearly contemptuous disregard, plopping on the couch in mud-encrusted boots and snuffing out his cigarettes on the door frames. Richard, naturally, used it as a stage set. The previous owners had hung old family portraits, some of which Grossman kept in place for period atmosphere. Fariña would study one for a moment and proceed to tell Joan, Mimi, and Bob the strange tales of its subjects. The young boy in the britches had been murdered by his mother for discovering her in a tryst with one of the carriage horses. The old woman in the snood was really the horse, in disguise. Most fascinating of all was the square silhouette on one wall where a hanging had been removed. The missing picture, Fariña said, no doubt had shown the visage of a ghost cursed forever to haunt the house. Dylan took this all as a bit melodramatic and snorted and called Richard "a silent movie actor." Since Fariña was anything but silent, that part of Bob's description must have been wishful thinking.

The Carmel contingent had just begun getting acquainted with Bearsville when Joan had to return to New York City for her annual outdoor concert at the Forest Hills tennis stadium. All four of the housesitters drove down together in the station wagon the day before the concert and stayed overnight in Manhattan, Bob and Joan in a room at the Hotel Earle on Washington Square Park, Mimi and Richard at the Foremans' house on Riverside Drive. The next afternoon they roamed the Village together like the tourists who wandered around looking for Bob Dylan and Joan Baez. Bob and Richard brought the sisters to Alan Block's Sandal Shop, where Joan bought shoes for all four of the Baez family women while Dylan and Fariña noodled with a dulcimer and a mandolin. On 8th Street, they wandered into a costume jewelry shop, and Bob and Richard decided to get their ears pierced. A woman of indeterminate age with dirty fingernails dipped a sewing needle into a bottle of rubbing alcohol and poked it through each of the fellows' earlobes while she tried unsuccessfully to guess who they were. Bob and Richard picked out small matching gold hoops.

Giving in to the tourist experience—or more likely, parodying it—Dylan had brought along an 8mm home-movie camera, which he used to shoot random images: street musicians, vendors, Mimi doing pirouettes, Joan sticking out her tongue. (With passersby frequently ogling him, especially in the Village, Dylan may have employed the camera as a means of deflecting attention or striking back at his fans, as well.) Bob told his companions that he was "just fucking around" with the camera. But Richard would have none of that. By midday, Dylan had agreed to co-produce a documentary on the Greenwich Village folk scene, or he allowed Richard to believe as much. They traded shooting duties, and Richard began conducting on-screen interviews, even though the equipment could not record sound. When they stopped at the Folklore Center waving the camera around, Izzy Young was impressed. In his next "Frets and Frails" column for *Sing Out!*, he wrote, "Bob [Dylan] and Dick Farina are doing a movie concerning a lot of people you read about, including myself."

Dylan made his usual surprise appearance in the second half of the Baez concert. Joan and Bob were clearly on different tracks, however, as Robert Shelton made clear in a *New York Times* review that was the first published notice of the professional schism between Bob and Joan. Despite his long allegiance to Dylan, Shelton was on Joan's side. He praised Baez for her political activism and chastised Dylan for a poor performance of new material Shelton considered substandard. "Miss Baez's political concerns were frequently obvious," he noted, recounting her lacerating criticism of Republican senator Barry Goldwater. "The soprano proved to be a much finer interpreter of Bob Dylan's songs than he was," Shelton continued. "He disappointed at least one listener with the lack of control of his stage manner [and] his raucously grating singing." (Dylan had drunk too much red wine; after the concert, he craned his head out of a window of the station wagon and, as a male fan came near, vomited on him.) Contrasting "the somewhat declining level of [Dylan's] new compositions," Shelton devoted a paragraph to two songs by other young composers that he considered "the best" of the concert's "gently philosophic work": Phil Ochs's antiwar "There But for Fortune" and Richard Fariña's "eloquent elegy on the death of six [sic] Negro girls," "Birmingham Sunday."

Drunk as he was, Dylan was determined to drive the station wagon that night. "I was never comfortable with Dick driving," Joan said. "[Fariña] wanted to be the best driver in the world, so he'd go fast, and he could never quite handle it. Bobby insisted on driving . . . and we got in the old station wagon. He was driving us all from the city to Woodstock—Mimi and Dick and Bobby and me and maybe somebody else. And he was driving horrendously. We were just all terrified. . . . We all said, 'Oh, Bobby, let me drive, hah hah,' you know, pussyfooting around, and he was having a wonderful time. 'Hey, I don't know what everybody's so fuckin' scared about. I can drive, right? I can drive.' I mean, if he'd taken his glasses off, it wouldn't have made any difference. He really nearly killed us. Finally, Mimi and I said, 'Oh, we have to go to the bathroom,' so he had to pull in, and we all got out of the car, and he got out of the car, and [Fariña] jumped in the driver's seat. And [Dylan] laughed when he came back from going to the bathroom, 'Oh, man, I can't believe it. Everybody's so fuckin' scared. Everybody's so chicken. . . .' And I said, 'Oh, shut up,' and he got in the backseat, put his head in my lap, and was asleep in about thirty seconds, sweet little baby."

In Bearsville the next day, Joan, Bob, Mimi, and Richard fell into a routine that they maintained for most of the month. Dylan and Fariña worked at their typewriters while the sisters kept each other company, as they had all done when they were together in California. Dylan was concentrating now on his "novel," a patchwork of sketches and experiments with language that he wrote in extemporaneous spurts, and Richard was still fussing with his book, a work in progress for so long now that it seemed almost purely an exercise in self-gratification, like Balzac's "Unknown Masterpiece." The men wrote independently, for the most part, Bob in his room (which was indeed "Bob's room" and locked, even when Dylan was not visiting the Grossmans, off limits to everyone but Joan),

Richard at a small round table by the pool. "It [was] very pretty, very quiet—nice place to work," Richard recalled. "It was especially nice during the days because everybody was doing something separate. Joanie and Bob would be off somewhere while Mimi and I would be somewhere else. I did a lot of cooking around that time, and we also played football together. As I remember, every morning Bob would get up and work." Every few days Dylan or Fariña would show the other a passage he particularly liked; but they never showed work with problems and rarely asked for criticism or advice. The one aspect of the writing life that Dylan and Fariña seemed equally eager to discuss was the matter of getting published. "What's a book agent supposed to do? What percentage do they get?" Bob wanted to know. "How much do you have to write to get a book contract?" Richard appeared to relish being the senior literary colleague, having had short stories and poetry published; "Dick was terribly envious of Dylan, because of his tremendous success in music," Mimi said. "Here was this younger guy making it in a much bigger way. The one edge he had on Dylan was as a serious writer, and he loved that. I know Dick wanted to be like Dylan and have Dylan's kind of success. But I could see when they were together in [Bearsville] that Dylan wanted what Dick had. He was trying to do what Dick did."

Since anyone who walked by the pool could glance over Fariña's pages, Richard soon became suspicious that Dylan was spying on him. "I guess Bob looked at Dick's typewriter or something," recalled Mimi. "Dick was convinced he was trying to steal from him." To trap Dylan, Richard decided to write something awful, something gimmicky, and leave it in his typewriter carriage all day; if he later saw the same idea in Bob's writing, he would know Dylan lifted it. Fariña wrote the silliest paragraph he could, and when he was done, he liked it so much, he hid it to prevent Dylan from taking it.

Fariña continued writing songs, and he and Mimi worked on their music, though only when Bob and Joan were out together. In Dylan's presence, Richard remained a novelist, not a musician, despite the recognition he was receiving for "Birmingham Sunday." The Fariñas were supposed to start recording for Vanguard in New York the following month, so they sneaked in rehearsals like kids trying forbidden experiments when the grown-ups were out of the house.

They had plenty of chances. In the afternoons, Joan would take Bob for long rides around the Catskill Mountains on the cherry-red Triumph 350 motorcycle he had purchased with Mary Travers's husband Barry Feinstein, who was a bike enthusiast as well as a photographer. Bob always held on behind her; although she had ridden motorcycles less than Dylan had, Joan felt more secure when she was driving. "I used to prefer to drive because he was a terrible driver, just terrible," Joan said. "I mean, I figured he was writing ten songs at once and trying to drive at the same time, and I always feared for us. So I'd always say, 'Could I drive?' He drove so sloppy, he used to hang on that thing like a sack of flour." They went antiquing, as they had enjoyed doing in California; Joan was drawn to paintings of the local countryside, Bob to anything that made music. One day he found a wind-up Victrola and a pile of 78-rpm records—a folk revivalist's dream strike of musical antiquities, worthy of Harry Smith himself—and they brought them to the Café Espresso, a European-style sandwich shop that the French chef Bernard Paturel had recently opened in Woodstock. Bob and Joan took a table, ordered some red wine, and spent the afternoon listening to the old recordings, which turned out to be of Caruso-era opera stars, and they sang along with mock grandiosity.

Killing another afternoon at the Café Espresso, Joan and Bob decided to draw portraits of each other in the notepad Dylan often carried to jot lines for songs or poems as they came to him. They took turns posing. For a while, Bob sat at a three-quarter angle from Joan, gazing pensively to one side, and Joan captured his likeness in a skillfully drafted sketch: he projected great seriousness, and she reflected it with formal precision. On her turn to pose, Joan made a buck-toothed funny face, as she had been doing for years at the sight of a camera lens, and Bob scrawled a few lines that suggested her in Thurber cartoon style. Posing again, Joan scowled and stuck out her tongue, and Bob scribbled a drawing, along with some words below her mouth: BAH DA BAH BOMB BOMB BOMB. The drawings were nearly identical to their music—Baez's accomplished, formal, nuanced, and austere, Dylan's spontaneous, naïve, piercing, and fearless. At one point, Bob or Joan suggested that they draw themselves, which was easy for Baez. She used to sketch herself to pass time in high school and knew how to produce a profile of herself in the proficient style of a sidewalk charcoal artist. On his turn, Bob drew the scantest suggestion of a face, with a preposterously enormous hook nose.

"Bob and Joan came in a lot, and he would order anything that was fried," Bernard Paturel said. "People would come up to me the next day and say, 'Bernard, I heard Dylan and Joan were in here yesterday. Why didn't you call me? I would have come and brought a lot of people—you would have a lot of business.' Well, that's why I didn't tell them. [Baez and Dylan] didn't want any attention. If they wanted a big party, they would bring Dick and Mimi. If Dick was there, there was a party."

Detached from the worlds of music and politics, alone but for Mimi and Richard, Baez and Dylan gave in to the sheer pleasure of each other's company in Bearsville. As Joan wrote in a letter to her mother,

> I've gotten very close to Bobby in the last month. We have such FUN! Wow and he takes baths and everything. . . . He is beautiful to me. He bought me a beautiful coat and a dress and earrings, and he's just a joy to be with. We understand each other's need for freedom and there are no chains, just good feelings and giggles and a lot of love. And I enjoy his genius. . . . Everything is cool. Mimi and Dick aren't too cool, but it comes and goes. I think Bobby will come and stay with me for a while if my house is done. . . . I really love him.

Enclosed in the same envelope was a second letter signed by Joan but really written by Bob, pretending to be her:

> It's me here. i'm up in woodstock at uncle alby's. nice house you oughta be here. swimming pool. all that stuff. i'm with you-know who. dick an mimi're also round the place but i've hardly seen

them sinse you-know-who got a hold on me. mummy you must
believe me. i was gonna stay at the foremans as planned i mean i
was all set to an everything. anyway when me an mimi got t town
right away first thing we did was to go there. an you know me i
was tired and it was already past noon an well i fuigureed like to
get t sleep you know an well i got in t bed y'know an jesus i pulled
back the blankets an who do you think was hiding under the quilt?
yeah him. i mean like i dont know if you'll believe me or not but i
swear t gawd he was rolled up like a ball inside the pillow.
mummy, i shit. the first thing i did was t call for mimi.

What, exactly, did Joan find none too cool about Mimi and Richard?
"As long as he was good to my sister, he was cool with me," Joan said.
"If he wasn't, he wasn't. I was sensing some sort of anxiety, and I didn't
like what I saw it doing to her." As Mimi recalled, the stress of preparing
for their upcoming recording session put a strain on their marriage, a
problem compounded by Fariña's frustration with his novel and Mimi's
own jealousy of Joan and Richard's new musical relationship. "We had
this recording date coming up in New York, and Dick was very nervous
about it," Mimi said. "It really meant a lot to him to do something really
good and original, and not just make a record. I think he learned his lesson in London. He was beginning to get recognition as a songwriter
through Joan, and she was anxious to hear his next songs, because Dylan
stopped writing the political things, so there was that. He felt the pressure, and I was feeling a little lost in the picture. And it all meant so much
to him, because he still didn't have a publisher for his book, so he didn't
have that validation."

When Dylan mentioned casually that he was going to be meeting a
book editor because Albert Grossman was negotiating to have his novel
published, Fariña congratulated him coolly—*hey, man, groovy*—and
went out for a long, long walk. When he returned with his pants and
shirtsleeves caked with dirt and thorns from treading deep in the woods,
Mimi could barely contain him. He paced around their room, ranting
about the advantages of fame and good management. *When we make it,*

he predicted to his wife, *they'll publish our grocery list, and it'll be better written than Dylan's poetry. If only Albert Grossman were managing us.* "He was terribly upset," Mimi said. "He never let himself look that messy." (Fariña always had his jeans dry-cleaned and pressed.)

Joan drove Bob to Manhattan on his motorcycle to meet Robert Markel, a young editor who had recently joined Macmillan and who knew Barry Feinstein through mutual friends. Grossman, by way of Feinstein, had contacted Markel about publishing Dylan. Feinstein proposed a book of his photographs with captions by Bob, but Markel was more interested in the prose-poetry Grossman said Dylan had been writing. Grossman's office gave Feinstein ten or fifteen pages of sample typescript to pass along to Markel, who found the work intriguing but inconclusive. "I liked it, because it had a freshness of expression," he said. "It was going down a path that I hadn't seen before. I didn't know quite what kind of an animal it was or what to call it or where it would go or how it would develop, but I also knew damned well that with Dylan's name on it and the fact that he was moving up the charts and whatnot that it would be a smart thing to publish him, if I could make something coherent out of it. Some things were unclear to me, and there were some things I didn't find to my liking, so we needed to get together."

Dylan requested that their meeting be held after business hours so he would not have to meet anyone at Macmillan except Markel. Joan and Bob switched places on Dylan's motorcycle a few blocks from the publisher's offices on Fifth Avenue and 12th Street in Greenwich Village, Bob at the handlebars when they arrived. He parked the bike on the sidewalk in front of the building, and they approached the receptionist, who had been told that Mr. Markel was expecting a gentleman but was unprepared for a windblown young couple in blue jeans, boots, and leather jackets. Markel came down from his office accompanied by a security guard and ushered his prospective new author and the author's girlfriend up a marble staircase, past the portraits of Yeats, Churchill, and other Macmillan writers, to Markel's small office along a windowless side wall. They were the only three people on the floor, as Dylan had requested.

"They seemed slightly ill at ease and very playful, I think trying to hide their nerves," said Markel. "There was a lot of chatter between them of a personal nature or some nature of which I wasn't included—inside jokes going back and forth. Almost the first thing that happened was that they said, 'What about the title?' and Joan Baez said, 'I have an idea for a title.' So I leaned forward with all of my attention, to show that I really cared about what her idea for a title was, and she said, 'Why don't you call the book *Fuck You?*' Now, that was a phrase that I had heard before, but it was not a phrase that one heard women use, by and large, especially in a place of business. She smiled as she said it, but there was a bit of a serious note there. So in order to show that I was taking all of the things they were saying seriously, I said, 'Well, that's an interesting idea. But I'm not certain it's going to work for this particular book.' " Bob mentioned another idea, *Side One*, and Markel agreed to it as a working title. (The final title would be *Tarantula*.)

The meeting lasted about fifteen minutes. Markel would ask a question, and Joan and Bob would whisper between themselves until they came up with an answer, and one of them would announce it. "The distinct impression I got was that Dylan wanted to show her off to me—'My girlfriend is the beautiful and sophisticated Joan Baez.' And he wanted to show me off to her, to impress her—'I have a contract with the Macmillan company, and I'm going to be an author with a capital A, underscored in italics. What about that?' Beyond that, he was really uncertain what the hell he was doing. Suddenly, they had to leave. They both seemed to have a very short attention span, and they got bored and left. But we had somehow covered everything it would usually take a two-hour luncheon to discuss." It was settled: Dylan would write a book for Macmillan. It would be an episodic collection of short prose-poetry pieces, about two hundred pages of typescript, to be delivered a year later for prospective publication at some point in 1966. (In a separate meeting with Albert Grossman and the Macmillan attorneys, the author's advance would be set at $10,000, to be paid upon signing, respectable for a first-time author at the time.) Already beginning to bring a literary quality to music of the rock and roll era, Dylan was now introducing the literary world to the rock and roll sensibility.

Richard Fariña could not forgive him for it. "Dick put years into that book [of his] . . . that he was trying to do as real literature in a radical young voice," Eric von Schmidt said. "He was really trying to do something revolutionary—a pop–rock and roll–college-drug-music novel and with pictures on top of that—and Dylan comes along and publishers are chasing after him, and Bob doesn't have any idea what he wants to do. Dick was really pissed."

Dylan knew he had fallen into his Macmillan contract and, indeed, privately resented the pressure he felt to prove himself between hard covers. As he explained in an interview (five years later), "When I suddenly began to sell quite a few records and a certain amount of publicity began to be carried in all the major news magazines about this 'rising young star,' well . . . book companies began sending me contracts, because I was doing interviews before and after concerts, and reporters would say things like, 'What else do you write?' And I would say, 'Well, I don't write much of anything else.' And they would say, 'Oh, come on. You must write other things. Tell us something else. Do you write books?' And I'd say, 'Sure, I write books.' After the publishers saw that I wrote books they began to send me contracts. . . . We took the biggest one and then owed them a book." In truth, there is no evidence that any publisher besides Macmillan approached Dylan. "You follow me? But there was no book. We just took the biggest contract. Why, I don't know. Why I *did*, I don't know. Why I was *told* to do it, I don't know. Anyway, I owed them a book.

"Boy, they were hungry for this book. They didn't care what it was. They just wanted . . . people up there were saying, 'Boy, that's the second James Joyce' and 'Jack Kerouac again,' and they were saying 'Homer revisited' . . . and they were all just talking through their heads. They just wanted to sell books, that's all they wanted to do. [My book] wasn't about anything . . . and I knew that—I figured they *had* to know that, they were in the business. I knew that, and I was just nobody. If I knew it, where were they at? They were just playing with me. 'My book.' "

At the end of the summer, Sally and Albert Grossman returned to

Bearsville, and Alfredo Dopico came to take Richard and Mimi to Manhattan for their first record date. Joan took the train back to California, and Bob stayed a little longer in his room at Grossman's house; though they were apart again, their relationship had survived—indeed, prevailed through—the shifts in their careers. Baez and Dylan kept in touch by phone while Bob was in Bearsville, working on his book and unwinding in the company of visiting friends (such as Neuwirth, Paul Clayton, and David Blue), clients of Albert's (including Odetta and Peter, Paul and Mary), and friends of Sally's (such as Sara Lownds, a former model and onetime *Playboy* bunny). "[He] and I talked in a playful way over that summer month about 'our futures,' " Joan recalled in her memoirs. "We even named a baby. I think the name was Shannon.

"As I remember it, [he] called me one day [from] Woodstock and, with what sounded like a party in the background, mumbled something about marriage. I do remember that I said no. It had not been a proposal; it had been a noncommittal continuation of our fun and games that might very well have led to a noncommittal joining of two lives in a noncommittal marriage. That is my memory. I'm sure [Dylan would] remember it differently, if at all." Remembering the same phone conversation somewhat differently herself (in an interview with Dylan biographer Anthony Scaduto around 1970), Joan said, "We talked about getting married. He was on the East Coast and I was on the West Coast when that came about in a phone conversation. And we kidded about it, because we knew, in a sense, we almost felt it was inevitable, too. . . . I think what happened was that I expressed it before he did. He would have, probably, eventually. But he was still in the joking stage, and I said, 'Oh, you know, it'd never work out' or something. . . . And after that was the switch, after that he was never . . . I mean, after that it was as though he was trying to get back at me. Ever after, it was as though he was playing around with my soul." When pressed to recall which account was more accurate and who really called whom, Joan answered quickly, "Either way—same thing. We both thought about it, and neither one of us wanted it bad enough. I think we both felt spurned, and we were both right." Around the Village, only one rumor about the relationship between Baez and Dylan was verifiable, Izzy Young reported in *Sing Out!* in the fall of 1964: They would get married, if they could only agree on whose last name to use.

W HATEVER TROPISM DREW both Joan Baez and Bob Dylan out of the city and into the woods as they became successful, a different impulse drove Richard Fariña, and Mimi followed him. Whether Joan and Bob were seeking escape, repose, or inspiration, Richard sought the isolation of cabin life only to work his way toward a victory. With success, he needed people. Now that he and Mimi were professional musicians, they had to get out of the Carmel Highlands. The Fariñas decided to move to Cambridge as soon as they finished recording in New York. "We both wanted to move," said Mimi. "I needed a break from Joanie. For Dick, I think it was about coming out of his shell." When his book was published, Mimi assumed, they would move from Cambridge to New York or another major city, perhaps San Francisco.

Mimi and Richard made their first record, *Celebrations for a Grey Day* (a variation of the title of the poem he wrote for Carolyn Hester), in two days of sessions at Manhattan's Olmstead Studios in early autumn 1964. All the songs were Richard's, with the exceptions of the traditional "Dog Blue," which was arranged by Mimi, and "Pack Up Your Sorrows," which was credited to Richard and Mimi's sister Pauline, from whom Fariña had taken the title phrase. It was a wildly adventurous and eclectic record. More than half of the songs were instrumentals built around Fariña's free approach to the dulcimer. He created songs like paella, rummaging around his memory for available ingredients—bits of Appalachian melodies, Irish cadences, Latin rhythmic patterns, modal ideas smuggled through unknown parties from the Middle East, and hints of the blues—that he chopped and mixed together. The lyrics are clearly the work of a skilled writer, disciplined if overly romantic and a bit too neatly crafted at points, as in "Another Country":

When we were apprenticed to roaming
We tried the hills of Spain
The roads were open, the company good
We rose where we had lain

Most extraordinarily, Richard pressed Maynard Solomon to allow him to record two songs that brought poetry together with folk music and rock and roll. Several others had combined folk and rock: Dylan had recorded one song, "Mixed-Up Confusion," with a rock band in November 1962, although the tune itself was fairly conventional and lyrically a throw-away, reportedly jotted down in a taxi on the way to the recording studio. (He would later dismiss it; "It didn't do anything, whatever it was supposed to do," Dylan said. "I didn't arrange the session. It wasn't my idea.") Since then, Bob had gone only as far as implying rock and pop through his chord changes, his driving guitar work, and his eruptive singing style. (Dylan would not record his breakthrough folk-rock album, *Bringing It All Back Home*, until the beginning of the following year.) The Animals, a rough-hewn combo from Newcastle, England, had given the folk standard "House of the Rising Sun" rock treatment, and it became a number-one hit. John Hammond, Jr., the twenty-three-year-old singer and guitarist, had recorded with a Canadian bar band, The Hawks (with Dylan in attendance at the sessions), but they were playing traditional blues songs. No one had recorded songs with mature, poetic lyrics and music in the rock style until Fariña's "One-Way Ticket" (a twelve-bar blues) and "Reno Nevada" (an innovative song in a sixteen-measure form, built on a riff related to Herbie Hancock's 1962 jazz composition, "Watermelon Man"). Both are road songs about journeys to the brink, with forceful, biting words. In "Reno Nevada," Fariña snarls,

You can walk down the street
Pass your face in the window
You can keep on fooling around
You can work day and night
Take a chance on promotion
You can fall thru a hole in the ground

For the instrumental break, Bruce Langhorne took a long electric guitar solo so raw that it nearly jeopardized the whole album; Seymour Solomon threatened not to release the record with that "abrasive noise," but he capitulated when Fariña said Solomon was correct about the solo and that that was precisely its intent.

"We all grew up with . . . radio music—it was not traditional music," Fariña said. "Only when popular music was in its very worst period, when nothing was happening there, did we turn to folk music. [Rock and roll] was part of everybody's music when they were growing up in America. It was part of high school in America. The first person that Dylan and I ever talked about when we hung out together was Buddy Holly." If so, neither of them had talked much about Holly since then, at least not in public. Everyone knew rock and roll was the music that Fariña, Dylan, and their peers grew up with—and grew out of. But virtually no one seemed to think of it as something that could grow up with its audience.

"Folk music, through no fault of its own, fooled us into certain sympathies and nostalgic alliances with the so-called traditional past," Fariña said, distancing himself from the culture of the music while he was experimenting with it. "The '30s, the highways and open roads, the Big West, the southern mountains, the blues, labor unions, Childe [sic] ballads—all . . . made their mark, almost as if Chuck Berry and Batman had really nothing to do with who we were, and Uncle Dave Macon or Horton Barker could do a better job of telling us. But the paradox was implicit: What the hell were rebels doing looking for roots? And how long would people with contemporary poetic sensibilities be content to sing archaic material? Some of us had been listening to AM radio for a number of years."

During the months between their recording sessions and the release of the album, Mimi and Richard made a new home with Lush in Cambridge. They rented half of one floor in a two-story row house on Putnam Avenue that had been divided into four one-bedroom apartments. The neighborhood was Massachusetts-Irish working-class. Kids everywhere. If Mimi left the apartment while Richard was rehearsing a song, she would have to step over the children sitting in the hall, listening through the door. The landlord prohibited pets, "but [Lush] knows about it," Richard explained in a letter to Alan Marcus, "and has learned the secret of canine invisibility." Mimi felt at home among the old friends who had stayed in (or had left and returned to) Cambridge—Debbie Green, Betsy and Bob Siggins, the Robinson sisters, the Greenhills, most of the original Charles River Valley Boys—although many of them privately distrusted Fariña. "People who knew her when she was young were very protective of Mimi, because they were older and she was shy," Debbie Green said, "and Fariña scared certain people away, because he wasn't one of the 'in' crowd in Cambridge and he certainly wasn't a New England type. There was a lot of bad-mouthing about Richard going on, but it was all behind Mimi's back." The Harvard Square scene had not changed much since the Baezes lived in Belmont. All the same clubs and coffeehouses were open, and the legend of Joan Baez still lingered in the coffeehouses half a decade after she had sung in any of them. "I was glad I was married and doing my own thing when I came back," said Mimi, who applied to the Boston Conservatory to study dance and was accepted. "There was a kind of clinging thing, where they didn't want to let Joanie go. It was much better for me to come back and be Mimi Fariña and not the little Joan." This was very much a return with a difference. "Richard loved Cambridge, too," Mimi added. "He really liked the stimulation of the city and the universities, where there were a lot of interesting people and he could talk about books and ideas." Richard, who had started his adult life as an aspiring artiste in College Town, relished being a working one in the quintessential American college town.

Comparing notes with the young songwriter Eric Andersen at a party in Betsy and Bob Siggins's house, Richard said he had been talking to Albert Grossman that day and heard that Dylan had just become a million-aire. "Keep writing songs," Fariña encouraged Andersen. (Grossman's early nurturing had paid off well: although none of Dylan's four albums had sold more than a few hundred thousand copies, Dylan's songs were on million-selling albums by hit acts such as Peter, Paul and Mary, and "Blowin' in the Wind" had been recorded by dozens of others, from Odetta to Kate Smith.) While money was still tight for Mimi and Richard, they were able to live on their advance from Vanguard and in-come from a new song-publishing contract with Witmark that Richard asked Albert Grossman to set up for him. Soon they were getting hired to perform publicly, beginning with the first of several engagements on a double bill with Mitch Greenhill at Club 47 on Saturday, September 26. (Tom Rush, Jim Kweskin, and Judy Collins had appeared there earlier that week.)

At first Mimi and Richard were an unknown musical quantity; their name was misspelled "Farinia" on the club's promotional materials. "Richard was the focus—he would do all the talking," recalled Mitch Greenhill. "Mimi actually was quiet and beautiful and intriguing from that point of view, whereas Richard was more get-out-there-and-grab-the-audience. The strongest part was his dulcimer. I hadn't really heard anybody play the instrument that way before. It was very driving, rhyth-mic, kind of rock and roll dulcimer playing. They had a mystique. I ac-tually felt quite a bit ignored on those gigs. I definitely felt kind of second-banana on the situation and was kind of struck by how happen-ing the Dick and Mimi show was. It really was quite together and dy-namic, and they went over very, very well."

Personally, however, Greenhill could never warm up to Richard. "I think he was creating himself in a way where I could kind of see the strings, whereas in Dylan's case, I couldn't see the strings—it seemed so organic," Greenhill said. "So Richard made me a little uncomfortable. Dy-lan was offensive in that he would really be *rude* to people, and Dick wouldn't really be rude to people. But Dick was like 'Look at me—here I am. Dig me!' Dylan was like, 'Look all you want. You'll never see me.' "

Mimi and Richard's impact at Club 47 was such that they were given a regular monthly slot. To fill out their sound and help ground their often ethereal music, they brought in Fritz Richmond of the Jim Kweskin Jug Band to play washtub bass. "I was sort of in awe of them," Richmond said. "They were sort of the perfect couple. And Mimi—she was the most beautiful woman I have ever seen. She was so pretty that I couldn't actually see her. If I looked in her eyes, I would be in danger of meltdown. It was distracting. Dick was very outgoing and gregarious. He always had a party going on, but it was on a very intellectual level. He liked to talk about great writers and philosophical ideas and so forth, and when we were doing those gigs, their audience was sort of like him. They got these shrinking-violet type of college girls coming in, and they marveled at Richard."

Meantime Richard's literary agent, Robert Mills, was now shopping a finished manuscript of Fariña's book and getting rejections that the author found heartening. "The book has been turned down now by Lippincott and Doubleday," Richard wrote to Eric von Schmidt. "Mills says he is encouraged, however, by the nature of both rejections, since they reinforce his (our) belief that the book *is* a book. . . . The fact that it is finished and circulating, and coming closer each time speaks for something positive." As von Schmidt recalled, "All he got was rejections on that thing since we were in London, and he announced every one to me like it was good news." Others with firm goals and strong personalities—such as Joan Baez, for instance—refused to take no for an answer. Fariña heard everything as yes.

WHEN HE WAS A BOY, Bob Dylan liked to make his own Halloween costumes. One year when he was nine or ten, he put his pajamas on backward, cocked an old fedora of his father's on his head jauntily, and strapped on a cap-gun holster. "Who are you supposed to be?" his younger brother

David asked. "If you don't know," Bob said, "I'm not going to tell you."

Some fifteen years later, Halloween night 1964, Dylan gave his first New York concert since his Carnegie Hall performance the previous October, and he was still playing with mysterious disguises. He performed solo, accompanying himself on acoustic guitar and harmonica to an audience overflowing onto folding chairs set up on the stage of the 2,600-seat Philharmonic Hall. Joan Baez (unbilled as usual) joined him for a duo set, and they looked and sounded beautiful—Bob sleek in jeans that fit and were clean, a black turtleneck, and a gray sport jacket, his thick hair brushed back; Joan sultry in fishnet stockings and a knee-length black cocktail dress that set off a long gold chain that twirled on her body as she swayed in time. Bob accompanied Joan while she sang "Silver Dagger"; for their duets, they did not only the now-familiar "With God on Our Side" and "It Ain't Me, Babe," but also a country-flavored love song recorded for *Another Side of Bob Dylan* but not issued on the album, "Mama, You Been on My Mind." With Columbia recording the show for a prospective "live" album (never commercially released), the program was exceptionally varied: Dylan offered up samples of everything he had written, from his early talking blues to the protest anthems to the relationship songs from his latest record. Bob was in good cheer all night, chatting with the audience between songs. "It's Halloween—I have my Bob Dylan mask on," he said. "I'm masquerading!"

The program booklet included a new prose-poem written by Bob Dylan for the occasion, "Advice for Geraldine on Her Miscellaneous Birthday"—a litany of aphorisms, mostly humorous, all cynical, ostensibly directed at a hypothetical friend or protégée but largely self-referential. It is a bitterly comic handbook of tips on aversion and distortion of identity: "be careful of enthusiasm . . . it is all temporary an' don't let it sway you . . . do Not create anything, it will be misinterpreted. it will not change. it will follow you the rest of your life. when asked what you do for a living say you laugh for a living . . . when asked if you care about the world's problems, look deeply into the eyes of he that asks you, he will not ask you again . . . when asked t' give your real name . . . never give it."

If he was masquerading, who was Bob supposed to be this time? In the opening paragraph of his *New York Times* review of the Philharmonic Hall concert, Robert Shelton referred to him as Dylan "the writer and folk musician." (In the closing sentence, much the same, Shelton called him the "brilliant singing poet laureate of young America.") Now publicized as an author contracted to a major publisher as well as an acclaimed songwriter, Bob certainly had literary credibility, whether or not he was indeed a writer *first*. As for being a folk musician, no one had much reason to think of Dylan as any other kind. Still, when he made his little joke about masquerading, the next song he played was something new, "If You Gotta Go, Go Now." A simple, heavily rhythmic tune with an indelible chorus about sex, it was rock and roll in everything but instrumentation, and Dylan was slashing at his Martin guitar as if it were a Stratocaster. He had his Bob Dylan mask on, and the person under it was Elston Gunn. Bob and his teenage rock and roll self sounded very much as if they wanted to switch places.

Instead, they united. On January 13–16, 1965, Dylan returned to Columbia's Studio A, accompanied by Baez on at least one of the first two days, to engage in an experiment. His current producer, Tom Wilson, had already tested the idea of giving Bob's music a rock treatment; a few weeks earlier, Wilson had tried overdubbing electric instruments and drums over several existing Dylan tracks (including the acoustic version of "House of the Risin' Sun" from Bob's first Columbia sessions) without Dylan's knowledge. Evidently satisfied with the results, Wilson prepared to bring out yet another side of Bob Dylan for his fifth album. On the first day of recording, Dylan sang and played acoustic versions of eleven new songs, accompanied by John Sebastian on bass. Over the following two days, he rerecorded nearly all of those songs with various configurations of musicians playing electrified instruments, rock and roll style. Neither Wilson nor Dylan seemed wholly certain what they wanted, other than spontaneity; they tried three more bassists, John Boone, Bill Lee, and Joseph Macho, Jr., and four electric guitarists with different approaches—the bluesy Bruce Langhorne and John Hammond, Jr., the pop-oriented Kenny Rankin, and the versatile studio pro Al Gorgoni. Dylan played acoustic guitar on most of the tracks, approximating the effect of the electric by use of dynamic strumming patterns, and traded off on the piano with studio musician Paul Griffin. (Bob had virtually no experience on the electric guitar and was not prepared to record on the instrument; he still formed his chords folk-style, on the end of the neck.) There were virtually no rehearsals or run-throughs, just recorded takes. "There was a whole bunch of studio cats, and we were unrehearsed," said Langhorne. "No lead sheets. Everyone would just start playin'. I don't even remember Bob runnin' through the songs once. It was sort of telepathic—'Let's do a take.' " In most cases, no more than one or two takes were attempted, and several tracks selected for the record (and eventually seen as classic, including "Subterranean Homesick Blues") are first takes. If Dylan and Tom Wilson were using the studio like a laboratory, grabbing sounds and styles, throwing them together, shooting them with electricity, they seemed to be trying to make explosions.

Most of Dylan's new songs (with the notable exception of "Mr. Tambourine Man," one of several tunes recorded in Bob's older style, with acoustic guitar) were created as spontaneously as they were recorded. Bob had written nearly all his new work in a few days, holed up alone in a studio apartment above the Café Espresso in Bearsville. He laid out dozens of photographs torn from newspapers and magazines in a montage on the floor and sat down amidst them with his guitar. Bernard Paturel stopped by a couple of times and watched as Dylan composed: Bob would start with a simple musical framework, a blues pattern he could repeat indefinitely, and he would close his eyes—he would not draw from the pictures literally but would use the impression the faces left as a visual model for kaleidoscopic language. He appeared to sing whatever came to him, disconnected phrases with a poetic feeling. When something came out that he liked, he scrawled it down hurriedly, so as to stay in the moment, and he would do this until there were enough words written for a song.

Walk on your tip toes
Don't try No Doz
Better stay away from those
That carry around a fire hose

Much as he drank coffee and red wine habitually while working at his typewriter, he chain-smoked marijuana while he composed this work.

The songs Dylan wrote for *Bringing It All Back Home* were verbal improvisations—strongly indebted to his recent prose-poetry but also a mutation of the talking blues and the lyric high jinks of Chuck Berry and Little Richard (as well as jazz "vocalese" and the century-old Negro tradition of "toasting," whether or not Dylan had any such historical references in mind). He was not pursuing refinement, sophistication, and clarity of expression, those ideals of the Cole Porter generation of songwriters, but their near opposites: kinetic energy, instinct, and ambiguity. As he explained in the liner notes to the album, "[I] have given up at making any attempt at perfection. . . . the Great books've been written. the Great sayings have all been said / I am about t sketch You a picture of what goes on around here sometimes. tho I don't understand too well myself what's really happening." When she watched him write, Joan Baez got the impression that Dylan hated to edit or revise a word once written, because he valued naturalness above all. "I'm not just . . . trying to invent some surrealistic rhapsody," Bob later said. "It's the sound and the words. . . . I'm not doing it to see how good I can sound or how perfect the melody can be or how intricate the details can be woven or how perfectly written something can be. I don't care about those things."

Made up of seven tunes recorded with a rock band (including "Subterranean Homesick Blues," "She Belongs to Me," and "Maggie's Farm") and four with acoustic guitar (among them "It's Alright Ma" and "It's All Over Now, Baby Blue"), *Bringing It All Back Home* is the manifesto of a new music. It is no darker than Dylan's Columbia debut, an album about death and pain. It is not as emotionally raw as *Another Side*; nor is it as melodic, varied, and well crafted as either *Freewheelin'* or *The Times They Are a-Changin'*. But it is faster moving, more alive, sexier, more urban, than anything Dylan had ever tried. By uniting his teenage musical passion, rock and roll, with his adult creative outlet, poetry, he found a new style he loved—"the sound of the streets," Dylan said. "That ethereal twilight light, you know. It's the sound of the street with the sun rays, the sun shining down at a particular time on a particular type of building. A particular type of people walking on a particular type of street. It's an outdoor sound that drifts even into open windows that you can hear. The sound of bells and distant railroad trains and arguments in apartments and the clinking of silverware and knives and forks and beating with leather straps. It's all—it's all there." No one had ever tried anything like it, except for Richard Fariña's experiment with two songs a couple of months earlier, although his album with Mimi had not yet been released.

The jacket cover for *Bringing It All Back Home*, which would be released on March 22, was designed to establish Bob's new identity at a glance. Dylan is thoroughly citified, dressed up in French cuffs and a black sport jacket and lounging in an opulent parlor—could it be a townhouse in England, home of the Beatles and the Animals? He is surrounded by deliberately strewn-about magazines and records (including albums by Lotte Lenya and Eric von Schmidt), demonstrative evidence of the subject's eclectic influences and interests. Dylan pets a small blue Persian cat and scowls at the camera while, in the background, Sally Grossman reclines in a red gown, smoking a cigarette. No work clothes, no snowy street, no folk guitars, no earth-sister girlfriend: this Dylan is not the hardscrabble troubadour of the working folk but a vaguely Edwardian young philosopher-aristocrat—a thinking dandy who has the leisure to delve into the world of ideas and music and looks none too happy with what he has found. A trick photo effect devised for the shoot by photographer Daniel Kramer (involving a double exposure and a jerry-built revolving camera back) distorts the edges of the scene, evoking the drug haze in which Dylan composed much of the album as well as its disorienting impact upon the listener.

Some of Bob's new music troubled Joan. She accepted much of it, especially the work overtly connected to the folk tradition, such as "Mr.

Tambourine Man" and "Gates of Eden." (At their heart, nearly all the tunes recorded for *Bringing It All Back Home*, including the rockers, had links to folk music; "Subterranean Homesick Blues," with its blues harmonies flexibly stretched over eighteen-measure verses, came out of a song by Woody Guthrie and Pete Seeger called "Take It Easy," which had a similar structure and the lyrics "Mom was in the kitchen, preparing to eat / Sis was in the pantry looking for some yeast / Pa was in the cellar mixing up the hops / And Brother's at the window, he's watching for the cops"; "She Belongs to Me" has the same melody and chord structure as von Schmidt's "Going Down to Melbourne"; and "Maggie's Farm" is a rewrite of a Seeger favorite about a hostile landlord, called "Down on Penny's Farm"—Dylan's second use of this material.) As Bruce Langhorne observed, "Bob still had folk music in his head, even though we were playing something else." On the recording of the comedic story-song "Bob Dylan's 115th Dream," you can hear Joan laughing in the studio. She even tolerated one song recorded with a rock band that seemed to be about her, "She Belongs to Me," despite its sarcastic lyrics. (The protagonist of the song has an Egyptian ring, like Joan; Dylan portrays her as an arrogant, pretentious artist.) "Oh, I didn't mind any way he might have used me or the idea of me or anything like that," she said, "and there was no way to be sure if he was really writing about me—I wouldn't ask him, and he wouldn't tell me. The songs he was doing weren't really about anybody or anything in particular, anyway." What disturbed Baez was the growing sense of nihilism in Dylan's words and music. "He criticizes society, and I criticize it," she said at the time, "but he ends up saying there is not a goddamned thing you can do about it, so screw it. And I say just the opposite. I am afraid the message that comes through from Dylan in 1965 . . . is, 'Let's all go home and smoke pot, because there's nothing else to do. . . . We might as well go down smoking.' " The rock sound of more than half the songs on *Bringing It All Back Home* only magnified that impression for Joan. "I didn't like what he was doing," she said. "It was haphazard, and it was sloppy and too negative for me. There was hardly anything positive in it. I thought he just went one step too far in a very negative direction."

Dylan was changing too quickly for his own management. Unable to anticipate the course Bob's music would be taking, Charlie Rothschild was working with Albert Grossman to organize a spring tour of concerts featuring Dylan and Baez together, playing acoustic guitars for college audiences. The notion was to capitalize on the publicity Bob and Joan had been garnering as a couple—"the folk king and queen greet their public," Rothschild said. They would be billed and promoted as equals; in the year and a half since Joan introduced the little-known boy poet to her audiences, Dylan had achieved professional parity with his mentor and lover.

That equilibrium seemed critical to everyone involved and impossible to maintain. Manny Greenhill entered into the negotiations of financial terms girded to protect his client from Grossman, only to undermine his own intentions. "Manny was a lovely man, but was not as astute a businessman as Albert was, and he was paranoid that Albert was about to put something over on him," Rothschild recalled. "We went to him, and we were offering a deal where we would guarantee Joan Baez X amount of money per concert, rather than a percentage of the profits. Manny assumed Albert was taking advantage of him, so he turned the deal around, and he said, 'I'll do it, providing that Bob be the one who gets the guarantee, and we keep a percentage.' Well, as it turned out, there were a number of places that didn't turn a profit, so Bob ended up with more money than Joan, because of her manager." Dylan would appear to take special delight in this irony. "Manny Greenhill—he's such a loser," Bob said. "You know, such a stone loser. I worked for the cat, I did [those] concerts with Joan Baez. And would you believe this—I wasn't big then, really—not really big. I made more than she did, because he just had his ass up his neck. He did not know. Albert tried to make a deal with him, and he came on like a businessman . . . and Albert said, 'Okay,' and stuck it [to] him."

Greenhill commissioned Eric von Schmidt to do a painting of Baez and Dylan for a tour poster. For a reference image, von Schmidt used the poignant photograph Richard Waterman had taken at Club 47 when Joan and Bob had been squabbling and she nestled aside him onstage, patting a tambourine as he sang. "I had to adapt it—it was like doing a Chinese puzzle," von Schmidt said. "Manny and Albert insisted [Baez and Dylan] had to be exactly the same size. Neither one could look more important than the other, and I had to do the type so neither of their names was first and neither of them was above the other." His solution was an off-kilter design whereby Joan's name and image appear first from left to right, but Bob's come first from top to bottom. It was equally lovely and ingenious, a Lautrec-influenced watercolor designed for silk-screening. Greenhill's office had several thousand posters printed in time for the first concert at the state college in Bridgewater, Massachusetts, in late February, and Richard Waterman was dispatched to hang them at other local colleges. He started in a dormitory at Quinnipiac College, hanging posters all around the first floor, then on each of the two floors above it; by the time Waterman returned to the ground floor on his way out, students had taken them all down and squirreled them away in their rooms. A few days later Albert Grossman called Manny Greenhill, ordering that all the posters distributed be removed and pulped. "Manny was very upset," Waterman said. "Grossman was upset. Albert said, 'Bobby doesn't like it,' so we had to print up new posters—just type. No pictures. Bobby thought Joan's face was too big and too much in the foreground, and he thought Eric had made his nose look too big."

From late February to March 24, Baez and Dylan gave at least six and perhaps as many as ten dual concerts at colleges on the East Coast. (The tour itineraries are lost, and oral history accounts vary.) They took turns opening for each other, and each performed a forty-minute set followed by a shorter closing set of duets. Joan used at least five minutes of her time each night to lecture the student audiences on human rights and pacifism. Bob played mostly newer songs, including the hard-driving acoustic numbers from *Bringing It All Back Home*, such as "It's Alright Ma (I'm Only Bleeding)"; he largely ignored the political and social material that had drawn Baez—and much of his college audience—to him. Neither Bob nor Joan seemed especially pleased with what the other was doing, and their duets of the same few songs were growing pat, although they did add two-part harmony arrangements of the traditional tune "Wild Mountain Thyme" (or "Purple Heather") to their repertoire.

"The kids were calling out for him to do the songs that meant something to them, like 'Masters of War' and 'With God on Our Side,' " Baez said. "He didn't care. They were reaching out to him, and he didn't care. He just wanted to rock and roll."

Dylan was no longer content in the low-key atmosphere of acoustic folk concerts. "We played ten concerts together and, like, then I knew that it was all over," Bob said. "She gets such a morgue audience. They're so morgue-y. The only thing that dragged me when I played with her was that the audience was just a morgue. It was like playing in a funeral parlor. They [were] just sort of little flashlight people." The audience on this joint tour was his as much as hers, however. In fact, Rothschild believed Dylan to be the larger draw at most locations. Seemingly resentful of the awe in which he was held and quick to blame Joan for it, Bob began moving to shed his association with the whole folk scene, including Baez.

"I loved the fame, attention, and association with Bob, but soon our real differences surfaced and began to dominate our relationship," Baez wrote in her memoirs, recalling this tour. "Once I asked him how he came to write 'Masters of War.' His reply was that he knew it would sell; I didn't buy his answer then and I don't now. Once he commented to me about the kids in the audience calling out for 'Masters of War': 'They think I'm something I ain't.' And then he joked about it and told me to take care of them and 'all that stuff.' I told him I'd do my best. We were outside somewhere; I was yanking up blades of grass, troubled that our paths were splitting and going in very different directions. I asked him what made us different, and he said it was simple, that I thought I could change things, and he knew that no one could."

Baez and Dylan were taking separate but adjacent rooms in hotels and scarcely talking at much depth or length, despite Joan's efforts to discuss the growing distance between them. Bob, who had always been his most communicative in song, suggested to Joan that they warm up their voices by trying the Righteous Brothers' 1964 pop hit "You've Lost That Loving Feelin'." "We made the college tour, but I wouldn't talk to her," Dylan recalled. "I mean, who needs that? College-boy shit, college girl. High school. Petty senior prom bullshit."

When they finally had their first honest conversation, a couple of weeks into the tour, it was brief but decisive. "The most real conversation I ever had with him, which was the beginning of Bobby and my splitting, was after the last concert we did together," Joan said. "He said—you know, you'd get these private-private talks, you'd have to go and hide under a couch somewhere and talk—and he hauled me off to the bathroom and said, 'Hey, hey—let's do Madison Square Garden.' And I suddenly had a really funny feeling, and I said, 'What are we gonna do with Madison Square Garden?' And he said, 'I don't know, man—it'll just be a gas to do Madison Square Garden.' I thought about it a minute. 'I'm scared,' I said. 'I think what it means is that you'll be the rock and roll king, and I'll be the peace queen,' and he always put me down when I talked like that. He'd say, 'Bullshit, bullshit.' . . . And he knew immediately what I meant when I said I'd be peace queen and he'd be rock and roll king, and he said, 'Hey, man—I heard those kids. I heard them, right? I can't be responsible for those kids' lives.' I said, 'Bobby, you rat, you mean you're gonna leave them all with me?' He said, 'Hey, hey—take them if you want them. But, man, I can't be responsible.' It didn't mean he didn't love them, you know. I think he was just afraid. But it was real. He meant it. That was the end of that tour. We didn't continue it."

This was in Pittsburgh on March 24, 1965. No concerts had to be canceled; the Baez-Dylan tour was over anyway. "It ran its course," Charlie Rothschild said. "When I got the idea to do the tour, Bob was in one place, and by the time we got into it, he was somewhere else." On March 26, Dylan was scheduled to begin promoting his new album at a record-release party in Los Angeles. *Bringing It All Back Home* was appearing in record stores, and a single of "Subterranean Homesick Blues" was playing on the radio, although most AM radio deejays seemed to prefer the flip side, the biting rock ballad about Joan, "She Belongs to

Me." (On the sleeve of the single, there was a reproduction of the cover of the British music magazine *Melody Maker*; it had pictures of Dylan, John Lennon, and George Harrison and the banner headline, "Beatles say—Dylan shows the way.")

While he was on the West Coast, Bob paid a visit to Joan in Carmel. He stayed just a few days, and they talked little more than they had during their joint tour. One night Joan made a big pot of beef stew and invited a few friends (including Nancy Carlen) for dinner; before the guests arrived, Dylan picked all the meat out and ate it, leaving the vegetables for everyone else. Before he went back east, Bob started writing a new song, another scathing mockery of romance, "Love Is Just a Four-Letter Word." The lyrics were unfinished, confused, unresolved. He left them behind with Joan, and she thought they matched her feelings perfectly.

S HORTLY BEFORE her twentieth birthday, Mimi Fariña had a dream about Aunt Tia and her boyfriend Rugger, and she knew it had to do with Joan and Bob and Richard. So long as Mimi and Joan were both content in their romantic relationships—or both without lovers—they got along fairly well. There was bound to be trouble between them now. Joan had confided with their mother about her recent frustrations with Bob, and Big Joan shared the news with Mimi. Unfortunately, life had never been better for Mimi and Richard. Richard's novel had been accepted for publication by Random House; they were collaborating on a one-act play with music and dance, to be produced by the Image Theatre Workshop in Cambridge; and their album *Celebrations for a Grey Day* was out, after a delay of more than a month while Vanguard dithered with production details. (Big Joan and Albert Baez first learned about Mimi and Richard's secret marriage in Paris when they read the album's liner notes.) "I was afraid to tell Joanie all the good things that were happening," Mimi said. "I know, when Dick and I were starting out and things were rough for us, it was hard to listen to all the great things [Joan would say] about her and Dylan."

The Fariñas spent the end of March and the first half of April in Manhattan navigating their turns in fortune. They drove with Lush from Cambridge in a rented car, and Judy Collins put all three of them up in her spacious apartment on the Upper West Side. The day they arrived, March 30, Richard and his agent, Robert Mills, met with Jim Silberman, the intellectually venturesome thirty-eight-year-old editor who had signed *Been Down So Long It Looks Like Up to Me*. Mills and Fariña picked up Silberman at Random House's offices on Madison Avenue and 51st Street, and the three of them walked to lunch. (Mimi did not come.) Fariña was wearing black velvet pants and a Chesterfield coat draped over his shoulders like a cape. "He was the first person I ever walked down Madison Avenue with who people just stopped and turned to look at," Silberman said. "He was very striking. He was immensely stylish, elegant, likable, charming. Dick had force in his personality, vividly. He was an actor. He wanted to be seen as dramatic. He wanted to be perceived as different. Clearly he was driven—the music career, the literary career. He was driven to do something and to be somebody. He had also read and studied literature, and he knew exactly what he was doing in his book, which was something very daring and smart."

In five years of writing and rewriting, Fariña had made *Been Down So Long It Looks Like Up to Me* something more than another first novel about college life. (It may or may not have been Richard's first novel at that; he told his Cornell classmates that he had spent one summer between terms secluded in a cabin writing a novel about his mother's family in Ireland, although he probably never finished that book, judging by the incomplete manuscript he gave his father.) Constructed in kaleidoscopic scenes set variously on campus, in Las Vegas, on a nuclear test site, in Cuba, and other points on the map of the early '60s, *Been Down So Long* has a carefully plotted story that turns on a matter of love. Fariña's stand-in, the narcissistic, moody, womanizing bohemian antihero

Gnossos Pappadopoulis, gets high and roams about musing on the meaninglessness of it all until he falls for a tender, delicate woman from Chevy Chase, Maryland; betrayed (or so Gnossos believes, Fariña remaining slyly vague on the matter), he seeks revenge through a vile but imaginative combination of sex and drugs. There is a great deal of sex and drugs in *Been Down So Long*, as there is in many of the pulp novels and college writing of its time. But Fariña manages to take his book into the realm of literature with seemingly boundless invention, a keen sense of the absurd, and a highly charged and surreal but utterly consistent tone. At points, especially in its more sedate, ruminative passages, the book also has a disarming tenderness.

"I thought it was great," Silberman said. "Very clever. There is just no question. I thought it was wonderful, lively—not quite what Pynchon said about it, but right up there." (The cover letter Mills had sent with the manuscript promised endorsements from Pynchon, Fariña's acquaintances Joseph Heller and Herb Gold, and Norman Mailer. However, Heller, who had met Richard in Europe, never read the manuscript; Herb Gold had no intention of helping Fariña; and if either Mills or Fariña had ever been in contact with Mailer, the evidence is lost and Mailer forgot about it.)

Silberman looked over samples of Eric von Schmidt's drawings that Fariña brought (without his agent's consent) and liked them but offered to publish the book in the conventional way; the text was sufficiently unconventional. Fariña's advance would be $1,800 paid in three equal installments, some of the raunchier passages would need to be cut, and the book would be published a year later, in the spring of 1966. "Dick had been waiting for this, to prove to himself that he really was good," Mimi recalled, "and I guess to prove it to other people, too. Pynchon was already a famous writer, but Dick could still beat Dylan [to publication]."

While they were in Manhattan, Mimi and Richard stopped by the Vanguard offices to pick up copies of *Celebrations for a Grey Day*. They were largely delighted with the package, especially the jacket cover, a black-and-white photo of the Fariñas playing their instruments under one of the tunnels in Central Park. Like most musicians listening to their own records, however, Mimi and Richard heard missed opportunities in the music; as Richard wrote to von Schmidt, "We're pleased, for the most part, although there is a restrained deliberateness about it all that would have been improved with a little looseness. It won't make the charts, of course, but I think we'll pick up a couple of friends." (The music press responded to *Celebrations for a Grey Day* favorably. "*Celebrations for a Grey Day* brings Richard Fariña with an outstanding dulcimer style," said *Sing Out!* in an uncredited review. "There is a little of Richard's singing and less of Mimi's . . . but this is only incidental to the consistently good instrumental music." In *The New York Times* Robert Shelton wrote, "The couple's chief innovations lie in two directions, the use of dulcimer and guitar to give an American-based raga sound, and the subtle use of 'folk rock' music, with electric guitar, piano and bass backing. The Fariñas have made an important debut disk—we can expect to hear a lot more about this talented couple.")

Judy Collins was making her fifth album while Mimi and Richard were visiting and decided to record "Pack Up Your Sorrows" along with songs by other young songwriters such as Dylan, Eric Andersen, and Gordon Lightfoot. A classically trained pianist and guitarist raised in a musical household (her father sang popular songs on radio and TV in Denver), Collins was a highly skilled and versatile musician with sophisticated, catholic tastes, far from another of the interchangeable "folk girls," as *Time* magazine mistakenly categorized her. She was also literate, warm, generous, and silly whenever possible. With her crooked nose, twisted smile, and enormous child's eyes, Collins was paranormally beautiful; another woman born into her skin would have been plain. She had grudging respect for Joan Baez, who had been known to do a cruel impersonation of Collins (distorting her features like a stroke victim), but she adored both Mimi and Richard, and they loved her in kind.

"That dog he had, Lush, loved him completely—he followed Dick everywhere," Collins said. "I felt the same way about him, as a lot of people did.

"Frankly, there were an awful lot of heavy vibrations in those years from a lot of people who were very serious about everything, and it became quite difficult at times just to deal with. I think he lightened things up in a wonderful way. He just had a capacity for enjoying life and for enjoying whatever situation he was in. He was also very deep. I think he had a very large capacity for feeling things about people and about life in general. He also had a kind of sizzling imagination. He was always reading interesting things and doing interesting things. I loved his songs because they had that rock and roll energy, but they had more than most songs in terms of literary content. They had something that I could get my brain around.

"Dick was completely different from Dylan, although they were both incredible writers. I couldn't talk to Dylan. When I first heard his first few great songs, I wanted to meet him. I wanted to meet the mind that created all those beautiful words. We set something up, and we had coffee, and when it was over, I walked away thinking, 'The guy's an idiot. He can't make a coherent sentence.' Of course, he was anything but an idiot—he was a genius. Dick could write a haunting, poetic song that moved you to tears, and he could sit down and talk and make you think or laugh. He could do anything and everything, and nothing would stop him from trying to."

At Collins's recording sessions, Richard played dulcimer on two tracks, "Pack Up Your Sorrows" and Gil Turner's civil rights anthem "Carry It On," which Collins rendered with dignity and restraint, aided substantially by Richard's sensitively rhythmic accompaniment. "His music was becoming more and more important to him and also to me," Collins later recalled (in the text she wrote for *The Judy Collins Songbook*). "On my fifth album, he played the dulcimer and Mimi and Bruce [Langhorne] and the dog and a bunch of other characters and I had the best time I think I ever had recording. . . . Lush leapt about in the middle of the studio, slamming into the microphones and entangling himself in the wires and Dick played the dulcimer and wrestled with Lush and we ended up making a beautiful album in the madness and fun." Fariña also wrote the album's liner notes, a portrait in verse, nearly all of which was coherent and lyrical.

Joan was returning to the East Coast herself and planned to visit Dylan, who was staying with the Grossmans. Since she would be in New York State so close to Mimi's birthday, the Fariñas decided to go to Bearsville to celebrate the occasion in advance. Bernard Paturel let them stay in the room above the Café Espresso, and Richard organized a lavish fête for his wife at the café. "Dick loved birthdays like a little kid," said Mimi, who got thoroughly drunk and stoned with her husband, Dylan, Victor Maymudes, and innumerable strangers. Paturel had never served so many people in one evening; "I don't know where Fariña found them all," he said. Joan sipped some wine and declined to smoke the marijuana, as usual. Surrounded by Bob, Mimi, Richard, friends, and dozens of her admirers, she felt alone. "It was a difficult time," Joan said decades later, still groping to understand it. "I felt isolated."

Dylan aggravated Baez's distress by avoiding her; he turned his back to her in groups and snapped at her in public. During dinner at the café with Mimi and Richard the night before Joan had to leave Bearsville to give a concert, he lashed out at Joan mercilessly, without evident provocation. Neither Joan nor Mimi would remember what prompted the outburst nor precisely what Bob said, but it had to do with Joan's appearance, and both sisters thought it was horribly cruel. When Joan bolted out of the restaurant, Bob started mocking her rage, grimacing and waving his arms in spastic jerks. Mimi rose from her seat, clutched Dylan's hair with both her hands, and yanked his head over the back of his chair. "Don't you ever treat my sister that way again!" she screamed in his face. "Do you understand me?" Dylan was choking and beginning to cry. Mimi released him and ran out to the patio in front of the café, where Richard was comforting Joan. "What a jerk!" Fariña said as he held Joan in his arms.

The following morning Richard drove Joan to the Poughkeepsie train station with Mimi and Bob. Joan kissed everyone, including Bob, good-bye. Shortly after they returned to Grossman's house, Mimi decided to unwind with a swim and began to enter a bedroom to change clothes when she noticed that Bob was in the room making a phone call.

"Don't worry," Mimi overheard him say. "She just left." The best Mimi could discern, Bob was making plans to meet a woman named Sara.

BOB DYLAN UNDERSTOOD how much Joan Baez had helped him. "I rode on Joan, man," he acknowledged in an interview with Robert Shelton (which the writer softened for use in his biography of Dylan). "You know? I'm not proud of it." But he felt he had honored any debt to Baez for her help in broadening his audience and facilitating his growth as a writer. "I didn't owe her nothing," Dylan said. "As far as I'm concerned, I paid her back." Had he agreed to participate in the Baez-Dylan joint tour as repayment for Joan's support? Were the songs he had written for her offerings of recompense? Or did he see the personal attention he had paid her over the past two years as compensation for Joan's professional help? Looking back upon this period, Baez would say she believed all of that likely. "I'm sure he thought of anything between us that didn't help him—and there wasn't a whole lot like that—as a big favor to me," Joan said.

Early in the spring of 1965, Baez learned that Dylan would be on a tour of Great Britain from the end of April to early June 1965, and she expected Bob to take her and introduce her to English audiences as she had done with him in America. "I assumed he was going to do what I did and have me come up and sing with him," she recalled. "I had a concert in England coming up myself after his, and I [had] never appeared there before, so I would have appreciated it if he would have given me a little boost like that. I thought he was going to do that. I would have liked it." Dylan invited Joan to join him, along with the Grossmans, Bob Neuwirth, and their entourage, but not on Baez's terms. "I didn't want her to sing with me—I wouldn't let her sing with me," Bob recalled a couple of years later. "I told her [up] front that she couldn't sing with me. . . . I told her before we left. And she came on like a little kitten. I told her in the States, and I didn't mention it ever again. . . . There is no place for her in my music. She don't fit into my music. Hey, I can fit into her music, but she doesn't fit into my music—my show. It would have been dumb. It wouldn't have added to me, and it would have been misleading to the audience." This was to be an acoustic tour, though; Dylan would be performing the same type of music he had been doing with Baez as recently as April 7, when he appeared in a concert of hers in Berkeley. Baez saw Dylan's move away from her as punitive, and she was crushed. "Bobby's rise had happened so fast that he was hotter than I was, and he didn't need me anymore," Joan said. "It was a big slap in the face." She decided to tag along even so, hoping that Bob's latent sense of duty and affection for her would eventually impel him to change his mind.

Unbeknownst to Baez—and, it seems, to nearly everyone else, including many of Dylan's usual confidants such as Victor Maymudes—Bob had been quietly pursuing Sally Grossman's friend Sara Lownds. Sara, who had changed her name from Shirley Noznisky, was a smoldering, girlish twenty-five-year-old beauty who had been a successful magazine model. She was also well read, a good conversationalist and better listener, resourceful, a fast study, and good hearted. She impressed some people as shy and quiet, others as supremely confident; either way, she appeared to do only what she felt needed to be done. Sara was not a music fan. The first time she was exposed to Bob Dylan, when Sally Grossman invited her to watch him on television, she was expecting to see Bobby Darin. She had a young daughter, Maria, from a brief marriage to fashion photographer Hans Lownds, and she was raising her in the Chelsea Hotel. "This was a woman with a great well of resources," said Richard Leacock, the documentary filmmaker; when Dylan and Grossman were planning the English tour, Sara was working for Time-Life Films, where she met Leacock and his fellow cinema-verité pioneer D. A. Pennebaker. "Sara was supposed to be a secretary," said Pennebaker, "but she ran the place." Dylan rented a room in the Chelsea Hotel so he could meet Lownds in private; he kept her as secret as he kept his parents and his brother, perhaps for the same reason. "He obviously fell for her," said Sally Grossman, "and he didn't like people prying into his family and the things that were really closest to him. If he was really serious about her, she had to be unknown. That was one of our [the Grossmans'] jobs, to help give him that privacy. Look—he just had a taste of a very public relationship [with Joan], and that wasn't working out very well, was it?" Strong but nonthreatening, impressive but unassuming, Sara seemed at least in part a combination of what Dylan loved best in Suze Rotolo and Joan Baez.

Through Sara's intervention, Albert Grossman contacted Pennebaker to explore the prospect of making some sort of movie about Dylan. After a few conversations and a meeting with Dylan and Neuwirth at the Cedar Tavern (wherein Dylan seemed fixated on determining if the slight, handsome filmmaker was homosexual), it was agreed that Pennebaker would shoot the English tour, cinema-verité style. Pennebaker, a jazz enthusiast, had only heard a few Dylan songs on the radio; he was primarily interested in probing Dylan's image, which evoked for him images of Lord Byron. "I was on a Byron kick," Pennebaker recalled. "The way I saw Byron, he invented the concept of 'Fuck you all, I'm above you as an artist, not below you, so screw you'—you know? I saw Dylan as a Byronesque pop figure, a guy who was inventing a whole new kind of mood in popular music. Here's this middle-class kid who goes out on the road, hangs out with people, and he becomes or he decides to become a kind of hobo-type character, and with all the romance that carries—the music, the freedom, everything that gets lost in the movement toward the middle class—and once he's made it, he looks out at everybody and says, 'Fuck you!'"

Dylan's first suggestion for the film became its opening sequence, a wittily literal portrayal of Dylan the street poet. Bob stands among hills of garbage and a cliff of scaffolding (on a street near the posh Savoy Hotel, where he stayed in London). He is wearing his folk uniform, blue jeans and a vest, and he is holding a stack of poster boards on which Pennebaker, Baez, and a few others had written words and phrases from "Subterranean Homesick Blues" in block letters. Deadpan as Buster

Keaton, Dylan holds up the cards, one by one, as the lyrics of the song race on the soundtrack. Allen Ginsberg, an ad hoc member of the ballooning Dylan entourage, drifts in and out of the background, as if to validate that all this subterraneanism is poetic.

Aside from that single planned sequence, Pennebaker shot whatever happened as the tour progressed. He and his sound engineer, Robert Van Dyke, adhering to the principles of cinema verité, strove to capture events with minimal intrusion or influence. Van Dyke used omnidirectional microphones placed out of his subjects' view, and Pennebaker looked through the viewfinder as little as possible; he preferred to rest the camera on his lap and gaze around the room nonchalantly, so most people would not realize the equipment was running. Still, for all their efforts to capture unadorned reality, they were largely filming a reenactment of another movie, *A Hard Day's Night*, itself a fanciful simulation of cinema verité. Director Richard Lester's fictional peek behind the scenes on a Beatles tour had been released the previous July, and it had influenced the behavior of the pop music audience, Bob Dylan, and the Beatles themselves. As John Lennon pointed out, not only did Beatle fans begin mimicking the riotous mobs in the film, his bandmates started adopting their movie personalities. Dylan's tour was like a reel added to the Beatles film: throngs of teenagers were waiting for him at Heathrow Airport; press crews followed him everywhere; girls threw themselves onto the hood of his limousine; kids mobbed the Savoy for a glimpse of the American singing poet—and of all four Beatles, who joined Marianne Faithfull and members of the Animals and the Rolling Stones at the parties Grossman threw for Dylan at the hotel. "Young people had worked themselves up for the Beatles and gotten fairly organized about it," said Karl Dallas, the English music writer. "When Dylan came over here, the same people were doing what they do, and Dylan was the fortunate recipient. Had he arrived a few years before or after that, he would have found quite a substantially different reception." When Dylan had done "The London Waltz" with Richard Fariña and Eric von Schmidt, there had been fewer people at the Troubadour than there would be outside the Savoy waiting to watch Dylan walk to his car three years later.

"It's never been like this before," Dylan said, reveling in the attention. "I seem to be more popular here than I am at home." With the endless queue of English journalists who interviewed him throughout the tour, Bob virtually re-created *A Hard Day's Night*'s press conference scenes. "Are you a mod or a rocker?" a reporter asks Ringo Starr in the film. "I'm a mocker," Starr replies. "What is your message?" a writer asks Dylan. "Keep a good head and always carry a lightbulb," Dylan says, brandishing an enormous theatrical lightbulb. Reporter: "Are your tastes in clothing changing?" Dylan: "I like to wear drapes, umbrellas, hats." His favorite composers? "Brown Bumpkin and Sidney Ciggy." His professional ambition? "To be a stewardess."

In his eight concerts all around England, Dylan sang in his old style, alone with his guitar and harmonica. Without a band, he could not perform his new music, a combination of the folk and rock styles; but he was living that union. Still singing folk, he had become a rock star. As the English music author and editor Ray Coleman wrote, "Dylan conquered Britain [and] 'Blowin' in the Wind' and 'The Times They Are a-Changin'' became favorites of the university students and the pop screamers. Dylan emerged from the relative obscurity of the folk world to the wider, more dangerous world of pop idol. For Dylan, it was fraught with trouble." Indeed, the adulation fed Dylan's ego, with perilous consequences for some of his personal and professional associations, especially his already tenuous relationship with Joan Baez. On May 5, Joan wrote a letter to Mimi from the Savoy:

Dearest Mimishka—I love you.

We're leaving Bobby's entourage. He has become so unbelievably unmanageable that I can't stand to be around him. Everyone traveling with him is going mad—He walks around in new clothes with a cane—Has tantrums, orders fish, gets drunk, plays his record, phones up America, asks if his concert tonight is sold out—stops all three limousines every morning to buy all the newspapers that might have his name in them. He won't invite me to sing with him even when the kids yell out my name and send petitions to him to have me sing. He doesn't speak to me, or anyone, really, unless it's "business," how many records he's selling, will his record be #1, etc. It's shocked me completely out of my senses and I'm fed up. Pride enters, too— it would be so great to have him invite me onstage the way I did with him in the states, and I realize that I can't take being *completely* ignored all the time—I mean, riding in limousine no. 2 has its advantages, but [it] is also an undeniable put down to a prima donna. Last night I was so incredibly battered by the whole thing that I cried through his entire concert (which was, by the way, a magnificent performance) drove 2 1/2 hours back to London, collapsed with Bobby Neuwirth, who has been an angel, and cried for another hour. Neuwirth is going mad with it all too, and it's made him sort of a brother of sympathy.

I think the Beatles are a little confused by Bobby, he got so drunk and they all had to be ha ha funny, so I made friend[s] with John's wife & Paul's girl and I think all of them—the girls & Beats will come to my concert.

Can't resist telling you I just called up the Lennons and maybe I'll go over there tonight *without* Bobby and really have a nice time.

Love to you & Ricardo and a hug to Lush.

Joanie

When he acknowledged Baez at all, Dylan chastised and ridiculed her. "He would fume at her so badly, he would spit at her," Robert Van Dyke said. "I had to cover the microphones with my hands, so they wouldn't get wet." En route to one concert, Dylan's train of three limousines came upon a truck full of Gypsies parked on the roadside. Joan, riding with D. A. Pennebaker in the second car, asked the driver to stop. "Joan went over to them and started to talk to them—I don't know why, and for some reason it really pissed Dylan off," Pennebaker recalled. "I was kind of curious, but I didn't try to film it. I think Joan wanted me to film her talking to the Gypsies, or at least that was the implication, and I kind of didn't. And Dylan got out of the car ahead of us, and he started to really kind of read the riot act to Joan about the Gypsies. He said, 'You know, I know what these people are like. I understand the way they live. You can't understand them.' And he stormed back into his limousine."

Joan held tight until Dylan called in Neuwirth as an ally. Pennebaker was filming Bob, Joan, and Neuwirth unwinding in the Savoy when Neuwirth struck the fatal blow to Joan's pride, an attack on her breasts. Neuwirth seemed to have been waiting for an opening; all Baez said was "Oh, God, I'm sleepy—I mean, I'm fagging out."

"Let me tell you, sister, you fagged out a long time ago," Neuwirth barked. "You fagged out before you even thought you were faggin' out. Oh, my God, there she is, Fang. Fang, you have one of those see-through blouses. Hey, she has one of those see-through blouses that you don't even wanna. That's Fang Baez. . . ."

"Oh, pardon me," Joan said in shock.

"I didn't mean to hurt your turtle," Neuwirth responded with a bite.

"God," Baez moaned, and left the room. She started packing and took the next flight she could book to Paris, where her parents were living again.

Dylan had prevailed. "There was no reason [for Joan to be in London]," Bob said. "But I don't care. I don't give a fuck."

A couple of weeks later, on May 23, Joan returned to London for her own concert at the Albert Hall. Dylan had promised to attend, then sent word that he was ill, and he was—in fact, he was suffering from a stomach ailment serious enough for him to be admitted to St. Mary's Hospital in Paddington. Having learned of the severity of his condition, Baez ignored her own emotional wounds and went to visit him. Sara Lownds met her at the door of Dylan's room; she and Bob had rendezvoused in Paris, then gone to Portugal, where Bob fell ill. "And that's how I found out that there was a Sara," Joan said. "All in all, the whole thing [with

Dylan in London] was the most demoralizing experience in my life. I have never understood how he could suddenly change, as if everything he had done before had never really happened."

For the title of the film about Dylan's spring 1965 tour of England, Pennebaker and Dylan used three emphatic words of the opening lines of "She Belongs to Me":

She's got everything she needs
She's an artist
She don't look back

Perhaps the song never was about Baez, but was really a self-portrait.

WELL AWARE OF how a dramatic appearance at the Newport Folk Festival could help a career, Mimi and Richard planned a big surprise for their debut at the 1965 event. The Fariñas were scheduled to appear on the New Folks program on the last afternoon of the four-day festival, Sunday, July 25, along with Gordon Lightfoot, Patrick Sky, and "Spider" John Koerner. Richard, drawing upon his expertise in such matters, was going to throw a party onstage. As he outlined the set with Mimi, they would begin with one of their quiet songs, perhaps "The Falcon" or "Birmingham Sunday." A third musician—Fritz Richmond on bass—would join them for the next tune, followed by a fourth player—Al Kooper on electric guitar—then a fifth—Kyle Garahan on harmonica—and a sixth—Bruce Langhorne on tambourine—until there was a full band behind them. The songs would build in tempo and drive, climaxing with the rock and roll numbers from their first album and a new, unrecorded rocker Fariña had written, "Hard-Loving Loser," and finally "Pack Up Your Sorrows." Maria Muldaur said she would sing and dance; even Joan was game to join in for the finale. All of the musicians worked out their parts during the first few days of the festival, careful to keep the scheme to themselves. "Dick had it all set up," Langhorne recalled, "so it would turn into this whole crazy dance party." It might not be folk music, but it would be festive.

Newport was jammed again, with attendance surpassing 70,000 on the festival's new site, thirty-four acres of hillside on the northern perimeter of the seacoast. The concessionaires brought 23,000 hot dogs and 8,400 pizzas. There were more than 150 musicians, among them the biggest attractions in the field, Joan Baez and Bob Dylan included. A film crew was shooting a documentary about the event. Still, six years after the initial Folk Festival, Newport had lost something; an atmosphere of familiarity and inevitability hung over the workshops on group singing with children and clog dancing, and the sight of uprooted old Appalachians wandering among the northeastern undergraduates had lost its novelty value. "Folk music wasn't the new thing anymore—it's that simple," George Wein said. "So you got a lot of people who had come to the festival before, and they're coming back because they enjoyed themselves in the past and want to have a good time again." Always an enactment of nostalgia, Newport had become nostalgic for itself. Still, as festival publicist Charlie Bourgeois added, "it was *the* story of the summer for the feature writers."

Since Baez and Dylan were estranged, the social scene at the Hotel Viking lost its romantic core. Joan spent most of her time with Mimi and their mother, who was visiting from Paris, and some of it with Donovan, the Scottish-Irish Dylan imitator she and Bob had met in London. The sisters dropped by the pool occasionally, but Bob stayed cloistered indoors. Without Baez and Dylan, no one poolside seemed to know which way to point his lounge chair.

The Fariñas, already nervous about their festival debut, squabbled on their first day in Newport. They were strolling the grounds when they bumped into a colleague from Cambridge who was friendly with Manny Greenhill. "I don't know who it was," Mimi said, "but he said, 'Hey, Manny was really upset when he read that you guys had signed with

Grossman.' I said, 'We didn't sign with Grossman.' And this person got out his program, and there was an advertisement in it—you know, 'Albert Grossman representing . . .' with a list of all his clients, and we were on there. Dick had done it without my knowledge—he had talked to Albert and worked this out and signed a contract with him to represent the two of us. I was very angry. We argued heavily about it when I realized what had happened. He didn't handle it honestly, but I understood why he did it. He wanted us to make it and start making some money, and he saw going with Albert and going to Newport as the big moves to do that."

For the first time since the Newport Folk Festival had been revived as a not-for-profit foundation in 1963, Joan Baez and Bob Dylan did not perform together. Baez was scheduled to appear on a roster with Josh White, Maybelle Carter, and the New Lost City Ramblers on the opening night, and Dylan was billed with Peter, Paul and Mary, Eric von Schmidt, and Ronnie Gilbert in the last evening concert of the festival. Having been a part of notable duets at Newport since she made her debut in 1959, Joan felt almost superstitious about carrying on the tradition and asked Donovan to join her as a surprise guest. They sang his country-pop love song "Colors," although Joan was clearly uncomfortable with the insipid tune. There seemed no reason for an important artist such as Baez to be in the company of a lightweight such as Donovan, aside from the fact that he looked, dressed, and tried to act exactly like Dylan.

Thanks to Grossman's influence, Mimi presumed, the Fariñas were given a slot in the New Folks program, the last event before the final night's evening concert. She dressed to look older, hiding her twenty-year-old dancer's shape in a long blue floral-print peasant dress with a ruffled neck and long sleeves, and he looked casually sleek in black jeans (dry-cleaned and pressed) and a body-hugging crew-neck shirt. Richard, like Dylan, Donovan, Bob Neuwirth, Peter Yarrow, and seemingly every other male at the festival, wore black Ray-Ban sunglasses, although the weather was cool and overcast with threatening gray clouds.

They strode onto the long, partially covered stage holding hands and began their set quietly, according to plan, with "Birmingham Sunday." However, the ballad was apparently not moving the festival crowd as it had in Mimi and Richard's club shows; people were squirming in their seats. Before the song was over, at least a dozen of them got up and left. Mimi was horrified; Richard stiffened, but he grinned and adhered to his plan, introducing Fritz Richmond. More people rose to leave, at which point Mimi saw a crack of lightning and realized it was raining on the audience. "We thought people were leaving because they didn't like us," Richard later recalled in a radio interview. "We saw uneasiness in the audience, and we didn't know it was the rain falling on them. We were angry. We didn't want anybody to leave. We were frustrated." When they finished their second song, about a third of the audience was on its feet, drenched. A summer storm was raging.

Peter Yarrow bolted out to tell Mimi and Richard to stop—the audience wanted to leave, and the rain was unsafe for everyone near the stage; the microphones and wiring were not weatherproof and needed to be shut off immediately.

Mimi watched Richard shrink. So much for his musical dance party. Too bad for those plans to make a sensational Newport debut. There went Mimi and Richard Fariña's grand bid for glory.

Yarrow hustled offstage, and Richard took the microphone to make an announcement. "Okay, everybody. Everybody get up from your seats now, okay?" he said, and started chuckling, as Mimi recalled. "You can't dance sitting down! Right? Okay—let's go! Let's boogie!" Richard waved Bruce Langhorne out from backstage with his guitar—an acoustic, owing to the circumstances (although the vocal mikes and amps were still getting dangerously wet). Fariña started the pounding rhythm of "Reno, Nevada," and Mimi bounced in time as he sang. "Yeah!" Richard shouted, now laughing uncontrollably. "C'mon!"

"We went from that straight into 'Hard-Loving Loser' and everything else we did that cooked," said Mimi. "I looked out, and the audience started dancing in the pouring rain. Everybody was getting soaked, and people were laughing and dancing to the music." It was quite a celebration for a very gray day.

"They turned that catastrophe into something everybody enjoyed," said Theodore Bikel, one of the directors of the festival. "I was afraid they were going to get electrocuted out there, which was quite possible. But it was apparent to me that they were not getting off the stage. Everyone was having the time of their lives."

As their finale, they did "Pack Up Your Sorrows," as planned, and Joan joined them as promised, sitting next to Mimi in the rain. At the end of the number, Joan rose from her stool and danced along with the crowd, giggling as she bowed her head back and let the torrent pour onto her face.

The festival could not continue, it was clear to Bikel; the evening concert would have to be canceled. "A perfect way to end the festival!" Bikel said, congratulating the Fariñas backstage. Mimi gave her husband a long, tight hug, and he roared in her ear, "We did it!"

Huddling backstage, Bikel, Pete Seeger, and others on the Newport board of directors chose to hold off announcing that the festival would be cut short; the seacoast weather was capricious and could improve in time to salvage at least some of the evening concert. Wet and confused, thousands of people wormed about for shelter, crunching together under the workshop tents and concession stands or retrenching in their cars. Musicians gathered in the lounge at the Viking, where talk of Mimi and Richard Fariña seemed to dominate the conversation. "They had a truly great moment, and everybody knew it," John Cooke said. "Really magical and historic." Even Dylan acknowledged Richard Fariña's resourcefulness sarcastically. "I was beneath the bleachers at Newport when he played in the rain, and I heard him totally go insane," Dylan said. "I hope he gets recognition till he puffs his face out."

As evening came, the sky cleared. Dylan got ready to go on as planned, performing his new music with members of the Paul Butterfield Blues Band. How much of fate has God delegated to the weather?

Some 15,000 people saw Dylan's set, and everyone who touched a different part of that elephant came away with his or her own mental picture of the beast. The facts are the following. Bob Dylan took the stage at nine fifteen. In place of his old work clothes, he was wearing motor-

258

cycle boots and a black leather blazer over a pressed white dress shirt with a gold tab pinning the collar tight. His hair and sideburns were long, and he had a sunburst Fender Stratocaster electric guitar, the model Buddy Holly played, strapped over his shoulder. A band of other musicians followed him—Mike Bloomfield of Butterfield's group on electric guitar, Al Kooper on organ, Barry Goldberg on piano, and the Butterfield rhythm section, Jerome Arnold on bass and Sam Lay on drums. They played three songs, "Maggie's Farm," "Like a Rolling Stone," and an early version of "It Takes a Lot to Laugh, It Takes a Train to Cry," and left the stage. A few minutes later Dylan returned alone with an acoustic guitar, and he sang two more songs, "It's All Over Now, Baby Blue" and "Mr. Tambourine Man."

From that sprang one of the most enduring myths of postwar popular culture: having affronted his fans by "going electric," Dylan was booed off the Newport stage, thrown from the temple for propagating a new faith in rock and roll too radical for his old followers to accept; humbled, teary-eyed, Dylan returned to sing in his folk style, an act of contrition. As a poetic allegory, the story dramatizes the emergence of a new music through the union of folk and rock with themes close to young people—generational conflict, style, and rage. But the mythic tale of Dylan's 1965 Newport performance has never borne scrutiny well.

The Newport audience was mostly young, predominantly college students and others their age. By July 25 they were thoroughly steeped in Bob Dylan's new music. *Bringing It All Back Home* and the single of "Subterranean Homesick Blues" had been in release for more than a third of the year. Dylan's current single, moreover, was "Like a Rolling Stone"—his venomous rock and roll masterpiece, written on his way back from London ("as a long piece of vomit," he said). It was a top-forty hit; you could hardly drive to Newport with the radio on and not hear it, repeatedly. ("Like a Rolling Stone" would peak at number two on the pop music charts on August 14, 1965.) While some folk traditionalists in the Newport audience may have been startled to hear "Maggie's Farm," far more had been listening to it for months. "It was a huge festival, not a recital for a musicological society," John Cooke said. "My own view, and I was sitting there, was that most people in that audience had heard 'Like a Rolling Stone,' and they probably bought tickets purposely to see Bob Dylan and hear it, not in some weird hope that Dylan would go back in time and do stuff he hadn't done on his last two albums." Nor could the sound of a group playing rock and roll on electrified instruments have come as much of a shock that evening. The Paul Butterfield Blues Band had done a whole set of hard-driving R&B on Sunday afternoon, the Chambers Brothers had played the same day, and both groups had gotten wildly enthusiastic receptions.

What about that booing, then? There was consternation during Dylan's first song, although accounts differ on its nature and intent. Historian and musician Sam Charters, who has studied Vanguard's archival recordings, the documentary film soundtrack, and private tapes of Dylan's set, insists the audience was not booing but hollering complaints about the sound quality. "There were no boos," he said, "and the complaints weren't about the music—my God, Dylan was the hottest thing going. The sound system at Newport was not set up properly for electric instruments, so people were yelling out because all they could hear was noise." As Jack Elliott put it, "The music was good. It sounded like horseshit." Among those who did hear booing, Geoff Muldaur assumed it was a reaction to the execution, not the style, of Dylan's music. "I don't believe people were booing because the music was revolutionary," Muldaur said. "It was just that Dylan wasn't very good at it. He had no idea how to play the electric guitar, and he had very second-rate musicians with him, and they hadn't rehearsed enough. It just didn't work. The musicians didn't play good. There's no doubt in my mind, people were booing because it stank."

Dylan was among those convinced the audience was booing him, and he attributed it to a faction of musical reactionaries. "It was in Newport—well, I did this very crazy thing," Dylan said. "I mean, I didn't really know what was going to happen, but they certainly booed, I'll tell you that. You could hear it all over the place. I don't know who they were, though, and I'm certain whoever it was did it twice as loud as they normally would. . . .

"I was kind of stunned," he recalled. "But I can't put anybody down for coming and booing. After all, they paid to get in. They could have been maybe a little quieter and not so persistent, though. There were a lot of old people there, too. Lots of whole families had driven down from Vermont, lots of nurses and their patients, and, well, like they just came to hear some relaxing hoedowns, you know, maybe an Indian polka or two. And just when everything's going all right, here I come on, and the whole place turns into a beer factory. . . .

"I think there's always a little 'boo' in all of us. I don't even understand it. . . . They can't hurt me with a boo. . . . There were a lot of people there who were very pleased that I got booed. I saw them afterward. I do resent somewhat, though, that everybody that booed said they did it because they were old fans."

Backstage, the traditional folk powerbrokers watched Dylan in exasperation. Folklorist Alan Lomax and Pete Seeger sputtered and fumed about this violation of everything Dylan represented, at least to them. Seeger at one point spouted something widely repeated as a threat to chop the power cord with an ax if Dylan were not pulled off immediately. (Years later Seeger would say he had indeed been furious, but only because the volume on the instruments was obscuring the socialist message of "Maggie's Farm.") When Dylan left the stage after only three songs—not in retreat, but because the band had only rehearsed those three—he walked into the wall of Lomax, Seeger, George Wein, Theodore Bikel, and Peter Yarrow (the latter two of whom had been arguing in Dylan's favor). "I told him, 'Bob—people are very upset,' " Wein recalled. "I didn't know how upset the audience was. Maybe they were thrilled. I was trying to keep things under control, and I knew people backstage were very upset. I said, 'Bob, you've gotta go back and sing something and calm things down.' He said to me, 'I only have my electric guitar.' I said, 'Does anybody here have a guitar for Bob Dylan?' Twenty people raised their hands with guitars. He picked one out of the air, and he did go out there."

Dylan would insist he was not upset by either the booing he thought he heard or the reaction he found backstage. "I wasn't shattered by it," he said. "I didn't cry." The strap on the guitar he borrowed was too short and pulled the instrument high up on his chest; he looked uneasy, and his singing was soft and vulnerable. He seemed wrought with emotion. There is a picture of this moment by photographer Rick Sullo, who was on the side of the stage and used a telephoto lens to catch Dylan close up, in profile. Bob is glaring ahead at the audience as he sings, and a tear trails from his left eye down his cheek.

That night the not-for-profit Newport foundation diminished its prospects of a budget surplus with an extravagant postfestival bash for performers and their guests at Nethercliffe mansion, which had served as festival headquarters. There were marble-topped tables overloaded with raw seafood, and a bar in every corner. The Chambers Brothers played for dancing—no folk music tonight; this was for fun. "After all this folk shit was over, we couldn't wait to get up and boogie," Maria Muldaur re-called. "The Chambers Brothers hadn't started playing yet, so Richard Fariña started one of his cutlery jams. He picked up some of the fine sil-verware from the mansion, and he did an incredible Cuban dance rhythm on one of the tables. Pretty soon a whole bunch of people are around him, jamming on the tables and the chairs with the cutlery. Then the Chambers Brothers pick up on it, and they lay a really funky blues shuf-fle over this rhythm. Richard gets up, and we start dancing, and Dylan is sitting in the corner—I mean, he's just curled up at a table by himself. So Richard goes, 'Maria, go over and ask Dylan to dance.'

" 'Ask who?'

" 'Go up to Bob and ask him to dance. He's looking really weird.'

"So I said, 'Okay.' I had never seen Bob dance before, but if Richard told me to do just about anything within reason, I would have done it, you know. So I go over by myself, and I say, 'Hey, Bob, how you doing?' His legs were wiggling like they always did, and he was just brooding in the corner with his legs wiggling. I put my hand on his shoulder and said, 'Would you like to dance?' And he looked up at me, and he said, 'I would dance with you, Maria, but my hands are on fire.'

"And I said, 'Okay then.'

"Dick was having a grand old time, celebrating his great moment in the rain. But Bob was looking like he was really down after his whole experience with that band. He didn't look like a guy who thought he had very much to celebrate."

A S SHE ASSUMED THE DUTIES of Peace Queen, speaking at antiwar rallies and to the press on issues of military policy, Joan Baez found herself vulnerable to charges of political naïveté. She had always acted intuitively; for the first time in her twenty-four years, she found her impulses inadequate. "I was tired of being a political nincompoop and a spiritual nincompoop at the same time," she recalled. As her guru Ira Sandperl described Joan's predicament, "She found herself among politically knowledgeable people, and while she had strong feelings, she didn't know any of the socio-economic-political-historical terms of nonviolence." So Joan asked Sandperl to begin tutoring her in the history and practice of pacifism. Teacher and student had weekly sessions alone in the house Joan had contracted to be built over the remains of an old adobe viaduct on a hill in the Carmel Valley. The construction was still under way around them, in fact; there had been some setbacks—partial dismantling and replanning because the designer Joan had hired, John Gamble, had no formal training and no architectural license. But the house was spacious and welcoming, oriented around a central combination kitchen–living room, which Gamble explained as the Chinese style. After a few weeks of private study, Baez realized a social approach might prove more stimulating to her while introducing others to pacifist ideas; she decided to offer organized classes with Sandperl at her new home. "I think people learn more from a bunch of people—if it's kept at the right number—than just two people," she said. "I thought it would be [an] intelligent idea to have a school." Thus she founded the Institute for the Study of Non-Violence, its first sessions conducted in front of Joan's stove shortly before the 1965 Newport Folk Festival.

The school soon took shape as the foundation for Baez's work as a social activist. It was to be an unconventional institution; the autodidact daughter of a professor, Joan remained ambivalent about organized education. Not long before, she had said she would like to see "every university in the country just fold up, because they turn out ping-pong balls"; indeed, she saw Sandperl's rejection of academia as a source of his authority. "He has no credentials that anybody should quote 'know' about him," Joan explained, "except that he left Stanford after three years because he said it was interfering with his education." Beyond lecture-talks with Sandperl, who sat next to Joan on the floor in jeans and Converse tennis shoes, the program Baez planned would include yoga-style exercise, silent meditation, and group meals. Her own role would be one of fellow student, "referee" between the loquacious Sandperl and the students she presumed he would intimidate, and sole financial benefactor. When the Monterey County Planning Commission alerted Baez that she was violating the local zoning code by operating an educational institution in her residence, she found a better site, a white adobe building on Carmel Valley Road that had previously served as a county schoolhouse, the laboratory for So Help Me Hannah Poison Oak Remedy, and a gun-shell factory, and she purchased it for $40,000. Joan put Sandperl on salary and hired a full-time school administrator, Holly Chenery. The Institute for the Study of Non-Violence offered a six-week course for $120 tuition, which covered lodging at a nearby apartment house. There were no entrance requirements. Despite an effort by a contingent of Carmel Valley residents to close the school on the grounds that it lowered property values, the institute was thriving by the end of the summer of 1965 with an enrollment of fifteen or twenty wide-eyed young acolytes. Joan was giving concerts only once every three or four months. Asked if she could foresee a time when she would drop music entirely and devote herself to the institute full time, she said, "I can see that happening, yes."

Joan wrote a letter to Mimi and Richard that July and followed it with several phone calls inviting them to move back to Carmel and join her at the school; Mimi could give dance classes, and Richard could help Joan and Ira do some writing. The institute was doing important work, and wouldn't it be fun to be back together again? Who knows where it could lead? With no more to accomplish in Cambridge, Richard responded enthusiastically to the offer, and it came just in time for Mimi. "I saw that as Joanie reaching out to us," Mimi recalled. "After the split with Dylan, she was finding herself, and there was a place for us to be together again. I thought that was positive, and I think Dick thought it was an opportunity for him. I was happy about the idea of doing something that didn't revolve around Dick. I needed that. So we decided to do it." Tension was developing between the Fariñas, and Mimi wanted to be near her sister. She wrote a letter to her mother about the problem but ended up mailing it to Lotte and Alan Marcus, elders she trusted and who knew both Mimi and Richard well:

> It's happened three times and each time he becomes very preoccupied with talk about dying and what does it all matter and so on. Then he'll poke at enough things to get me mad and then say that we just can't make it—can't get along—we're always unhappy—he's always somewhere else in his mind, what does it all mean—stupid house—no—yes—no—yes I've decided it's final—I'm going to leave—you're just not what I need—you're not a woman—I need to be free. It usually lasts a night and the next morning or the day after he tells me how he was incredibly drunk and on just three glasses of so & so. . . . I finally got mad last night and told him if he was going to go then to do it & quit playing games. He wept & carried on, and I was very disturbed to say the least.

Mimi gave the Marcuses instructions to send any response to Mimi care of the Boston Conservatory, because Richard always got the mail first and opened everything addressed to his wife.

Joan found Mimi and Richard a gingerbread house on Mt. Devon Road, off Route 1; though only twenty by thirty feet, it had a view of the Pacific in the winter when the eucalyptus trees thin. Before the Fariñas left for California, Richard arranged for the singer and songwriter Tom Rush to take over their apartment in Cambridge. Fariña took Rush into the bedroom alone for a private talk. "I want to show you a couple of things," Fariña said in hushed tones, and he handed Rush an X-ray of his skull. "I have a metal plate in my head," Richard confided, as Tom Rush recalled. "If you're ever with me and I hurt my head, kill me." The second item was a silver-plated .38-caliber revolver. "I'm leaving this with you, because I can't take it across state lines," Richard said. "But don't worry. It doesn't work." For reasons Rush never understood, Fariña left the X-ray as well as the pistol with him.

"I don't know why he couldn't take an X-ray across state lines," Rush said, "and I don't know why he left it with me. I don't know why he had the thing in the first place—hell, I don't know if it was really his head."

There was not a great deal for Mimi and Richard to do at the institute. Mimi led the students in simple dance movements as part of the daily exercise program, but Joan and Ira kept postponing their writing, and Richard ended up cooking the lunches. (Although the Fariñas were not on salary, Joan paid the cost of their relocation to California and helped cover their living expenses, and meals at the school were free.) Most days Mimi and Richard worked on new music for a couple of hours, which was good for their marriage. In the evenings, they would often socialize with Joan, which was not. Richard fixated on Joan. Together at the Fariñas' house for dinner (something fabulously scrumptious Richard just threw together), any random stimulus—the scratch of a knife on a plate, a word of idle conversation—would trigger his pinball imagination, and he would start ad-libbing dialogue in character. Joan would jump in the improvisation as if on cue. Both quick-witted, gifted mimics, they played off each other with competitive fury, like bebop musicians in a cutting contest. As Joan described these sessions, "The laughing was steady from that point on with pauses for eating and changes of character. Dick commanded and directed the show, swaying the tide of nonsense. . . . Before a night was over he would have gone German officer, gone Festus Turd from Texas, gone Indian foreign exchange student, gone paralyzed, gone weightless, gone blind, and gone mad. I would go with him, because I loved it. It was crazy, and it was fun, and the night roared by as we laughed ourselves teary-eyed." In a Carmel restaurant one evening, Joan pretended she was blind, pawing everyone's food and knocking over glasses; Richard became her English manservant. Another night out somewhere else, Richard was a magician and Joan his assistant; he seemed close to demonstrating his knife-throwing act but announced a change in the evening's program and instructed Joan to pull the tablecloth out from under the dinner dishes on his signal—"Abracadabra!" Mimi and Joan cried out in laughter and pain as they picked up all the broken plates and glasses, while Richard took off his shoes and socks. He was a swami, preparing to walk on the glass. Mimi roared every time— "Who wouldn't?" she said, giggling at the memories years later; but she could not keep up with Joan and Richard—who could?

"When Joanie and Dick got together," Big Joan said, "everybody else was an outsider. They were onstage, and nobody could join them. I think they could have done something fatal, because they'd get into it, and I was afraid they would do *anything*. Joanie would have loved to have had a partner like that."

Baez's friends in the Carmel area began growing suspicious of Richard's intentions, just as the Cambridge circle had several years earlier. "It just began to be very clear that Dick was preying on Joan now that Dylan was out of the picture," Nancy Carlen said. "Everybody around Joan noticed it. We all talked about it. He was becoming obsessed. Everybody was troubled by it, but nobody said anything to Joan about it—[nor] to Mimi—that I knew of. We just sort of hoped it would blow over."

Through Joan's influence, Mimi and Richard were invited to perform at Carnegie Hall on September 24 with nearly eighty other singers, actors, and groups participating in a pair of antiwar benefits, the "Sing-In for Peace in Viet Nam." Vanguard covered the airfare for Mimi and

Richard, because they were due in New York to record their second album, and Joan pitched in to bump them to first-class so they could keep her company. "There we were," Richard wrote in a letter to Eric von Schmidt, "belching back marinated oysters over the Great Salt Lake, dipping lewd lobster tail chunks in parsley butter over Chicago. . . . And then zoom, out of the plane into Carnegie Hall to wage war against the war-wagers in Viet-Namara." There is no record of what Joan or Mimi and Richard performed, but *The New York Post* reported, "The crowd (estimated at 2,800) reserved some of its strongest applause for a non-musical statement by folksinger Joan Baez. 'I make one request to the men in the audience—don't cooperate with the draft.' " A folksinger mainly in name, Baez was now making more news for what she said than for what she sang.

Mimi and Richard recorded their second album, *Reflections in a Crystal Wind*, at Olmstead Studios again during the last few days of the month. Pretentious title aside, it advances the innovations of their first album in strides. Only four of the record's thirteen tracks are instrumentals (including one by Mimi, "Miles," a dissonant homage to the jazz trumpeter), but they are more coherent and unified as compositions than the anomalous experiments in sound and texture on *Celebrations for a Grey Day*. The musical reference points are unusually varied for an album in the pop-folk genre; as Richard, in his liner notes, aptly described the piece "Dopico," an instrumental dedicated to his Cuban friend, "Call it an Afro-Indian Pachanga for Alfredo and his Italian chariot. Those with an ear to the Caribbean Ground and an eye to explosive horizons will recognize The Superman Club in Old Havana, narcotized cous-cous in Alexandria, and certain of the more maniacal diversions up for grabs at the Tangier Bazaar. Olé." Another four of the songs are full-tilt rockers deepened by Fariña's dense but cogent lyrics, played by a five-piece band featuring Bruce Langhorne on electric guitar and Felix Pappalardi (later of Mountain and producer for Cream) on electric bass. "I was really impressed with what Fariña was doing," recalled Alvin Rogers, who played drums on the sessions. "There weren't a lot of songwriters doing that poetic thing who understood the importance of rhythm like he did."

Among the rockers on the album, "Hard-Loving Loser" is certainly most distinctive for the wry humor in its portrayal of a social misfit blessed with a compensatory gift:

> *He's the kind of artist rents a groovy little attic*
> *And discovers that he can't grow a beard*
> *He's a human cannonball, comes in for a landing*
> *And he wonders where the net disappeared*
> *But when he takes off his shoes, it won't come as news*
> *That they're lining up in threes and in two*
> *He's got them fainting on the floor*
> *Got them begging for some more*
> *And they call him whatever they choose*

By a couple of methods subtle and not so, Richard used the record to advance his standing as a musician. In the credits he provided, the Fariñas are described as "accompanying themselves on guitar and dulcimer," blurring who played which instrument, the guitar carrying its associations with the au courant folk-rock, the dulcimer with the declining folk. (Much the same, Richard recorded three songs as a solo singer for the Elektra anthology album *Singer-Songwriter Project* in this period, credited as "Richard Fariña, with dulcimer and guitar accompaniment"; but he declined to add the name of the guitarist, his wife.) On the cover of *Reflections in a Crystal Wind*, moreover, the billing of the artists has been transposed; Mimi and Richard Fariña on their first album, they are now Richard and Mimi Fariña. Her husband approved the text without mentioning the change (whether he initiated it or allowed it to pass), and Mimi never noticed it on her own. She was highly unlikely to do so, of course, since many words shifted their positions when she read them. (Released in December 1965, *Reflections in a Crystal Wind* would be named one of the ten best folk albums of the year by *The New York Times*.)

On the last day of recording with Mimi, Richard had lunch with his agent and his editor again to plan for the publication of *Been Down So*

Long It Looks Like Up to Me the following April. Fariña continued to
lobby for von Schmidt's illustrations but settled on Eric doing a painting
for the cover—something frenzied and kinetic, like the text, Silberman
suggested. Richard had a number of suggestions for the publishing party.
There should be live music and dancing, he said, and he recommended
the Chambers Brothers, who were friends of his. Robert Mills drank
four martinis, his usual, and warned that any overt drug imagery on the
cover could hurt the book's sales. To get that endorsement Fariña had
promised from Thomas Pynchon, Richard asked Silberman to contact
the writer formally. "I got the distinct impression that he didn't want
Pynchon to think he was overstepping boundaries," remembered Silberman, who had met Pynchon several years earlier, before *V.*, when Silberman was editing the literary magazine *Dial* and Pynchon was a young
writer trying to get short stories published. Silberman had rejected Pynchon's submissions but recommended him to the agent Candida Donadio. "Herb Gold and Jim Silberman," Pynchon later reminisced in a
letter to Mimi. "Probably if it hadn't been for those two guys, I'd be in
some other racket now." When he received Silberman's inquiry about
Fariña's book, Pynchon responded positively, with a caveat. "Sure I'll
give a comment on Dick Fariña's book," Pynchon wrote to Silberman.
"Provided of course that you editorial guys haven't massacred it beyond
recognition or something. I mean it does happen. The last I saw the book
was August of 1963, and then I was left more or less cliffhanging because
Dick had the last couple chapters off with somebody else. What I read I
like and was wondering when somebody would come along smart
enough to pick up on it. Glad it was you."

As soon as he read the edited manuscript, Pynchon wrote Fariña:

> Holy shit man. How would "holy shit" look on the book jacket?
> What I mean is you have written, really and truly, a great out-of-
> sight fucking book. For Jim Silberman I will get up something
> phrased more acceptable to the family trade and all. But to you,
> wild colonial maniac, about all I can say is holy shit. . . . This
> thing man picked me up, sucked me in, cycled, spun and cen-

trifuged my ass to where it was a major effort of will to go get up and take a leak even, and by the time it was over with I know where I had been.

If you want comparisons, which you don't, I think most of Rilke.

If you want complaints, sorry, I don't have any against you; only what appear to be RH editors screamin ick, ick.

He signed the letter "Pyñchoñ."

Following up with Silberman, Pynchon sent the editor an extravagant blurb:

It's been a while since I've read anything quite so groovy, quite such a joy from beginning to end. This book comes on like the Hallelujah Chorus done by 200 kazoo players with perfect pitch, I mean strong, swinging, skillful and reverent—but also with the fine brassy buzz of irreverence in there too. Fariña has going for him an unerring and virtuoso instinct about exactly what, in this bewildering Republic, is serious and what cannot possibly be— and on top of that the honesty to come out and say it straight. In spinning his yarn he spins the reader as well, dizzily into a microcosm that manages to be hilarious, chilling, sexy, profound, maniacal, beautiful and outrageous all at the same time.

Pynchon did voice one objection to the editing, however. At Silberman's recommendation, Fariña had cut a passage involving a ribald word game wherein the titles of literary works are amended to include the word "cunt." Richard had devoted five pages to this: "The Cunt Also Rises," "Brave New Cunt," "The Catcher in the Cunt," "Winnie the Cunt," and so on. "Why the hell did you guys cut the Anthropomorphic (Gynecomorphic?) Game?" Pynchon asked Silberman in his letter. "You couldn't have been worried about Redeeming Value. It's funny—how much more redeeming can you get?" In closing, Pynchon encouraged Silberman, "I doubt very much that any puff from me will help your sales. The book will be a success even if you put it out with a puffless, blurbless, photoless, pure white (or better black) jacket to it. It is that good a book."

When they returned to California, the Fariñas spent more and more time at Joan's house, clowning, feasting on peasant concoctions, and listening to music. Richard was rummaging through his sister-in-law's record cabinet one evening when he found a pile of old 45-rpm singles from the Baez sisters' teen years—the first songs Joan had learned to sing, like "Young Blood" and "Annie Had a Baby." Fariña put a stack of them on the turntable and made some glib remarks in a slick disk-jockey's baritone. Picking up the cue, Joan chimed along with the records, singing in a bright, playful voice. "That's how Dick got the idea that I had to do a rock and roll album," Joan recalled. "It had never occurred to me. I loved the music, but I never seriously considered singing it. Dick got this brainstorm. He could be terribly persuasive, and it started to sound like a good idea."

Dylan, among others, thought that Joan needed stronger musical guidance than she was getting from the Solomons and Manny Greenhill. "I feel sorry for her, knowing that I don't have to feel sorry for her, because she would definitely not want me to feel sorry for her or anybody to feel sorry for her," Dylan said. "I feel sorry for her, because she has nobody to ask—she has nobody to turn to that's going to be straight with her. About her school, yes. But when she is going to make a record, I mean, how can [Ira Sandperl] be straight with her? She has nobody." She used to have Bob Dylan, of course. In his absence, Richard Fariña seemed eager to try his hand at steering Joan in a different creative direction. Baez agreed to make that rock and roll album, with Fariña supervising the project as the producer. The challenge could help "get me more excited about music," she said, and possibly even lead to a hit record, which "wouldn't be bad."

Neither Baez nor Fariña appeared any more concerned about the fact that Richard had never produced an album (not even one of his records with Mimi) than Joan had been troubled by the fact that the designer of her house had no architectural training or that the leader of her school distrusted formal education. This was the 1960s. The establishment had proven the hazards of overconfidence in institutions and authority; it was time for a new generation to test the risks of overvaluing novelty and experimentation.

Joan and Richard bought dozens of new 45s and listened to them with Mimi at Baez's house. If she liked a record, Joan would sing along and try it out. Richard weighed in—*Yeah, groovy!* or *No, this is a drag*—and when they all liked something, they danced. Most of the songs Joan and Richard agreed to record veered more toward light pop than rock and roll: up-tempo ballads by Burt Bacharach and Hal David such as "My Little Red Book," "Always Something There to Remind Me," Paul Simon's "Homeward Bound," Lennon and McCartney's "Yesterday." (Jazz singer Mel Tormé chose two of the same songs, "My Little Red Book" and "Homeward Bound," for his venture into rock-era pop, the album *Right Now!*, that year.) Joan wanted to include Dylan's beautiful "One Too Many Mornings" (from *The Times They Are a-Changin'*), and they both thought it would be nice to include a couple of Fariña's compositions, "Pack Up Your Sorrows" and "A Swallow Song." Taken in by the spirit of trying new sounds and untested ideas, Baez wanted to write a song, too. She collaborated with Kim Chappell to set a poem of Richard's, "All the World Has Gone By," to music. Fariña thereby shared songwriting credits with two of the three Baez sisters, Pauline and Joan.

Maynard Solomon, who had produced all six of Baez's albums for Vanguard, was deeply upset to hear of Joan's intentions. On principle, nonetheless, he assented to the project as he had always supported his best-selling artist. "I said yes, and I watched Richard trying to invent the wheel, trying to learn how to be a producer on the job, and it didn't work," Solomon recalled. "I tried to help him by bringing in a first-class pop-rock arranger, Trade Martin, so that at least there would be some modicum of professionalism. But, you know, I might have been wrong in that. It's possible that given enough time and experimentation, Richard would have come up with some extraordinary new sound that none of us had been able to imagine. I tend to doubt it."

Mimi and Richard flew to New York from San Francisco on February 15, 1966, shortly after the release of *Reflections in a Crystal Wind*, and stayed on the East Coast for the next six weeks, promoting the album together (a concert in Boston, a week-long run at a Philadelphia club, an appearance on Pete Seeger's educational-TV show) while Richard prepared for Joan's recording sessions. Baez arrived a couple of weeks later for her annual New York concert (March 13 at Philharmonic Hall) and rehearsals Richard had set up with a small group of veteran New York studio pros led by Trade Martin. "I was the guy they brought in to make sure everything went right at the session, and stuff like that," Martin recalled. "But I didn't really have to do that. I did a lot of the arrangements, and Richie [Fariña] ran the show from the rehearsals on. Richie seemed to me always to have that ability of knowing what was, what felt, sounded, or worked, or not."

At her concert, Joan gave the audience a brief talk about Mimi and Richard—rather, Richard and Mimi Fariña—and brought them out to do a few songs. They proved to be a leavening addition to Baez's show. "A thread of melancholy spun through the entire first part of the afternoon," critic Robert Sherman wrote in *The New York Times*. "Beautiful as Miss Baez's singing was, one longed for an occasional touch of lightness. A delightful change of pace followed the intermission [when] Miss Baez ushered on stage her sister and brother-in-law . . . [who] launched into an energetic, not to say frenetic ballad, which seemed to be called 'The House Un-American Blues Activities Dream.' It was to quote a phrase from the tune, 'a hippy, hoppy' sort of affair, with Richard strumming his dulcimer, Mimi singing with guitar and Joan herself whopping a tambourine and doing some of the niftiest dance steps west of [the discotheque] Arthur. It is hardly a masterpiece but it gave the program a rhythmic lift, and a vivacity it had lacked earlier."

However unprofessional Fariña may have seemed by Maynard Solomon's standards, he managed to audition and hire musicians, book studio time, lead rehearsals, rent instruments and equipment, and keep meticulous notes of each activity and expense for the Vanguard accountant. The atmosphere at the recording sessions, conducted at Olmstead Studios over the last weeks of March, was affable and lively, not much like Joan's austerely efficient past sessions but fitting for the tone of the music. On the first day of taping, Joan danced into the sound booth and boomed, "Ready, ready, ready to rock and roll!" She was having fun, and it shows in the tracks she recorded; her voice was sunny, and she let the words twirl and bounce around the light pop melodies. Listening to this bright, almost silly music decades later, you can picture Richard Fariña in the control booth after a take, encouraging his singer, "Yeah, groovy!"

Guitarist Al Gorgoni, a New York pop journeyman who had played on nearly three dozen top-ten singles (including Simon and Garfunkel's "Sounds of Silence" and Van Morrison's "Brown-Eyed Girl"), took the job expecting "a stuffy full-of-itself Joan Baez vibe." He was surprised, he said, to find Joan "having the time of her life" and Fariña, whom Gorgoni had never heard of, leading the sessions like a studio pro. "He was very intelligent and perceptive and talented and, you know, very able to express himself very well," Gorgoni said. "He kept things from getting too heavy—that's a big job with Joan Baez—but you knew what he wanted from you."

Baez certainly recognized the record's publicity value—the Peace Queen folk-goddess madonna sells out!—and for the first time submitted to interviews about an album while it was still in the works. She allowed columnist Dick Schaap of *The New York Herald Tribune* to observe the recording sessions, and she sat (with Richard at her side) for an interview about the album with a writer for *The New York World-Telegram*. Her fans were "petrified already," she told Schaap. "They've been writing to me. 'Don't go rock and roll,' they tell me. 'It's dirty and sinful. You can't do it.' It's a big departure for me." When she was asked if it was really rock and roll she was singing, Richard answered, "It's folk-rock, with some hard rock in it." Joan interjected, "I hate to call it anything. It's different. That's all." In one interview, Joan mentioned casually that she had begun working on a book as well. Reporter G. Bruce Porter asked her if she could describe it, and Baez hesitated. Fariña answered for her, "It's about love."

When Dylan heard about Baez's new music, he lashed out. "Hard-rock record!" Bob exclaimed to Robert Shelton. "Hey, let me tell you right now, she's going to make a hard-rock album, but . . . she ain't never going to find her people. Nobody's going to put up with her. She just don't—she hasn't got that much in common with the street vagabonds, man, who play insane instruments. She's not that kind of person. Her family is a very gentle kind of family. She's very fragile and very sick.

"Hey, listen—I would never put her down. She's talking about making a rock-and-roll record, and she thinks it's so easy—you go in with electric guitar, drums, bass, electric piano, and organ and make a rock-and-roll record—I resent that. It's the thing to do, it's to tell all the teenyboppers, 'I dig the Beatles,' and you sing a song like 'Yesterday' or 'Michelle.' Hey, God knows, it's such a cop-out, man."

In thanks for producing her album, Joan bought Richard a heavy gold-link bracelet. Mimi found it—or "maybe just the idea of it," she said—distasteful. "I was feeling kind of squeezed out. Dick was, 'Joanie said this,' and 'I think Joanie should do this.' " Mimi was looking forward to the imminent publication of Richard's novel, "so we could all move on."

A S HE ASSUMED THE DUTIES of Rock and Roll King, recording and performing his own style of corrosively poetic rock, Bob Dylan found himself vulnerable to charges of opportunism and perfidy. Folk loyalists booed at the concerts he began giving after the 1965 Newport Folk Festival with the Hawks, the crackerjack R&B band he had heard recording with John Hammond, Jr., and hired to back him. (The group's leader, the drummer and singer Levon Helm, was reluctant to let the group work with Dylan at first. Helm thought of Dylan as "a strummer" and found his songs limited musically; after a few practice sessions together, though, Helm began to hear the blues in Dylan's music.) With the follow-up to his half-electric *Bringing It All Back Home*, the blazing *Highway 61 Revisited*,

Dylan's metamorphosis into an Elvis of the mind appeared complete, and the dejected folk establishment tore into him with ravaging essays and cynical reviews. He was playing to a larger audience now, however. *Highway 61 Revisited* was not only a startling musical achievement—a rock and roll motorcycle trip through Dylan's America in nine works of swerving, blurry imagery (including "Ballad of a Thin Man," "Just Like Tom Thumb's Blues," and "Like a Rolling Stone")—it was also Dylan's best-selling album by far, his first to reach a spot as high as number three on the *Billboard* album charts. "His move into that music just seemed so calculated," said Geoff Muldaur. "It just seemed to me like he decided, 'Okay, now I'm going to be a rock and roll star and sell a lot of records.' " Bob's response was one that only further vexed his critics: he disavowed the whole folk genre and most of his own work in it. Dylan was not adopting a pose to capitalize on the popularity of rock, he said; he had been posing in Greenwich Village to cash in on the folk craze.

"I have not arrived at where I am at now," Dylan said. "I have just returned to where I am at now. I never considered myself a folksinger. They called me that if they wanted to. I didn't care. I latched on, when I got to New York City, because I saw [what] a huge audience there was. I knew I wasn't going to stay there. I knew it wasn't my thing. I knew that Woody did this kind of thing and Woody was famous, and I used it.

"I became interested in folk music because I had to make it somehow," he contended. "Sure, you can make all sorts of protest songs and put them on a Folkways record, but who hears them? The people that do hear them are going to be agreeing with you, anyway. You aren't going to get somebody to hear it who doesn't dig it. If you can find a cat that can actually say, 'Okay, I'm a changed man, because I heard this one thing or I just saw this one thing . . .'

"I was doing fine, you know, singing and playing my guitar. It was a sure thing—don't you understand? It was a sure thing. I was getting very bored with that. I couldn't go out and play like that. I was thinking of quitting. Out front, it was a sure thing. I knew what the audience was gonna do, how they would react. It was very automatic. Your mind just drifts unless you can find some way to get in there and remain totally there. It's so much of a fight remaining totally there all by yourself. It takes too much. I'm not ready to cut that much out of my life. You can't have nobody around. You can't be bothered with anybody else's world. And I like people. What I'm doing now—it's a whole other thing.

"Folk music," he said decisively, "is a bunch of fat people."

Dylan painted most of the singer-songwriters to come out of folk with a broad stroke of tar. Asked for his opinion of the folksinger Ewan MacColl, portrayed in England as Dylan's counterpart, he snapped, "He's the worst, I think." About Phil Ochs, he said, "Phil Ochs' writing, I have no respect whatsoever for." On Tom Paxton: "I have no respect whatsoever for Tom Paxton."

Richard Fariña? "I don't have any respect for his writing. I used to dig him a lot more when he wasn't so really uptight. He has nothing to say. He's the best of all the bullshitters, that's really where it is at with him. Fariña jumped on the wagon. Hey, Fariña knows nothing about music, that's his hang-up. Fariña is a—he's doing a bad thing, although I don't resent that. I don't think about it. He is taking his music too lightly. He thinks that anybody can write a song that makes rhyming sense and is a little weird and—I've tried to listen to all his songs. I haven't heard them all, but I've heard his [second] album [with Mimi]. I haven't heard the other ones. I have heard all his songs, and I didn't like any of them. They were all shucks. You can put this down. I'm not judging them as a shuck. I'm not telling somebody else that they are a shuck. Believe me, I wouldn't want anybody else to think they are a shuck. I hope that he becomes a millionaire."

While the brush was wet, Dylan continued his ongoing repudiation of Joan—and included Mimi with her. "I couldn't care less [about Baez]," he said. "She's neither here nor there. She's just Joan Baez. Mimi is just a lamp—a lamp, that's all she is."

Dylan's harshest and most lucid attack on the folk community came in the form of a new single released while "Like a Rolling Stone" was still on the charts. Recorded four days after the Newport Folk Festival and released in the first week of September, "Positively 4th Street" was

Bob Dylan's valedictory to the Greenwich Village scene. Musically, the song is a throwback to his early folk songs, despite its pop-rock arrangement and electric instrumentation. The melody is pleasantly conversational, just eight bars that repeat for twelve verses. The song has no bridge or chorus; it does not build melodically or harmonically but gains intensity through the cumulative effect of its relentlessly combative lyrics. It is a knockout accomplished by incessant, strategically placed jabs.

The victim of the song is either one of the folk diehards who had charged Dylan with betraying the music's ideals or, more likely, a stand-in for them all. "You say I let you down," Dylan sings. "You say you lost your faith . . . Don't you understand that's not my problem?" While the lyrics keep the issues at stake artfully vague, Dylan's title signals the song's thematic terrain. Greenwich Village's West 4th Street was where Bob made his Gerde's debut, where he lived (on and off with Suze Rotolo) during his breakthrough years, and where he met Joan Baez. (Dylan had also lived on the 4th Street in Dinkytown.) There were rumors connecting "Positively 4th Street" with Joan Baez, Irwin Silber, Izzy Young, Tom Paxton, Peter Yarrow, and Richard Fariña (with no evidence that Richard spread such talk himself). "It was a contest to be Bobby's target," Dave Van Ronk said. "I should have sold raffle tickets." Winning would have been a dubious honor; the subject of "Positively 4th Street" is prey to a twisted psychology close to sadism. "You got a lotta nerve / to say you are my friend," the singer charges in the opening verse. "When I was down / you just stood there grinning." Once he establishes himself as a wounded victim, Dylan uses this justification to rip his opponent apart, grinning back at him: "I wish that for just one time / you could stand inside my shoes / You'd know what a drag it is / to see you." Clearly, Dylan had not abandoned the fiery indignation of his protest songs, any more than he had forsworn the melodic and harmonic traditions of folk music. He had taken everything he had learned, recombined it, amplified it (literally and figuratively), and made it personal.

Once he was using the Hawks, Dylan seemed to want to play with the band constantly, and Albert Grossman saw to it that he had the opportunity. "He got the bug, big time," said bassist Rick Danko. "He was what you call a real road dog. You never got to sleep [in his company]." Beginning in the autumn of 1965, Dylan and the Hawks were booked somewhere virtually every night—October 22, Providence, Rhode Island; October 23, Burlington, Vermont; October 24, Detroit, Michigan—or they were traveling, promoting a show (with another of Dylan's put-on interviews), or rehearsing. Bob hardly stopped long enough for his own wedding to Sara Lownds, a small private ceremony in the chambers of a State Supreme Court judge in Mineola, Long Island, on Monday, November 22. Under a directive from Dylan, the marriage was kept so secret that his parents, his brother David, and most of his closest old friends knew nothing about it. "Getting married, having a bunch of kids, I have no hopes for it," Bob told reporter Joseph Haas of the *Chicago Daily News* a week after the ceremony. When pressed, Dylan denied it; Ramblin' Jack Elliott would recall seeing Dylan around Christmastime and congratulating him. "I said, 'Bob, I heard you got married. Better luck than I had!' And he was shocked. 'I'm not married, Jack. We're old buddies. Don't you think I would have told you if I got married?' " Nora Ephron finally broke the news in the *New York Post* on February 9, 1966—"Hush! Bob Dylan Is Wed"—although the newlyweds had managed to keep part of their life private. Sara and Bob Dylan were parents of a young son, Jesse Byron Dylan, born in January.

Dylan was back on the road with the Hawks (and without his wife) a week after the wedding. Cheered in some cities, booed in some, Bob was indifferent to the audience, absorbed in the exhilaration of trailblazing a new music. "Keep playing, no matter how weird [the crowd] gets," Dylan told the Hawks. He was making rock and roll a modern art, a form of idiosyncratic, frequently obtuse personal expression. "I'm not interested in myself as a performer," he pronounced in January 1966. "Performers are people who perform for other people. Unlike actors, I know what I'm saying. It's very simple in my mind. It doesn't matter what kind of audience reaction this whole thing gets. What happens on the stage is straight. It doesn't expect any rewards or fines from any kind of outside agitators. It's ultrasimple and would exist whether anybody was looking or not."

Like a jazz musician, Dylan was improvising, and he entrusted his bandmates with inextricable parts of the creative process. "Nobody [in the band] knew what to do," Rick Danko said. "Bob didn't tell us. Shit, he didn't know. He was making it up as he went along, and we just made it up with him." Erratic, impenetrable, contemptuous and thrillingly so, the sound of Bob Dylan and the Hawks was not popular music by any existing definition; Dylan, who resisted the label *rock and roll* and hated the then-voguish term *folk rock*, called it "vision music."

By spring 1966, as his relentless tour with the Hawks carried him around the world, Dylan was visibly debilitated from his grueling schedule, the unabating controversy his music stirred everywhere, and his drug intake, which appeared to be increasing. There is no knowing exactly what Dylan was ever on, which drugs, how often, in what combination. He had been smoking marijuana since his early days in the Village, if not before, and he told Robert Shelton in March 1966 that he had used heroin in the past but had shaken it. Dylan and Fariña had traded tales of their LSD experiences; and Donn Pennebaker, who was on the tour to shoot footage for a TV special Dylan was contracted to make, assumed Bob had to be taking handfuls of amphetamines to function at his pace. According to Al Aronowitz, the journalist who had introduced Dylan to the Beatles and had brought marijuana for them all (the first any of the Beatles had tried, Aronowitz said), "Bob got his kicks when he wanted. We smoked some pot. Everybody did. He tried some harder stuff, but he kept it under control. Then he lost it a little when he got into the rock thing. Drugs are part of that life, and he wasn't prepared for it. Not many of them are."

With a single from his new album in progress (*Blonde on Blonde*), Dylan made his first explicit statement about drugs in music—"Rainy Day Women #12 and 35," a party song about torment and escape that encapsulates his experiences on tour with the Hawks in the form of a schoolyard chant.

They'll stone you when you're riding in your car
They'll stone you when you're playing your guitar
But I would not feel so all alone
Everybody must get stoned

(Released in mid-April, the song would reach number two on the pop-record charts and be the biggest hit of Bob Dylan's recording career.)

Albert Grossman apparently saw no business risk in Dylan's drug use. Indeed, Grossman (now representing the Hawks, whom he later renamed The Band) did nothing to inhibit it. "Albert's benevolence was insidious," said one of his clients, a singer who had known Grossman since the time he was auditioning women to join Peter Yarrow and Noel Stookey in a new folk trio. "He was not into excess himself, but he encouraged it in his clients. It was a source of his power. He was bacterious [sic]. He made sure his clients had anything and everything they wanted, which made them all the more dependent upon him. If Bob had been my client, I would have put road people on who made sure he didn't get any drugs or certainly wouldn't have supplied them to him. Albert made sure to do exactly the opposite. Bob always had all the drugs he wanted, and I know they started getting to him."

As Dylan and the Hawks began the European leg of their world tour at the end of April 1966, Bob was skeletal and green. He gave hypnotic performances, on the whole, though his music and singing style had so much in common with the surreal, distorting effects of hallucinogens that he may or may not have been high on something much of the time. Donn Pennebaker, among others, was growing concerned. "He was obviously starting to lose it," Pennebaker recalled. Backstage during an intermission one night, Bob was wandering around alone, disoriented, and his stream-of-consciousness rambling offstage was sometimes far more incoherent than usual. "Nobody could go on like that much longer," Pennebaker said. The filmmaker began to wonder if Dylan would ever make it home.

MIMI FARIÑA WAS NOT PREPARED for her twenty-first birthday. She still felt like a child. Although she had been a married woman for nearly three years, had recorded two well-regarded albums, and had performed in concerts and nightclubs around the country, she had done all of that under her husband's wing. Mimi had no driver's license, no checking account; she never carried money. Richard not only opened her mail but usually answered it. Ill equipped for the adult world, Mimi felt like Richard's insults were right: *she was not a woman*, and she blamed herself for allowing Fariña to repress her. Mired in feelings of inadequacy and self-loathing, Mimi wept through her shower on the morning of April 30, 1966, while Richard, primping himself at the bathroom mirror, chatted to her obliviously the whole time: "I'm going to let my hair grow longer—I can't get it the way I want it."

The couple had been squabbling for several weeks leading up to this day. At one o'clock that afternoon, there was to be a book-signing party for Richard, whose novel had been published two days earlier, at the Thunderbird bookstore and café in the Carmel Valley. "For almost a month when we got close to his book coming out, we argued a lot," Mimi remembered. "It was sinking in to both of us that he had this big thing about to happen, and there was no place for me in it. He started putting pressure on me to do something on my own—dancing or something that I could do without him, and I was feeling that he was trying to get rid of me, at the same time I felt terrible about turning twenty-one and not having gone to college and not really being ready to do anything without him. I don't know if he was really trying to hurt me or if he was trying to encourage me, but I took everything negatively because I felt so insecure." When Mimi saw printed copies of *Been Down So Long It Looks Like Up to Me*, she was unsure how to take the dedication: "This one's for Mimi." Was he merely signaling that the book was the first of many to come? Or was he hinting that the next one would be for someone else?

Richard was thoroughly prepared for the book signing. He had gone to the beach over the past several afternoons to get a deep tan, and he had his favorite black jeans, a new pair in the flared style, cleaned and pressed; to preserve their appearance, he was planning to wear older blue jeans in the car, then change pants at the bookstore before the event began. But he did nothing to acknowledge that the day was also special for Mimi: no gift, no card, no flowers; he never even said "Happy Birthday." With her sister Joan visiting their parents in Paris, Mimi felt alone—worse, "like I was disappearing, when I was supposed to be growing up." She exploded to Richard right before they were due to leave for his event. "I don't know what I said, I was so upset," she recalled. "I just didn't understand. It was so unlike him to completely forget my birthday. I didn't understand how he could be so self-centered." Richard stormed out of the house, and Mimi wandered around their yard, pulling out weeds. When they had both calmed, they got into their car and drove away in silence.

The Thunderbird was a good bookstore in an angular modern building on the periphery of the Carmel Valley business district. It had framed photographs of famous authors hung between the shelves and a patio furnished like a Parisian café. Richard was euphoric at the event; he chatted author chat with the two or three dozen friends and Carmel locals who came to congratulate him. Sitting at an oblong metal table on the patio under cloudless April skies, he grinned as he inscribed each of the books with one word—*Zoom!*—and signed his name.

"I remember sitting next to him and feeling superfluous but trying to smile and keep a classic face, whereas I was crying inside," Mimi said. "I was still feeling just terrible. And then at some point, it was over."

Mimi's sister Pauline, who had recently moved with her second husband, Peyton Bryan, to a cabin a few miles away from the Thunderbird in the Carmel Valley, invited Mimi and Richard to come to her house afterward. When the Fariñas arrived, they found a celebration under way in front of the cabin. It was a birthday party for Mimi. "Dick organized this whole thing with me so it would be a big secret," Pauline recalled. Mimi turned to Richard, who was beaming smugly. "Happy Birthday to you!" he said, half-singing and doing a little dance. Most of Mimi and

Richard's friends from the Carmel area were there—Barbara Warner, Colleen Creedon, Mimi's cousin Mary Henderson, as well as a few acquaintances of Pauline and Peyton's who were gathering to go out with the Bryans after the party. A table was set up on the lawn with a birthday cake and a few bottles of wine and soft drinks. One by one, everyone gave Mimi a kiss or a hug. The owner of the Thunderbird, Jim Smith, tried to make a joke to the effect that Mimi was so old that she might as well die now, and handed her a bouquet of calla lilies. "Today you are twenty-one," he said. "These are for the wake."

Richard was flying—*Zoom!* He was finally a published author, autographing his novel for all those old Carmel friends and neighbors who knew him when (and had probably doubted him). *Zoom!* He had pulled off a surprise party for his wife's birthday, and he was Mimi's hero again. *Zoom!* Is that wine? A toast to Mimi! *Zoom!* To Gnossos Pappadopoulis!

"Hey, whose Harley is that?" Richard yelled when he noticed a red, new-model Harley Davidson Sportster parked among the cars herded around the Bryans' house. "Let's go for a ride!" It belonged to a friend of Pauline's husband, Willie Hinds, a marine biologist at the Hopkins Marine Station in Pacific Grove by day, a bartender at a biker hangout in Cannery Row called the Palace by night. He had long, wavy blond hair and a thick mustache that ended in curlicues, like that of Buffalo Bill Cody, the road-show cowboy, who was Hinds's apparent role model. "I liked riding with the outlaws and meeting those interesting people, even though I wasn't quite one of them," Hinds recalled. "I liked being with the freethinkers, you know, the doper hippies." He had not smoked any marijuana that day but fully intended to do so later. "Fariña had this great big smile and this exuberance of 'Hey, wow! Let's keep this party going!' so I said, 'Sure, let's go.' " Hinds and Fariña barely knew each other.

Richard changed into his new hip-hugging black jeans and asked Mimi to hold his car keys and wallet while he went riding. "That was a little strange," Mimi thought, "because I couldn't drive the car, and he never let me have his wallet. I remember holding it and wanting to look through it, because I had never held it in my hands before." Hinds hopped on the motorcycle, Fariña slid on the pillion—neither had a helmet—and they roared past the cabin: *Zoom!*

The roads of the Carmel Valley make for thrilling rides, as Pete Seeger had pointed out when he introduced Mimi and Richard on his television music program *Rainbow Quest* that March:

> I wonder how many of you viewing have ever seen pictures of the coast around Carmel, California. It's only in the last few years they've had roads there, because the mountains tumble down into the sea, and pine trees cling to the rocks, and the Pacific Ocean sometimes is full of fog, and it rolls up and gets up to the top of the hill and all of a sudden the fog evaporates. And when it does clear off, why, you get the most magnificent views you could imagine. You're lucky people to live there.

The evening fog was just forming as Hinds and Fariña looped around Carmel Valley Road.

About half an hour after the men left the cabin, around seven-fifteen p.m., Mimi thought she heard a siren in the distance, and she began to worry. Pauline suggested she calm down with a glass of wine; she was old enough now. But Mimi persisted, and Pauline agreed to take her for a drive along the mountain roads; Hinds's wife, Madonna, and Pauline's five-year-old son, Nick, hopped in the backseat of Peyton's blue-and-white 1953 Chevrolet. Coming upon highway patrol cars about five miles away from the house, Mimi and Madonna Hinds rushed out of the car. Madonna did the talking. "Motorcycle accident . . . ," Mimi heard the officer say. "The driver got scratched up . . . the other guy wasn't so lucky."

"Where's the driver?" Madonna asked.

"The hospital."

"What about the other guy?" Mimi interjected.

"I'm sorry, ma'am, we can't give that information," the officer answered, as Mimi recalled. "He didn't have any identification."

Mimi handed him Richard's wallet, and the officer said, "He's at the morgue, ma'am."

Her head spinning, Mimi got back in Pauline's car with Madonna and told her sister to rush them to the morgue; she could not remember exactly *what* the morgue was, but she pictured Richard sitting there, waiting to give her another of his big surprises.

Hinds and Fariña had been on their way back to Pauline and Peyton's house. They cruised along the snaking curves, gaining speed. After one sharp right turn, the road twitched left. Hinds threw his body weight from one side to the other, leaning hard to ride the motorcycle low to the ground, but Richard was fighting him, trying to keep the bike straight. "I made that turn a hundred times going faster," Hinds said. They missed the road and ran up a five-foot embankment. Fariña flew off the backseat and over two fences into a rocky clearing. Hinds plowed through a barbed-wire fence and crashed into a wooden one, which stopped the motorcycle; his head was cut, and the barbed wire had ripped his arms apart. According to the coroner's report, Richard Fariña died of pulmonary edema resulting from a laceration of the brain; when he landed on the ground, his head apparently smashed against a rock, killing him almost instantly. An autopsy also showed multiple rib fractures, contusions in the right lung, laceration of the spleen, and multiple abrasions on the upper and lower extremities; Fariña was severely mangled. (The coroner's report, which was highly detailed on the state of Fariña's brain and skull, made no mention of a metal plate.)

Mimi stayed at Pauline and Peyton's house for the next few days and made the arrangements for Richard's burial. "I grew up fast," Mimi recalled. Friends brought some of Mimi's clothes and things from her house and helped her find a simple pine coffin and a grave site near the ocean. Richard's mother and his father, who had not spoken in years, flew in from New York together. Pynchon came from Los Angeles to be a pallbearer. Judy Collins interrupted her touring schedule for the funeral and sang "Amazing Grace" a cappella over Richard's grave. Big Joan offered to come immediately from Paris, but Mimi discouraged her.

"I told mother there were a lot of people around and things were very hectic," Mimi remembered. "I said, 'I'd rather have you here when this part is over and everybody else is gone. That's when it would be really nice to have you here—come then.' " (Dr. Baez recalled, "I was immersed in my work, and so I don't think I was paying too much attention to what was going on.") Joan, who had sent a birthday telegram that Mimi received the day after Richard's death (DEAR MIMI—CONGRATULATIONS—HAVE A CIGARETTE—I LOVE YOU—YOUR SISTER—CIAO JOANIE), explained on the phone that she had concert commitments remaining in Europe and promised her sister to be with her as soon as her schedule allowed. "I had a responsibility to the audience, and I wanted to sing some of Richard's songs and tell them about him," Joan recalled. "I knew that's what Richard would have wanted." Mimi told Joan she understood, although she disagreed about Richard's probable wishes. "What he would have wanted," Mimi said, "was for her to stop everything and have a nervous breakdown, because she couldn't go on without him."

It was more than a week after Richard's death when Mimi returned to her house to get more clothes. There was a bouquet of orange roses, now dead, arranged in a copper kettle on the kitchen table, alongside a pair of shoes Mimi had ogled when she noticed them in a store window, and a birthday card from Richard. He must have put it all together after their argument on the morning of her birthday, while she was outdoors pulling weeds, Mimi realized. She was supposed to find it waiting for her when they came home from her surprise party.

Willie Hinds's motorcycle license was suspended pending an investigation of the crash by the California Department of Motor Vehicles. Blood tests showed that neither Hinds nor Fariña had been intoxicated, although Richard's blood-alcohol level was elevated. However, the highway patrol reported that Hinds's motorcycle had been traveling at a "terrific" speed, perhaps as fast as ninety miles per hour. Prior to the investigation, there had been no question that Hinds had been driving the motorcycle at the time of the accident; his proximity to the vehicle when it crashed and the barbed-wire cuts on his arms clearly indicated that he was at the handlebars. His license could likely be revoked, and he could be held liable for civil charges of wrongful death, should Mimi decide to sue. "The DMV called me in on an investigation to find out what had happened," Hinds explained, "and so I went to see a lawyer to find out what I should do about this, and he said, 'Don't say anything,' so I went in there and didn't say anything, and they suspended my license until I came in and said, 'I don't know who was driving,' and then they gave me my license back." Ever since, Hinds maintained that he and Richard might have switched places during the ride, but he could not recall. Mimi never sued.

The press coverage of Fariña's death—"Cycle Kills Singer Kin of Baez," "Teen Idol Farina Dies in Crash"—predictably emphasized his relationship with Joan and inflated his popularity, much as Fariña himself had always done; and it tended to romanticize his death on a speeding motorcycle and the irony of it having occurred on the publication date of his first novel, as Richard certainly would have appreciated. The first item in the "Talk of the Town" section of the May 14, 1966, issue of *The New Yorker* was an homage to Fariña. It began, "Everyone's death is to some degree outrageous, but there are people who, by virtue of their youth and talent, make the outrage of their deaths felt like a blow in the face. These deaths are sometimes all the harder to bear because the occasion of them is so sadly appropriate."

Yet no way of dying except old age was appropriate for Richard Fariña, he so relished life. Who reveled in the act of living more than this man who tried to make every meal a banquet, every task a mission, every conversation a play, every gathering a party? Reckless and prone to delusions of exemption, he tempted death, but only because he never considered it seriously. "When you've walked a little with death," he told Judy Collins in a letter, "you learn to court it, play with it, defy it if you choose, because having turned, you possess the choice. What I am saying is that you mustn't be afraid." Fariña may have glamorized Dylan as a doomed figure—"There was . . . the familiar comparison with James Dean . . . an impulsive awareness of his physical perishability," he wrote. "Catch him now . . . Next week he may be mangled on a motorcycle." But Richard had too little awareness of his own perishability. To Fariña, surely, there was nothing appropriate about smashing up in a motorcycle accident; that sort of thing was for Bob Dylan.

O N THE DAY FARIÑA DIED, Dylan was communing with Hamlet's ghost at Kronborg Castle. He and the Hawks were in the midst of a European tour, with a concert scheduled in Copenhagen the following evening. Bob stood at the foot of the sixteenth-century monument, rubbing his chin in mock-contemplation, while Donn Pennebaker rolled film. The scenario was Dylan's idea, Pennebaker said—"a joke on the literary world and some sort of riff on contemplating the meaning of life and death. At that point," Pennebaker said, "Bob wasn't taking anything seriously, especially the meaning of life and death."

No one involved in the tour would remember if Dylan ever heard the news about Fariña. Not much about the outside world was penetrating Grossman's tour machinery. Dylan, the band, and their entourage chugged from one city to another, doing the concerts and the absurdist press conferences, getting high, running for three and four days straight without sleep. "I was straining pretty hard and couldn't have gone on living that way much longer," Bob recalled. "Those were . . . my wild, unnatural moments." Offstage Dylan would tell one of the members of the Hawks a bit of a story, then tell it again minutes later. In his dressing room after one concert, apparently very high, Dylan mistook Rick Danko for a roadie and asked him if the mail had come yet and if Danko would go buy him a box of cookies. The bassist at first assumed Dylan was using drug code, but soon he realized Bob was serious about wanting mail and cookies; he was longing for comfort and home.

In the last week of May, the tour reached London. Dylan gallivanted with various members of the Beatles and the Rolling Stones and one evening took a limousine ride through the city with John Lennon. Pennebaker sat next to the driver in the front, his camera pointed at the backseat. Dylan's skin was blue, and his head and arms flopped about like a marionette's. He might have imagined that he was parrying with Lennon in Pickwickian repartee, but he was whispering unintelligibly. Lennon recoiled on the other side of the seat and struggled to put on a good face for the camera. "Come, come, boy—pull yourself together," he half-joked in a comic military-commander's voice. Dylan's state deteriorated. He leaned over the seat and vomited on the floor of the vehicle, and Pennebaker turned the camera off.

"We went straight to his hotel," Pennebaker remembered. "John and I picked him up and hauled him upstairs and got him into his room. We laid him down on his bed, and he looked really weird. We sat on his bed and just looked at him. He looked dead. We went downstairs and back outside, and John said, 'Well, I think we just said good-bye to old Bob.' "

And they had; the next time Pennebaker would see Dylan, he would be a new Bob.

When Dylan returned to America in early June, it was the first opportunity he had since his wedding more than six months earlier to spend time with his family in the house Grossman found for them in Woodstock, a spacious fieldstone-and-glass chalet surrounded by pines. But there was little time for domestic life: Albert had already booked another tour, more than sixty-four shows with the Hawks across the United States, beginning on August 6 at the Yale Bowl in New Haven. Before leaving, Dylan also had to catch up on two other items of unfinished business. He had to complete his book, which was scheduled for publication that fall, and he had to screen and edit all that footage D. A. Pennebaker had shot in Europe for a TV special. Dylan worked on the film at his home for three days without sleep. If touring with the Hawks had nearly killed him, this sort of home life was no remedy.

On Tuesday, August 2, 1966, *The New York Times* published a two-sentence news item noting that Bob Dylan had canceled his upcoming concert at Yale because of injuries sustained from an accident the previous Friday (July 29, sixty days after Fariña's crash). The next issue of *Time* filled out the story:

Every folksinger worth his guitar has got to have a motorcycle. It's a symbol of status, or maybe antistatus. Such a symbol comes dear, as it did to promising young Singer Richard Fariña, who died in a cycle accident in April. Folk Hero Bob Dylan, 25, was luckier—but not by much. He was buzzing along on his Triumph 500 near Woodstock, N.Y. when the rear wheel froze, flipping him off and onto the pavement. Dylan was rushed to a doctor and will spend at least two months in bed, recuperating from a neck fracture, a concussion (he wasn't wearing a helmet), and severe face and back cuts.

Albert Grossman's office confirmed that all of Dylan's outstanding concert commitments were hereby called off. Robert Markel at Macmillan was told the book would be delayed indefinitely. The TV special was postponed.

Unlike Richard Fariña's accident, precisely what happened to Bob Dylan on July 29 is impossible to reconstruct with authority. (There are no public records, because police were not called to the scene and there was no governmental investigation nor a civil suit; and Dylan's medical records are private.) In the weeks after the event, information about Dylan's condition was so scarce that Bob's own parents knew no more than the general public. Beatty Zimmerman learned of the accident from a friend who heard about it on Paul Harvey's radio show; that evening she and Abe watched Walter Cronkite hoping to learn more. (Bob had never given his parents his new home phone number, and Grossman's staff would not return their calls for more than a month.) In early August, the Zimmermans received a phone call from a reporter in Detroit asking them about the funeral arrangements; Dylan's father had to call Robert Shelton to make sure his son was not dead. More rumors spread: Dylan was mauled beyond recognition and undergoing radical plastic surgery; he was paralyzed; there had been no accident, and Dylan was drying out from heroin addiction. Rick Danko insisted Dylan never fell off his motorcycle but was pushed. According to Danko, who swore Bob entrusted him with the true story, a young woman in Woodstock who had to wake up early for her job at a hospital was fed up with Dylan revving his engine at a stop sign in front of her house after midnight; she hid behind a bush near the sign one night, and when Bob started revving, she jumped out and shoved him over.

Dylan's own stated recollections of the accident have varied over the years:

"It happened one morning after I had been up for three days. I hit an oil slick."

"The back wheel locked, I think. I lost control, swerving from left to right. Next thing I know I was in some place I never heard of—Middletown, I think—with my face cut up, so I got some scars and my neck busted up pretty good. I saw my whole life pass before me."

"It was real early in the morning on top of a hill near Woodstock. I can't even remember how it happened. I was blinded by the sun. . . . I was drivin' right straight into the sun, and I looked up into it, even though I remember someone telling me a long time ago when I was a kid never to look straight at the sun. . . . I went blind for a second and I kind of panicked or something. I stomped down on the brake, and the rear wheel locked up on me, and I went flyin'. . . . [Sara] was followin' me in a car. She picked me up. Spent a week in the hospital, then they moved me to this doctor's house in town. In his attic. Had a bed up there in the attic with a window lookin' out. Sara stayed there with me."

Dylan would be much more consistent on the subject of the accident's influence on him. "I had that motorcycle accident. . . . When I woke up and caught my senses, I realized I was just workin' for all these leeches. And I didn't want to do that. Plus, I had a family, and I just wanted to see my kids [his son and Sara's daughter]," Dylan said. "The turning point was . . . in Woodstock, a little after the accident. Sitting around one night under a full moon, I looked out into the bleak woods and I said, 'Something's gotta change.'

"It came time. . . . You know, sometimes you get too close to something and you got to get away from it to be able to see it, and something like that happened to me at the time."

When Donn Pennebaker visited Dylan in his home that August, Bob was wearing a neck brace but seemed healthy otherwise—hardier than the filmmaker had ever seen him, in fact. Pennebaker left convinced, as others soon became, that the motorcycle accident had been real but was the least of Dylan's recent problems. Overworked and overdrugged, overexploited and overindulged, Dylan had nearly succumbed to the demons that assault every rock and roll king—and he was trying to serve triple duty as a novelist and television producer. The accident gave Dylan the gift of that "impulsive awareness of his physical perishability"; from there, Bob came to a new appreciation of his life and his family. "What I've been doin' mostly," Dylan explained to a reporter shortly after his accident, "is seein' only a few close friends, readin' little about the outside world, porin' over books by people you never heard of, thinkin' about where I'm goin', and why am I runnin', and am I mixed up too much, and what am I knowin', and what am I givin', and what am I takin'." Dylan realized he could easily have died on his motorcycle, as Fariña had, instead of living to ponder the meaning of life and death— and sound rather seriously like Hamlet after all.

About twenty years later, Dylan saw Mimi Fariña at a fund-raising event in San Francisco, the first time they had talked since the events of 1966. They spoke briefly. "Hey, that was a drag about Dick," he told her. "It happened right around my thing, you know. Made me think."

For a year and a half after his accident, Dylan stayed in seclusion at home in Woodstock while rock musicians absorbed and drew upon his ideas—and took them to progressively extravagant lengths. The trio of Dylan records uniting poetry with elements of folk and rock and roll— *Bringing It All Back Home, Highway 61 Revisited,* and the double album *Blonde on Blonde*—came to be acknowledged as pop masterworks and chartered a whole new style of music. Dylan's "electric" set at the 1965 Newport Folk Festival took on the aura of myth; and the Hawks shows, largely misunderstood or dismissed in their time, found their audience belatedly through bootleg records that circulated widely in the absence of new Dylan records. When Bob began making music again, it was wholly for his own pleasure. Jamming on barn-dance instruments with members of the Hawks, Dylan reanimated the unpretentious, home-grown spirit of Harry Smith's *Anthology of American Folk Music* in the basement of a pink house the band rented in Saugerties, the next town east of Woodstock.

AFTER THEIR RELATIONSHIPS with Bob and Richard, Joan and Mimi slowly rediscovered each other as grown-up individuals. But it took a while. For a few months after Fariña's death, both women were tangled in Richard's affairs.

Fariña had been under assignment to write an essay for *Esquire* when he died. John Berendt, a senior editor at the magazine, had read advance galleys of *Been Down So Long It Looks Like Up to Me*, was "completely enchanted," and commissioned Richard to write something comparably fabulous about the contemporary undergraduate scene. After Fariña's accident, Berendt asked Thomas Pynchon to fill in and write an homage to his departed friend, but Pynchon considered the idea exploitative. Berendt turned to Joan, who drafted an affectionate, intimate portrait that had no relationship to the title *Esquire* gave it, "Introduction to (and Conclusion of) a Future Hero." "I'll tell you what he was in my eyes," Baez wrote. "He was my sister Mimi's crazy husband, a mystical child of darkness—blatantly ambitious, lovable, impossible, charming, obnoxious, tirelessly active—a bright, talented, sheepish, tricky, curly-haired, man-child of darkness. . . . He'd won me full over by the end, from a hostile, critical in-law of Dick the intruder to a fond friend. By the end we sisters and many other people had some of Dick's blood running in our veins, and mad Irish Cuban thoughts in our heads."

At the same time, Joan proceeded to extricate those mad thoughts of Richard's from her head. She canceled the release of the album Fariña had produced for her and pronounced the whole idea an indefensible lapse in judgment and abrogation of her principles. "I realized when I was listening to the tapes and trying to put the record together that something was wrong," Baez explained. "And I never could figure it out until we were reading Gandhi [at the institute] and he said something about art. He said how you could never accept art for art's sake. Then he said he rejected it. He didn't say it was necessarily bad, he said he rejected it because it didn't represent truth, it wasn't involved with truth, and I realized that that was really what was wrong with that record. Not that it was false or lies or anything, but just that it had nothing to do with anything meaningful, most of it. The rock songs are not necessarily untrue, but what Gandhi also said was that art must elevate the spirit. Rock and roll does not elevate my spirit." Baez assented only to the release of a single of two of Fariña's songs, "Pack Up Your Sorrows" and "A Swallow Song." (Dumped in the marketplace with no promotion or support by Baez, the record failed efficiently.) When Mimi began working on an album of unreleased material by the Fariñas (including Richard's "Farewell to Bob Dylan," the captious "Morgan the Pirate," recorded with Mimi singing lead), Joan allowed her sister to include one more track from the Baez "rock" record, "All the World Has Gone By" (the song Joan and Kim Chappell had written to Fariña's words).

As Joan and Mimi both became involved with new men, the sisters grew closer. In 1968 Joan married the antiwar activist David Harris, with whom she had her only child, a son, Gabriel, the following year. Mimi moved to an apartment on Telegraph Hill in San Francisco. She and Pynchon became close friends, visiting briefly; she dated a bit and married record producer Milan Melvin (for whom Joan wrote "Sweet Sir Galahad," only the second song she had ever composed) the same year Joan married; but she had no children and kept the name Fariña. (Mimi and Milan Melvin separated after two years.) "It made a big difference that we got in relationships that weren't so tied in with music, so they didn't get the competitive juices going for Joan and me," Mimi said. "We went in different directions with different guys, and that seemed to make us appreciate what she and I had in common more." In 1967 Joan and Mimi had started singing together again, recording duets ("Catch the

Wind," "I Am a Poor Wayfaring Stranger") released on Joan's albums and performing duo sets at Newport and other folk festivals. "There's a very strong tie between Mimi and me when we sing together," Joan explained. "We harmonize with such facility. For me, there was always an additional pathos when we sang because Mimi seemed so fragile, and there were all our sisterly issues to deal with. There was bound to be rivalry between us. In spite of that, or maybe sometimes because of it, there's something special about our duets."

Baez and Dylan never severed their ties. When Bob dove back into performing several years after his motorcycle accident, he invited Joan to join him, Bob Neuwirth, Jack Elliott, and their gypsy band on the Rolling Thunder Revue. The best song Joan ever wrote is her lament to her affair with Bob, "Diamonds and Rust":

> *Now I see you standing with brown leaves falling all around and the*
> *snow in your hair*
> *Now we're smiling out the window of that crummy hotel over*
> *Washington Square*
> *Our breath comes out white clouds, mingles, and hangs in the air*
> *Speaking strictly for me, we both could have died then and there*

Dylan mentioned Baez little in the years after his marriage to Sara. But when they separated after twelve years of marriage and four children, Bob turned to Joan and lived with her again for a few weeks.

As Joan wrote in her memoir, Mimi never really let go of Dick. She founded the charitable organization Bread and Roses, in addition to recording and singing with Joan and others from time to time. Still, Mimi said more than thirty years after Fariña's death, "I'll always love Dick. He was an impossible act to follow." Serving as a conscientious steward of Fariña's legacy, Mimi oversaw the preparation of an album of their music, *Memories*, and an anthology of Richard's unpublished short stories, essays, and poetry, *Long Time Coming and a Long Time Gone*. She sanctioned a disappointing movie adaptation of *Been Down So Long It Looks*

Like Up to Me (with a young and unknown Raul Julia) and a short-lived Off-Broadway play constructed from Richard's music and writings (with a young and unknown Richard Gere).

Fariña's only novel remains in print, now published as a Penguin Twentieth-Century Classic, with an introduction by Thomas Pynchon. Evidently, Richard never started the next book he said he planned to write, although he had described it to Jim Silberman, his editor at Random House; it was to be a memoir of his experiences with Mimi, Joan Baez, and Bob Dylan.

ACKNOWLEDGMENTS

NOTES

BIBLIOGRAPHY

INDEX

ACKNOWLEDGMENTS

I have to thank my brother Chuck first, for introducing me to the characters in this book nearly forty years ago.

For their trust, their generosity, and their help in countless ways, I am immeasurably indebted to Joan Baez Sr., Albert Baez, Joan Baez, Pauline Bryan, and, most especially, Mimi Baez Fariña. Only my wife, who lived with this book and me for the past five years, was more essential to its coming to be; if it were not dedicated to Karen, this one, too, would be for Mimi.

Eric von Schmidt shared his memories and insights, his papers, and his tapes; he painted the cover illustration; and he became the best kind of friend, one who knew when to leave me alone and when not.

Tom Costner, who not only was a key player of this story but also put years into researching it for a prospective book about Richard Fariña, allowed me to reap the benefits of all his work. I doubt I wrote it as well as he would have.

Thomas Pynchon let me in, answering all my questions. No words are adequate to thank him.

Richard Farina Sr. and his nephew Omar Lugonis granted me unlimited access to the Farina family archive with no conditions. This book would not have been possible without their gracious support.

My editors Jonathan Galassi and Paul Elie helped mold this book since it was an idea for a proposal. Paul, especially, was nothing short of a collaborator every step of the way.

I owe a great deal to the boundlessly supportive Chris Calhoun.

Jaime Wolf selflessly passed along his extensive research materials on Richard Fariña, a priceless resource.

Ron Cohen, the guardian angel of folk studies, took me under his wing.

Many people close to my subjects shared their correspondence, tape recordings, and photographs, as well as their memories. Among them, I am particularly indebted to Izzy Young (the living encyclopedia of the Greenwich Village folk scene), Art D'Lugoff, Harold Leventhal, Alan Marcus, Nancy Carlen, C. Michael Curtis, John Byrne Cooke, Carolyn Hester and David Blume, Mitch Greenhill, and Sally Grossman.

The heart of this book comprises the recollections of the people who granted me interviews, in some cases many over several years. My first interviews for an article that became the genesis of this book, conducted in 1974, included conversations with several people now dead: Mike Porco, Phil Ochs, and David Blue. In the years to follow, I spoke with Susan Alevizos, Ted Alevizos, Jackie Alper, Eric Andersen, Paul Arnoldi, Alfred F. Aronowitz, Albert Baez, Joan Baez, Joan Baez Sr., Paula Ballan, Mary Beal, Harry Belafonte, John Berendt, Roy Berkeley, Theodore Bikel, Diane Divers Blair, Allan Block, Charlie Bourgeois, Oscar Brand, Marshall Brickman, Pauline Baez Bryan, Peyton Bryan, Peter Cadle, Emil Cadoo, Candie Carawan, Guy Carawan, Nancy Carlen, Martin Carthy, Yves Chaix, Len Chandler, Samuel Charters, Joyce Kalina Chopra, Paul Cleaver, Bob Cohen, John Cohen, Paul Colby, Judy Collins, Jim Connor, John Byrne Cooke, Tom Costner, Colleen Creedon, Agnes "Sis" Cunningham, Arline Cunningham, C. Michael Curtis, Karl Dallas, Barbara Dane, Rick Danko, Owen de Long, Art D'Lugoff, Gladys Dobell, Tasha Doner, Alfredo Dopico, Pru Ducich, Jack Elliott, Mimi Fariña, Richard Farina Sr., Humberto Fariñas, Bob Fass, Barry Feinstein, James Field, Hans Fried, Ronnie Gilbert, Sidsel Gleason, Herbert Gold, Lorraine Gordon, Al Gorgoni, Deborah Green, Mitch Greenhill, Dick Gregory, Dan Griffin, Sally Grossman, John Hammond, Rutha Harris, Steve Harris, Bess Lomax Hawes, Fred Hellerman, Pauline Henderson, John Herald, Carolyn Hester, Jenny Hicks, William E. Hinds, Jac Holzman, Sam Hood, John

Lee Hooker, Clay Jackson, Matt Jones, Robert L. Jones, Sue Jones, Anthea Joseph, Artie Kaplan, David Kapralik, Bill Keith, Lionel Kilberg, John Koerner, Barry Kornfeld, Dan Kramer, Bart Kraus, Jim Kweskin, Jack Landron (Jackie Washington), Bruce Langhorne, Carol Langstaff, Dudley Laufman, Richard Leacock, David Leshan, Julius Lester, Harold Leventhal, Everett Lilly, Byron Linardos, Richard Lockmiller, Caridad Lugones Fariñas Ugarte, Omar Lugones, Severa Fariñas Lugones, Robert J. Lurtsema, Tommy Makem, Jenny Mansbridge, Alan Marcus, Anina Marcus, Lotte Marcus, Nick Marden, Robert Markel, Trade Martin, Victor Maymudes, Marjorie McClain, James McConkey, Janet McGuinness, Alice McSorley, Val Miller, Geoff Muldaur, Maria Muldaur, Charles Neblitt, Fred Neil, Odetta, Milt Okun, Jon Pankake, Bernard Paturel, Tom Paxton, Brian Peerless, D. A. Pennebaker, Thomas Pynchon (by fax), Bernice Johnson Reagon, Jean Redpath, Fritz Richmond, Jean Ritchie, Alvin Rogers, Hugh Romney, Jim Rooney, Charlie Rothschild, Susan Rotolo, Peter Rowan, Tom Rush, Eric Sackheim, Faith Sale, Kirkpatrick Sale, Irene Saletan, Tony Saletan, Peter Schickele, Norman Seaman, John Sebastian, Peggy Seeger, Pete Seeger, Selma Shapiro, David Shetzline, Brian Shuel, Bob Siggins, Betsy Siggins-Schmidt, Ethan Signer, Irwin Silber, Jim Silberman, Judy Silver, Penny Simon, Patrick Sky, Ralph Lee Smith, Don Sollash, Maynard Solomon, Seymour Solomon, Mark Spoelstra, George Sprung, Rick Stafford, Peter Stampfel, Peter Stanley, Ellen Stekert, John Stein, Noel Stookey, Todd Stuart, Terri Thal, Mary Ann Tharaldsen, Mary Travers, Robert Van Dyke, Dave Van Ronk, Eric von Schmidt, Helen von Schmidt, Barbara Walters, David Warner, Richard Waterman, George Wein, Eric Weissberg, Kristin Osterholm White, Cynthia Williams, Honey Williams, John Williams, Eric Winter, Bill Wood, Peter Yarrow, Bob Yellin, Izzy Young, and Richard Zaffron.

Marsha Maguire and her staff facilitated my use of the Robert Shelton Archive and other materials at the Experience Music Project.

Mitch Blank and Ian Woodward provided me with rare audiotapes and documents, as well as their expertise and advice.

For diligent and fastidious research, I am deeply indebted to my principal researcher, Deirdre Cossman, as well as to Dorian Tenore-Bartilucci, Nina Wright, Amy Beth Aronson, Thomas McNulty, Steve Ellworth, Brian Mikesell, Tanya Elder, Allison Paulo, Margaret Cossman, and Karen Schoemaker.

Frank McGarry gave me musical suggestions.

For help of all sorts, I thank Jeff Rosen, Millie Rahn, Robert L. Jones, and Tracy Reid of Festival Productions, Bill Pagel and the people of Boblinks, the Folk Alliance, the research staff at the Library of Congress, Aurore Eaton and the Cambridge Historical Society, the Lincoln Center Library for the Performing Arts, Malcolm Taylor of English Folk Dance and Song Society, the Monterey Historical Society, Paula Gabbard, James Gavin, Al Simmons, Lellie Pittman, Duane Martuge, Ken Peplowski, Bruce Pollock, Ruth Kadish, Joanne Hajdu, and Elba Flambury.

For transcribing my interview tapes, I thank Dorian Tenore-Bartilucci, Dorian Palumbo, Amanda Blair Ellis, and Ruth Reif.

For reading the manuscript at various stages and offering incisive suggestions, I am very grateful to Robert Polito, Ron Cohen, Eric von Schmidt, Tom Costner, Lisa Merrill, Robert Dunn, Jaime Wolf, and, especially, once again, Karen, who read the wet pages every night.

And I thank my children Victoria and Jacob for pitching in with myriad tasks, for excusing my habitual absences, and for enduring all that folk music playing in the house.

All quotations in this book come from the author's interviews, unless otherwise noted here. The quotes from Thomas Pynchon are from an interview with Pynchon conducted by fax, as well as from letters from Pynchon to Mimi Fariña. Most of the quotes from Bob Dylan are from transcriptions of interviews with Dylan conducted by Robert Shelton, in repository at the Experience Music Project in Seattle. (All such material from Shelton's interviews appears for the first time or for the first time in unaltered form in this book.) Sources for other quotes and excerpts from publications not attributed in the text follow.

3 In the winter of 1949: There is family disagreement on this timing. In her self-published book *Fund Raiser for a Ph.D.: Our Boarding House*, Joan Baez Sr. foreshortens the time the Baezes lived in the house by three years. According to Elliott Henderson, his mother, Tia, and her sister Joan reunited in 1946.

6 "I asked him how": Joan Baez, introduction to Ira Sandperl, *A Little Kinder* (Palo Alto: Science and Behavior Books, 1974), p. vii.

9 At the end of the high school concert: In an interview with Robert Cantwell for his book *When We Were Good*, Dave Guard (who died in 1991) said he first heard Pete Seeger at a Weavers concert in San Francisco in 1957. However, Seeger kept a letter that Guard had written him after they had met at the same concert in Palo Alto that Joan Baez had attended in 1954. The Kingston Trio played at the Purple Onion for eight months in 1957.

19 "It's as if": Nat Hentoff, "A Talk with Joan Baez," *Hi Fi/Stereo Review*, November 1963.

23 "We were passionately": Quoted in John McPhee, "Sibyl with Guitar," *Time*, November 23, 1962.

23 "In my tender narcissism": Joan Baez, *And a Voice to Sing With* (New York: Summit Books, 1987), p. 51.

26 Taped in May 1959: *Folksingers 'Round Harvard Square* was reissued in November 1963 under the title *The Best of Joan Baez*.

27 "I don't know": Hentoff, "A Talk with Joan Baez."

30 Bob Gibson began his set: Joan Baez's own website, the booklet for her CD set *Rare, Live & Classic*, and other sources cite the date of her Newport debut as Saturday, July 11, 1959. However, it was Sunday, July 12, according to festival records and newspaper articles published at the time.

30 She stood alongside Gibson: In *And a Voice to Sing With*, Joan Baez describes playing guitar with Bob Gibson during her Newport debut. But photographs and recordings of the performance show that she sang without a guitar.

31 "If I hadn't 'introduced' Joan": Bob Gibson and Carole Bender, *I Come for to Sing* (Naperville, Ill.: Kingston Korner, 1999), p. 37.

64 "Go back to that night": Quoted in David A. DeTurk and A. Poulin, Jr., eds., *The American Folk Scene* (New York: Dell Publishing, 1967), p. 214.

68 "a preoccupation with death": David Zimmerman, unpublished portion of an interview with Robert Shelton, Experience Music Project.

70 "because it looked better": Barry Miles, ed., and Pearce Marchbank, comp., *Bob Dylan in His Own Words* (New York: Quick Fox, 1978), p. 19. Dylan also told Robert Shelton, "Straighten out . . . that I did not take my name from Dylan Thomas. I mean, that should be very obvious. Please say that I did not take my name from Dylan Thomas."

70 "He's the greatest": Quoted in Anthony Scaduto, *Bob Dylan: An Intimate Biography* (New York: Grosset and Dunlap, 1971), p. 56.

70 "genius genius genius genius": Quoted in "Let Us Now Praise Little Men," *Time*, May 31, 1963.

71 On the way back to Minnesota: Dylan has told varying accounts of his trip to New York. Although he probably arrived with Fred Underhill, he may have shared a ride with a Dave Berger.

72 "Man, I could whip": Quoted in "Let Us Now Praise Little Men," *Time*, May 31, 1963.

74 "He's so goddamned real": Gil Turner, "Bob Dylan—A New Voice Singing New Songs," *Sing Out!* October 1962.

76 It was a Monday: Baez, in her memoir, describes first meeting Bob Dylan under Michael New's "watchful eye." She was writing figuratively; she and Mimi were with their friend John Stein, and New was not there.

82 Thal wanted to play a tape: A bootleg has circulated among collectors that is widely understood to be of the tape Terri Thal brought to Massachusetts. It was recorded at the Gaslight and has been dated September 6, 1961. But Thal's trip preceeded that date by several months. Either the Gaslight recording has been misdated or Thal brought a different tape to Massachusetts. The latter is more likely, since Dylan had been recorded at the Gaslight on several occasions.

86 "Richard and I were talking": Quoted in Scaduto, *Bob Dylan*, 93.

87 "I put a lot of faith": Quoted in Bob Spitz, *Dylan: A Biography* (New York: W.W. Norton, 1989), p. 161.

87 Unlike virtually every notable folksinger: Some early books about Dylan claim that he recorded as a sideman for the singers Harry Belafonte and Victoria Spivey before his sessions with Carolyn Hester. Later research by discographers has proved otherwise.

88 During the summer of 1961: In *And a Voice to Sing With*, written in the mid-1980s, Baez recalls moving to the West Coast at Christmastime 1960, around the time her first Vanguard record was issued. However, according to research conducted in 1962 for *Time*'s cover story on her, she told Manny Greenhill in spring 1961 that she was planning to move, and she made the move that summer.

88 "She was a star": *Time* research file from 1962.

91 Albert Grossman came to Gerde's: Charlie Rothschild and Terri Thal also claim responsibility for booking Dylan at Gerde's.

102 Young reserved Carnegie Chapter Hall: Confused with Carnegie Recital Hall in many works about Dylan, Carnegie Chapter Hall (later renamed Kaplan Space) is a smaller room on a floor above Carnegie Recital Hall (later renamed Weill Hall). In 1961 Carnegie Chapter Hall had no permanent seats but was typically set up with about two hundred folding chairs.

106 "writing like I thought Woody": Quoted in Sy Ribakove and Barbara Ribakove, *Folk-Rock: The Bob Dylan Story* (New York: Dell Publishing, 1966), p. 24.

107 "How many nights": Quoted in Robert Shelton, *No Direction Home: The Life and Music of Bob Dylan* (New York: Beech Tree Books, 1986), pp. 131–32.

108 He told her in the first week: In the liner notes he wrote for his album with Eric von Schmidt, Fariña claimed to have gone to England in "the tail end of 1961." But his father and his wife remember celebrating New Year's with him in Brooklyn and seeing him off the following week.

111 On a warm, hazy morning: According to John Cooke, this event occurred in mid-June 1962. Mimi and other participants have placed the date in April.

117 "Your silence betrays you": Quoted in Scaduto, *Bob Dylan*, 118.

123 The editors of *Time*: Two errors in the *Time* cover story would be perpetuated for years: that Joan was born in Boston and that her last name is pronounced "Buy-*ezz*." She was born on Staten Island, where her father worked briefly, and the correct pronunciation of her last name is closer to "Bize."

134 "Man, there's things": Richard Fariña, unpublished text for prospective book of biographical essays on folksingers, to be illustrated by Eric von Schmidt.

134 "Take Joanie, man": Quoted in Richard Fariña, "Baez and Dylan: A Generation Singing Out," *Mademoiselle*, August 1964.

139 Bob was carrying a crate: There is some dispute over Dylan's participation in this recording session. According to numerous published sources, Dylan sang and played harmonica on several tracks recorded on January 14; but his name is not listed on the original session logs for that date, and he cannot be heard on the masters provided to the author by producer Tom Costner.

141 This time Dylan was involved: In most discographies, Dylan is cited as performing on six tracks from these recording sessions: "Glory, Glory," "You Can Always Tell," "Xmas Island," "Cocaine," "London Waltz," and "Overseas Stomp." But the master tapes show that the tracks of "You Can Always Tell," "Overseas Stomp," and "London Waltz" released on the album are takes recorded on January 14 *without* Dylan. He did record three complete takes of "Overseas Stomp" on January 15, but none was used on the released al-

bum. He also appears to have recorded a take of "Xmas Island"; one is listed on the January 15 session logs as having been recorded with Dylan, although the recording does not exist on the master tapes. The take may have never been recorded, or it may have been erased before the next track was taped.

146 "I was quietly jealous": Baez, *And a Voice to Sing With*, 84.

147 "I was basically a traditional": Quoted in Phil Hood, ed., *Artists of American Folk Music* (New York: GPI Books, 1986), p. 72.

160 "I had barely finished": Baez, *And a Voice to Sing With*, 92.

161 Joan drove him back: In May 1963, Baez and Dylan spent just a few days at Joan's house in the Carmel Highlands. Published accounts of a visit lasting two weeks or longer at this time have evidently confused this with a longer and more substantive period a few months later.

176 "[I remember] being very huffy": Baez, from an unpublished interview by Jaime Wolf for a prospective biography of Richard Fariña.

180 Richard would write an account: Fariña was free with the facts in his *Mademoiselle* article about the Monterey Fair. He claimed to have spent two and a half years in Europe, although he had spent only one and a half; he described an argument over civil rights with a fortune teller, which never occurred, according to Bart Kraus; and he said Mimi was preparing for their wedding during the fair—while she was sick in bed.

182 Joan, who convinced Bob: Shelton, in his cover story on Baez and Dylan in the March 1964 issue of *Hootenanny*, wrote, "A call from Dylan convinced Joan to make an important performer's appearance at the Aug. 28 March on Washington." According to Baez, she persuaded Dylan to participate.

184 "The only way": Quoted in Scaduto, *Bob Dylan*, 208.

190 On the evening of Saturday, October 12: Numerous secondary sources, including Bob Dylan and Joan Baez websites, and several books cite the date of this concert as October 6. Primary materials show that it was held on October 12.

192 "It seems to be": Quoted in Clinton Heylin, *Bob Dylan: The Recording Sessions 1960–1994* (New York: St. Martin's Press, 1996), p. 26.

193 "100% Hootenanny": "WCPO 100% Hootenanny," *Billboard*, August 3, 1963.

203 "There aren't any finger-pointing": Quoted in Nat Hentoff, "The Crackin' Shakin' Breakin' Sounds," *The New Yorker*, October 24, 1964.

203 "The songs [on *Another Side*] are insanely": Quoted in ibid.

211 "All I can say is politics": Quoted in Scaduto, *Bob Dylan*, 177.

216 "I was never comfortable": Quoted in ibid., 204–5.

217 "It [was] very pretty": Fariña, unpublished portion of an interview with Robert Shelton, Experience Music Project.

218 "I used to prefer to drive": Quoted in Scaduto, *Bob Dylan*, 204.

223 "When I suddenly began to sell": Quoted in Jann Wenner, "The Rolling Stone Interview," *Rolling Stone*, November 29, 1969.

223 At the end of the summer: In *And a Voice to Sing With*, Baez suggests that after she, Mimi, and Richard vacationed together at Grossman's house in the summer of 1964, Dylan visited her in Carmel and wrote "The Lonesome Death of Hattie Carroll." The Carmel visit

when he wrote that song actually came first. When pressed for clarification on the timing of the phone conversation in which she and Dylan discussed marriage, Joan said it probably occurred after the summer 1964 vacation.

224 "[He] and I talked": Baez, *And a Voice to Sing With*, 93–94.

224 "We talked about getting married": Quoted in Scaduto, *Bob Dylan*, 197.

227 "We all grew up with": Fariña, interview with Robert Shelton, Experience Music Project.

227 "Folk music, through no fault": Fariña, liner notes for the album *Singer-Songwriter Project*, Elektra Records, 1965.

235 "the sound of the streets": Miles, *In His Own Words*, 33.

240 "The most real conversation": Quoted in Scaduto, *Bob Dylan*, 196.

246 Neither Joan nor Mimi would remember: A version of this story in at least one account of Dylan's life would confuse it with a squabble involving Alfredo Dopico the previous August. But Richard's friend was not in Bearsville with the Fariñas in April 1965.

248 She had a young daughter: According to several sources, Sara had been married to Playboy Enterprises executive Victor Lownes. She had indeed dated Lownes, but she married photographer Hans Lownds. The confusion has led to her name being misspelled as Lowndes.

251 "It's never been like this . . . I seem to be more popular": Quoted in Shelton, *No Direction Home*, 289, 290.

260 "It was in Newport": Transcription of press conference in San Francisco, December 3, 1965.

261 "I was kind of stunned . . . I think there's always a little 'boo' ": Miles, *In His Own Words*, 33, 28.

263 "I was tired of being": Quoted in DeTurk and Poulin, *American Folk Scene*, 235.

263 "She found herself": Quoted in Joan Didion, "Just Folks at a School for Nonviolence," *New York Times Magazine*, February 27, 1966.

264 "every university in the country": Quoted in DeTurk and Poulin, *American Folk Scene*, 236, 239.

264 "I can see that happening": Quoted in ibid., 249.

266 "The laughing was steady": Joan Baez, "Introduction to (and Conclusion of) a Future Hero," *Esquire*, September 1966.

275 "Ready, ready, ready": Quoted in Dick Schaap, "From the Sublime," *New York Herald Tribune*, April 4, 1966.

275 "petrified already": Ibid.

275 "It's folk-rock, with some hard rock": Ibid.

275 "I hate to call it anything": Ibid.

275 "It's about love": Quoted in G. Bruce Porter, "Joan Baez Probes the Whys of Angry Young Americans," *New York World-Telegram*, March 14, 1966.

277 "I have not arrived": Miles, *In His Own Words*, 46, 61, 74.

280 "Keep playing": Quoted in Tony Glover, booklet with CD *Bob Dylan Live 1966*, Sony Music, 1998.

290 "I was straining pretty hard": Miles, *In His Own Words*, 34.

293 "It happened one morning": Quoted in Shelton, *No Direction Home*, 374.

293 "The back wheel locked": Quoted in Miles, *In His Own Words*, 33.

293 "It was real early in the morning": Quoted in Sam Shepard, "True Dylan," *Esquire*, July 1987.

293 "I had that motorcycle accident": Quoted in Clinton Heylin, *Bob Dylan: Behind the Shades III: The Biography—Take Two* (London: Viking, 2000), 176.

293 "The turning point": Miles, *In His Own Words*, 34.

294 "What I've been doin' ": Quoted in Michael Iachetta, "Scarred Bobby Dylan Is Coming Back," *New York Daily News*, May 8, 1967.

295–96 "I realized when I was listening": Quoted in DeTurk and Poulin, *American Folk Scene*, 243–44.

297 "There's a very strong tie": Quoted in booklet with CD *Rare, Live & Classic*, Vanguard Records, 1993.

BIBLIOGRAPHY

The following is a selection of books drawn upon for this work.

Archer, Jules. *The Incredible Sixties: The Stormy Years That Changed America*. New York: Harcourt Brace Jovanovich, 1986.

Baez, Joan. *Daybreak*. New York: Dial Press, 1968.

————. *And a Voice to Sing With*. New York: Summit Books, 1987.

Baez, Joan, Sr., *Fund Raiser for a Ph.D.: Our Boarding House*. Privately published, 1994.

Baggelaar, Kristin, and Donald Milton. *Folk Music: More Than a Song*. New York: Thomas Y. Crowell, 1976.

Benson, Carl. *The Bob Dylan Companion: Four Decades of Commentary*. New York: Schirmer Books, 1998.

Bluestein, Gene. *Poplore: Folk and Pop in American Culture*. Amherst: University of Massachusetts Press, 1994.

Blumberg, Rhoda Lois. *Civil Rights: The 1960s Freedom Struggle*. Boston: Twayne Publishers, 1991.

Bohlman, Philip V. *The Study of Folk Music in the Modern World*. Bloomington: Indiana University Press, 1988.

Bookbinder, David. *What Folk Music Is All About*. New York: Julian Messner, 1979.

Bowden, Betty, ed. *Performed Literature: Words and Music by Bob Dylan*. Bloomington: Indiana University Press, 1982.

Brand, Oscar. *The Ballad Mongers: Rise of the Modern Folk Song.* Toronto: Minerva Press, 1967.

Cadle, Peter. *Nights in the Cellar.* London, England: Bunjies, 1994.

Cantor, Norman F. *The Age of Protest: Dissent and Rebellion in the 20th Century.* New York: Hawthorn Books, 1969.

Cantwell, Robert. *When We Were Good: The Folk Revival.* Cambridge, Mass.: Harvard University Press, 1997.

Carawan, Guy, and Candie Carawan. *Sing for Freedom: The Story of the Civil Rights Movement Through Its Songs.* Bethlehem, Pa.: Sing Out, 1990.

Chamber, Judith. *Thomas Pynchon.* New York: Twayne Publishers, 1992.

Clark, Jim. *The Folk Music Yearbook (1964 Edition).* Fairfax, Va.: Jandel Productions, 1964.

Cohen, Ronald D., ed. *Wasn't That a Time! Firsthand Accounts of the Folk Music Revival.* Metuchen, N.J.: Scarecrow Press, 1995.

Collins, Judy. *The Judy Collins Song Book.* New York: Grosset and Dunlap, 1969.

———. *Trust Your Heart.* Boston: Houghton Mifflin, 1987.

Cott, Jonathan. *Dylan.* Garden City, N.Y.: Doubleday, 1984.

Cunningham, Agnes, and Gordon Friesen. *Red Dust and Broadsides: A Joint Autobiography.* Amherst: University of Massachusetts Press, 2000.

Davidson, Sara. *Loose Change: Three Women of the Sixties.* New York: Doubleday, 1977.

Denisoff, R. Serge. *Great Day Coming: Folk Music and the American Left.* Urbana: University of Illinois Press, 1971.

———. *Sing a Song of Social Significance.* Bowling Green, Ohio: Bowling Green Popular Press, 1972.

Denisoff, R. Serge, and Richard A. Peterson. *The Sounds of Social Change: Studies in Popular Culture.* Chicago: Rand McNally, 1972.

DeTurk, David A., and A. Poulin, Jr., eds. *The American Folk Scene: Dimensions of the Folksong Revival.* New York: Dell Publishing, 1967.

Dunaway, David. *Pete Seeger: How Can I Keep from Singing*. New York: Da Capo Press, 1981.

Dunson, Josh. *Freedom in the Air: Song Movements of the 60's*. New York: International Publishers, 1965.

Dylan, Bob. *Tarantula*. New York: Macmillan, 1966.

———. *Writings and Drawings by Bob Dylan*. New York: Alfred A. Knopf, 1973.

———. *Lyrics 1962–1985*. New York: Alfred A. Knopf, 1996.

Fariña, Richard. *Been Down So Long It Looks Like Up to Me*. New York: Random House, 1966.

———. *Long Time Coming and a Long Time Gone*. New York: Random House, 1968.

Fishel, Elizabeth. *Sisters*. New York: William Morrow, 1979.

Flanagan, Bill. *Written in My Soul*. Chicago: Contemporary, 1987.

Forcucci, Samuel L. *A Folk Song History of America*. Englewood Cliffs, N.J.: Prentice-Hall, 1984.

Fuss, Charles J. *Joan Baez: A Bio-Bibliography*. Westport, Conn.: Greenwood Press, 1996.

Gans, Terry. *What's Real and What Is Not: The Myth of Protest*. Munich: Hobo Press, 1983.

Garman, Bryan K. *A Race of Singers: Whitman's Working-Class Hero from Guthrie to Springsteen*. Chapel Hill: University of North Carolina Press, 2000.

Gibson, Bob, and Carole Bender. *Bob Gibson: I Come for to Sing*. Naperville, Ill.: Kingston Korner, 1999.

Gill, Andy. *Don't Think Twice, It's All Right: Bob Dylan, the Early Years*. New York: Thunder Mouth Press, 1998.

Gitlin, Todd. *The Sixties: Years of Hope, Days of Rage*. New York: Bantam Books, 1987.

Gold, Herbert. *Bohemia*. New York: Touchstone, 1994.

Goldsmith, Peter D. *Making People's Music: Moe Asch and Folkways Records*. Washington, D.C.: Smithsonian Institution Press, 1998.

Goodman, Fred. *The Mansion on the Hill: Dylan, Young, Geffen, Springsteen, and the Head-On Collision of Rock and Commerce*. New York: Times Books, 1997.

Gray, Michael. *Song & Dance Man III: The Art of Bob Dylan.* London, Eng.: Cassell, 2000.

Gross, Michael. *Bob Dylan: An Illustrated History.* New York: Grosset and Dunlap, 1978.

Guthrie, Woody. *Bound for Glory.* 1943. Reprint New York: E.P. Dutton, 1976.

———. *Seeds of Man.* New York: E.P. Dutton, 1976.

———. *Pastures of Plenty: A Self-Portrait.* Edited by Dave Marsh and Harold Leventhal. New York: Harper Perennial, 1990.

Hammond, John. *John Hammond On Record.* New York: Summit Books, 1977.

Hampton, Wayne. *Guerrilla Minstrels.* Knoxville: University of Tennessee Press, 1986.

Helm, Levon. *This Wheel's on Fire: Levon Helm and the Story of the Band.* New York: William Morrow, 1993.

Herdman, John. *Voice Without Restraint: Bob Dylan's Lyrics and Their Background.* New York: Delilah Books, 1982.

Heylin, Clinton. *Bob Dylan: Behind the Shades: The Biography—Take Two.* London: Viking, 2000.

———. *Bob Dylan: A Life in Stolen Moments: Day by Day 1941–1995.* New York: Schirmer Books, 1996.

———. *Bob Dylan: The Recording Sessions 1960–1994.* New York: St. Martin's Press, 1996.

Holzman, Jac, and Gavan Daws. *Follow the Music: The Life and High Times of Elektra Records in the Great Years of American Pop Culture.* Santa Monica, Calif.: FirstMedia Books, 1998.

Hood, Phil, ed. *Artists of American Folk Music.* New York: GPI Books, 1986.

Hoskyns, Barney. *Across the Great Divide: The Band and America.* New York: Hyperion, 1993.

Humphries, Patrick, and John Bauldie. *Absolutely Dylan.* New York: Viking Studio Books, 1991.

Johnson, Tracy. *Encounters with Bob Dylan: If You See Him, Say Hello.* San Francisco: Humble Press, 2000.

Klein, Joe. *Woody Guthrie: A Life.* New York: Ballantine Books, 1980.

Kramer, Daniel. *Bob Dylan: A Portrait of the Artist's Early Years.* New York: Citadel Underground, 1991.

Krogsgaard, Michael. *Positively Bob Dylan: A Thirty-Year Discography, Concert, and Recording Sessions Guide, 1960–1991.* Ann Arbor, Mich.: Popular Culture, 1991.

Laning, Dave; Karl Dallas; Robin Denselow; and Robert Shelton. *The Electric Mouse: The Story of Folk Into Rock.* London: Methuen, 1975.

Lawless, Ray M. *Folksingers and Folksongs in America.* New York: Meredith Press, 1960.

Lee, C. P. *Like the Night: Bob Dylan and the Road to the Manchester Free Trade Hall.* London: Helter Skelter Publishing, 1998.

Lieberman, Robbie. *My Song Is My Weapon: People's Songs, American Communism, and the Politics of Culture, 1930–50.* Chicago: University of Illinois Press, 1995.

Marcus, Greil. *Invisible Republic: Bob Dylan's Basement Tapes.* New York: Henry Holt, 1997.

Matteo, Steve. *Dylan: The Life and Music of America's Folk-Rock Icon.* New York: Metro Books, 1998.

McDarrah, Fred W. *Greenwich Village.* New York: Cornith Books, 1963.

McGregor, Craig, ed. *Bob Dylan: A Retrospective.* New York: William Morrow, 1972.

McKeen, William. *Bob Dylan: A Bio-Bibliography.* Westport, Conn.: Greenwood Press, 1993.

Mehnert, Klaus. *Twilight of the Young.* New York: Holt, Rinehart, and Winston, 1977.

Miles, Barry, ed., and Pearce Marchbank, comp. *Bob Dylan: In His Own Words.* New York: Quick Fox, 1978.

Noebel, David A. *The Marxist Minstrels: A Handbook on Communist Subversion of Music.* Tulsa, Okla.: American Christian College Press, 1974.

Okun, Milt. *Something to Sing About!* New York: Macmillan, 1968.

O'Neill, William L. *Coming Apart: An Informal History of America in the 1960's.* Chicago: Quadrangle, 1971.

Orman, John. *The Politics of Rock Music.* Chicago: Nelson-Hall, 1984.

Pennebaker, D. A. *Bob Dylan: Don't Look Back*. New York: Ballantine Books, 1968.

Pollock, Bruce. *When Rock Was Young*. New York: Holt, Rinehart, and Winston, 1981.

————. *When the Music Mattered: Rock in the 1960's*. New York: Holt, Rinehart, and Winston, 1983.

Ribakove, Sy, and Barbara Ribakove. *Folk-Rock: The Bob Dylan Story*. New York: Dell Publishing, 1966.

Riley, Tim. *Hard Rain: A Dylan Commentary*. New York: Alfred A. Knopf, 1992.

Ritchie, Jean. *The Dulcimer Book*. New York: Oak Publications, 1974.

————. *Jean Ritchie's Dulcimer People*. New York: Oak Publications, n.d.

Rodnitzky, Jerome L. *Minstrels of the Dawn*. Chicago: Nelson-Hall, 1976.

Rosenberg, Neil V. *Transfoming Tradition: Folk Music Revivals Examined*. Chicago: University of Illinois Press, 1993.

Sandperl, Ira. *A Little Kinder*. Palo Alto, Calif.: Science and Behavior Books, 1974.

Santelli, Robert, and Emily Davidson, ed. *Hard Travelin': The Life and Legacy of Woody Guthrie*. Hanover, N.H.: University Press of New England, 1999.

Scaduto, Anthony. *Bob Dylan: An Intimate Biography*. New York: Grosset and Dunlap, 1971.

Schumacher, Michael. *There But for Fortune: A Life of Phil Ochs*. New York: Hyperion, 1996.

Seeger, Pete. *The Incomplete Folksinger*. New York: Simon and Schuster, 1972.

Shelton, Robert. *No Direction Home: The Life and Music of Bob Dylan*. New York: Beech Tree Books, 1986.

Shelton, Robert, and David Gahr. *The Faces of Folk Music*. New York: Citadel Press, 1968.

Spitz, Bob. *Dylan: A Biography*. New York: W.W. Norton, 1989.

Thompson, Toby. *Positively Main Street*. New York: Coward-McCann, 1971.

Thomson, Elizabeth M., ed. *Conclusions on the Wall: New Essays on Bob Dylan*. Manchester, Eng.: Thin Man Press, 1980.

Thomson, Elizabeth, and David Gutman, eds. *The Dylan Companion: A Collection of Essential Writings About Bob Dylan*. New York: Dell Publishing, 1990.

Tick, Judith. *Ruth Crawford Seeger: A Composer's Search for American Music*. New York: Oxford University Press, 1997.

Vassal, Jacques. *Electric Children*. New York: Taplinger Publishing, 1976.

Viorst, Milton. *Fire in the Streets: America in the 1960s*. New York: Simon and Schuster, 1979.

Von Schmidt, Eric, and Jim Rooney. *Baby, Let Me Follow You Down*. Garden City, N.J.: Anchor Books, 1979.

Walker, Franklin. *The Seacoast of Bohemia*. San Francisco: Book Club of California, 1966.

Williams, Don. *Bob Dylan: The Man, the Music, the Message*. Old Tappan, N.J.: Fleming H. Revell, 1985.

Williams, Paul. *Bob Dylan: Performing Artist 1960–1973*. London: Omnibus Press, 1994.

Williams, Richard. *Dylan: A Man Called Alias*. New York: Henry Holt, 1992.

Woliver, Robbie. *Bringing It All Back Home: Twenty-Five Years of American Music at Folk City*. New York: Pantheon Books, 1986.

Young, Israel G. *Autobiography: The Bronx: 1928–1939*. New York: Folklore Center Press, 1969.